Deadly Justice

Deadly Justice

A Statistical Portrait of the Death Penalty

FRANK R. BAUMGARTNER

MARTY DAVIDSON

KANEESHA R. JOHNSON

ARVIND KRISHNAMURTHY

COLIN P. WILSON

OXFORD
UNIVERSITY PRESS

OXFORD
UNIVERSITY PRESS

Oxford University Press is a department of the University of Oxford. It furthers
the University's objective of excellence in research, scholarship, and education
by publishing worldwide. Oxford is a registered trade mark of Oxford University
Press in the UK and certain other countries.

Published in the United States of America by Oxford University Press
198 Madison Avenue, New York, NY 10016, United States of America.

Library of Congress Cataloging-in-Publication Data
Names: Baumgartner, Frank R., 1958–, author.
Title: Deadly justice : a statistical portrait of the death penalty /
Frank R. Baumgartner, Marty Davidson, Kaneesha R. Johnson,
Arvind Krishnamurthy, Colin P. Wilson.
Description: New York, NY : Oxford University Press, 2017. |
Includes bibliographical references and index.
Identifiers: LCCN 2017030287 | ISBN 9780190841539 (bb : alk. paper) |
ISBN 9780190841546 (bc : alk. paper)
Subjects: LCSH: Capital punishment—United States. |
Capital punishment—United States—Statistics.
Classification: LCC KF9227.C2 D39 2017 | DDC 364.660973—dc23
LC record available at https://lccn.loc.gov/2017030287

TABLE OF CONTENTS

FIGURES

TABLES

PREFACE

This book has been a long time coming. The senior author (Baumgartner) has been involved in the study of public policy since the 1980s; the younger authors were all born more recently than that. In 2008, Baumgartner and coauthors published *The Decline of the Death Penalty and the Discovery of Innocence*, his first in-depth exploration of the death penalty, or any other criminal justice issue. That book focused on the analysis of framing, assessing how the debate around the death penalty had been transformed by the newfound attention to the issue of innocence. The impact of framing on public policy had long been a central part of his research agenda, but he had never applied it to issues of criminal justice. In writing a book-length treatment of the death penalty, naturally he was compelled to learn a lot about the substance of the matter. Over more than 15 years working in the area, he has learned a lot about criminal justice and the death penalty, visiting prisons, meeting dozens of exonerees, and teaching hundreds of students about the intricacies and contradictions of the US death penalty. So while his first book was narrowly focused on a particular question about the death penalty (framing), this one is more general. Hopefully it will be of interest to a more general audience as well.

One cannot study the death penalty without becoming aware of the acute importance of race and poverty. In recent years, in fact, much of Baumgartner's research agenda has moved to the analysis of the impact of race, gender, and ethnicity on the provision of various public policies, in particular in the criminal justice system—concerns that previously had not been central parts of his research focus. This shift in focus has led to an eye-opening and disturbing journey into the world of criminal justice.

This book is very different from the 2008 book, which had a strong focus on innocence. The current book provides a more general overview of our collective 40-year experience with the "modern" death penalty. It is a work of social science, but inevitably, it covers a lot of law. None of the authors is a lawyer. In particular, we are not attempting to defend any client or prosecute any case. Rather, we are looking, often from 30,000 feet, at trends and patterns that are apparent in the system as a whole. This approach will make the book seem quite different from the type that might be assigned in law schools or be written by law professors. We make no apologies for that, especially because excellent scholars such as Carol Steiker and Jordan Steiker, David Garland, Brandon Garrett, and Evan Mandery have recently published excellent works with closer legal analyses. We focus here on the trends, the patterns, and the correlations that are apparent in the system now that we have had 40 years of experience with it. Lawyers, of course, will continue to focus on their individual clients and on the evolution of constitutional jurisprudence. But even they, we hope, will also be interested to see what the general empirical trends are. Indeed, our hope is that many different groups will learn from our research, from students to activists to legal professionals to members of the general public, not to mention the justices of the US Supreme Court and judges and justices on lower courts throughout the country. We believe we have written the book in a way that allows anyone to read it; it requires no prior knowledge of the topic or legal training. Occasionally that may mean that we introduce or explain topics that insiders might find superfluous. We beg their patience as we don't want the book to be read only by insiders. Similarly, those being introduced to the death penalty for the first time here may occasionally find the constitutional details and our reviews of multiple Supreme Court cases to be tedious. We ask their forbearance as well because we want the book to address concerns that also are of interest to the specialized audience.

Our Website

Our website (https://www.unc.edu/~fbaum/books/DeadlyJustice) includes all the data reported in the book and will be regularly updated so that readers can see how the trends we describe have progressed in the period since the book was published. We also provide the computer code necessary to replicate each figure and map in the book. The website provides links to a wide variety of useful sites where we have retrieved information for this book, to sites providing the full text of the major US Supreme Court decisions we cite, and a variety of other resources. We encourage readers to visit our site and to contact Frank Baumgartner with any suggestions or corrections. The website will continually evolve and be improved, but it will always be the place to go to get the data we report here and to learn more about the topics covered in this book.

ACKNOWLEDGMENTS

Frank Baumgartner would like to thank many institutional supporters of this research, as well as a number of individuals. Institutional supports are, first, the Richard J. Richardson Distinguished Professorship in Political Science, which he holds. Funds associated with that professorship have been invaluable throughout this project, including supporting the teaching-focused activities that we describe in the epilogue, in particular all the expenses associated with a public speakers series. The Department of Political Science and various units at the University of North Carolina at Chapel Hill have been extremely supportive, not least by providing a steady stream of outstanding graduate students and, particularly for this project, undergraduate students who have worked over the years to make this book possible. A fellowship from the university's Institute for African-American Research in fall 2015 provided very helpful time for research. Although that support was directed toward a project analyzing racial dynamics in traffic stops, this book benefited from it as well. The Institute for Advanced Study in the Humanities, at the University of Edinburgh, was generous to afford a quiet and enjoyable place to finalize many chapters of the book during May and June 2016.

Numerous individuals have been helpful in sharing insights and data throughout the years during which this book has been either percolating or in active production. These include Henderson Hill, Robert Smith, and Stefanie Faucher of the Eighth Amendment Project; Richard Dieter and Robert Dunham of the Death Penalty Information Center; and John Sides of the *Washington Post* Monkey Cage blog for publishing some essays derived from this research. Many scholars of the death penalty have supported our efforts: Michael Radelet, Jeff Fagan, Sam Gross, Barbara O'Brien, Catherine Grosso, Brandon Garrett, and Lee Kovarsky, to name a few. Many of those involved in the death penalty community in North Carolina have been very helpful, including Richard Rosen, Gretchen Engel, Adam Stein, Jane Stein, Gerda Stein, and Jay and Kay Ferguson; Ken Rose has been particularly

helpful. Isaac Unah, a colleague at UNC, has been particularly supportive throughout this project and has generously provided good insights into the process.

Michael Radelet, Scott Phillips, Dick Dieter, Rich Rosen, Brandon Garrett,
Gerda Stein and Ken Rose, Lisa Miller, and Julia Schlozman all provided written
comments on our first draft, for which we thank them. Rich Rosen and Gerda Stein
took the time to go virtually line by line through the manuscript, providing dozens
of pages of close edits, which were invaluable. They each shared much of their wisdom, drawing from decades of work in the field. It is a pleasure to have such generous colleagues. Stein's comments on the wording and nuances of how to discuss
mental health issues, and Rosen's advice about how to frame complicated constitutional issues (or sometimes simpler ones) certainly improved the quality of the
manuscript dramatically. Sam Gross provided critical and detailed comments on
chapter 9 that helped us avoid many errors.

UNC students who worked closely with Baumgartner on senior theses related
to the death penalty (some parts of which have made their way into these pages)
include Woody Gram (the geography of the death penalty, 2015); Anna Dietrich
(rates of reversal, 2014); Alex Loyal (state legislation on the death penalty, 2013);
Lindsey Stephens (the creation of the North Carolina Office of Indigent Defense
Services, 2012); and Alissa Ellis (mental disabilities, 2011). Alisa Mastro (at
Georgetown Law by the time the project was over) helped develop a comprehensive literature review of race-of-victim effects in capital charging and sentencing
studies, leading to a 2015 publication (Baumgartner, Grigg, and Mastro 2015). It is
a pleasure to work with such students. UNC colleague and friend Nikhil Kaza made
our maps. Finally, he thanks his wife, Jennifer Thompson, for all she does for him
and for so many others.

Marty Davidson would like to recognize and thank Dr. Baumgartner and the
other coauthors for the incredible opportunity to participate in this research project. He would also like to thank his family members and friends who have supported him in this effort.

Colin Wilson expresses his sincere gratitude to Dr. Baumgartner for the numerous opportunities he has provided, not the least of which being the chance to participate in this project. The faith that Baumgartner has shown in his undergraduate
students is a testament to his excellence as an educator, and for that, no thanks could
ever be enough. Wilson would also like to thank his parents for providing him with
unwavering support and instilling in him the values that drive him to seek knowledge and effect change.

Arvind Krishnamurthy would first like to thank Dr. Baumgartner for providing
the incredible opportunity to work on this book. Dr. Baumgartner's commitment
to his students is an embodiment of the words "educator," "teacher," and "scholar."
Krishnamurthy also thanks Dr. Thomas Carsey for recommending that he take a
course with Dr. Baumgartner. Finally, he extends his sincere gratitude to his loving
family for their immeasurable support, encouragement, and passion.

Kaneesha Johnson thanks Dr. Baumgartner for his unbridled commitment to encouraging young scholars to engage in research and push on the boundaries of their abilities. Johnson would also like to thank the guest speakers in Dr. Baumgartner's death penalty undergraduate seminar, whose stories and work toward ensuring justice in the capital punishment system are admirable. Finally, she thanks her friends and family, whose support and encouragement have instilled and fostered a sense of curiosity that has been immeasurable in her academic pursuits. We all thank Justin Cole for preparing the index.

1

Furman, Gregg, and the Creation of the Modern Death Penalty

Our story begins on June 29, 1972, with the US Supreme Court ruling in *Furman v. Georgia*[1] and three companion cases, overturning the death sentences duly imposed under procedures the Court said were not acceptable.[2] The sweeping decisions had immediate implications that led to the invalidation of every capital punishment law in the country. Just months earlier, California had ruled that its own death penalty violated the state constitution (*People v. Anderson*). Through these monumental decisions, more than 600 individuals on death row, including some notorious killers such as Charles Manson and Sirhan Sirhan (who had killed Robert Kennedy in 1968), saw their death sentences commuted to life in prison, and many subsequently became eligible for parole. The US Bill of Rights explicitly mentions "capital" crimes in the Fifth Amendment, and both the Fifth and the Fourteenth Amendments discuss the conditions under which a person may be "deprived of life," leaving no doubt that the framers of the Constitution envisioned a system where states could deprive criminals not only of their liberty or property but indeed of their life. Since colonial times, more than 16,000 individuals have been executed by judicial authorities in our country (see Banner 2002; Espy and Smykla 2005; Allen and Clubb 2008; Bowers, Pierce, and McDevitt 1984). So *Furman* was a bombshell.

Political response to *Furman* was swift and fierce. President Richard Nixon, California governor Ronald Reagan, and politicians throughout the county lambasted the Court's decision and vowed to bring back the death penalty as quickly as possible. As we will see later in this chapter, state legislatures moved with unprecedented speed to rewrite their laws to meet constitutional muster. By 1976, the first cases made it to the Court, and in *Gregg v. Georgia* (1976), the Court affirmed Georgia's condemnation of Troy Gregg, whose sentence came about using the revised death penalty law that Georgia had passed in 1973, less than a year after the *Furman* decision. (*Gregg* was accompanied by decisions affirming death penalty systems in Florida and Texas, and reversing mandatory systems in North Carolina and Louisiana, as we explain later.)

A Simple Question: After Forty Years, Does the Evidence Show That the Modern Death Penalty Meets the Goals of *Gregg* or Fails the Test of *Furman*?

The motivating question for this book is very simple. The Supreme Court ruled in 1972 that the death penalty was unconstitutional for a variety of reasons that we will review in this chapter. Then, in 1976, the Court ruled that revised procedures had the promise of avoiding the faults that had led it to invalidate the older laws. So our question is: Given forty years of experience with the new, improved, death penalty, can we say that it seems to be in the "safe zone" of constitutional acceptability, given the standards that the Court imposed in *Furman*? If we were to review the entire system again today, would it again fail the *Furman* test, or would it pass the *Gregg* test?

We cannot overstate the sea change in the legal environment that the *Furman* and *Gregg* decisions mark. Figure 1.1 shows historical trends in executions from 1800 to 2015.

The first recorded execution occurred in 1608, but Figure 1.1 begins with the turn of the nineteenth century. The number of executions grew with the country's population, showed various rises and falls, and reached a peak of 197 executions in 1935. From there they began a precipitous decline, falling below 100 in 1952 and reaching zero by 1968, where the number remained through 1976. "Modern" executions began with Gary Gilmore's death by firing squad in Utah in 1977 and rose through the 1990s, reaching a peak of 98 executions in 1999, and have declined again since then.[3] Figure 1.2 zooms in on the period since 1900. Figure 1.2A shows

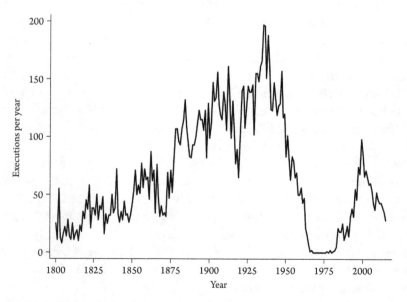

Figure 1.1 Judicial Executions, 1800–2015. Source: For the modern era, the Carolina Execution Database; for the historic period through 1972, Espy and Smykla 2005.

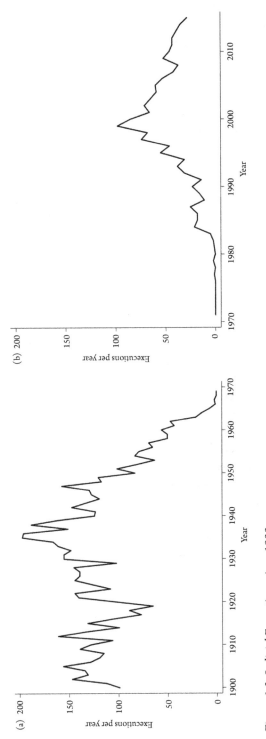

Figure 1.2 Judicial Executions since 1900.
A. Before *Furman*. Source: See Figure 1.1.
B. After *Gregg*. Source: See Figure 1.1.

executions before *Furman*, and Figure 1.2B shows those after *Gregg*. Our book focuses on the 1,422 executions that are represented in Figure 1.2B.

The "old" death penalty died with *Furman*, and the new one rose following *Gregg*. The justices mandated various improvements in procedures to ensure that the "modern" death penalty would be reserved only for the most deserving criminals, those whose unspeakable deeds truly merited their assignment to the category of the "worst of the worst." The justices insisted on bifurcated trials, proportionality review by state appellate courts, and federal review of every death sentence before it could be carried out, and following from this an entire jurisprudence developed around the idea that "death is different." In fact, as Carol Steiker and Jordan Steiker (2016) have recently argued, the automatic federal review of all death cases led to a remarkably fast accrual of new federal jurisprudence. Unlike any other area of the law, the Supreme Court has been intimately involved in the modern death penalty. In effect, the Court owns the new death penalty, and according to the Steikers' remarkable new analysis, it has created a system rife with internal paradox, partly, they argue, because the Court has been unwilling explicitly to recognize an elephant in the room, namely, race. In any case, the modern death penalty is distinguished by a jurisprudence based on the "death is different" idea: whatever rules and safeguards generally apply in criminal proceedings, these are not enough. Special provisions must be put in place to guarantee that if we are going to carry out the ultimate punishment, we do so fairly and without regard to extraneous factors, such as race. The Steikers suggest that the Court will be forced to evaluate the system comprehensively before too long. We agree. When it does, this book will provide useful empirical evidence about how the system has worked over the modern period.

In this chapter we first review the decisions in *Furman* and *Gregg* to understand exactly why the death penalty was found unconstitutional in 1972 but acceptable following the reforms states put into place immediately after *Furman*. Following these reviews, we attempt to summarize a complicated question that we seek to answer in later chapters: Exactly where is the constitutional "sweet spot" where the death penalty is acceptable, according to these two monumental decisions? With that, we explain the structure of the chapters to come.

The *Furman* Decision

The landmark decision, argued on January 17, 1972, and decided on June 29, 1972, for the first time in the United States struck down all existing death penalty statutes under the cruel and unusual punishments clause of the Eighth Amendment.[4] The Court consolidated four cases and heard their oral arguments together, issuing the *Furman* decision at the same time as companion cases *Jackson v. Georgia* and *Branch v. Texas*. (The fourth case, *Aikens v. California*, was rendered moot before the *Furman* decision was rendered, when the California Supreme Court ruled the state's death penalty law unconstitutional as a matter of state law; see *People v. Anderson* (1972).) These decisions led to the invalidation of forty death penalty statutes across the United States and to the commutation of more than 600 death sentences.

Furman and its associated cases involved three petitioners: William Furman, who had been convicted in Georgia of murder, and Lucius Jackson and Elmer Branch, who had been convicted of rape in Georgia and Texas, respectively. Furman committed murder while robbing his victim's house. At trial in an unsworn statement, Furman said that while he was trying to escape from the home, he fell, and the weapon that was in his possession discharged, killing the victim. This contradicted a previous statement in which he said that while fleeing, he turned and blindly fired a shot. In either rendition of the event, the shooting occurred during the commission of a felony (a home robbery), making the crime eligible for the death penalty. Neither Branch nor Jackson had killed his victim. All three defendants were black males and had been given the death penalty by juries that had received no specific guidelines or limitations on their discretion. That is, the juries were to decide, with no guidance from the court, whether the defendant should live or die.

In a 5–4 decision, the Court held that the imposition of the death penalty in these cases was cruel and unusual and therefore in violation of the Constitution. However, the justices could not reach a consensus on the rationale. The five justices of the majority agreed that the penalty was cruel and unusual, therefore violating the Eighth Amendment, but for different reasons. For Justices Brennan and Marshall, the death penalty itself was inherently unconstitutional; Justice Douglas found it to be racially discriminatory; Justice Stewart found it to be "wanton and freakish" or arbitrary; and Justice White noted it was so infrequently used as to serve little purpose. The Court concluded based on the evidence that the punishment was unequal and was often discretionary and haphazard. In fact, one of the defining elements of *Furman* is that no single overarching theme emerged from the five justices who voted in the majority. Rather, the five votes came about for various reasons, which we review here. While two justices were prepared to rule that the death penalty is inherently unconstitutional, the others used narrower arguments: capriciousness, cruelty, arbitrariness, lack of deterrence, the rejection of retribution, the racially biased nature of sentencing, and infrequency of use.

A Blanket Rejection: The Death Penalty Is Inherently Cruel and Unusual

Justice William Brennan and Justice Thurgood Marshall both held that the death penalty was unconstitutional per se, that is, that the penalty was inherently unconstitutional. This view, however, did not sway the other justices, even those concurring.

Justices Douglas, Stewart, and White based their views on narrower rulings, particularly on the issue of the death penalty's uneven application.[5]

Arbitrariness, Capriciousness, and Bias

The key organizing principle of the *Furman* decision was capriciousness. The death penalty was inflicted only on a small proportion of all those potentially eligible for it. It was, in the words of Justice Stewart, like being struck by lightning:

> These death sentences are cruel and unusual in the same way that being struck by lightning is cruel and unusual. For, of all the people convicted of rapes and murders in 1967 and 1968, many just as reprehensible as these, the petitioners are among a capriciously selected random handful upon whom the sentence of death has in fact been imposed. My concurring Brothers have demonstrated that, if any basis can be discerned for the selection of these few to be sentenced to die, it is the constitutionally impermissible basis of race. But racial discrimination has not been proved, and I put it to one side. I simply conclude that the Eighth and Fourteenth Amendments cannot tolerate the infliction of a sentence of death under legal systems that permit this unique penalty to be so wantonly and so freakishly imposed. (309–310, citations omitted)

As we will see in later chapters, and as Scott Phillips and Alena Simon (2014) have argued, the justices had two concerns about arbitrariness. One was freakishness, the idea that a random handful of guilty inmates are selected for a more severe punishment than others. The other is bias: that this handful is not, in fact, a random selection but is indeed selected with a greater probability among those with white victims, or among defendants who are themselves not white. Justice Douglas highlighted bias in writing that the death penalty is unacceptable if it discriminates "by reason of race, religion, wealth, social position, [and] class, [and] if it is imposed under a procedure that gives room for the play of such prejudices" (Douglas, in *Furman*, 242).[6]

As Phillips and Simon explain, the justices saw evidence in *Furman* that just 15 to 20 percent of eligible defendants were sentenced to death and concluded that this low percentage opened the door for the play of various unacceptable biases to creep into the decision-making process. Whether these were overt prejudices based on race, class, or gender, or whether they were more subtle influences, the result was unacceptable in either case. Whether bias came from "the impermissible basis of race" or whether it was merely random, in either case it was disallowed. The justices were seeking a "guided discretion" and "narrow targeting" system that would target only certain crimes but lead to the vast majority of offenders to be sentenced to death (see Phillips and Simon 2014).

While they may have meant slightly different things, all five concurring justices (Brennan, Stewart, White, Marshall, and Douglas) noted the problem of capriciousness. No other single argument gained as much attention. For this reason, legislators responding to *Furman* sought to ensure some greater degree of guidance, and the Court in *Gregg* focused on the issue of avoiding arbitrariness in the modern death penalty. We will return to this issue throughout the book.

Lack of Deterrent Effect

Another reason voiced by Justices White, Marshall, and Brennan was the lack of deterrent effect of capital punishment. A long line of studies has been directed toward the deterrent effect of the death penalty. One of the first attempts to look at deterrence was conducted by Thorsten Sellin for the Model Penal Code Project of the American Law Institute. Sellin (1959) found that the death penalty did not appear to have any influence on homicide rates. Another prominent study was conducted by Isaac Ehrlich (Sellin's most forceful critic) and published in 1975, just as the justices were preparing to consider the arguments in *Gregg*. While Ehrlich was careful to make clear the uncertainties of his study, one bottom-line conclusion became the takeaway used in future discussions: Ehrlich concluded that the "average tradeoff between the execution of an offender and the lives of potential victims it might have saved was of the order of magnitude of 1 for 8 for the period 1933–67 in the United States" (1975b, 398). Ehrlich's study drew wide attention because it contradicted a long line of evidence on the topic. It also drew a great deal of criticism regarding the statistical methods that it employed. Ehrlich's study was complex and his conclusions more nuanced than this one-for-eight summary statistic, as we will review in chapter 15. But the study appeared in 1975, carried the imprimatur of a respected University of Chicago economist, appeared in the *American Economic Review*, the top journal of that profession, and was prominently referenced by US solicitor general Robert Bork in *Gregg*. Deterrence was a hotly contested element for the justices in *Furman*, but for three of them at least, the lack of a proven deterrent effect was a reason to reject the punishment. In *Gregg* the situation was reversed, and several of the justices cited a possible deterrent effect in providing their reasoning for why the death penalty should be affirmed.

A Four-Pronged Test

Justice Brennan laid out a four-part test for acceptance of a punishment. First, he argued, "[A] punishment must not be so severe as to be degrading to the dignity of human beings" (271). Second, the state "must not arbitrarily inflict a severe punishment" (274). Third, the "severe punishment must not be unacceptable to contemporary society" (277). Finally, "[A] severe punishment must not be excessive. A punishment is excessive under this principle if it is unnecessary: the infliction of a severe punishment by the State cannot comport with human dignity when it is nothing more than the pointless infliction of suffering. If there is a significantly less severe punishment adequate to achieve the purposes for which the punishment is inflicted, the punishment inflicted is unnecessary, and therefore excessive" (279, citations omitted). Justice Brennan concluded that the death penalty failed each of the four principles and is therefore unconstitutional.

On the issue of arbitrariness, Brennan argued that a punishment widely used would unlikely be used in an arbitrary manner, but if it were extremely rare, then it was more likely to be arbitrary: why certain individuals received it but others did not would not be a problem if virtually everyone within a class of offenders received the punishment. We will return to this issue repeatedly in the chapters to come.

On the issue of acceptability to contemporary society, Brennan added these elements: "The acceptability of a severe punishment is measured not by its availability, for it might become so offensive to society as never to be inflicted, but by its use" (279). We will return to this question repeatedly as well.

Evolving Standards of Decency

Given that the death penalty is explicitly referenced in the Fifth Amendment as well as in the Fourteenth Amendment, one cannot argue that it is inherently unconstitutional, given the meaning of the Constitution at the origin, nor the intent of the framers; this point is often brought up by supporters of the death penalty. Therefore, it is essential to make the case that "originalism" is not at issue, but rather that the Constitution is a living document to be interpreted by contemporary standards. The evolving standards of decency argument surfaced in multiple opinions, including that of Brennan with reference to whether the punishment is excessive.

The Court first recognized this concept in *Weems v. United States* (1910). In this case, Paul Weems was convicted of fraud and sentenced to 15 years in prison, to hard labor, and to being chained from wrist to ankle. The Court ruled that the punishment did not fit the crime and, most notably for our purposes, that the Eighth Amendment "is not fastened to the absolute but may acquire meaning as public opinion becomes enlightened by a humane justice."

In *Trop v. Dulles* (1958), the Supreme Court was again faced with the question to what extent the state may punish a person based on his or her crimes. In 1944 Albert Trop, a private in the US Army, escaped from a military stockade at Casablanca following his confinement for disciplinary action. The day after his escape, Trop willingly surrendered. Trop was subsequently sentenced to three years hard labor, loss of all pay, and dishonorable discharge. Almost a decade later, in 1952, Trop applied for a passport, his application was denied on the grounds that he lost his citizenship due to his dishonorable discharge for wartime desertion. The Court held that this was a cruel and unusual punishment. The Court stated that citizenship is not a license that expires upon misbehavior; it can only be renounced voluntarily by express language and/or conduct. Because Trop did not demonstrate disloyalty toward the United States or involve himself directly with a foreign state, his convictions did not warrant his denationalization. The *Trop* decision introduced the core idea that the Eighth Amendment must "draw its meaning from the evolving standards of decency that mark the progress of a maturing society" (*Trop v. Dulles* (1958)) and has become a critical element in the discussion of the constitutionality of the death penalty in subsequent cases. The majority opinion in *Trop* was written by Chief Justice Earl Warren. References to this decision are sprinkled throughout the concurring opinions in *Furman* and in later opinions throughout the modern period.

The Dissenting Justices

If there were five votes to invalidate, there were four to retain. Chief Justice Burger and Justices Blackmun, Powell, and Rehnquist argued that because the death penalty has been used throughout our history, and is widely accepted, it cannot suddenly be found to be unconstitutionally "cruel" (381). They further argued that such judgments should be left to elected officials in legislatures (384). They dismissed arguments about the low frequency of use; defended the prerogatives of the jury and state legislatures (which "express the conscience of the community" and "maintain a link between contemporary community values and the penal system") (388); defended the value of retribution (394); and presaged that because "no majority of the Court" existed "on the ultimate issue presented in these cases, the future of capital punishment in this country has been left in an uncertain limbo" (403). The dissenters also provided what would become a well-used playbook for states to rewrite their statutes in a way that would please the Court: avoid capriciousness by narrowly targeting the offenses possibly punishable by death, divide the trial into two parts with the post-guilt phase focusing solely on the question of whether the crime and the defendant together deserve to be put to death, and have a mechanism to ensure "proportionality"—that the penalty be reserved only for those who are among the worst of the worst. As we will see, states rapidly revised their laws to do exactly this. If the Court ruled that the ultimate punishment had become capricious and biased, then the states could satisfy the Court if they ensured that it was more equitably applied.

The Aftermath

Evan Mandery (2013) and David Garland (2010) give excellent reviews of the political response to *Furman*. To put it mildly, it was powerful. Particularly in the South, the decision was met with derision. The same Court that had forced integration of the schools (*Brown v. Board*, 1954) and protected the rights of criminals (*Miranda v. Arizona*, 1966) had now intervened to counteract the will of 40 elected state legislatures throughout the country. In the wake of Woodstock, Vietnam, assassinations, and riots, and with a recent dramatic rise in violent crime, the response was the fastest in modern US legislative history. President Nixon responded within twenty-four hours, vowing to fight the unelected justices. In California, Governor Reagan moved quickly, and in November 1972 voters had re-established the death penalty by popular referendum with a 70–30 vote. Elected officials throughout the South saw *Furman* as an attack on southern values, an "illegitimate attack on the region's cultural traditions by outside elites" (Garland 2010, 248). Capital punishment thus became a major front in a cultural war (Sarat 1999).

The legislative response was rapid. The *Furman* decision was announced in June 1972; already before the end of the year, Florida had taken legislative action to re-establish capital punishment (see Ehrhardt and Levinson 1973). The legislature met in special session on November 28, passed the law on December 1, and the law was signed by the governor on December 8, 1972, effective immediately. By the end of the following year, 16 states had followed suit, and by the end of 1974, 28 states had re-established. By the time of the *Gregg* decision in 1976, 35 states had re-established, in one of the quickest diffusions of legislative enactments in US history. Figure 1.3 shows the rapid legislative response.

Table 1.1 gives the exact dates of these enactments, also indicating when the states abolished, if they did. Note that the states listed at the bottom of the table were abolitionist throughout the modern period.

As of 1960, the death penalty was available at least in theory in all US states and jurisdictions except for Michigan, Wisconsin, Maine, Minnesota, Alaska, and Hawaii: a total of 47 jurisdictions.[7] By 1965, Vermont, Iowa, and West Virginia had abolished, leaving 41 states, the District of Columbia, the federal government, and

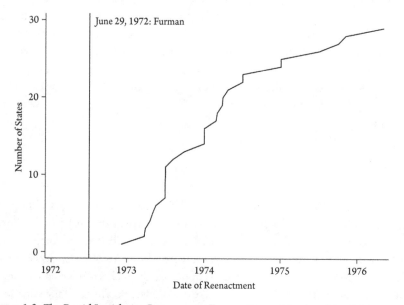

Figure 1.3 The Rapid Legislative Response to *Furman*. Source: Moody and Lee 1999.

Table 1.1 **State Enactments and Abolitions of Capital Punishment**

State	Date of Establishment	Year of Abolition	State	Date of Establishment	Year of Abolition
Florida	12/8/1972		New York	9/1/1974	2007
Wyoming	2/24/1973		Colorado	1/1/1975	
New Mexico	3/23/1973	2009	Kentucky	1/1/1975	
Idaho	3/27/1973		Maryland	7/1/1975	2013
Georgia	3/28/1973		Missouri	9/28/1975	
Nebraska	4/20/1973		Virginia	10/1/1975	
Indiana	4/24/1973		Washington	11/4/1975	
Oklahoma	5/17/1973		Alabama	3/7/1976	
Texas	6/14/1973		Oregon	12/7/1978	
Rhode Island	6/26/1973	1984	South Dakota	2/27/1979	
Nevada	7/1/1973		Massachusetts	11/13/1979	1984
Utah	7/1/1973		New Jersey	8/6/1982	2007
Louisiana	7/2/1973		US military	12/31/1983	
Arkansas	7/24/1973		US federal	12/31/1987	
Arizona	8/8/1973		Kansas	4/22/1994	
Connecticut	10/1/1973	2012	*Consistently Abolitionist Jurisdictions*		
California	1/1/1974		Michigan		1846
Montana	1/1/1974		Wisconsin		1853
Ohio	1/1/1974		Maine		1887
Tennessee	2/27/1974		Minnesota		1911
Pennsylvania	3/26/1974		Hawaii		1957
Delaware	3/29/1974	2016	Alaska		1957
North Carolina	4/8/1974		Vermont		1964
New Hampshire	4/15/1974		Iowa		1965
Mississippi	4/23/1974		West Virginia		1965
Illinois	7/1/1974	2011	North Dakota		1973
South Carolina	7/2/1974		District of Columbia		1981

Note: Nebraska's legislature voted to abolish in 2015, but a 2016 referendum reversed this decision. Delaware's Supreme Court ruled in 2016 that the state's law is unconstitutional.

Source: Dates of establishment: Moody and Lee 1999; year of abolition: Death Penalty Information Center 2017.

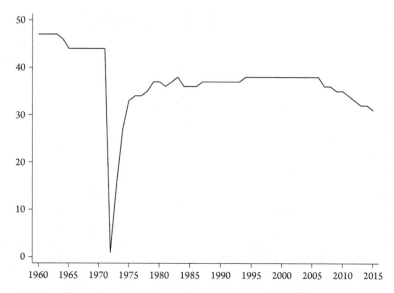

Figure 1.4 Death Penalty Jurisdictions over Time. Note: Includes the federal government and the U.S. military.

the military as retentionist jurisdictions. All 44 of these laws were invalidated in 1972, with Florida reinstating before the end of that year. Figure 1.4 traces the number of jurisdictions with the death penalty as of December 31 of each year.

Following *Furman*, the modern death penalty returned quickly, though it never reached its previous levels. Modern figures reached a maximum of 40 jurisdictions on December 31, 1983, when the US military re-enacted the death penalty. The following day, January 1, 1984, Rhode Island and Massachusetts abolished their systems. The number again rose to 40 after the US federal government and Kansas adopted in 1987 and 1994, respectively. Beginning in 2007, a downward trend has brought the number from 40 to 33 as of December 31, 2015.[8]

The *Gregg* Decision

Just over four years after the *Furman* decision, on July 2, 1976, the Supreme Court announced its decision in *Gregg v. Georgia* (and companion cases) to reaffirm the constitutionality of the death penalty and resume the practice of capital punishment in the United States. Troy Gregg was found guilty of murder and armed robbery after killing two men he was traveling with, stealing both their car and their money. Gregg was sentenced to death on two charges. In *Gregg*, the Court dismissed the idea that capital punishment was unconstitutional per se, but it also declared in *Woodson v. North Carolina* (1976) that mandatory death penalty statutes would violate the Eighth Amendment's cruel and unusual punishment clause. In the four cases decided on July 2, 1976, the Court attempted to establish a clear rule: that the modern death penalty be "narrowly focused" with guarantees of "proportionality"—that it be reserved for the "worst of the worst." In validating the Georgia law with *Gregg*, the Court also validated laws in Florida and Texas. In *Profitt v. Florida*, the Court accepted a system that used similar aggravating and mitigating factors as in Georgia, but that differed by making the jury's decision only advisory to a judge, who would impose the final sentence. In *Jurek v. Texas*, the Court affirmed a system that did not have aggravating and mitigating circumstances but rather used a set of "special circumstances," including consideration of future dangerousness; the Texas law defines a set of crimes eligible for capital punishment but does not use aggravating and mitigating circumstances.

On the same day that the Court affirmed the new systems in Texas, Florida, and Georgia, it rejected mandatory death sentencing schemes in *Woodson v. North Carolina* and *Roberts v. Louisiana*. The states could not make death the only sentence for capital crimes; individualized assessments based on the circumstances of the crime and the characteristics of the defendant were required. Clearly, the Court was willing to affirm a range of approaches as the three laws deemed acceptable were in fact quite different from one another. What they had in common was a system to ensure "narrow targeting" and an individualized ruling, not a blanket or mandatory sentence for all offenders guilty of one of the specified crimes.

In establishing the necessary safeguards to prevent arbitrary punishment, the US Supreme Court outlined two meanings of excessiveness: (1) the punishment must not involve the unnecessary and wanton infliction of pain, and (2) the punishment must not be grossly out of proportion to the severity of the crime. It also sought to force the states to create safeguards in capital punishment procedures to ensure fair application of the punishment.

One of those safeguards recognized as essential by the court in *Gregg* was a bifurcated system, in which there are two phases of a capital trial, the guilt phase and the sentencing phase. In the first, the question is guilt or innocence. If the defendant is found not guilty, there is no penalty phase; the accused goes free. If the verdict is guilty of capital murder, then the penalty phase follows immediately, and the same jury that just found the defendant guilty then hears evidence about aggravating and mitigating factors before deciding on a punishment: life in prison, or death.[9] The sentencing phase permits the comparison of aggravating and mitigating factors, allowing the jury to find that, even if the defendant is guilty, mitigating factors might suggest that he or she does not deserve the ultimate punishment.

In the sentencing phase, the jury was also provided with specific guidelines, which required it to find beyond a reasonable doubt that the defendant had engaged in at least one of the enumerated aggravating circumstances (10 in the case of the Georgia law considered in the *Gregg* decision). These aggravators included whether the accused had a prior conviction of capital felony, had escaped from custody, had created a great risk of death to more than one person in a public place, or had acted as either the agent of or the principle for another in the commission of a murder. Shortly following the 1976 *Gregg* decision, the Court ruled in *Lockett v. Ohio* (1978) that mitigating factors could not be limited to a list defined by statute; the jury could consider any mitigating factor that it chose. (We review state aggravating and mitigating laws in chapter 5.)

At the same time as the Court accepted *Gregg* and *Profitt* with their lists of aggravators and mitigators, however, it also accepted Texas's system in *Jurek*. Texas had neither aggravators nor mitigators. What it had in common with the other two systems validated by the Court, however, was a specified set of crimes that were death-eligible (e.g., killing a police officer or jail guard, committing murder while simultaneously committing a robbery; see chapter 5 for more detail) and a set of "special issues." These included whether the crime was deliberate, whether the inmate posed a threat of future dangerousness, and (in some circumstances) whether the victim had provoked the offender. As we review in greater detail in chapter 5, these are not necessarily the same as mitigators. For example, having been the victim of childhood abuse or suffering from mental illness is typically considered a mitigator under the Georgia and Florida laws (and, following *Lockett*, which came in 1978, any number of mitigators must be available to a jury), but under the Texas law affirmed by the Court in 1976, such factors could potentially add to the jury's calculation of the likelihood of future dangerousness. Clearly, in affirming *Jurek* at the same time as *Gregg* and *Profitt*, the Court was showing it was willing to accept a wide range of approaches to the question of "narrow targeting."

As discussed earlier, if the problem in *Furman* was the low percentage of eligible offenders who were sentenced to death, the solution would be narrow targeting and reduced discretion. Justice White, in *Gregg*, wrote that because the Georgia law "narrowly defined" the crimes eligible for death, and because these "are limited to those which are particularly serious or for which the death penalty is peculiarly appropriate," then "it becomes reasonable to expect that juries . . . will impose the death penalty in a substantial portion of the cases so defined. If they do so, it can no longer be said that the penalty is being imposed wantonly and freakishly or so infrequently that it loses its usefulness as a sentencing device. There is, therefore, reason to expect that Georgia's current system would escape the infirmities which invalidated its previous system under Furman" (*Gregg*, 222, quoted in Phillips and Simon 2014, 87). We will return consistently to this question of "narrow targeting" leading to death for a "substantial portion" of offenders in the chapters to come; generically, we will refer to this as "reliability." A reliable system will be one that targets and imposes. An arbitrary system is the opposite: a wide range of criminals are eligible, but a small fraction are chosen as if "struck by lightning."

In *Gregg*, concurring Justices White and Rehnquist, joined by the chief justice, wrote as follows:

Georgia's new statutory scheme, enacted to overcome the constitutional deficiencies found in *Furman v. Georgia*, 408 U.S. 238, to exist under the old system, not only guides the jury in its exercise of discretion as to whether or not it will impose the death penalty for first-degree murder, but also gives the Georgia Supreme Court the power and imposes the obligation to decide whether in fact the death penalty was being administered for any given class of crime in a discriminatory, standardless, or rare fashion. If that court properly performs the task assigned to it under the Georgia statutes, death sentences imposed for discriminatory reasons or wantonly or freakishly for any given category of crime will be set aside. (156)

So, the justices expected the state to avoid "discriminatory, standardless, or rare" application of the death penalty. The problem of "arbitrary" clearly had several meanings: racially biased, completely random, or imposed only in a small percentage of all eligible cases.

The Georgia system approved by the Court also provided a list of mitigating factors for the jury to take into consideration. These included the circumstances such as whether the offender was a youth, the offender's cooperation with the police, and the emotional state of the defendant at the time of the offense. The new Georgia statute also included a mandatory review of the death sentences by the Georgia Supreme Court. At the time of sentencing, the jury was to be informed by the judge that it could recommend the death sentence or life in prison without the possibility of parole; the jury was not required to impose the death penalty after finding the defendant eligible for the crime, it was merely authorized to do so. The defendant was also entitled to an automatic appeal to the state supreme court, and the state was required to ensure that the punishment was "proportionate," in light of the punishments given out across the state to others convicted of similar crimes. Thus, the state appellate courts could reduce a death sentence to life in prison if they found that the jury had imposed death in a situation similar to one where other juries had not.

A key question for future consideration is whether courts have followed through with effective proportionality review. As any social scientist would argue, this would have to involve a review of all capital-eligible homicides, not just those receiving death. That is, if the penalty is to be proportional, one would want to assure both that those not receiving death were among the least aggravated cases, and that those receiving it were among the most aggravated. In the legal tradition, however, only death cases have been reviewed. The courts have long held that lesser punishments may be handed out as an act of mercy, but that harsher penalties must be reviewed. As we will see in chapter 5, all systematic reviews of state proportionality review have found that death sentences are not typically reserved only for the most heinous crimes or deserving killers. While many death sentences have been overturned, no state system has been found to be deficient. The Court may have to confront this issue in the future. When and if it does, proportionality should be assessed by a review not only of death cases but of all death-eligible cases. From an outside perspective, there may be no other element in the Court's jurisprudence in *Gregg* and related decisions that has resulted in such a complete failure as proportionality review. Virtually every academic study conducted by rigorous standards has found egregious failure. And, yet, as we will see in later chapters, the Court ruled in *McCleskey v. Kemp* (1987) that such studies were irrelevant. According to prominent legal scholars Carol Steiker and Jordan Steiker, the *McCleskey* decision was "the most significant missed opportunity for heightened reliability review," since "the Baldus study findings were a more powerful indictment of the American death penalty than the facts before the Court in *Furman*" (2016, 174). (We review the Baldus study in a later chapter; it involved a comprehensive review of all death-eligible homicides in Georgia and showed that, controlling for legally relevant factors such as heinousness, the death penalty was given out disproportionately in cases with white victims and black defendants, among other elements of bias or caprice.) But, in the face of powerful evidence of racial discrimination (not proven in *Furman*), the Court refused to budge or to reinforce its "death is different" perspective. If racial disparities were to invalidate the death penalty, couldn't that logic be used to challenge criminal convictions throughout the entire justice system? Such was the fear of "too much justice," and such was the logic of refusing relief in *McCleskey*.

Rulings in *Gregg* also addressed the question of "evolving standards of decency." These issues had previously been raised in *Furman*, but the justices clearly recognized the rapidity and enthusiasm with which states reinstated their death penalty laws. The Court noted in *Gregg* that there is wide support for the punishment, at least partly shown by the rapidity with which elected representatives of the people in so many states re-enacted their capital statutes. Justice Stewart, who in *Furman* had declared that the punishment was "unique . . . in its absolute renunciation of all that is embodied in our concept of humanity" (306), found in *Gregg* that the punishment no longer went against standards of decency. The idea was that the widespread effort to reinstate the death penalty showed that American society regarded the punishment as appropriate, which therefore made it appropriate. Justice Warren Burger also held that it was appropriate for the Supreme Court to endorse the views of the majority as reflected in these "evolving standards" (Zimring and Hawkins 1986, 46).

The common themes of dissent in *Gregg* echoed the concurring opinions in *Furman*, that the death penalty violated the Eighth and Fourteenth Amendments based on evolving standards of decency, the denial of human dignity, the lack of wide public knowledge and an uninformed citizenry, and its excessiveness in both its lack of deterrence and its unacceptable retributive qualities. Justice Brennan again read evolving standards of decency in regard to the death penalty itself, instead of toward the procedures used to carry it out. Moral concepts require us to hold that the law has progressed to a point where we should declare that the punishment of death, "like punishments in the rack, the screw, and the wheel, is no longer morally tolerable in our civilized society" (229). Justice Marshall also maintained his position that the death penalty remained an unconstitutional practice on all grounds, reasserting his general opposition, rejecting the deterrence evidence presented in *Gregg*, and again rejecting the public opinion argument as based on inadequate information. In response to his fellow justices' understanding that the widespread reinstitution of the death penalty equated to public support of the punishment, Justice Marshall maintained that the public's lack of knowledge of the nature of capital punishment rendered this argument invalid.

So what occurred between *Furman* and *Gregg* that led some justices to revise their opinions about the acceptability of the ultimate punishment? Franklin Zimring and Gordon Hawkins (1986, 67) suggest that two events influenced Justices White and Stewart: the impact of *Furman* on public opinion toward the death penalty, and the legislative response to *Furman*. Evan Mandery (2013) also notes that the justices themselves seem to have been surprised by the strength of the political opinion and the legislative response to their 1972 decision. Between *Furman* and *Gregg*, crime rates were rapidly increasing, and so it is also possible that public sensitivity to crime was also heightening due to the increasingly complete reporting of crime by criminal justice agencies (O'Brien 1996), as well as the growing focus on crime in the mass media, creating the context for rapid increases in public support of the death penalty.

We would add to this that in *Furman* and its companion cases the justices were ruling on decades of use of capital punishment, with plentiful evidence and experience about how the system had been working in practice. Four years later, in *Gregg* and its companion cases, they were looking at new systems that had been designed to avoid those flaws but were completely untested. One set of decisions, we could say, was based on empirics; the other, on theory. In any case, a new era of capital punishment opened up.

The Court Struggles with Sentencer Discretion

For much of the last half century, the US Supreme Court has struggled with deciding how much, if any, discretion to allow or require in the process leading up to a capital sentence. The Court first addressed this issue in detail in *McGautha v. California* (1971). There, the Court rejected due process challenges to death sentences imposed in Ohio and California under systems that had "no governing standards," and that left the decision of life or death completely to the discretion of the jury. Justice Harlan wrote for the Court, joined by Justices Burger, Stewart, White, and Blackmun and with Justice Black concurring in a separate opinion. (Brennan, Douglas, and Marshall dissented.)

Some excerpts from *McGautha* are worth considering:

> [P]etitioners contend that to leave the jury completely at large to impose or withhold the death penalty as it sees fit is fundamentally lawless, and

therefore violates the basic command of the Fourteenth Amendment that no State shall deprive a person of his life without due process of law. Despite the undeniable surface appeal of the proposition, we conclude that the courts below correctly rejected it. (196)

The Court found that

[t]o identify before the fact those characteristics of criminal homicides and their perpetrators which call for the death penalty, and to express these characteristics in language which can be fairly understood and applied by the sentencing authority, appear to be tasks which are beyond present human ability. (204)

Further, Harlan wrote that "'the factors which determine whether the sentence of death is the appropriate penalty in particular cases are too complex to be compressed within the limits of a simple formula'" (205). In particular, the Court was unwilling to accept that a full set of possible mitigating factors could be created, or that a judge could preclude a jury from considering whatever mitigating facts it chose:

It is apparent that such criteria [i.e., lists of aggravating and mitigating factors] do not purport to provide more than the most minimal control over the sentencing authority's exercise of discretion. They do not purport to give an exhaustive list of the relevant considerations or the way in which they may be affected by the presence or absence of other circumstances. They do not even undertake to exclude constitutionally impermissible considerations. And, of course, they provide no protection against the jury determined to decide on whimsy or caprice. In short, they do no more than suggest some subjects for the jury to consider during its deliberations, and they bear witness to the intractable nature of the problem of "standards" which the history of capital punishment has from the beginning reflected. Thus, they indeed caution against this Court's undertaking to establish such standards itself, or to pronounce at large that standards in this realm are constitutionally required.

   In light of history, experience, and the present limitations of human knowledge, we find it quite impossible to say that committing to the untrammeled discretion of the jury the power to pronounce life or death in capital cases is offensive to anything in the Constitution. The States are entitled to assume that jurors confronted with the truly awesome responsibility of decreeing death for a fellow human will act with due regard for the consequences of their decision and will consider a variety of factors, many of which will have been suggested by the evidence or by the arguments of defense counsel. For a court to attempt to catalog the appropriate factors in this elusive area could inhibit, rather than expand, the scope of consideration, for no list of circumstances would ever be really complete. The infinite variety of cases and facets to each case would make general standards either meaningless "boiler-plate" or a statement of the obvious that no jury would need. (207–208)

Then, just one year later in *Furman*, a majority of the justices found that the results of just such a discretionary system violated the Eighth Amendment's prohibition against cruel and unusual punishments. What had changed? Justices Brennan and Marshall, of course, believed that the death penalty itself was unconstitutional; they had also dissented in *McGautha*. Justice Douglas had dissented in *McGautha* as well, but in *Furman* these three were joined by Justices Stewart and White, who had been in the majority in *McGautha*. Rather than find against jury discretion, the majority in *Furman* ruled that the way in which this discretion was used rendered existing procedures allowing such discretion unconstitutional. Douglas cited racial discrimination; Stewart discussed the arbitrary nature of the death penalty (like being "struck by lightning"); and White held that its rarity of use itself rendered the penalty unjustified as a deterrent or for retribution.

Four years later the Court returned to the troubling question of how much discretion to allow in capital sentencing. In *Woodson v. North Carolina*, the Court rejected a mandatory death sentencing scheme, ruling that there must be individualized consideration by a capital sentencer to allow the judge or jury to consider both the particulars of the crime and the character of the defendant. Justice Stewart wrote for the majority:

> A process that accords no significance to relevant facets of the character and record of the individual offender or the circumstances of the particular offense excludes from consideration in fixing the ultimate punishment of death the possibility of compassionate or mitigating factors stemming from the diverse frailties of humankind. It treats all persons convicted of a designated offense not as uniquely individual human beings, but as members of a faceless, undifferentiated mass to be subjected to the blind infliction of the penalty of death. (304)

On the same day in 1976, however, in *Gregg v. Georgia* and its companion decisions, the Court also gave its acquiescence to systems that, in the Court's eyes, seemed to promise some degree of guidance to a capital sentencer in order to rationalize the imposition of death. Under these "guided discretion" schemes, the Court held, such safeguards as bifurcated trials, jury instructions, and proportionality review would ensure that the problems of arbitrariness and caprice which it found to have inflicted the historic discretion-laden death penalty would no longer be present in the modern period. If the evidence in this book were to show that such problems continue to plague the modern death penalty, then we would be back to where the Court was in *Furman*. If there is inevitably to be jury discretion, since it is impossible to lay out beforehand a clear set of guidelines, there must be safeguards to ensure that this discretion is used in a manner that does not violate the equal protection clause or other elements of constitutional protection. Just how much "guidance" there can be to a jury that in the end cannot be given clear instructions is a matter at the crux of the debates we will be reviewing throughout the book. How to create a fair and reliable system when the fundamental decision at the core of it—who deserves death—cannot be specified is indeed a puzzle. And, as we will see, it is perhaps an unsolvable one.

Testing the "Marshall Hypothesis"

Justice Thurgood Marshall famously wrote that the US public was far less enthusiastic for the death penalty than it appeared because, he suggested, the public knows so little about the punishment. Marshall also felt that a simple response to a public opinion survey might not reveal a true public attitude, since that attitude would most likely be based on a great deal of ignorance or on assumptions about what the penalty probably is or should be, not what it really is. He hypothesized that with greater knowledge of the facts would come less support. The following is an extended excerpt from Justice Marshall's opinion in *Furman*:[10]

> While a public opinion poll obviously is of some assistance in indicating public acceptance or rejection of a specific penalty, its utility cannot be very great. This is because whether or not a punishment is cruel and unusual depends, not on whether its mere mention "shocks the conscience and sense of justice of the people," but on whether people who were fully informed as to the purposes of the penalty and its liabilities would find the penalty shocking, unjust, and unacceptable.
>
> In other words, the question with which we must deal is not whether a substantial proportion of American citizens would today, if polled, opine that capital punishment is barbarously cruel, but whether they would find it to be so in the light of all information presently available.
>
> This is not to suggest that with respect to this test of unconstitutionality people are required to act rationally; they are not. With respect to this judgment, a violation of the Eighth Amendment is totally dependent on the predictable subjective, emotional reactions of informed citizens.
>
> It has often been noted that American citizens know almost nothing about capital punishment. Some of the conclusions arrived at in the preceding section and the supporting evidence would be critical to an

informed judgment on the morality of the death penalty: e.g., that the death penalty is no more effective a deterrent than life imprisonment, that convicted murderers are rarely executed, but are usually sentenced to a term in prison; that convicted murderers usually are model prisoners, and that they almost always become law-abiding citizens upon their release from prison; that the costs of executing a capital offender exceed the costs of imprisoning him for life; that while in prison, a convict under sentence of death performs none of the useful functions that life prisoners perform; that no attempt is made in the sentencing process to ferret out likely recidivists for execution; and that the death penalty may actually stimulate criminal activity.

This information would almost surely convince the average citizen that the death penalty was unwise, but a problem arises as to whether it would convince him that the penalty was morally reprehensible. This problem arises from the fact that the public's desire for retribution, even though this is a goal that the legislature cannot constitutionally pursue as its sole justification for capital punishment, might influence the citizenry's view of the morality of capital punishment. The solution to the problem lies in the fact that no one has ever seriously advanced retribution as a legitimate goal of our society. Defenses of capital punishment are always mounted on deterrent or other similar theories. This should not be surprising. It is the people of this country who have urged in the past that prisons rehabilitate as well as isolate offenders, and it is the people who have injected a sense of purpose into our penology. I cannot believe that at this stage in our history, the American people would ever knowingly support purposeless vengeance. Thus, I believe that the great mass of citizens would conclude on the basis of the material already considered that the death penalty is immoral and therefore unconstitutional.

But, if this information needs supplementing, I believe that the following facts would serve to convince even the most hesitant of citizens to condemn death as a sanction: capital punishment is imposed discriminatorily against certain identifiable classes of people; there is evidence that innocent people have been executed before their innocence can be proved; and the death penalty wreaks havoc with our entire criminal justice system.

Our book is drawn in part from a desire to test the Marshall Hypothesis. But in constructing the book we have come to understand that we must go far beyond this single hypothesis. And while Justice Marshall was in a position to make judgements, we are not. Our moral sense of whether the death penalty is right or wrong is no better than anyone else's, and, because we do not sit on the US Supreme Court as Marshall did, our opinions on the moral issue are completely irrelevant to public discussion. But we can contribute to the debate nonetheless.

We therefore propose a slight revision to the Marshall Hypothesis and use that to motivate this book. The death penalty is an area where there is a lot of moral feeling but, as the justice wrote, very little understanding of the facts. We believe that everyone is entitled to his or her abstract moral position, but that everyone benefits from understanding the facts. Whether these facts lead, as Marshall expected, to a lessening of support for the death penalty is one possibility. But, more generally, we believe that the death penalty, like any other public policy, must be assessed by its record. With 40 years of experience with the "modern" death penalty, with the increased safeguards put in place by the US Supreme Court in 1976, we are now in a place where we can step back and assess the record. Also, as we noted earlier, members of the Court ruled in 1972 based on accumulated facts; in 1976 they ruled based on theoretical understandings of how the states' newly devised systems would work. Today, we can assess the "modern" system based on the empirics, since we have 40 years of experience to show how it really has worked.

But one thing is clear: we cannot assess and develop opinions about a hypothetical death penalty we might wish we had.[11] Nor should we limit our acceptance of the death penalty to abstract issues of morality without understanding how it really works. Rather, everyone concerned with this ultimate punishment should be interested in how it actually functions. We believe the pages to follow will contain many surprises for most readers. Thus, with this book we make a plea for all those concerned with the death penalty to assess it not as we might wish it were, but as it actually is. With those facts in place, each reader can draw whatever conclusions he or she deems appropriate.

Assessing the Modern Death Penalty

Some elements of the disagreements among the justices cannot be assessed empirically. Whether retribution is a sufficient justification for the death penalty, for example, is a question of morality; some of the justices rejected the idea, and others accepted it. On the other hand, a great number of the differences between the justices were essentially empirical ones. Is the death penalty imposed in an arbitrary manner? Can we impose "proportionality" so that it is reserved only for the worst offenders? Throughout the remainder of this book, we will focus on these empirical questions, knowing that they do not answer all of the questions—people will continue to disagree on the issue of retribution, for example—but with the hope that empirical evidence about how the system has worked over 40 years of experience will be of interest to many.

Phillips and Simon (2014) note that one of the key elements in *Gregg* was to put a limit on the set of crimes for which the death penalty could be administered. The solution to the arbitrary and capricious problem was to narrow the scope of eligible crimes and to impose death on the vast majority of offenders who committed death-eligible crimes. In other words, if the application of the punishment is uniformly and systematically imposed on virtually all those guilty of the specified crimes, then the punishment will remain constitutional. If, by contrast, it is "wantonly and freakishly" imposed on a tiny fraction of killers within a certain category, then it will have failed the *Furman* test. We will return to this concept of reliability repeatedly in the chapters to come.

As many commentators have noted (see, e.g., Garland 2010), the *Furman* and *Gregg* decisions are anticlimactic and disappointing to many. Capital punishment was abolished in 1972 on the basis of procedural and empirical flaws: it was "wanton and freakish." But it was not wrong in the abstract; only two justices agreed with this. When *Gregg* validated the new state laws, it did so with a heavy focus on procedural issues. It was not a ringing endorsement of the moral superiority of a death penalty system over one without capital punishment. Rather, it was a statement based on confidence that newly devised procedural safeguards would ensure that the punishment would be reserved only for the most deserving, not a random or biased selection of defendants. The result of this procedural focus was the beginning of an entirely new jurisprudence, one that required repeated Supreme Court review and that led to various complicated, expensive, arcane, and confusing procedures. In the years that have followed, the arcane nature of capital punishment jurisprudence has been striking. Entire specializations of the law have been built up around capital law, and new professions (such as mitigation specialists) have emerged. The debate moved from one of abstract morality to one of federalism, judicial interpretation, and procedural fairness. Such is the law.

In the years since the *Gregg* decision, many elements of capital jurisprudence have evolved. Congress passed the Antiterrorism and Effective Death Penalty Act of 1996 (AEDPA), designed to curtail appeals and limit delays, in sum, to "get the process rolling." Ironically, as we will see, the law was passed at the year of peak application of the death penalty. In spite of the legislators' most sincere intentions, AEDPA did not usher in a new, quicker, streamlined process. Rather, reversals continued to be common, delays continued to grow, and court decisions limited the use of the death penalty more and more. In 2005 the Court eliminated executions for those who were minors at the time of the trial; in 2002 it eliminated their use for those with severe intellectual disabilities. In sum, in the later chapters we will review a number of trends in our attempt to assess where the accumulation of 40 years of experience leaves us. Are we in that constitutional "sweet spot" or not?

Structure of the Book

We begin in chapter 2 by reviewing the process associated with a capital prosecution. As is clear from the previous paragraph, one of the defining elements of the modern death penalty system is its focus on procedural fairness. We move in chapter 3 to review the history and scope of homicide, as we cannot understand our topic without first understanding its root cause. In chapter 4 we then compare homicide victims and offenders with the victims and offenders in execution cases to explore the patterns of difference between those homicides that lead to execution versus those that do not. In chapter 5 we review state laws on aggravating and mitigating circumstances; chapter 6 reviews state-by-state and county-level variability in the use of capital punishment; chapter 7 discusses what happens after a death sentence is imposed: is the inmate executed, or is the sentence more likely to be reversed? Chapter 8 reviews delays from sentence to execution; chapter 9 reviews exonerations; chapter 10 focuses on methods of execution; chapter 11 reviews how often executions are stayed or canceled; chapter 12 focuses on the issue of mental illness among those condemned to die; chapter 13 reviews evidence about public opinion over time and from place to place; chapter 14 considers cost; chapter 15, deterrence; chapter 16, evidence that the death penalty has been in steep decline over the past 20 years; and in chapter 17 we review the accumulated evidence about whether the modern system lives up to the promise of *Gregg* or fails the test of *Furman*.

In each chapter, we present empirical evidence or background information that should allow us to inform a set of conclusions on these issues, which were central to the decisions in *Furman* and *Gregg*. Does the death penalty comport with "evolving standards" and "community values"? Is it cruel and unusual? Is it narrowly targeted to the worst of the worst? Does a high percentage of all those committing eligible crimes receive a sentence of death, or is the penalty imposed in a "wanton and freakish" manner only on a small percentage of those eligible for it? Are certain classes of offenders or victims particularly targeted for death, such as the poor, minorities, or those who kill whites, females, or both? Is the penalty imposed relatively fairly across geographical units in those states that have the death penalty? Are there elements that can be considered to be torture, or is any unnecessary pain avoided? Is there evidence that the death penalty deters crime or serves other important penological purposes beyond the next most severe punishment, life in prison without the possibility of parole? Does the public support the death penalty? Are members of the public well informed about it? Does variability in use of the death penalty correspond to "community values," or is it affected by such things as electoral politics, the personality of a district attorney, or the calculations of elected judges about the need to be "tough on crime" before an election? Is retribution a sufficient justification for the penalty, and if so, is this justification invoked fairly and evenly across cases? We will raise other questions, of course, but our theme will be to let the evidence speak. It speaks volumes.

Further Readings

American Bar Association (ABA). 2013. The State of the Modern Death Penalty in America: ABA Death Penalty Due Process Review Project, Key Findings of State Death Penalty Assessments 2006–2013. www.americanbar.org/dueprocess.

Banner, Stuart. 2002. *The Death Penalty: An American History*. Cambridge, MA: Harvard University Press.

Bedau, Hugo Adam, ed. 1997. *The Death Penalty in America: Current Controversies*. New York: Oxford University Press.

Bedau, Hugo, and Paul Cassell, eds. 2004. *Debating the Death Penalty*. New York: Oxford University Press.

Blecker, Robert. 2013. *The Death of Punishment: Searching for Justice among the Worst of the Worst*. New York: St. Martin's.

Garland, David. 2010. *Peculiar Institution: America's Death Penalty in an Age of Abolition*. Cambridge, MA: Harvard University Press.

Hatch, Virginia Leigh, and Anthony Walsh. 2016. *Capital Punishment: Theory and Practice of the Ultimate Penalty*. New York: Oxford University Press.

Mandery, Evan J. 2012. *Capital Punishment in America: A Balanced Examination*. 2nd ed. Sudbury, MA: Jones and Bartlett Learning.

———. 2013. *A Wild Justice: The Death and Resurrection of Capital Punishment in America*. New York: Norton.

Moody, Christopher Z., and Mei Hsien Lee. 1999. Morality Policy Reinvention: State Death Penalties. *Annals of the American Academy of Political and Social Science* 566:80–92.

Oshinsky, David M. 2010. *Capital Punishment on Trial:* Furman v. Georgia *and the Death Penalty in Modern America*. Lawrence: University Press of Kansas.

Sarat, Austin. 2001. *When the State Kills*. Princeton, NJ: Princeton University Press.

Steiker, Carol S., and Jordan M. Steiker. 2016. *Courting Death: The Supreme Court and Capital Punishment*. Cambridge, MA: Harvard University Press.

Zimring, Franklin E. 2003. *The Contradictions of American Capital Punishment*. New York: Oxford University Press.

2

The Capital Punishment Process

Condemning a citizen to death and carrying through to execution is the only punishment that can never be reversed, and as such it calls for a unique process to avoid errors.[1] Accordingly, the US Supreme Court has adopted a "death is different" logic, imposing particular requirements and allowing for special processes to apply to capital punishment, many of which have no counterparts in other areas of criminal justice. Following the *Gregg* decision, the Supreme Court mandated measures in both the trial and the appeals process that are designed to limit the chances of the arbitrary application of the death penalty. This chapter lays out the pretrial, trial, and appeals process an inmate facing execution will likely complete, a process that will be referred to throughout the book. Because criminal justice is a state matter, each state lays out its own particular processes, and we cannot explain each one here. Rather, we attempt to give an overview of how the process works in most states, with any important peculiarities laid out in the relevant sections of this chapter and those that follow.

Pretrial

Capital trials involve only those inmates accused of particularly heinous crimes. The first thing to keep in mind is that none of these trials are "garden variety"—all involve first-degree murder. Therefore, the point of reference in comparing capital trials to others is to other similar trials. Trials for first-degree murder are serious affairs, considering what has occurred to the victims and what may happen to the defendant. But when the defendant is on trial for his or her life, the stakes are even higher. No wonder, then, that capital trials are highly emotional. Even before the trial, the stakes are high.

Pretrial Detention

Inmates accused of crimes are presumed to be innocent. However, judges may set bond at various levels, ranging from none ("free on own recognizance"), when they expect that there is no danger that the defendant will fail to appear for trial, to various levels of monetary commitment. Bonds are supposed to ensure that the accused will appear at trial; in some circumstances, bond can be denied to ensure the protection of the community. In capital cases, the accused are usually detained before trial; that is, there is no bond. Rather than go home to prepare for trial (or continue to work and pay for attorneys), capital defendants are typically kept in jail before trial. Because the trials can sometimes take years, many inmates begin their incarceration period well before they are convicted. Typically, they are held in county jails, but in many cases they are held in maximum security prisons. North Carolina, for example, houses "infamous" or other pretrial detainees who cannot be held by the county sheriff at Raleigh's Central Prison. Although they are called "safekeepers" rather than inmates, and they are not held on death row, they are not free. So the first difference in a capital trial occurs well before the trial itself. The accused is typically held in detention from the moment he or she is arrested.

Bryan Stevenson notes that his (innocent) client Walter McMillan in Alabama was actually housed on death row before being tried. As Stevenson notes, "[I]t is illegal to subject pretrial detainees . . . to confinement that constitutes punishment" (2014, 52), but the authorities did it anyway to increase pressure on the defendant to plead guilty. While it is certainly extremely rare—and illegal—to house an accused inmate on death row, typically those accused of first-degree murderer are denied bail and thus are held in custody before trial.

Notice of Intent, Discovery, and Preparing for Trial

Although the particulars differ from state to state, a capital prosecution begins when the district attorney (DA) informs the court that he or she intends to seek death. In some states this will be reviewed and approved by a judge; in others the DA acts with complete discretion. Once the DA declares the intent to seek death, the case proceeds as a capital one, following different rules than a non-capital case, even a non-capital murder case.

Due to the serious nature of the charges, the discovery period in capital cases is often a long one and may rely heavily on experts to build effective cases on both sides. It is considered the responsibility of the court to ensure indigent defendants obtain the services needed to develop an effective defense not only for the guilt phase but also for the potential sentencing phase. In contrast to a non-capital trial, a capital trial will potentially involve a penalty phase, and preparation for that begins immediately. This means that the prosecution is expected to disclose to the defense prior to trial any potential mitigating factors found in its discovery, in addition to its obligation to provide other exculpatory evidence. Mitigation specialists, psychologists, investigators, jury consultants, and other experts may be part of the pretrial team that develops a picture of the defendant, on both sides. These procedures differ from state to state and have been revised over time. Many active death states provide few guarantees for a robust defense or mitigation team, and many inmates currently on death row were tried and sentenced under systems that have since been revised. One reason for dramatic reductions in the numbers of death sentences imposed nationally and in particular states may be improved safeguards and increased resources for the defense. Unfortunately for many currently on death row, these reforms have not been made retroactive.

One of the most important differences that sets the modern death penalty apart from its historical counterpart is the creation of a specialized legal community. Capital jurisprudence has evolved into a complex legal specialty, so attorneys must specialize in it to do it well; courts have (slowly and incompletely) come to recognize that standards of practice must be higher when a life is on the line, mitigation evidence must be gathered, and a range of other characteristics define the difference between a capital and a non-capital murder trial (see Steiker and Steiker 2016, 195ff.). We will review this in somewhat more detail in chapter 15 on cost.

Appointing Capital Counsel

Perhaps the most important implication of the state's decision to seek death is a different process for appointing defense counsel, though of course this differs by state and has been subject to greater scrutiny over time. The vast majority of capital defendants are indigent; that is, they require a state-appointed attorney and are guaranteed under the Constitution the right to have one "promptly appointed" (18 U.S.C. § 3005; White 2006). Unfortunately for these indigent defendants, court-appointed capital defenders often lack the resources and experience needed properly to represent their clients, and the quality of their counsel can strongly affect the outcome of trials.

It should come as no surprise that state legislatures place funding defense costs for a subset of those accused of the most vicious crimes at the very bottom of their budgetary priorities. Though the states differ, many have or previously had both woefully inadequate levels of support for their capital defense attorneys and low standards for practice. According to Steiker and Steiker, these issues have particularly affected the southern states. Comparing the dramatic differences in rates of execution between Texas and California, they write:

> The difference in legal culture so evident between California and Texas is the legacy of a much older and broader phenomenon. It is no accident that so many of the executing states are concentrated in the South, as that region has a history of incomplete conversion to a due process culture of criminal adjudication. It is notable that the Supreme Court began its foray into the constitutionalization of criminal procedure in the capital trial of the Scottsboro Boys, which was emblematic of the "legal lynchings" that often passed for Southern justice, particularly in cases of alleged

black-on-white violence. The wholesale criminal procedure revolution
wrought by the Warren Court in the 1960s was in large part an attempt
to bring outliers—again mostly Southern states—up to a national standard of due process in criminal cases. The ability to expedite executions in
many states is at least partly due to the incomplete success of the Warren
Court's project—the result of Southern resistance to norms dictated by
the same Court that sought to impose national values of racial justice. Or,
from the perspective of the symbolic states, the *inability* to expedite executions is attributable not merely to less deeply held political commitment at
all levels to the policy of capital punishment but also to entrenched expectations about what the judicial process ought to look like in capital cases.
For example, it would simply be unthinkable—far outside the norms of
the reigning legal culture—for lawyers in California to fall asleep during
capital trials, for trial judges to ignore such behavior, or for appellate courts
to excuse it, as has happened in Texas more than once. (Steiker and Steiker
2016, 148–149)

Stephen Bright (1994) suggests that poor lawyering is a major cause of death
sentences; that is, individuals who are sentenced to death are not those who are
most deserving but rather those with the worst lawyers. And, as the Steikers make
clear, poor lawyering is not equally accepted in capital cases in all areas of the country. It is more accepted in the South, where hostility to the Warren Court's "rights
revolution" of the 1960s was stronger and deeply shared through many parts of the
judicial system.

The Supreme Court was slow to push the states to improve their capital defense
services, often affirming lower court actions accepting woefully poor performance
by counsel. The Supreme Court established the "Strickland test" in 1984 to determine quality of counsel; when the test is applied, a defendant must show that
representation "fell below an objective standard of reasonableness" and that such
performance prejudiced the defendant. However, this test was created with the
caveat that the guarantee of effective assistance will "improve the quality of legal
representation" and ensure that the trial is fair, "with a fair trial being defined as one
'whose result is reliable'" but not perfect (White, 2006, 14).

The Steikers point out: "When the Court first articulated the right of criminal defendants to receive effective assistance of counsel, it went out of its way to
insist that the standard should not differ because the defendant faced the death
penalty" (2016, 169–170), adding that "the purpose of reviewing claims for ineffective assistance 'is not to improve the quality of legal representation' but to
provide relief where the adversarial system totally broke down" (170). A successful challenge on these grounds had to show that the attorney's performance was
"'outside the wide range of professionally competent assistance'" and also that
the errors made

"actually had an adverse effect on the defense." As a result of this lax approach, state and lower courts routinely denied relief in cases involving manifestly poor representation in capital cases. Especially during the first two decades post-*Furman*, capital defendants were often represented by court-appointed lawyers lacking the experience, resources, or commitment to mount an appropriate defense. In a number of states, attorney fees were capped at absurdly low amounts, effectively guaranteeing that defense lawyers would conduct minimal investigation, employ no experts, and confine their efforts to off-the-cuff cross-examination of state witnesses. (170)

In sum, when the state has sought to kill, it has not easily provided the resources to mount a defense equal to the challenge presented, and the Court long accepted lax standards that perpetuated a "caste" system that denied the poor the type of defense that could save their lives (see Justice Douglas in *Furman*; Steiker and Steiker 2016, 170).

With all this in mind, some states have implemented reforms that move in the right direction. Others, like Alabama, have seen powerful nonprofit law firms such as the Equal Justice Initiative raise funds privately to improve indigent defense. In New Mexico, which abolished capital punishment in 2009, minimum standards included being a member of good standing of the state bar, a minimum of five years of active criminal litigation experience, and completion of capital defense training provided by the state (NMSA §5-704). In North Carolina, legislation passed in 2000 established Indigent Defense Services (IDS) in 2001, a statewide office that works closely with the nonprofit Center for Death Penalty Litigation (CDPL). Each defendant is entitled to two CDPL-affiliated attorneys. Prior to the reform, local judges assigned local bar members, not necessarily those specializing in capital law, for a set fee to represent each client. (That fee was often as low as $5,000.) The judge then had to approve budgetary requests for the defense (such as hiring an investigator or an expert or mitigation specialist), whereas the state had its own budget. The reform thus sought to eliminate this disparity, creating something closer to a level playing field between the two sides. Crucially, IDS and CDPL, not local judges, appointed counsel and managed their budgets. Only trained, qualified, and specialized attorneys were appointed. Not surprisingly, death sentencing rates plummeted in the state after this equalizing reform was put into place, leading to a situation in which more than two-thirds of the inmates on death row as of 2015 were sentenced under procedures and with defense lawyers funded through a system that is no longer in place because of its recognized inadequacies (see Baumgartner 2015). These examples are but the tip of the iceberg, but they illustrate the idea that taxpayer support for the legal defense of accused murderers is an extremely unpopular budget item, and there is little political will to fund such programs. Stephen Bright (1994) provides ample examples of how a bad lawyer can spell trouble in the complex and arcane world of capital litigation.

Plea Bargaining

With the state seeking death, and the inmate in pretrial confinement, many inmates plead guilty to murder with the agreement that the state will seek "only" the penalty of life without parole (LWOP). This process, known as "plea bargaining," is a common legal tool within today's criminal justice system, at both the state and the federal level. In fact, "[O]ur criminal justice system is almost exclusively a system of plea bargaining, negotiated behind closed doors and with no judicial oversight" (Rakoff 2014).

Plea agreements may be made at any point from soon after charges are filed to any period before the trial is complete. Indeed, the vast majority of individuals facing criminal charges will choose a plea bargain over the option of going to trial. According to a US Department of Justice summary of the process, "While there are no exact estimates of the proportion of cases that are resolved through plea bargaining, scholars estimate that about 90 to 95 percent of both federal and state court cases are resolved through this process" (Devers 2011, 1; Bureau of Justice Statistics, 2005; Flanagan and Maguire, 1990). This high rate of usage represents a relatively new shift in legal practices within the United States. For most of common-law history, plea bargains were actively discouraged (Alschuler 1968, 1979). Only when our criminal justice system became swamped with increased criminal caseloads did prosecutors begin to use plea bargains as a means to expedite backlogs.

On its surface, a plea bargain appears as an opportunity for the defendant to consider his or her choices while facing the threat of criminal trial. The defendant weighs the proposed punishment offered by the state in exchange for a guilty plea against the probability of receiving a harsher sentence through criminal trial. If it is certain that a harsher sentence will be handed down through trial, the defendant is wise to choose the plea bargain. Of course, there is always an element of risk in a trial, but in fact the vast majority of trials end in a verdict of guilty. Therefore, inmates can be under a lot of pressure to accept a plea, since the alternative is often a high probability of a harsher sentence. Of course, once the trial starts, a plea is unlikely, since both sides would have had ample opportunity to come to such an agreement if it had been possible to avoid the time-consuming and costly preparations for a major trial. (Paradoxically, in the context of a capital case, plea bargaining does not typically lead to a dramatic reduction in cost as compared with a system without capital trial, for reasons we address in chapter 14, but which amount to each side doing due diligence, given that a life is on the line. A capital trial typically involves extensive investigation not just into the evidence of guilt but also of mitigation factors, and these investigations must play a powerful role in each side's estimate of the likely final outcome of the trial, and therefore the best plea bargaining strategy. So, while a plea bargain can avoid some court costs, it does not necessarily come at a lower financial cost than if a death sentence were not available.)

Proponents of plea bargains often tout this rational-probabilistic framework and associate plea bargains with better legal outcomes for the entire criminal justice system. Without plea bargains, they argue, limited scarce resources would be redirected from other aspects of the criminal justice system to help accommodate the extra burden of increased criminal trials. This stance, however, ignores how plea bargains often "take place in the shadow of prosecutors' preferences, voters' preferences, budget constraints, and other forces" (Stuntz 2004, 2550). While theoretically every accused has the right to a full hearing in court, in fact, the vast majority of US criminal cases end in plea bargains, with negotiated settlements taking place without any jury involvement Thus, the right to have one's case heard in open court is often more a theoretical promise than a practical reality, even in the case of capital crimes (Kuziemko 2006).

While there are various reasons why plea bargains are disproportionately used, legal considerations alone do little to explain why plea bargains are used at consistently high rates across the United States. Rather, structural-psychological factors help to provide a better interpretation. Uncertainty, money (or lack thereof), self-interest, and demographics all help to explain how plea bargains are influenced (Bibas 2004). Because of these factors, opponents challenge the "fairness" of voluntary settlement, definitions of who should be considered innocent (should an individual who did not commit a crime but who pleaded guilty to a crime be considered innocent?) and suggest that conflicts of interest permeate the plea bargaining process (Schulhofer 1992). Plea bargains certainly help explain why some individuals ended up on death row whereas others did not.

Death Qualification

Jurors in capital cases must be "death-qualified," which means the juror is one who, should the defendant be convicted, states that he or she would be capable of sentencing that person to death. Death-qualified jurors do not precommit to doing so, but if they indicate that they could not bring themselves to sentence a person to death, they are excused from jury service. Lawyers and others familiar with the death penalty understand the concept of "death qualification," but for those considering the topic for the first time, or those who have not studied it in detail, this is one of the most surprising, puzzling, and troubling aspects of the death penalty system. Under long-standing legal doctrine, prospective jurors may be excluded from service in a capital trial if they are systematically opposed to capital punishment to such an extent that they could not vote for death. The logic is that a juror must be willing to apply the law. Of course, excluding all such individuals dramatically reshapes the jury pool, making it subject to the opposite type of bias. Death-qualified juries not only exclude all those unsupportive of death but also are more prone to find guilt (see Oberer 1961; Cowan, Thompson, and Ellsworth 1984; Haney 2005). This was challenged in 1968, and the Court recognized the possible bias toward finding guilt, ruling in *Witherspoon v. Illinois* that states could exclude jurors who were categorically opposed to the death penalty but could not exclude those who were merely hesitant about it. The Court here recognized the argument that death qualification could result in juries that were overly predisposed to findings of guilt.

Death qualification of all juries in the United States considering a crime with the possible penalty of death is one of the most significant elements of any capital trial. There are two stages to a capital trial, of course, but just one jury. That means that the filtering effect meant to affect the second stage (e.g., being willing to consider the penalty of death) also affects the first stage, the finding of guilt. Death-qualified juries are significantly more likely to defer to the prosecution, and ensuring that all members of the jury share this perspective also significantly reduces the diversity of opinions present in the jury room (see Cowan, Thompson, and Ellsworth 1984). Far from a jury of one's peers, or one that represents the diversity of opinion and values within a community, death qualification results—uniquely in American law—in juries predisposed both to guilt and to death as a punishment. As we will see in later chapters, death qualification renders even more puzzling the fact that death sentences are so rare. With more than 700,000 homicides in the United States since 1976, there have been just over 8,000 death sentences in the modern era; even with death qualification, the death penalty remains a rare punishment in comparison with the large number of homicide prosecutions throughout the country.

Death qualification also generates a perverse and costly incentive for prosecutors to seek death even if they do not expect to get it, do not want it, or would be satisfied with a lesser sentence. By seeking death, they can guarantee a death-qualified jury, which means one more likely to find in favor of guilt. Given the prosecutor's likely desire to get a guilty verdict, death qualification thus creates an incentive to seek death. This is but one of the many elements of the death penalty process that relate only indirectly to the death penalty itself; starting down the path toward a capital trial increases the likelihood of findings of guilt.

Supreme Court rulings on death qualification have actually reinforced its strength in the years since *Witherspoon*. The ability to exclude jurors was expanded in the *Wainwright v. Witt* (1985) decision giving a trial judge the authority to exclude a juror whose concern about the death penalty might "substantially impair" his or her ability to vote for death. (That is, the prospective juror did not have to be "categorically opposed" to the punishment in all cases.) In 1986 the Court ruled in *Lockhart v. McCree* that general pro-prosecution bias associated with death qualification (e.g., filtering out prospective jurors who may be less willing to vote for guilt as well as death, or disproportionately including jurors inclined to be sensitive to prosecution arguments) could not be used as a grounds to appeal guilt; defendants would have to prove bias in their individual case, not in the abstract.

This decision essentially puts the same burden on the defendant making a jury bias claim as *McCleskey v. Kemp* (1987) imposed on those making a racial bias claim: the Court required individualized proof of intent to discriminate, not a general empirical finding of disproportionate impact (no matter how powerful that evidence might be). More recently, in *Uttecht v. Brown* (2007), the Court ruled that considerable deference must be given to the trial judge, since only he or she can see the demeanor of the juror. This decision was made in the context of a case in which the judge had dismissed a juror who repeatedly asserted being able to apply the law but was excused anyway based on other statements the judge considered to be equivocal; the Court refused to overrule the judge.

To the uninitiated, it may seem shocking that so many Americans are excluded from service on capital juries through the doctrine of death qualification. Of course, the impact of these decisions is not neutral with regard to gender, race, or many other factors. Death qualification results in juries that are whiter, more male, and more favorable to the prosecution, and it categorically excludes millions of Americans from jury service on the basis of their political beliefs or religious attitudes. And yet, it is a matter of settled law. One must be willing to impose the law. Perhaps no other element of the US death penalty is so surprising to those not already familiar with it.

Trial

Jury Selection

Launching the trial stage, jury selection is a critical step in the capital process, with special guidelines put in place by the courts, such as death qualification as reviewed in the previous section. This jury is particularly important because it will determine not only the guilt or innocence of the defendant but also the penalty in the second stage of the trial if the defendant is found guilty.

In any criminal trial, prospective jurors may typically be excused for two reasons: "for cause" and peremptorily. An excusal for cause would be, for example, if the prospective juror was an acquaintance of the defendant or one of the witnesses. Judges decide on whether to excuse individual jurors for cause and do so in large numbers; a prospective juror may also be excused if he or she states that serving on the jury would create a hardship such as lost wages or difficulties arranging for childcare. Other jurors can be rejected using what are called "peremptory challenges," where either the state or the defense can simply strike them, with no reason given. The number of peremptory challenges in a criminal case is typically six, but in capital cases this number is often doubled as it is, for example, in North Carolina. This means that either side can reject 12 individuals from the jury pool for no reason. Evidence suggests that these strikes are often used to exclude blacks (see Stevenson 2014). Defense attorneys may use them to exclude individuals who appear overly deferential to the police or to authorities. It is illegal under *Batson v. Kentucky* (1986) for the state to use race (or gender) as the basis for its strikes, even peremptory ones. As we will discuss in later chapters, however, there has been little implementation of this ruling. Many capital juries have no black members.

The Bifurcated Trial

The two-part capital trial begins with the guilt phase, a trial period that runs relatively similarly to that for an average violent or major criminal trial. The trial begins with opening statements from both the prosecution and the defense, with each side giving a preview of the case to set the tone for the type of arguments it will be making over a trial that could run several weeks. At this stage in the capital process, the burden of proof is not on the defendant but instead on the state, and so the prosecution presents its case first, seeking to convince the jury beyond a reasonable doubt that the defendant committed the crime. Following the conclusion of the prosecution's presentation, the defense has the opportunity to respond. It may present alternative evidence, such as an alibi, argue that the crime was committed by another, or argue that the state has not proven its case. Many capital defendants face multiple charges: attempted murder, robbery, kidnapping, or others. These charges, not being capital, may lead to findings of guilt or innocence, and each may be subject to its own punishment. The fact that defendants often face multiple charges explains how individuals can sometimes be sentenced to what seem like extraordinary punishments, such as life in prison, plus 10 years. To an outsider, this may seem fanciful, but in the legal system, each separate conviction brings its own penalty. In any case, for the capital murder charge, juries may render one of four possible outcomes: (1) guilty of capital murder, (2) guilty of a lesser offense, (3) acquittal, or (4) mistrial.

If the verdict is guilty of capital murder (or first-degree murder, depending on the language used in the state), the penalty phase follows. In this phase, the same judge, attorneys, and jurors sit to weigh the aggravating and mitigating circumstances associated with the crime. Aggravating factors typically must be found to have been proven beyond a reasonable doubt, though the states differ in exactly how this is done, and some do not require that the jury be unanimous or that the jurors agree on which aggravating factor was proven. In any case, there is typically some emphasis on demonstrating that at least one aggravator was present, so that the case qualifies under the law for the death penalty. At the same time, in all states but Texas, the jury may consider any type of mitigating evidence that is presented to it. Sentencing phases can be quite extensive, as the defense team knows that the life of their client lies in the hands of the same 12 individuals who rendered the verdict of guilty of a capital crime. Of course, not all defense attorneys do present a full mitigation dossier, but the penalty phase is their opportunity to do so. Texas, the most prolific executing state, has a different process, as explained in chapter 1. The similarity between Texas and the other death penalty states is that there are two phases of the trial, and that only certain crimes make one eligible for death. Texas places particular emphasis on the jury's estimate of the inmate's "future dangerousness."

We review the aggravating and mitigating circumstances allowed in each state in chapter 5, but the process is simply that testimony is heard on both sides, and the jury then reconvenes no longer to consider guilt but to determine punishment. If the verdict is death, then the defendant is condemned. If the verdict is life, then the inmate is sentenced to the specified alternative punishment, which is LWOP.[2] If a death sentence is determined and approved by the judge,[3] then the inmate is condemned to die. However, as we will see in chapter 7, the appeals process is often successful, and in fact most condemned inmates are not put to death. Rather, either they languish on death row while their appeals continue, or their sentences are overturned and they are given a lesser penalty even after initially being condemned to die. In fact, just 16 percent of condemned inmates in the modern period have been executed (see chapter 7).

The Appellate Process

Appeals for death sentences come in two stages: direct appeals, which are automatic, and postconviction appeals, which follow rules relatively similar to those for any other criminal conviction. Direct appeals, which are a distinctive feature of the post-*Gregg* death penalty system, serve as a means to require state appellate courts to review the proportionality of the sentence (e.g., to make sure that different individual trial courts were indeed selecting only the "worst of the worst" for the harshest punishment) and to allow a review by the federal courts before an execution could ever be carried out in any state. Accordingly, the issues that can be raised can differ in direct and postconviction appeals. Direct appeals, being automatic, typically focus on issues that arise from the record of the original trial. Postconviction appeals may raise issues such as suppressed evidence, newly discovered evidence, ineffective assistance of counsel, and other matters not considered in the original trial.

While the Court focused significantly in *Gregg* and related cases on the need for proportionality review, it soon moved back from what seemed like a firm requirement. A 1984 California case significantly reduced its seeming commitment to proportionality review. In *Pulley v. Harris* (1984), the Court ruled that petitioner Harris was not entitled to habeas relief on the grounds that California did not conduct a proportionality review, and it noted several factors. First, while *Gregg* seemed to require proportionality review, in fact it did not. Instead, the Court ruled that in *Gregg*, Justices Stewart and Powell "suggested that some form of meaningful appellate review is required . . . those Justices did not declare that comparative review was so critical that, without it, the Georgia statute would not have passed constitutional muster" (*Pulley v. Harris*, 45). Continuing, the majority wrote:

[T]he concerns expressed in *Furman* . . . can be met by a carefully drafted statute that ensures that the sentencing authority is given adequate information and guidance. As a general proposition, these concerns are best met by a system that provides for a bifurcated proceeding at which the sentencing authority is apprised of the information relevant to the imposition of sentence and provided with standards to guide its use of the information . . . .

In short, the Court of Appeals erred in concluding that *Gregg* required proportionality review. (*Pulley v. Harris*, 46)

The Court also noted that Texas and California did not have proportionality review at all, but that their systems were constitutional because, for example, in the case of Texas, the state has narrowed its definition of capital murder, thereby reserving it only to those with aggravating circumstances before "a death penalty can even be considered" (48). Further, by "authorizing the defense to bring before the jury at the separate sentencing hearing whatever mitigating circumstances relating to the individual defendant can be adduced, Texas has ensured that the sentencing jury will have adequate guidance to enable it to perform its sentencing function" (48). In sum, proportionality review is actually not required, the Court clarified in 1984. Rather, capriciousness and arbitrariness can be avoided by narrow targeting and by the bifurcated trial.

Federal jurisprudence and law moved further toward the timely enforcement of death sentences after the 1996 passage of the Antiterrorism and Effective Death Penalty Act (AEDPA). This law required inmates to file their federal appeals within one year and dramatically increased the burden on the inmate seeking reversal. Under AEDPA, only "unreasonable" rulings can be overturned, not just erroneous or questionable ones. Although the distinction may not seem profound, it is. Since AEDPA, death row inmates have significantly reduced powers to appeal. A lower court simply being wrong is not a reason for reversal; the court must have been "unreasonable." A puzzle that we will examine in two later chapters is that while AEDPA clearly succeeded in its intent to limit the ability of death row inmates to succeed in federal court, it appears to have made no impact on reducing either the high rates of reversal (chapter 7) or the length of time that inmates spend on death row before execution (chapter 8).

Direct Appeal

Following *Gregg v. Georgia*, state appellate courts review verdicts and sentences in death sentence cases on "direct review." The direct appeal is automatically given to everyone who has received a sentence of death and is typically made to the state's highest court. While many states make this appeal mandatory for every person given the death penalty, other states allow this to be left to the discretion of the inmate. If the court reverses the conviction or sentence, then the case will go back to the trial court. If the state appellate court affirms the conviction and sentence, then the defendant may seek a writ of certiorari with the US Supreme Court. The Supreme Court is not required to hear the case; if the writ is denied, the defendant's direct appeal is over.

Appellate review differs from the original trial because, on appeal, the inmate is no longer covered by the presumption of innocence. Rather, the presumed guilty inmate is faced with proving that there was a mistake during the trial or sentencing phase. While each state differs in their appellate process, the following is a general guideline of what the process entails.

Any appellate court may overturn either the conviction or the death sentence, and if it does so, the judgment is vacated and the issue returns to the court. At that point the district attorney may request a new trial or sentencing hearing. If the DA does not seek a new trial, the conviction is thus vacated and the inmate goes free. In most states, if the death sentence is overturned (but not the conviction), the inmate will automatically be sentenced to LWOP unless the DA seeks death in a subsequent trial. Many death row inmates have had their initial death sentences overturned only to see them imposed a second or a third time. More, however, remain in prison for life after their death sentence is overturned. We discuss "reversals" in chapter 7.

Postconviction Appeals

Once an inmate has completed all direct appeals, and not found relief, he or she begins a process of postconviction appeals through both the state and federal courts. At this stage, however, with direct appeals completed, the governor or other authorized agent may set the inmate's execution date (see chapter 11).

State Review

Following any criminal trial, a convicted inmate may file a postconviction motion with the original trial judge seeking redress of flaws in the trial (e.g., Brady violations [improperly withheld evidence known to the state but not turned over as required to the defense]; ineffective assistance of counsel; false instructions to the jury) or relating to events that have come to light since the trial, such as recanted witness testimony or newly discovered evidence. This is a daunting process at this point; the inmate is now presumed guilty, the verdict and death sentence have been affirmed on direct appeal, and the motion goes back to the same trial court where the original trial occurred, perhaps to the same judge. In rare cases the judge may allow a hearing to consider the new evidence, but typically the motions are denied and may then be appealed up through the state appellate system to the state supreme court. Again, the outcome of these appeals may be nothing at all (affirmation) or the reversal of the original conviction or the death sentence.

Strict deadlines apply to all these procedures, and issues already considered by the courts may not be raised a second time. That is, once an inmate raises, for example, the issue of "ineffective assistance of counsel" and this claim is rejected, the matter is legally closed and may not be raised again. New motions must comply with the same deadline requirements and make different claims. Effectively this means that there is but "one shot" at postconviction motions, unless and until new evidence is discovered that the court had previously not been able to consider. This, of course, is rare.

Federal Review

After the state postconviction process has been exhausted, a defendant will typically take his or her case to federal court, submitting a habeas corpus petition in district court. Such a petition must be based on the denial of federal constitutional right. The defendant, referred to as the "petitioner" in federal court, must file within strict time limitations, and failure of the defendant or counsel to meet those limitations can preclude any review of the case in federal court. If granted, the petitioner will prepare for his or her federal hearing. If the court agrees with the petitioner and reverses the sentence or conviction, the case will go back to the state trial court. If the federal district court affirms the conviction and sentence, the petitioner may file an appeal with the federal court of appeals. Again, the case will be either reversed or affirmed. If affirmed, the petitioner will have one last chance to appeal to the US Supreme Court for review. A petitioner who is unsuccessful throughout the federal habeas process has exhausted his or her constitutional rights and may move to seek executive clemency. At the same time, the state may move to schedule the execution, as the inmate has exhausted all the mandated reviews and the death sentence has been affirmed by numerous courts.

The Antiterrorism and Effective Death Penalty Act of 1996

In the years since the *Gregg* decision, many elements of capital jurisprudence have evolved. Death sentences followed the *Gregg* decision quickly: more than 200 per year from 1981 onward, even reaching 301 in 1986. But the number of executions grew only slowly, as we saw in Figure 1.2B. Political leaders were clearly frustrated by what they considered "excessive appeals," and these pressures reached a peak in the mid-1990s. During this time not only did death sentences and executions reach their historic peaks, but public opinion in favor of the death penalty did as well (see chapter 13). Political sentiment reached perhaps its most enthusiastic support of the death penalty during this period. One of the most prominent manifestations of the pro–death penalty feeling among politicians was the Antiterrorism and Effective Death Penalty Act, which passed the Senate by a vote of 91 to 8 and was signed into law by President Bill Clinton in 1996. The act was designed to curtail appeals and limit delays, to "get the process rolling." It made numerous adjustments to federal habeas review, dramatically limiting the rights of a state inmate to make use of the federal system for relief on constitutional grounds. Under AEDPA, in order for a defendant to successfully appeal where the Constitution has been misapplied, he or she must prove that the state court's decision was "contrary to" Supreme Court precedent, not simply erroneous or questionable. As mentioned earlier, AEDPA reduced the time limit for federal appeal, but its most prominent adjustment was to raise the standard for reversal: only "unreasonable" state decisions were subject to change by the federal courts, not just erroneous ones.

Ironically, AEDPA was passed when the death penalty was experiencing peak application, and in spite of legislators' sincere intentions, AEDPA did not usher in a quicker and streamlined process leading inexorably from sentence to execution. On the contrary, reversals continued to be common, delays continued to grow, and court decisions limited the use of the death penalty more and more. Further, executions and death sentences have declined precipitously from their levels at the time the law was signed. So while the law resulted in significant limitations to the federal habeas rights of prisoners, it simply has not accomplished its overall goals.

A study by John H. Blume (2006) shows that although AEDPA had the potential to restrict habeas, it made a difference in only a handful of cases, and the Supreme Court has been just as involved in reviewing state court convictions as before the law was passed. Blume and others (see Stevenson 2002; Hammel 2002) speculate that the reason AEDPA had more "hype" than "bite" is because of how poorly it was drafted. Blume (2006) suggests that the most convincing explanation for the relative failure of AEDPA was the fact that the Supreme Court had already begun to curtail the writ. Further, he holds that AEDPA may have had a weaker impact because judicial actors believe that it is not up to Congress to determine how much habeas is enough; they view that responsibility as residing with the courts.

While the writ of habeas corpus persists, the "bite" that the AEDPA was able to effectively deliver is the dramatically reduced statute of limitations in the process. Although many death row prisoners have already felt the damage imposed by AEDPA's statute of limitations, and although the law was clearly designed to make it much harder for inmates to gain federal relief, it never achieved its goal. Or, perhaps more accurately, in the complex federal system with multiple layers of review and multiple angles on which to seek review, defense attorneys have found other ways to seek redress for erroneous or faulty decisions by state courts.

Death Warrants, Stays, and Executions

While the process differs from state to state, commonly at the completion of direct review, the competent authority (governor, attorney general, director of the prison, sometimes the local district attorney who sought the conviction) may set or ask for an execution date to be set. A death warrant is then issued, typically scheduling the execution for 30 to 90 days from the date the warrant is issued (though sometimes much longer, if there are many inmates scheduled for execution). Each state differs, of course.

Issuing a death warrant is a necessary but not a sufficient step in carrying out an execution. As we will review in detail in chapter 11, many death warrants are later canceled. Attorneys may accelerate their appeals once a warrant is issued, as this obviously moves their client to the highest priority compared with others. And, while direct appeals may have been exhausted, various postconviction motions may remain available. States, if they choose, may set dates for execution after the direct appeals have been denied, however. In fact, some states do not set dates promptly; others routinely set the dates even though there is little likelihood that the execution will be carried out. Dates are "stayed" (canceled or postponed) on a routine basis, and this can happen at any time from the issuance of the warrant to the very last minute. Sometimes death sentences are fully reversed after a warrant has been issued; in other cases the execution date is merely postponed while additional hearings are set, only to be reinstated later. As of June 2017, the DPIC website lists scheduled executions in Ohio out to March 2021. The site lists 22 scheduled executions for 2017 (of which 12 were already stayed or rescheduled); 14 for 2018; 10 for 2019; 8 for 2020; and 2 for 2021. While Texas, Virginia, and Missouri have scheduled execution dates listed, only Ohio has publicly listed execution dates more than six months in advance on the DPIC site.

If the execution does go forward, and 1,422 of them have been carried out in the modern period, each state specifies the procedures to be followed. Typically, the inmate is moved to a waiting area near the execution chamber a few days before the scheduled execution, which typically occurs at night with just a few observers (selected family members of the inmate or of the victim, often one or a few journalists). The cause of death is listed on the death certificate as "homicide." The family may retrieve the inmate's body, or it may be buried in a pauper's grave.

Clemency

The last chance for a defendant to reverse a death sentence is through seeking clemency or a commutation. The clemency process differs from state to state but typically involves the governor or a board of advisers (board of pardons or board of clemency) or a combination of these (see DPIC for individual state procedures). Clemency is mercy, or a unilateral decision by the state to forgo or reduce a judicial penalty though it may have been justly imposed. Through long-standing Anglo-American legal tradition, the chief executive typically has the right to issue such decisions. These are not reversals of the finding of guilt but rather reductions in the sentence imposed, from death typically to life in prison without the possibility for parole. In previous periods of US history, it was not uncommon for governors to grant clemency in large portions of death penalty cases, because of concerns about the fairness of the original trial, because of potential racial bias or proportionality concerns, or for other reasons. In the post-*Gregg* period, executive clemency is extremely rare, and those constitutional or due process concerns are supposed to be handled through the courts. In chapter 7 we give statistics on how often clemency has been granted. For federal cases, the president has similar rights of clemency to most governors. The US president does not have the power to grant clemency to an inmate who has been convicted in state court, which applies to the vast majority of inmates.

Pardon

In addition to the power of clemency, which means substituting a lesser sentence for a harsher one, governors typically have the power of pardon. A pardon implies not a finding of innocence of the underlying crime but a forgiveness of the penalty. With a pardon, the individual goes free but is not considered innocent. Pardons are typically given for relatively minor crimes, not those that lead to the death penalty. Such pardons, sometimes called "pardons of forgiveness," do not directly concern us here. We are more concerned with "pardons of innocence." With a pardon of innocence, available only in a few states, the governor formally recognizes that the individual did not in fact commit the crime. This may follow an exoneration. With an exoneration (see later), charges are dropped and the individual reverts to his or her pretrial presumption of innocence that all Americans enjoy. However, there is often no official finding that the individual was, in fact, innocent. Because the inmate was convicted, but those charges were later dropped, doubts can persist. A pardon of innocence is an official acknowledgment that the individual was innocent. Because our system is designed to prove guilt but to assume innocence, innocence lost can be very difficult to regain, at least in the eyes of all. A pardon of innocence, very rarely issued, is an official statement by the highest official in the state government that the person was wrongfully convicted. It may open the way to some form of compensation.

Exonerations

As we will discuss in detail in chapter 9, a total of 156 individuals have been exonerated since 1973 after serving time on death row. In an exoneration, the individual walks out of prison with charges dropped. While a great number of individuals eventually succeed in their death penalty appeals and have their sentence reduced to life in prison, exonerations are different. In these cases, when the original finding of guilt is vacated on appeal, either the district attorney decides not to refile the case, dropping all the charges, or the individual is tried again and found not guilty. The fact that 156 individuals have been exonerated and 1,422 have been executed has led many to believe that the system is just too prone to error; after all, 156/1,422 represents just a little more than one exoneration for every nine executions. While death sentences are reversed in very large proportions (see chapter 7), the individuals remain guilty; the issue is typically whether they deserve death versus a lighter sentence. In exoneration cases, guilt itself is found to be lacking; these are tragic errors, many times including the wrongly incarcerated inmate suffering through the imposition of death warrants, which later are canceled. Often, the inmate has initially been sentenced to death; then the death sentence may be overturned and the inmate remanded to prison for life; and then, sometimes years later, the inmate is fully exonerated. North Carolina's Leon Brown, for example, was convicted of a horrific crime in 1984, at the age of 15. Sentenced to death, he remained on death row until that sentence was overturned. At his second trial, he was convicted of rape, not murder, and sentenced then to life in prison. He was exonerated (with his brother Henry McCollum, who spent the entire time on death row) in 2014. The two brothers had each spent more than 30 years wrongfully incarcerated. (We discuss this case in more detail in chapter 7.)

Compensation and Official Immunity

Individuals who are released from prison after a wrongful conviction may erroneously believe that they will easily be able to gain compensation, but typically they are not automatically entitled to any. Prosecutors investigate possible criminals and do not press charges on a routine basis. Naturally, they may not know immediately who committed the crime. But imagine you were being investigated for an extended period of time for a serious crime, such as capital murder. During that time you may be held in jail pending trial, and you may sell your house (if you have one) to raise money for your defense—in short, your life would be completely upended. Similarly, for lesser crimes, many individuals are investigated with an eye toward prosecution, or are even prosecuted and then acquitted at trial. Does the state owe them something for this? The state has routinely said no. We cannot expect that no one other than the guilty will be investigated or tried, and it is inevitable that being investigated or accused of a serious crime (or even a minor one) would be extremely upsetting. It could easily lead to divorce, bankruptcy, unemployment, and many other horrible consequences. A 2015 report by the Center for Death Penalty Litigation that reviewed capital prosecutions in North Carolina found 56 cases in which prosecutors sought death but which ended in acquittal or dismissal of charges; these presumably innocent defendants spent a total of 112 years in jail (CDPL 2015, 5).

Now, if one holds that officials acted in bad faith, for example, that one was targeted because of a personal vendetta by the police or prosecutor, it may be possible to sue for damages in civil court. But in general, the state owes a defendant nothing at all for what can amount to lost years. And with pretrial detention, even those not convicted of any crime may be held in jail. Of course, many individuals accused of tax evasion and other white-collar crimes face huge legal bills and potentially other negative consequences from what could end up being erroneous charges leading to acquittal at trial. The good news for such individuals is that they are acquitted. The bad news may be a mountain of legal bills, loss of income, loss of job, and potentially other consequences. Given the logic of how prosecution works, and the inevitable fact that each investigation may not be targeted at the guilty, it makes sense why there is no automatic compensation for those who suffer through the courts, and perhaps why this philosophy holds as well for those wrongfully sentenced to death.

Not only is financial compensation difficult, but oftentimes no officials are held accountable even when the most egregious injustices occur, such as when innocent people spend decades on death row under threat of execution. This is because of another long-standing tradition of Anglo-American law: judicial immunity. Imagine for a moment being a judge, overseeing hundreds or thousands of cases over a period of time. Say that a defendant who had appeared in your courtroom was found guilty, then appealed the sentences saying that you, as judge, had erred in a ruling during the extensive trial, and that the defendant succeeded in his or her appeal. Naturally, the defendant, who suffered from your erroneous ruling, might be upset. However, in US courts, no judicial official is liable for mistakes made in good faith. This immunity covers all court officials, including not only the judge but also prosecutors and members of their team, including detectives and investigators. The bar for suing a judicial official is extremely high and is rarely reached.[4] We discuss judicial and prosecutorial immunity in more detail in chapter 9.

Some states have limited laws allowing for compensation for those found to have been wrongfully convicted. Some inmates have collected large sums in the form of compensation, but these have typically come from civil lawsuits against the city, county, police department, or other government agency shown to have negligently or willfully contributed to their suffering. For example, a civil suit might hold that a city or other agency failed properly to train its employees so that they could avoid errors, or to implement procedures that could recognize and correct errors more quickly. If successful (no sure bet), such a suit would allow some compensation even without holding accountable any individual who may have contributed to the error. A surprising number of those who are wrongfully convicted see no compensation at all (see Norris 2012; Simms 2016). Based on conversations with many individual exonerees known to the senior author of this book, few elements are more frustrating than the lack of accountability for those individuals they feel contributed to their tragic experience.

Waiving the Right to Appeal

Because direct appeal is available for all inmates, regardless of any alleged flaws in their trials, some inmates seek to waive their right to appeal. Many such inmates suffer from mental illness or are unable or unwilling to see the process continue; they prefer to give up. Others may regard their own death penalty as a fitting punishment, one that matches the crime of which they were convicted. In order for a waiver of appeals to be granted, the court must first find that the inmate is competent in his or her decision to seek the waiver. The first time the court was faced with the challenge to determine competency to waive appeals was in *Rees v. Payton* (1966); the Court ruled there that the state must evaluate the mental competency of the inmate to waive appeals over the advice of his or her attorneys. In some cases, the inmate's desire to forfeit the right to appeal conflicts with the state's interest in preservation of life (Blank 2006), causing major conflict and sometimes a serious ethical quandary for the inmate's legal team. The notion of competency will be explored further in chapter 12. About 10 percent of all inmates executed in the modern period have been "volunteers"—that is, inmates who have instructed their attorneys to cease filing appeals. Some inmates adopt this suicidal strategy right from the beginning, and others decide to stop participating in the appellate process only after many years of frustration. We discuss "volunteers" in greater detail in chapter 12.

Conclusion

The death penalty process is exhausting, peculiar, and frustrating to all those involved. Because of our nation's history with the death penalty, and especially the *Furman* and *Gregg* rulings, an arcane and sometimes convoluted set of rules has developed around the punishment. Trials with the possibility of death are unlike "normal" murder trials. From the beginning of the process through to the end, special provisions abound. The result, particularly as regards the process of appeals, is that capital law is not like criminal law in general, and to do it competently attorneys must specialize in particular aspects of it. Further, in contrast to the pre-*Furman* era, when capital trials were similar to non-capital trials in that the goal of the defense attorney was an acquittal or conviction on lesser charges, in the modern era mitigation evidence can be paramount. The defendant need not be found guilty of a lesser charge to avoid death; rather, during the penalty phase convincing evidence must be presented about mitigation. Thus, entire new legal specialties have arisen (see Steiker and Steiker 2016, 195–203).

This chapter has done nothing more than introduce some generic vocabulary so that the material covered in later chapters can be more easily understood. But to understand the logic, perhaps we can return to the discussion from chapter 1. In *Furman*, the Court essentially indicated its lack of trust that the states could implement the death penalty fairly. This monumental decision cleared the nation's death rows, reducing the sentences of hundreds of murderers and violent rapists. In *Gregg*, the Court found constitutionally acceptable a process that, on paper, seemed to guarantee that the death penalty would only be imposed for a narrow class of clearly delineated crimes, and with vigorous state and federal review to ensure that it was imposed only on the worst offenders. Much to the regret of the conservative wing of the Court, the modern death penalty involves more Court review than the older system, which left the states on their own. Following *Gregg* and the other 1976 cases, the Court tried to assure that the states fulfilled their promises to have a rational and fair capital punishment system by imposing a number of exceptional requirements for capital cases. This unprecedented federal involvement in what is traditionally a state activity, criminal justice, remains unique in American jurisprudence. As Steiker and Steiker (2016) have argued, the exceptional involvement of the Court in capital cases, but not in others, has created numerous internal tensions leading the Court continually to revise its rulings in the area, constantly tinkering with the machinery of death, trying to perfect a system that has never worked even as its proponents wished it would.

Further Readings

Bohm, Robert M. 2012. *Deathquest: An Introduction to the Theory and Practice of Capital Punishment in the United States*. 4th ed. Waltham, MA: Anderson Publishing.

California Attorney General's Office, Office of Victims' Services. n.d. *A Victim's Guide to the Capital Case Process*. Sacramento, CA: Office of the Attorney General. http://oag.ca.gov/sites/all/files/agweb/pdfs/publications/deathpen.pdf.

Dow, David R. 2005. *Executed on a Technicality: Lethal Injustice on America's Death Row*. Boston: Beacon Press.

———. 2010. *The Autobiography of an Execution*. New York: Twelve.

Dow, David R., and Mark Dow, eds. 2002. *Machinery of Death: The Reality of America's Death Penalty Regime*. New York: Routledge.

Lyon, Andrea D. 2010. *Angel of Death Row: My Life as a Death Penalty Defense Lawyer*. New York: Kaplan.

Sheffer, Susannah. 2013. *Fighting for Their Lives: Inside the Experience of Capital Defense Attorneys*. Nashville, TN: Vanderbilt University Press.

Temple, John. 2009. *The Last Lawyer: The Fight to Save Death Row Inmates*. Jackson: University of Mississippi Press.

Welty, Jeffrey B. 2013. *North Carolina Capital Case Law Handbook*. 3rd ed. Chapel Hill: University of North Carolina School of Government.

White, Welsh S. 2006. *Litigating in the Shadow of Death: Defense Attorneys in Capital Cases*. Ann Arbor: University of Michigan Press.

3

Homicide in America

In order to understand the death penalty, we must first clearly understand criminal homicide, the unlawful killing of another.[1] Compared with other similar countries, the United States faces an epidemic of homicides, and this has been true throughout our history. Further, homicides tend to be committed by young men, and their victims tend to be young men as well. The vast majority of homicides occur within the same race: whites kill whites, and blacks kill blacks, on average. The numbers of black and white homicide offenders and victims are roughly similar, though blacks are a smaller share of the population. Women commit relatively few homicides, and they are a small minority of all homicide victims.

These simple facts are clear from the data and are widely known among criminologists and others who study crime. But they differ sharply from common cultural myths and media portrayals that often seem to suggest that homicides affect different populations than the raw numbers make clear. One particular element that is poorly understood is that the same demographic groups—young men, particularly those of color—are both the most common offenders and the most likely victims of homicide. Despite the frequency of these homicide events, the death penalty is rarely imposed when a black male murders another black male. Later chapters will examine this phenomenon further. In this chapter we review these basic statistical trends and patterns surrounding who commits homicide in the United States, who the victims of homicide tend to be, and the interaction between the two. Understanding homicides establishes a foundation for analyzing which ones lead to the death sentence or execution of the offender, and which ones do not.

The Extent of Homicide

The United States stands out on the global stage as a hotbed for homicide. This phenomenon is not a recent one but has been a significant trend for decades. Figure 3.1 shows the number of homicides from 1960 to 2014, the most recent year available, based on the US Department of Justice (DOJ) Uniform Crime Reports (UCR). From 1960 through 2014, the reports list a total of 952,772 homicides, with more

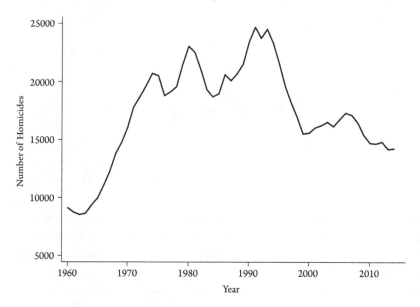

Figure 3.1 US Homicides, 1960–2014. Source: US DOJ, Uniform Crime Reports.

than 794,142 occurring since the states began reinstating their death penalty statutes in 1973[2] after *Furman*.[3]

Crime of all kinds rose dramatically during the 1960 to 1975 period, as homicides rose from fewer than 10,000 annually to more than double that number, eventually reaching a peak of almost 25,000 in the early 1990s. Numbers have declined
significantly since then, but they have remained around 15,000 over the past several
years, even as violent crime generally has dropped from its peaks of the 1990s.

While the trends in United States homicide data are remarkable, so is how the United
States compares with other advanced democracies across the world. Figure 3.2 shows
how the US homicide rate compares with the rates in a number of relatively similar countries. Among other nations with advanced democracies, similar to the United States, the
next most homicidal country is Canada, which still experiences only a quarter of the
number of homicides per capita that the United States does (see also Roth 2009).

Homicide rates in the United States tend to be on the order of about 5 homicides
per 100,000 population. So, on average, a city of 1 million might see 50 homicides in
a year, with some fluctuation depending on the particular city in question. By contrast, a German city with a population of 1 million might see 10 deaths by homicide.
The striking disparity between the United States and other similar nations in regard
to homicide trends speaks to a radically different culture that pervades the United
States, setting it apart from other nations. Determining why the United States experiences homicides at such greater levels than comparable countries is problematic to
say the least. A number of theories regarding race relations, substance abuse, income

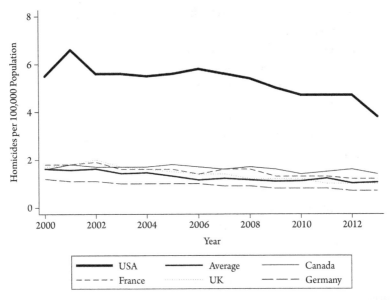

Figure 3.2 US Homicide Rates Compared. Source: UN Office of Crime Reporting. Average includes the following countries: Australia, Austria, Belgium, Canada, Czech Republic, Denmark, Finland, France, Germany, Greece, Hungary, Iceland, Netherlands, Norway, Poland, Slovakia, Slovenia, Spain, Sweden, Switzerland, and the United Kingdom.

inequality, gender relations, and more seek to explain the fluctuations in homicide rates, but none can completely explain why the United States is so dramatically set apart in this arena (Roth 2009). While causes of the trend cannot be inferred, the data explicitly show that homicide in the United States is abundant and persistent through time.[4]

Who Commits Homicide?

To look at the patterns of who commits and who is the victim of homicide, we cannot rely only on aggregate statistics about the total number of homicides, as in the figures in the previous section. For the United States, we can use a massive database compiled by James Fox of Northeastern University, showing the number of offenders and victims by race, gender, and age, for each US state and for each year from 1976 through 1999 (see Fox 2001). Obviously, to study offenders, the database must be based only on those homicides that were "cleared" by the police, or resulted in the identification of the perpetrator. In any case, this is a large proportion of all homicides, and the trends reported here do not appear to depend on these clearance rates, which have declined over time. In looking at the question of who commits homicide, and who are their victims, we will see that homicide is, in general, a young man's game, and that killers tend to kill others similarly situated to themselves: young black men kill other young black men, and young white men tend to kill other young white men. Of course, as we will see later, the different combinations of killer and victim demographics lead to dramatically different odds that an execution will follow. Before looking at those compelling questions, we first simply review the characteristics of killers and their victims here. We also show the geographical range in homicides and homicide rates, showing how widely this varies across the major cities and regions of the country; some places are much more violent than others.

Figure 3.3 shows the percent of homicides committed by different race and gender combinations. It is clear from the figure that homicides are committed by men: in 1999, 46 percent of offenders were black men; 41 percent white men; 5 percent black women; 5 percent white women; and the rest were members of other racial categories. Of course, there are far fewer blacks than whites in the United States, so the rate of homicide offending is much higher per population among blacks. Figure 3.4 shows these rates, per 100,000 population, and Figure 3.5 drills down for more detail among black men of different age groups.

Homicide rates among black men have historically been much higher than in other population groups and were extraordinarily high in the early 1990s, when they reached levels of almost 100 per 100,000 population. Rates for the other population groups average 10 for black females, 9 for white males, 1 for white females, and 6 for other races during this period. The spike in homicides was not generalized

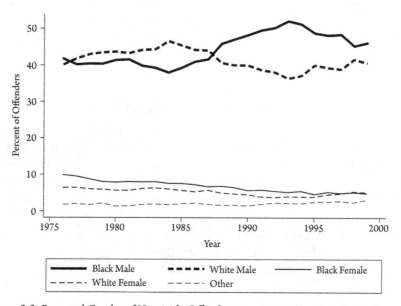

Figure 3.3 Race and Gender of Homicide Offenders. Source: Calculated from Fox 2001.

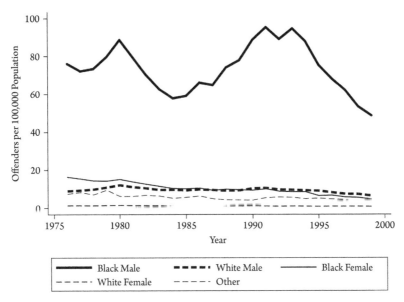

Figure 3.4 Homicide Offender Rates. Source: Calculated from Fox 2001.

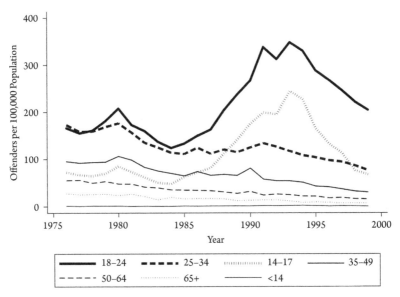

Figure 3.5 Homicide Offender Rates among Black Males of Different Age Groups.
Source: Calculated from Fox 2001.

among black men of all adult age groups. Figure 3.5 shows that it was extremely concentrated in the younger age groups.

Beginning in the mid-1980s, homicide rates among young black men, particularly those aged 14 to 17 and 18 to 24, reached unprecedented levels. Offense rates in other age groups continued a steady decline, even in the 25–34 age group. As we will see in later chapters, public rhetoric about the "war on crime" and the need for greater use of the death penalty was strongest in this period, growing from the 1980s through the mid-1990s, corresponding to a truly historic peak in homicides, particularly by young black men.

Who Are the Victims?

Men not only are statistically the most likely to commit homicide but also are the most likely to fall victim to homicide. Figure 3.6 replicates the analysis shown in Figure 3.3 but focuses on victims of homicide rather than offenders.

About 70 percent of homicide victims are males, divided roughly equally between whites and blacks. In 1999, 37 percent of victims were black males, 36 percent white males, 15 percent white females, 9 percent black females, and 4 percent persons of other races. The increase in black male homicide offending in the 1980s and 1990s led to an increase in black male victimization as well. Figure 3.7 shows how these numbers translate into victimization rates. Clearly, homicides tend to occur within

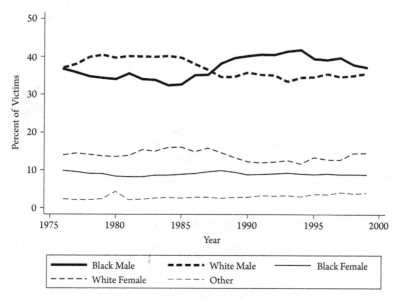

Figure 3.6 Homicide Victims by Race and Gender. Source: Calculated from Fox 2001.

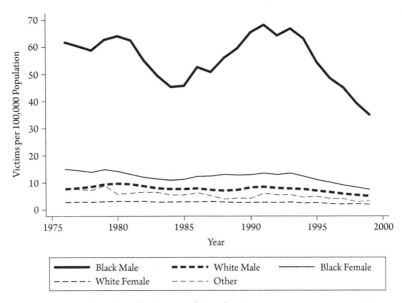

Figure 3.7 Victimization Rates by Race and Gender. Source: Calculated from Fox 2001.

racial categories, as blacks (males and females) have the highest rates on average and in every single year.

The victimization rate among black males is more than five times higher than in any other group. White females, by contrast, average just 2.7 homicide victims per 100,000 population, compared with 7.7 for white males, 12.2 for black females, and 55.6 for black males. There is clearly both a race and a gender effect; women are less victimized than men, but blacks are much more victimized than whites. Black women are victimized at alarming rates, many times more than white women, and significantly more than white men. As we will see later, however, those who kill white women, the group least likely overall to be victimized, are particularly likely to be executed. Those who kill black women have a significantly lower rate of execution. While our focus is largely on the black males because of their extraordinary victimization rates, it is important to consider the high victimization rates of black women.

Figure 3.8 shows the extremely high rates of victimization in that group, broken down by the same age categories as in Figure 3.5 above.

Just as the 1980s and 1990s saw a proliferation of black male homicide offenders, particularly among younger men, these data make clear that the primary victims of this crime wave were other similarly situated individuals. With more than 150 homicide victims per 100,000 population, younger black men were victimized at truly astounding rates. Given that the homicide offenders and the homicide victims tend to be concentrated in the same demographic groups, it is worth questioning why our collective and media attention on young black men has focused on their

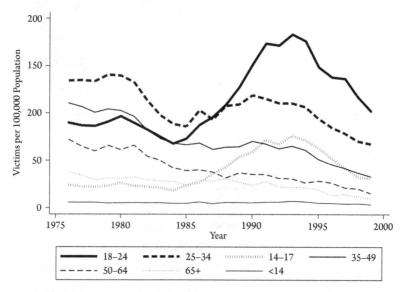

Figure 3.8 Black Male Victimization Rates by Age Group. Source: Calculated from Fox 2001.

outsized position as offenders, when in fact they are also the social group most likely to pay the burden as victims for this high rate of homicide. In the next section, we look at statistics showing that, in fact, homicide offenders and victims tend to be from the same racial groups, and that the vast majority of victims are male, no matter what the gender of the offender.

Offender-Victim Combinations

To best understand the nature of homicide in America, it is important to go beyond knowing who the offenders and victims are. Rather, it is crucial to examine the interaction of these two factors, that is, which offenders are killing which victims. It is widely accepted in the field of criminology that crime is generally committed intraracially; white offenders have white victims, black offenders have black victims, and so forth. This pattern is important to document given the common misconception among whites that white individuals are particularly vulnerable to black offenders; in fact such cross-racial homicides are relatively rare. We can show this by noting the combinations of offender and victim race and gender, again based on US DOJ figures.

Using the same DOJ Supplementary Homicide Reports used by Fox, we compare the offender-victim characteristic combinations for single-offender, single-victim homicide incidents. Table 3.1 shows the victim-perpetrator combinations of such incidents in 2013.

Table 3.1 Race/Gender Comparisons of Homicide Victims and Perpetrators, 2013

Victim Race/Gender	Perpetrator Race/Gender											
	White Male		White Female		Black Male		Black Female		Missing		Total	
	N	%	N	%	N	%	N	%	N	%	N	%
White male	1,688	57.12	226	64.76	281	10.70	20	7.25	71	23.13	2,286	35.09
White female	938	31.74	88	25.21	130	4.95	6	2.17	24	7.82	1,186	18.21
Black male	244	8.26	19	5.44	1,753	66.73	178	64.49	56	18.24	2,250	34.54
Black female	26	0.88	4	1.15	421	16.03	67	24.28	13	4.23	531	8.15
Missing	59	2.00	12	3.44	42	1.60	5	1.81	143	46.58	261	4.01
Total	2,955	100.00	349	100.00	2,627	100.00	276	100.00	307	100.00	6,514	100.00
% of perpetrators	45.36		5.36		40.33		4.24		4.71		100.00	

Note: Calculated from US DOJ Supplementary Homicide Reports (2013). The table includes only those homicides with a single offender and a single victim, which were 51.92 percent of all known homicides in 2013. Omitted cases include those where the offender was unknown (29.08 percent of cases) as well as those with multiple victims and/or multiple offenders. The table also excludes perpetrators and victims of other or unknown race. Reading down the columns of the table shows the percent of each type of victim, separately for each type of offender. While the data are incomplete because they exclude some categories, they present a good representation of black-white and male-female differences in offender-victim combinations.

This analysis shows that assertions made by criminologists regarding the intr-aracial nature of violent crime hold true for homicide, as it is committed in the United States as of 2013. In the first column, the table shows that for white male perpetrators, most of their victims are also white males, with the next largest group being white females. Fewer than 10 percent of their victims are cross-racial. Similarly for white female perpetrators, fewer than 10 percent kill blacks. Things are the same among blacks: black males have fewer than 15 percent white victims, with 64 percent of their victims being black males as well. Black females have fewer than 10 percent white victims. The last row of the table also shows that homicides are largely committed by men: in 2013, 45 percent of homicides were committed by white men, 40 percent by black men, 5 percent by white women, 4 percent by black women, with about 5 percent committed by individuals of unknown gender.

The patterns shown in Table 3.1 are very stable over time. We repeat the analysis for each year from 1998 to 2013 in Figure 3.9. Each of the four panels shows a different type of offender, and the vertical bars show the percentage of their victims of the different racial and gender groups (again, excluding persons of races other than black and white). Each bar represents a different year, so the stability in the patterns is made clear.

Figure 3.9 shows that, clearly and consistently, homicides in the United States tend to be committed by people of similar race as their victims. Women are rarely the perpetrators, and in fact statistically they are rarely the victims. While these patterns are true for homicides as a whole and are consistent over time, we will see in later chapters that the death penalty is not applied equally across these types of homicides. Homicides with female victims are much more likely to lead to a death sentence or to an execution, as are those with white victims. Further, female homicide offenders are rarely sentenced to death, compared with their proportion of all homicide offenders, which as we have seen is already low at around 10 percent. Black offenders are less likely to see the death penalty when their victims are also black but are much more likely to receive a death penalty or be executed when their victims are white. For white offenders, interracial crimes are rarely punished by execution. These patterns are the subject of the next chapter.

The Geography of Homicide

Different cities across the United States have vastly different homicide rates. In later chapters we will show that the same is true for executions: even within the same state, some jurisdictions see a great number of executions while most see none at all. In this section we explore the geographical distribution of homicides, since this is an obvious point of comparison. If the nation's homicide hot spots are not also where the executions are concentrated, we have to wonder what is causing some jurisdictions to have so many executions compared with others. If it is not homicide that drives executions, then what is it?

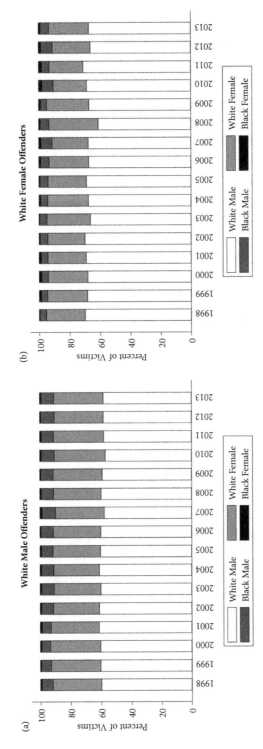

Figure 3.9 Victim Characteristics of Homicide Offenders by Race and Gender, 1998–2013. Note: See Table 3.1 for an explanation of the data source.

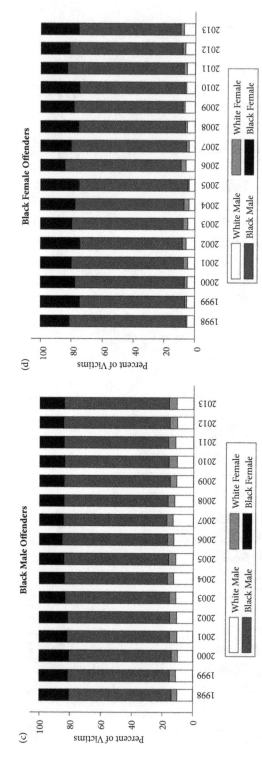

Figure 3.9 Continued

The US DOJ makes available county-level homicide reports through its annual publication and databases associated with the UCR; these are made available through the National Archive of Criminal Justice Data at the University of Michigan's ICPSR. We compiled all available county-level homicide reports, which ran from 1984 through 2012.[5] The resulting database includes 3,144 observations (one for each US county) for each year from 1984 to 2012: a total of 91,176 observations covering 29 years.

Figure 3.10 shows the number of homicides across all the counties of the United States. Most counties have relatively few homicides, thankfully enough. The figure leaves blank any county with fewer than 100 homicides cumulatively over the 29-year study period, some 2,593 counties; these are generally small rural counties, and they average 23 homicides across those years, less than 1 per year. Small dots appear in 494 counties with 100 through 1,999 homicides; larger dots represent 28 counties with 2,000 through 4,000 homicides. Above this are 22 counties with the highest homicide numbers in the country; the size of the circle associated with those counties is proportionate to the number of homicides. Los Angeles County, California, leads the nation with almost 35,000 homicides, followed by Cook County, Illinois (Chicago), with almost 19,500 killings. For ease of comparison to later maps on executions, states with the death penalty are shaded in light gray, and abolitionist states are in darker gray.[6]

We showed earlier in this chapter that the United States has an average of about 5 homicides per year per 100,000 population; the map in Figure 3.10 makes clear that those homicides are unequally distributed across the territory. Figure 3.11 makes this even clearer by focusing on the homicide rate. Here the rate is not an annual one, as in Figure 3.2, but compares the number of homicides across 29 years to the 2010 population of that county. Homicide patterns tend to be very stable over time, so combining years simply has the effect of averaging out any small annual differences. As before, the map leaves blank any county where the numbers might be based on very few observations: a population below 10,000 and fewer than 100 homicides; this leaves 2,177 counties. Of these, the map indicates with a small black dot those 919 counties with 1 to 3 homicides per 100,000; larger black dots for those 25 counties with 3 to 5 homicides; and larger circles for those 23 counties with the highest rates of homicide per population; these circles are sized proportionately to the homicide rate.

The geographical centers of greatest homicide rates clearly center in a mid-Atlantic corridor from Richmond, Virginia, through Philadelphia and up the Mississippi River from New Orleans to St. Louis. This is quite a different configuration from the previous map, which shows New York–Philadelphia–Baltimore, Los Angeles, Houston, Chicago, and Detroit as major centers of homicides, with Miami, Atlanta, Dallas, and St. Louis as important centers as well. When we look at the most violent communities in the country based on homicides rates per capita, it is clear that most are within states that have the death penalty on the books, and, strikingly, that none are in Texas. We will see later of course that Texas and Houston in particular are where very large percentages of executions occur.

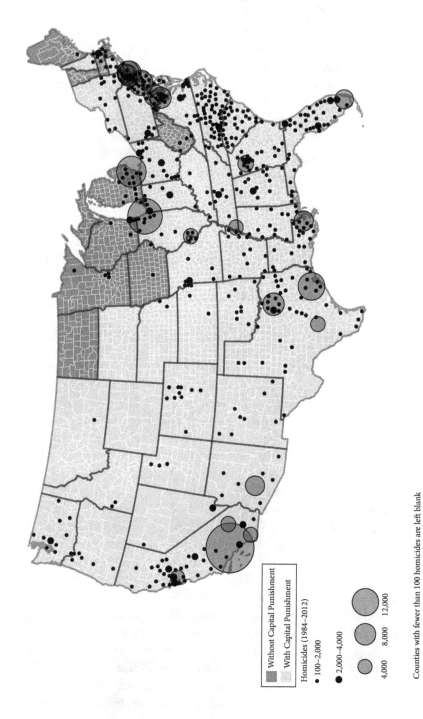

Without Capital Punishment

With Capital Punishment

Homicides (1984–2012)

· 100–2,000

● 2,000–4,000

4,000   8,000   12,000

Counties with fewer than 100 homicides are left blank

Figure 3.10 Homicides by County, 1984–2012

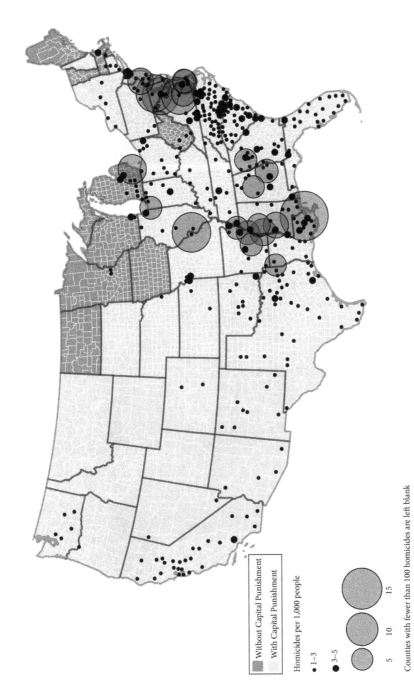

Figure 3.11 Homicide Rates by County, 1984–2012

Table 3.2 **Top Homicide Rate Counties in the United States**

County	State	2010 Population	Homicides, 1984–2012	Homicides per 100,000 Population	Annualized Homicide Rate
Orleans	LA	343,829	7,041	2,048	70.61
St. Louis City	MO	319,294	4,462	1,398	48.19
DC	DC	601,723	7,685	1,277	44.04
Baltimore	MD	620,961	7,847	1,264	43.57
Richmond	VA	204,214	2,514	1,231	42.44
Wayne	MI	1,820,584	15,111	830	28.62
Washington	MS	51,137	364	712	24.55
Philadelphia	PA	1,526,006	10,561	692	23.86
Hinds	MS	245,285	1,626	663	22.86
Chicot	AR	11,800	73	619	21.33
Petersburg	VA	32,420	197	608	20.98
Portsmouth	VA	95,535	574	600	20.70
Martinsville	VA	13,821	81	588	20.27
Phillips	AR	21,757	127	581	20.05
Norfolk	VA	242,803	1,387	571	19.70
Macon	AL	21,452	122	568	19.57
Leflore	MS	32,317	181	559	19.29
Jefferson	AR	77,435	418	539	18.60
Crittenden	AR	50,902	273	535	18.46
Lake	IN	496,005	2,647	534	18.40
Fulton	GA	920,581	4,893	531	18.33
Jefferson	AL	658,466	3,416	519	17.89
Caddo	LA	254,969	1,284	504	17.37

Note: Figure 3.2 shows how the United States compares to other countries. Using the same 2013 figures as reported there, these localities could be compared to national figures in Brazil (26.5), Colombia (31.8), South Africa (31.9), El Salvador (39.8), or Honduras (84.3). These are some of the most homicide-prone nations in the world.

The counties with the top homicide rates are listed in Table 3.2. Because these homicide rates are calculated over 29 years, Table 3.2 also shows an "annualized" rate of homicides per 100,000 population, which is comparable to the numbers shown in Figure 3.2. If the overall US average of about 5 per 100,000 was extremely high by international standards, New Orleans's rate of homicide, above 70, puts that county in the range of the most violent countries in the world. Clearly, there are many communities in the United States where levels of violence are similar to what one might observe in parts of Central America, as the note to the table makes clear.

Conclusion

Through a wide variety of data analyses, this chapter offers a picture of American homicide in terms of who is killing, who is getting killed, how often, and where. In sum, we find that the United States stands alone among comparable nations in terms of sheer number of homicides, homicides are generally committed by young males, homicide is largely intraracial, the most common offenders and victims of homicide are young black men, and homicide is largely concentrated in hotbed areas that have rates similar to those of dangerous developing nations. These patterns may surprise many readers; most Americans are not aware of how comparatively violent our nation is. But the violence is not random; it follows certain patterns. In the next chapter, we look at which homicides are likely to be treated with the harshest possible punishment. We will see that death sentences are particularly focused on those rare cases where black offenders cross the racial line and kill whites, particularly women. In the opposite case, where whites kill blacks, the odds of execution are vanishingly small. When we add gender into this comparison, the differences become even greater, as we will see in the next chapter. The death penalty is intended to be the most severe punishment, reserved for the most heinous homicide offenders. With a thorough understanding of how often homicide occurs in the United States, where homicide is occurring, and the characteristics of both offenders and their victims, we can turn our attention to analyzing which homicides actually yield executions, and whether or not these trends suggest that executions are focused on certain kinds of offender-victim combinations, in preference to others. As the next chapter will show, all homicides are definitely not equal in the face of the law.

Appendix on Data Sources: FBI versus CDC Reports on Homicide

Both the FBI and the Centers for Disease Control and Prevention (CDC) track homicide deaths in the United States, and the numbers they report are slightly different. While the CDC numbers cover more homicides, they do not contain any information about the offender. In order to link the offender and victim data, we use the FBI statistics here. But we want to reassure our readers that our analysis would be similar if we were to use the CDC numbers instead.

In 2014, the Bureau of Justice Statistics (BJS) published a report comparing these two major measures of homicide in the United States, weighing the various advantages and drawbacks of each (BJS 2014). The following is a brief summary of that report, with particular attention given to why the FBI Supplemental Homicide Reports (SHR) are better suited for our analysis of homicide trends.

The FBI SHR make up one part of the greater Uniform Crime Reporting Program used by policymakers, researchers, and law enforcement alike for a variety of purposes. Data for the SHR are gathered from those crimes that are reported to law enforcement agencies across the 50 states and the District of Colombia. Data are submitted to the Uniform Crime Reporting Program on a voluntary basis. By contrast, the Fatal Injury Reports kept by the CDC, developed form the National Vital Statistics System, are collected from registration systems that are legally responsible for keeping records of events such as births, deaths, marriages, and divorces on a national level. State laws require that medical examiners or coroners investigate all homicides or unexpected deaths. Death certificates, by law, are then submitted to state vital statistics offices and subsequently forwarded to the National Center for Health Statistics maintained by the CDC. The nature of this data collection methodology more readily inclines the CDC data for use in a public health context, whereas the data collection process used for the SHR leaves that source more disposed to use in a law enforcement/criminal justice policy context. However, we should make clear that the CDC typically is more complete. For 2013, the FBI reported 12,546 homicides, whereas the CDC reported 16,121, a difference of more than 25 percent. With more than 3,500 homicides "missing" from the FBI reports, why do we use that data source?

There are two reasons for our use of the FBI data over the more complete CDC numbers: offender information and geography. Each report on a homicide event in the FBI data includes information regarding the circumstances surrounding the incident; the weapon used to commit the crime; the relationship between the victim and the offender (spouse/significant other, parent/child, acquaintance, stranger, etc.); and, a crucial point in our analysis of homicide trends in the United States, the demographic characteristics of both the offender *and* the victim of the crime. The relationship between victim and perpetrator of a homicide in terms of demographic characteristics (principally gender and race) is a crucial factor in our understanding of who is killing whom and how that contrasts with who is getting executed for killing whom. By contrast, CDC data report only the information that can be found on a death certificate, which consists of age, race, ethnicity, marital status, educational attainment, residence, cause of death, and nature of the injuries sustained. In addition, the CDC data do not annually report any information related to the offender. Given that much of the analysis conducted in our book revolves around the demographic characteristics of the offender and the sentence that said offender receives in relation to those demographics, a database that focuses purely on information relating to the victim is of limited use.

A second reason for our use of FBI data has to do with geography: the FBI reports relate to the place where the crime occurred, whereas the CDC numbers relate to the place of residence of the deceased. Typically this may not be an important difference, but in this chapter and in chapter 6 we compare homicides and executions on a county-by-county basis. Here we need to know where the crime occurred, not the legal residence of the victim.

In any case, while the CDC reports a higher number of homicides, and many have noted that the FBI numbers are underreported, patterns of who is victimized by race and gender, which are at the core of our analysis here, are not greatly affected. In 2013, for example, while the CDC reported 28 percent more homicides than the FBI, the CDC reported that 78.94 percent of those victims were male (calculated from Xu et al. 2016, Table 12); the FBI reported that 79.40 percent of victims were male. Racial breakdowns were also very similar across the two data sets. In general, breakdowns of the proportions of victims from different demographic groups are close across the two data sources. Although the numbers are higher with the CDC because of the voluntary nature of the FBI reporting, and the fact that many homicides have unknown offenders, we use the FBI numbers because they allow us to link the victim to the offender, because they link to the geographical location of the crime, and finally because doing so makes little difference in the substance of the patterns we document.

Further Readings

Bureau of Justice Statistics (BJS). 2014. *The Nation's Two Measures of Homicide.* Washington DC: Bureau of Justice Statistics.

Collins, Randall. 2008. *Violence: A Micro-sociological Theory.* Princeton, NJ: Princeton University Press.

Grinshteyn, Erin, and David Hemenway. 2016. Violent Death Rates: The US Compared with Other High-Income OECD Countries, 2010. *American Journal of Medicine* 129 (3): 266–273.

Hawkins, Darnell F., ed. 2003. *Violent Crime: Assessing Race and Ethnic Differences.* New York: Cambridge University Press.

Pinker, Steven. 2011. *The Better Angels of Our Nature: Why Violence Has Declined.* New York: Penguin.

Riedel, Marc, and Wayne Welsh. 2014. *Criminal Violence: Patterns, Explanations, and Interventions.* 4th ed. New York: Oxford University Press.

Roth, Randolph. 2009. *American Homicide.* Cambridge, MA: Harvard University Press.

Zimring, Franklin E. 2007. *The Great American Crime Decline.* New York: Oxford University Press.

4

Comparing Homicides
with Execution Cases

In the previous chapter we considered who commits homicides and the characteristics of their victims.[1] This chapter will assess which homicides lead to execution for the offender, with particular attention paid to the race and gender of the victim. Given that capital punishment is intended to be reserved for the "worst-of-the-worst" homicide offenders, it is important to understand which homicides lead to execution and which do not. Ideally, one would expect the patterns in execution to coincide with those of homicides; however, the data regarding the offenders and victims of execution cases show stark disparities.

This chapter begins with an observation of characteristics of those executed. This analysis is brief, however, because our focus quickly shifts to a more important concern: Who is the victim, and what are the combined characteristics of the offender and the victim? We show dramatic disparities in sentencing and execution based on these factors, as others have done before us (Baldus and Woodworth 2003). For example, John Donohue (2014) recently reviewed all capital-eligible homicides in Connecticut and concluded that death sentences were not reserved for the most heinous crimes but instead were largely dependent on geography and victim race. Our analysis of victim characteristics in homicide and execution cases confirms these findings and shows their scope on the national scale. We also note, as others have done, that particular offender-victim combinations are particularly prone to execution: black-on-black homicides are unlikely to result in execution; black-on-white are particularly so (especially if the victim is female); and white-on-black crimes almost never result in execution. Our data in the previous chapter were the most comprehensive we could find relying on official statistics from the US government relating to homicides. In this chapter we compare these to a comprehensive database of every execution in the modern period. Given that there are hundreds of thousands of homicides, we cannot replicate here the careful studies of each eligible homicide as Baldus, Donohue, and others have done before. But we corroborate their findings that race and gender combinations of victims and offenders have startling effects on the likelihood of execution. In a later chapter we will review the heinousness of crimes eligible for death, and whether the evidence shows that execution is reserved for those who have committed the most heinous crimes. In the sections that follow, we focus on race and gender combinations of offenders and victims, and we document disparities in the implementation of the death penalty that will surprise anyone not already familiar with how the system works.

As we point out in chapter 7, there is a big difference between a death sentence and an execution; in fact, most death sentences are later overturned. Therefore, we recommend care in reading, since our comprehensive data refer to executions, not death sentences. For the 8,000-plus death sentences in the modern period, no comprehensive database allows the same kind of analysis we can do for the 1,400-plus execution cases. Much of the published literature, including that which we review in this chapter, refers to death sentences, not executions. However, whether we look at sentences or executions, when we compare them to homicides, we find vast differences. The patterns we describe in this chapter, with certain types of homicide victim-offender combinations much more likely to lead to execution than others, also hold when we look at death sentences rather than executions. The numbers are not identical, of course, but the patterns are robust.

Offender Race and Gender

While the characteristics of the offender alone are not the most significant factors in determining whether or not he or she will be executed, it is still important to recognize the disparities between homicide offenders in general and those offenders who are executed for their crimes. Table 4.1 presents an overview of the race, gender, and race-gender combination of offenders executed between 1976 and 2015.

We saw in the previous chapter that homicides follow relatively similar patterns over time, so in Table 4.1 we compare all execution cases with the data we presented in Table 3.1, which provides data on all homicides for 2013, the most recent year available. Of course there could be slight annual variations, but the stark patterns remain clear: white males are slightly *over*-represented among those executed; black males are slightly *under*-represented; and females of both races are significantly less likely than males to be executed. This finding that, among males, the racial dynamic seems to disadvantage white homicide offenders is perhaps surprising, and we will return to it later in the chapter. However, it is no mistake; it is a robust finding no matter which year we consider.[2] Although this disparity may seem counterintuitive, further analysis (provided later in this chapter) shows that the race of the offender alone is only a small, and statistically less significant, piece of the puzzle when determining which homicides lead to execution. Characteristics of the victims are more important. Together, the combination of offender and victim characteristics plays a powerful role. Because most homicides

Table 4.1 **US Executions by Race and Gender of Offenders**

Offender	Homicides		Executions	
Characteristic	Number	Percent	Number	Percent
White	3,304	50.72	777	54.64
Black	3,903	44.57	482	33.90
Other or unknown	307	4.71	163	11.46
Total	6,514	100.00	1,422	100.00
Male	5,582	85.69	1,407	98.95
Female	625	9.59	15	1.05
Unknown gender	307	4.71	—	—
Total	6,514	100.00	1,422	100.00
White female	349	5.36	10	0.70
White male	2,955	45.36	767	53.94
Black female	276	4.24	4	0.28
Black male	2,627	40.33	478	33.61
Other or unknown	307	4.71	163	11.46
Total	6,514	100.00	1,422	100.00

Note: Execution data ranges from 1976 to 2015; homicide data for 2013, from Table 3.1.

occur within race (as we saw in chapter 3), the race of offender and the race of the victim are highly correlated. Thus the "direct effect" of the race of the offender may not remain when we look in greater detail at the victims. We turn to that now.

Victim Race and Gender

Table 4.2 presents an overview of both executions and homicides by victim characteristic for the United States as a whole. The following sections will take a more in-depth look at the individual effect of race, gender, and the interaction of the two on whether or not a homicide offender is executed. Since 1976, a total of 1,422 executions have taken place. Those inmates had a total of 2,222 victims.

As we can see in Table 4.2, the victims of executed death row inmates are most commonly white females—38 percent. Almost as common are the executions of inmates who murdered white males—37 percent. Only 15 percent of victims of executed defendants have been black, whereas black victims constitute nearly half of US homicide victims. The data clearly allow us to see the emergence of a racialized and gendered victim hierarchy in determining who receives the death penalty

Table 4.2 **US Executions and Homicides by Race and Gender of Victims**

Victim	Homicides		Executions		Executions per 10,000
Characteristic	Number	Percent	Number	Percent	Homicides
Whites	252,366	50.77	1,678	75.52	66
Blacks	229,801	46.23	342	15.39	15
Others or unknown	14,863	2.99	202	9.09	136
Total	497,030	100.00	2,222	100.00	45
Males	379,164	76.29	1,139	51.26	30
Females	117,234	23.59	1,083	48.74	92
Unknown	632	0.12	—	—	—
Total	497,030	100.00	2,222	100.00	45
White female	68,576	13.80	851	38.30	124
White male	183,756	36.97	826	37.17	45
Black female	44,779	9.01	165	7.42	37
Black male	185,003	37.22	178	8.01	10
Other or unknown	14,916	3.00	202	9.09	135
Total	497,030	100.00	2,222	100.00	45

Note: Homicide data ranges from 1975 to 2005; execution data ranges from 1976 to 2015.

and who does not. This hierarchy places a premium on white lives over black, and female victims over males. Perhaps there is an assumption that female victims are less likely to be blameworthy than black males. Recall from the previous chapter that black males are both the most common offenders and the most common victims of homicide. Clearly, when we get to the death penalty, the data suggest that the odds of execution strongly depend on the race and gender of the victim, and black males are at the bottom of this hierarchy. The most common victims of homicide are the least likely to have their killers later executed.

Victim Race

In response to congressional concerns, the US General Accounting Office (GAO) conducted a systematic review of studies on racial bias, identifying 28 high-quality empirical studies conducted in the post-*Furman* period and finding that 82 percent concluded that those who murdered whites were more likely to be sentenced to death than those who murdered blacks, controlling for legally relevant factors (GAO, 1990). Coming from an arm of the US Congress, the GAO report had considerable impact, confirming as it did a long line of research. Michael Radelet's 1989 study of nearly 16,000 executions dating back to the 1600s found that there had been only 30 cases in which a white offender was executed for the murder of a black individual. More recently, a study of more than 4,600 Connecticut murders found that black defendants were three times more likely than whites to receive the death penalty when the victim was white (Donohue, 2014). In addition, a comprehensive study regarding victim effects found that those accused of killing white victims were four times as likely to be sentenced to death as those accused of killing black victims (Baldus, Pulaski, and Woodworth, 1983). Our own review of published studies reinforces and updates the 1990 GAO study.

Discussions surrounding the impact of victim race on criminal punishment have led scholars to this unfortunate conclusion: the judicial system places more value on the lives of whites, resulting in disproportionately harsh treatment of black criminals who have white victims (American Civil Liberties Union Capital Punishment Project 2007; Baldus, Pulaski, and Woodworth 1983; Fins 2015). The pattern presented in Figure 4.1 corroborates this assertion. With this side-by-side comparison we can see that the murderers of black victims are significantly less likely to end up

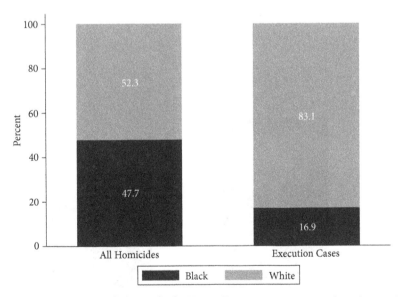

Figure 4.1 Executions and Homicides by Victim Race. Note: Executions refer to the period from 1976 through 2015, with 1,422 offenders and 2,222 victims. Homicides refer to the period from 1976 through 1999 as reported by the US DOJ. Individuals of races other than black or white constitute 2.2 percent of all US homicide victims and 9.4 percent of the victims for all US execution cases. This figure does not include victims of races other than white or black.

being executed than killers of whites. Looking only at black and white victims (i.e., excluding people of other races), just 16.9 percent of execution cases involve black victims, while roughly half of all homicide victims are blacks.

Victim Gender

As outlined earlier, victim effects are not only racialized but also highly gendered. Prior research suggests that murderers with female victims face a higher likelihood of being charged with a capital crime as well as a higher likelihood of being sentenced to death (Royer et al. 2014). The data represented in Figure 4.2 corroborate this claim. Overall, female victims of executed inmates are disproportionate to the rate of female victims in all US homicide cases. Less than a quarter of all homicide victims are female, while nearly half of the victims of executed inmates are female.

Female victims are over-represented among execution cases, accounting for a nearly equal percentage of executions as for their male counterparts, but only 24 percent of total homicides. Such a trend suggests that a premium tends to be placed on female lives, much like the premium placed on white lives in comparison to black lives. The interaction of these two factors is explored further in the next section.

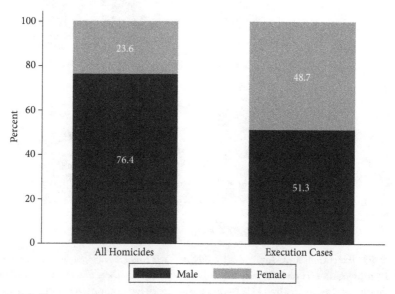

Figure 4.2 Executions and Homicides by Victim Gender. Note: Executions refer to the period from 1976 through 2015, with 1,422 offenders and 2,222 victims. Based on all homicides from 1976 through 1999 as reported by US DOJ.

Victim Race and Gender

Figure 4.3 shows the odds of execution for the four combinations of race and gender for black and white victims, using the data from Table 4.2. The table shows a comparison of homicides from 1975 through 2005 with executions over the modern period, and Figure 4.3 simply illustrates the ratios calculated from these comparisons. Among killers who were later executed, 178 had black male victims, but there were a total of 185,003 black male victims overall during the period of comparison. Dividing one into the other shows that there is a .10 likelihood (approximately one case in 1,000) that such a homicide would lead to an execution. White female victims associated with executions numbered 851 in Table 4.2; there were 68,576 white female victims overall; that ratio is therefore 1.24. Two important details emerge here. First, the odds of execution are very low: below 2 percent even for killers of white females. Second, of course, is the stark hierarchy that the figure makes clear.

Victim-Offender Combinations

As described in chapter 3, homicides are primarily intraracial activities, with intraracial homicides accounting for 89 percent of all cases and 72 percent of cases that led to executions. We find, however, that intraracial homicide is less likely to result in execution, particularly in the case of black-on-black crime. This is particularly significant when assessing which homicides tend to result in execution, given that the

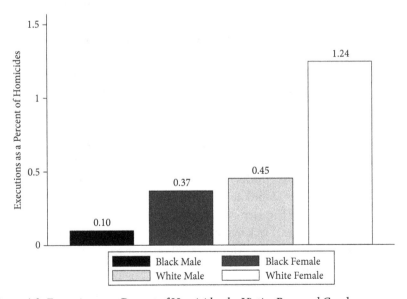

Figure 4.3 Executions as a Percent of Homicides, by Victim Race and Gender.

vast majority of homicides committed by blacks have a black victim. Overall, black/ white killer/victim combinatorial relationships constitute about 99 percent of all cases. Homicides in which "other" races are killers, victims, or both are comparatively rare and are over-represented among cases that lead to executions. Because the vast majority of homicides concern black or white killers or victims, in any combination, we will focus on those demographics in the analysis here.

Black-on-white murders are over-represented among execution cases, appearing at twice the proportion that they occur in all homicides. A study conducted in Philadelphia between 1983 and 1993 found that, after controlling for the defendant's criminal background and the gravity of the crime committed, black defendants were sentenced at a rate that was 38 percent higher than for other defendants. Further, the researchers found that the death penalty was more likely to be given in cases where black defendants have nonblack victims, and least likely in the case where a nonblack defendant has a nonblack victim (Baldus et al. 1998). The finding of racial disparities in different studies makes it appear as if blacks are over-represented on death row; however, this is not the case. This trend of black-on-black under-representation and black-on-white over-representation has persisted over time. As a baseline, white-on-white murders delineate an almost consistent 1:1 ratio of cases that led to executions versus all homicides in general. In comparison, there is a persistent bias toward executing black murderers of white victims and against executing white murderers of black victims. Additionally, there have been substantial lengths of time during which no white murderers were executed for killing black victims. Given the numbers and trends, the disparity in the death penalty's treatment of different victims appears to be chronic. Placing more value on the lives of whites has resulted in the harsher treatment of blacks in the judicial system, and consequently, on death row (American Civil Liberties Union Capital Punishment Project 2007; Fins 2015; Baldus, Pulaski, and Woodworth 1983).

In Table 3.1, we showed the breakdown of homicide perpetrators and their victims, using the year 2013 as an example, and later noting that the trends are highly stable over time. Table 4.3 looks at this same relationship, focusing on cases that lead to execution.

A number of trends represented in this table are particularly striking. First is the infrequency of executions that result from black male on black male homicide particularly when one considers the high number of such homicide cases. Just 99 black male inmates were executed for killing another black male; of all black males executed, only 21 percent of their victims were black males. Black males, we know from Table 3.1, mostly kill other black males; in fact, 67 percent of their victims overall are black males. These crimes are extremely unlikely to be represented on death row or followed by an execution.

On the other hand, in cases in which a black male murders a white female (just 5 percent of all homicides committed by black males in Table 3.1), they are much

Table 4.3 Race and Gender Comparisons between Execution Victims and Perpetrators

Perpetrator Race/Gender	Victim Race/Gender											
	White Female		White Male		Black Female		Black Male		Other		Total	
	N	%	N	%	N	%	N	%	N	%	N	%
White female	1	10.0	9	90.0	0	—	0	—	0	—	10	100.0
White male	317	41.33	401	52.3	9	1.2	11	1.4	29	3.8	767	100.0
Black female	1	25.0	0	—	0	—	3	75.0	0	—	4	100.0
Black male	121	25.3	162	33.9	64	13.4	99	20.7	32	6.7	478	100.0
Other	33	20.3	51	31.3	5	3.1	7	4.3	67	41.1	163	100.0
Total	473	33.3	623	43.8	78	5.5	120	8.4	128	9.0	1,422	100.0

more likely to be executed. In fact, the table shows that 121 black males have been executed for killing white females, and just 99 have been executed for killing black males. But white females constitute only 5 percent of the victims of black male homicide offenders, and black males constitute 67 percent of their victims. The rare black male/white female homicide is a particular flash point for the death penalty, as previous researchers have also found.

Table 4.3 also clearly shows that murder of a white woman leads to the most instances of executions, a point that has been well covered earlier in the chapter. As we saw in chapter 3, however, and following from the generally intraracial characteristics of homicide, far more white males murder white females than do black males. However, black males are far more likely to be executed for killing a white female than are white males. In other words, while murdering a white woman leads to a higher likelihood of being executed no matter who is the killer, this likelihood increases disproportionately when the perpetrator is a black male. This distinction is crucial when considering the roles of both the homicide victim characteristics and the perpetrator characteristics.

While this chapter has shown that the race and gender of the victim are both highly indicative of the likelihood of execution, the race of the perpetrator has a significant impact as well. At the beginning of this chapter, the race and gender of the offender were shown to be less significant in determining the outcome of execution when analyzed on its own. However, the interaction between offender and victim characteristics proves to have a far more striking effect, serving to emphasize that it is not necessarily who is doing the killing that matters, but who it is that was killed, and by whom. In this light we can see that black males not only are valued less as victims of homicide but also are treated more severely for committing homicide outside of their race. With these data in mind, one must consider the problematic nature of a system that punishes certain individuals for the crimes that they commit against one race and gender, but not for the crimes that similar individuals commit against their own race and gender.

Females Executed

As we noted in chapter 3, and again in Table 4.1, the vast majority of homicides in the United States are committed by male offenders; about 90 percent of offenders are male. However, when we look at the 1,422 inmates who have been executed during the modern period, only 16 have been female. Women, then, constitute about 10 percent of homicide offenders, but just 1 percent of those executed. Further, the crimes for which women are executed are much more likely to involve family members, in particular their own children. In this section, we focus on the rare cases where women have been executed and explore the differences in the crimes that lead to this as compared with those more typical for male inmates who are executed.

Throughout US history, female offenders have typically been given capital sentences for the murder of someone well known to them (i.e., a spouse, child, or other relative), forming a striking contrast with death-sentenced males, who are almost always convicted for killing strangers, often in conjunction with another felony (e.g., robbery, rape). Timothy Kaufman-Osborn (2002, chap. 6) explores this history, noting a number of pertinent facts. From 1608 to the modern period, 537 women have been executed, compared with more than 19,000 men, so women account for less than 3 percent of the total executed over US history. Some periods stand out for anomalies: the late seventeenth century, when 27 white women were executed for performing witchcraft in New England, and the period during and after the Civil War, when many black women were executed in the South. (Blacks account for two-thirds of all the women executed, of which half were executed during this period.) Black women were executed for a variety of crimes, including "petty treason" or rebellion against their slave master. White women, except for the accused witches, were killed almost always for the crime of homicide. In the twentieth century, two-thirds of the women executed have been white. Kaufman-Osborn cites Kathleen O'Shea, who writes that half of the women on death row suffered from a history of abuse and were there for killing their abusive spouse, partner, or lover (see also American Civil Liberties Union Capital Punishment Project 2004; O'Shea 1999, 2000; Leonard 2002). Kaufman-Osborn writes:

> Indeed, throughout U.S. history, the typical victims of women given capital sentences have been persons well known to them. This pattern contrasts sharply with that of death-sentenced men, who, as a rule, are convicted of killing strangers in conjunction with some other felony; the convenience store robbery gone awry is the paradigmatic example. (2002, 167)

The trends that Kaufman-Osborn discusses remain true today. Table 4.4 shows the characteristics of the 21 victims of the 16 women who were executed from 1976 through 2015.[3] As the table clearly indicates, a majority of women are executed for killing either a spouse or significant other (boyfriend, girlfriend, etc.) or children. Only 3 victims were strangers to their offender, a trend that stands out for female offenders in comparison to male offenders. As mentioned previously, men are far more often executed for the murder of a stranger in conjunction with another crime or aggravating circumstance as determined by state law. In only two cases was a female offender executed for murder in conjunction with another offense, namely, a robbery. Female offenders who have been executed often satisfy the requirement for aggravating factors relating to murder for monetary gain. In one case, an offender was sentenced for murdering a police officer.

In certain respects, it not terribly surprising that women are executed for committing domestic murder (i.e., the murder of a spouse, child, or significant other) rather than for killing a stranger, given that women are more likely than men to have

Table 4.4 **Relationship of Victim to Offender, among Females Executed**

Victim Relationship to Offender	Number	Percent
Spouse/significant other	9	42.9
Child	6	28.6
Acquaintance	2	9.5
Stranger*	4	19.0
Total	21	100.0

Note: Data are based on information gathered by the DPIC with slight adaptation based on information gathered from the Clark County Prosecutor website.

* Includes a police officer murdered by Lynda Lyon Block.

such victims. More troubling, however, are the implications of this pattern. If execution is reserved for the "worst of the worst" and thus reflects society's deepest fears, this seems to be the man who kills a stranger, or the woman who kills a family member. The fact that such a high percentage of women on death row were convicted of killing their abusive partners is particularly troubling. Men are rarely executed for the crime of killing their spouse.

In any case, women are rarely executed, and when they are, it is typically for a different set of crimes: killing their children or their (sometimes abusive) spouse or partner (see Kaufman-Osborn 2002, chap. 6). One possible explanation for the difference is that juries perhaps see female defendants as less likely to pose a threat to others in the future, or because they see a greater likelihood of rehabilitation. But the United States has executed hundreds of women over the years, including 16 in the period from 1976 to 2015.

Empirical Studies of Charging and Sentencing

A large and important literature consists of "Baldus-type" studies in which scholars, typically law professors working in concert with statistically trained social scientists, have attempted to assess possible bias in death penalty systems by looking at large numbers of death-eligible crimes and evaluating based on the records which cases led to either capital prosecution or death sentences. We refer to these as "Baldus-type" studies because the leader in this field was David Baldus of the University of Iowa. He led the team that assessed Georgia's death penalty system as argued before the US Supreme Court in *McCleskey v. Kemp* (1987).

McCleskey was a landmark case in many ways, especially for the decision to ignore powerful statistical evidence of racial disparity and, as the Steikers have argued, as perhaps the greatest missed opportunity to ensure serious proportionality review. Mr. McCleskey was a black male convicted and sentenced to death for killing a white police officer during a robbery. The case hinged on whether the State of Georgia could be shown to sentence such offenders disproportionately to death because of the combination of the race of the offender and the victim, and powerful evidence of such disproportionality was presented by Baldus as part of the legal brief. According to Lee Kovarsky:

> Justice Powell was the swing vote in *McCleskey*, and became convinced, as the litigation progressed, both that the Baldus Study was methodologically sound and that he did not want to go down the slippery slope of permitting statistical evidence alone to sustain litigation under the Equal Protection Clause. The result of Justice Powell's conclusions was the controlling opinion in *McCleskey*, in which he conceded the statistical correlations presented in the Baldus Study, but argued that they were insufficient to prove a constitutional violation because "[a]pparent disparities in sentencing are an inevitable part of our criminal justice system." (2016, 321)

Indeed, the Court held in *McCleskey* not only that statistical patterns were irrelevant but also that one of the reasons it so held was the fact that the "Petitioner's claim, taken to its logical conclusion, throws into serious question the principles that underlie the entire criminal justice system. His claim easily could be extended to apply to other types of penalties" (281). In his dissent from this decision, Justice Brennan wrote that "such a statement seems to suggest a fear of too much justice" (339). In contrast, in an internal memo to the other justices, Justice Scalia, wrote: " 'Since it is my view that the unconscious operation of irrational sympathies and antipathies, including racial, upon jury deliberations and (hence) prosecutorial decisions is *real . . . and ineradicable*, I cannot honestly say that all I need is more proof' " (Scalia 1987, quoted in Haney López 2015, 80). Anthony Amsterdam, a longtime attorney for the National Association for the Advancement of Colored People Legal Defense Fund, referred to *McCleskey* as the *Dredd Scott* of our time (see Mandery 2013, 429). Justice Brennan eventually declared that he "would no longer tinker with the machinery of death" because of the failure of the Court to devise a mechanism to ensure that it be administered fairly (see *Callins v. Collins* (1994), quoted in Mandery 2013, 435). Presented with powerful statistical evidence of racial disparities, the Court ruled that evidence of patterns is not only irrelevant, but indeed that considering it would potentially create havoc throughout the judicial system.

Table 4.5 presents a summary of 13 major empirical legal studies on the factors that influence capital punishment. These studies were selected because each focuses on the post-*Furman* era application of the death penalty in one particular state, using regression analysis to determine the factors that affect capital charging

Table 4.5 Summary of Published Empirical Studies of Proportionality

Author and Year	Study Basics					Legally Relevant Factors							Extralegal Factors			
	State	Time	Sample Size	Source of Data	Number of Variables in Regression	Heinousness	Number of Victims	For Gain	Previous Violent Felony	Sexual Assault	White Victim	Black Victim	White Defendant	Black Defendant	Gender of Victim	Geography
Baldus et al. (2002)	NE	1973–1999	185 death-eligible homicides	Table 4, p. 553	12		x				xx		xx			✓✓
Unah and Boger (2001)	NC	1993–1997	3,990 homicides	Tables 6 & 7	37	✓✓	xx	xx	✓✓		✓✓			xx	xx	
Donohue* (2011)	CT	1973–2007	205 death-eligible homicides	Tables 22 & 23, p. 179	12	x✓	✓✓	✓x		✓x	✓✓	xx		x		
S. Phillips** (2009)	TX	1992–1999	504 capital murders	Table 7, p. 746	27	✓✓	✓✓	✓✓	✓✓	✓✓	✓✓	✓✓		✓✓	✓✓	✓
Songer and Unah (2006)	SC	1993–1997	2,319 nonnegligent homicides	Table 3, p. 195	19		✓	✓✓	✓✓	✓	✓			x	✓	✓
Paternoster et al. (2004)	MD	1978–1999	1,202 death-eligible homicides	Tables 6B & 7B, pp. 67–73	118	✓✓	✓✓	✓✓	✓x	✓✓	✓✓			x		✓✓
Baldus et al. (2012)	US Army	1984–2005	105 death-eligible cases	Table 12, p. 1,289	15		✓✓				✓✓			xx		
Paternoster, Lee, and Rocque (2016)	GA	1995–2004	1,317 death-eligible cases	Tables 7.3 & 7.4	29			✓		✓	✓	x	✓	x	✓	✓

Keys and Galliher (2016)	OK	1973–2010	3,395 homicides	Tables 9.2 & 9.3	29			√√			x√	xx		x	xx	√√
Barnes, Sloss, and Thaman (2008)	MO	1997–2001	1,046 intentional homicides	Tables 7.3(a) & (b) pp. 69–70	10						√x	√x	xx	xx		√√
Williams and Holcomb (2001)	OH	1981–1994	5,319 homicides	Table 4, p. 17	12			√		√	√			√		
Radelet and Pierce (2002)	IL	1988–1997	5,310 first-degree murders	Table 31a, p. 57	28	√	√	√	√	√	√	x	x			
Baldus, Pulaski, and Woodworth (1983)	GA	1973–1978	594 cases where death penalty was sought	p. 694	26	√	√	√	√	√	√				√	
Number of studies in which factor was found to be statistically significant						7/8	10/13	9/10	5/8	9/10	14/18	4/10	1/6	3/15	5/9	8/8

Note: A check mark denotes that the factor studied was found to be statistically significant. An "x" denotes that the factor was found to be not statistically significant. If a column is blank, the factor was not evaluated by the study. Alpha levels differed between studies. If the "x" or check mark is underlined, the study evaluated the factors with regard to sentencing. If the "x" or check mark is not underlined, the study evaluated the significance of the factor in charging. Some studies evaluated both charging and sentencing.

* Donohue presents only defendant/victim race pairs and classified racial categories as "white" and "minority." Because all cases where the victim was white were statistically significant, this column received a check for significance. Similarly, for this table, Donohue's labeling of "minority" is used as black. Because all cases where the victim was a minority were *not* statistically significant, this column received an "x" for not statistically significant.

** Phillips does not provide statistical significance alongside coefficients, but we have confirmed our coding of his study through personal correspondence. In S. Phillips, Potter, and Coverdill 2012, 140, Table 4, having a white female victim is significant in the capital charging model.

Source: Compiled by the authors from the sources indicated.

and/or sentencing. The first study selected is described in John Donohue's report *Capital Punishment in Connecticut, 1973–2007: A Comprehensive Evaluation from 4686 Murders to One Execution* (2011), which presents a summary of the regression-based studies on capital punishment since 2001. Included in this list were studies by Pierce and Radelet (2002), S. Phillips (2009), Williams and Holcomb (2001), Paternoster et al. (2004), Barnes, Sloss, and Thaman (2009), Baldus et al. (2002), Unah and Boger (2001), and Songer and Unah (2006). Two authors included in Donohue's list—Raymond Paternoster and David Keyes—published recent regression-based studies on the factors that affect capital charging and sentencing. As a result, the studies by Paternoster, Lee, and Rocque (2016) and Keys and Galliher (2016) were added to the table. Finally, the foundational study by Baldus, Pulaski, and Woodworth (1983) used in *McCleskey v. Kemp* was included. More studies that conduct regression analysis within a particular state, analyzing the factors that influence capital charging or capital sentencing, may exist: Table 4.5 is by no means a comprehensive list of such work. However, the 13 studies included cover 12 jurisdictions and are among the most prominent and influential studies of their kind. Together, they represent the "state of the art" in empirical assessments of proportionality.

Many of the studies listed in Table 4.5 include the analysis of thousands of death-eligible homicides and control for dozens of relevant variables. In the last row of the table we summarize how many of the studies found the indicated variables to be important predictors of capital charging or of death sentencing. Looking first at the legally relevant factors, heinousness, number of victims, previous violent felony convictions, and sexual assault at the same time as the murder are consistently found to be predictors; these are found in almost every study that assessed them. Clearly, legally relevant factors play very important roles in determining who gets death. When we continue with extralegal factors such as race, gender, and geography, we find that having a white victim is a powerful predictor in 14 of 18 studies; having a female victim is statistically significant in 5 of 9 studies; and geography is relevant in each of the 8 studies that assessed it. Legally relevant factors matter. But, controlling for these, factors that are supposed to be legally irrelevant also come into play. As we saw in earlier sections of this chapter, many of these are powerful indeed.

Conclusion

Homicides typically occur among young men of the same race. Black men are both the most common offenders and the most common victims of homicide. However, their killers rarely face the death penalty. Women constitute just 10 percent of all those who commit homicide, and about one-quarter of all homicide victims. Killers of women, however, are much more likely to face execution, as are killers of whites. When we combine the race and gender of homicide offenders and victims, we gain a powerful insight into the types of crime that are considered the most egregious: when a black male kills a white female, odds of execution nationally are more than 10 times greater than when a black male kills another black male. Such "garden variety" crimes—statistically the most common category of crime per capita—are highly unlikely to be met with death. When a white person kills a black victim, especially a male victim, odds of execution are vanishingly small. In fact, in many US states, such an execution has never occurred. Women are rarely executed, but when this occurs, is it typically for the crime of killing their (abusive) partner or their child. If justice were blind, we might wonder whether any of these patterns would appear.

Further Readings

Abrams, David, Marianne Bertrand, and Sendhil Mullainathan. 2012. Do Judges Vary in Their Treatment of Race? *Journal of Legal Studies* 41 (2): 347–383.

American Civil Liberties Union Capital Punishment Project. 2004. *The Forgotten Population: A Look at Death Row in the United States through the Experiences of Women.* American Civil Liberties Union. https://www.aclu.org/files/FilesPDFs/womenondeathrow.pdf.

———. 2007. *The Persistent Problem of Racial Disparities in the Federal Death Penalty.* June. https://www.aclu.org/persistent-problem-racial-disparities-federal-death-penalty.

Baldus, David C., George Woodworth, Catherine M. Grosso, and Aaron M. Christ. 2002. Arbitrariness and Discrimination in the Administration of the Death Penalty: A Legal and Empirical Analysis of the Nebraska Experience (1973–1999). *Nebraska Law Review* 81 (2): 486–756.

Baldus, David C., George G. Woodworth, and Charles A. Pulaski Jr. 1990. *Equal Justice and the Death Penalty: A Legal and Empirical Analysis.* Boston: Northeastern University Press.

Baumgartner, Frank R., Amanda Grigg, and Alisa Mastro. 2015. #BlackLivesDon'tMatter: Race-of-Victim Effects in US Executions, 1977–2013. *Politics, Groups, and Identities* 3 (2): 209–221.

Baumgartner, Frank R., Emma Johnson, Colin P. Wilson, and Clarke Whitehead. 2016. These Lives Matter, Those Ones Don't: Comparing Execution Rates by the Race and Gender of the Victim in the US and in the Top Death Penalty States. *Albany Law Review* 79 (3): 797–860.

Blume, John, Theodore Eisenberg, and Martin T. Wells. 2004. Explaining Death Row's Population and Racial Composition. *Journal of Empirical Legal Studies* 1 (1): 165–207.

Donohue, John J., III. 2014. An Empirical Evaluation of the Connecticut Death Penalty System since 1973: Are There Unlawful Racial, Gender, and Geographic Disparities? *Journal of Empirical Legal Studies* 11 (4): 637–696.

Eberhardt, Jennifer L., Paul G. Davies, Valerie J. Purdie-Vaughns, and Sheri Lynn Johnson. 2005/06. Looking Deathworthy: Perceived Stereotypicality of Black Defendants Predicts Capital-Sentencing Outcomes. *Psychological Science* 17 (5): 383–386.

Leonard, Elizabeth Dermody. 2002. *Convicted Survivors: The Imprisonment of Battered Women Who Kill.* Albany: State University of New York Press.

O'Shea, Kathleen A. 1999. *Women and the Death Penalty in the United States, 1900–1998.* 2nd ed. Westport, CT: Praeger.

———. 2000. *Women on the Row: Revelations from Both Sides of the Bars.* New York: Firebrand.

Paternoster, Raymond, Robert Brame, Sarah Bacon, Andrew Ditchfield, David Biere, Karen Beckman, Deanna Perez, Michael Strauch, Nadine Frederique, Kristin Gawkoski, Daniel Ziegler, and Katheryn Murphy. 2003. *An Empirical Analysis of Maryland's Death Sentencing System with Respect to the Influence of Race and Legal Jurisdiction, Final Report.* http://www.aclu-md.org/uploaded_files/0000/0377/md_death_penalty_race_study.pdf.

Paternoster, Raymond, Robert Brame, Sarah Bacon, and Andrew Ditchfield. 2004. Justice by Geography and Race: The Administration of the Death Penalty in Maryland, 1978–1999. *University of Maryland Law Journal of Race Religion Gender and Class* 4 (1): 1–97.

Pierce, Glenn L., and Michael L. Radelet. 2002. Race, Region, and Death Sentencing in Illinois, 1988–1997. *Oregon Law Review* 81 (1): 39–96.

——— . 2005. The Impact of Legally Inappropriate Factors on Death Sentencing for California Homicides, 1990–1999. *Santa Clara Law Review* 49:1–31.

Radelet, Michael L., and Glenn L. Pierce. 1991. Choosing Those Who Will Die: Race and the Death Penalty in Florida. *Florida Law Review* 43 (1): 1–34.

Rattan A., C. S. Levine, C. S. Dweck, and J. L. Eberhardt. 2012. Race and the Fragility of the Legal Distinction between Juveniles and Adults. *PLoS ONE* 7 (5): e36680.

5

Capital-Eligible Crimes

Is the Death Penalty Reserved for the Worst of the Worst?

The US Supreme Court has consistently upheld the decision that the death penalty is constitutional if reserved for the worst of the worst.[1] A key flaw noted by the justices in *Furman* was that the death penalty was not systematically reserved for such inmates but was handed down capriciously. For capital punishment to remain constitutional, the death penalty must be "narrowly targeted" on only a specified set of particularly deserving murders, and it should be imposed on a "substantial proportion" of all those convicted of such crimes. Standardization and predictability must replace arbitrariness and caprice. "Individualized sentencing" means that characteristics of the crime as well as those of the criminal must be considered, with those who are less culpable punished by a lesser sentence such as life in prison. Of course, we also noted that the Court has also consistently refused to provide clear written guidelines as to exactly where the line is between life and death (see *McGautha v. California*, 1971). "Guided discretion" means that capital sentencers must be guided, but they must also retain their discretion, and no law that specifically lays out the precise conditions for life and death for all criminals guilty of any particular crime, no matter how heinous, has ever been found to be constitutional by the Court. In *Woodson v. Gregg* (1976), a companion case of *Gregg v. Georgia*, the Court rejected a mandatory death sentence for all those convicted of a class of identified crimes. Writing for the court, Justice Potter Stewart stated, "A process that accords no significance to relevant facets of the character and record of the individual offender or the circumstances of the particular offense excludes from consideration in fixing the ultimate punishment of death the possibility of compassionate or mitigating factors stemming from the diverse frailties of humankind" (*Woodson v. North Carolina*, 304).

In *Gregg*, the justices wanted to validate a system of "guided discretion" that would direct the nation's harshest penalty toward criminals whose acts were truly wanton, and who themselves were the most culpable. Writing for the Court, Justice Stewart reiterated the purpose of the death penalty as described by *Furman*, namely, that it was intended for times when a sentencing body had to consider a "matter so grave as" to determine "whether a human life should be taken or spared." During these times, discretion had to be "suitably directed and limited so as to minimize the risk of wholly arbitrary and capricious action" (189). That is why *Furman* invalidated existing death penalty laws that failed to achieve this goal, and why *Gregg* attempted to correct these flaws by instituting "guided discretion" and a proportionality review–based system that reserved the death penalty for the "worst of the worst." Consistently, the Court has ruled that sentences must consider not just the circumstances of the crime but also the "character and record of the individual offender" (*Woodson v. North Carolina*, 304).

In *Zant v. Stephens* (1983), the Court reviewed its own rulings in *Gregg* and *Furman*, noting that Georgia's system had been deemed acceptable in *Gregg* based on the clear identification of "at least one valid statutory aggravating circumstance" and that the state Supreme Court reviewed every death sentence to ensure against disproportionality:

> These elements, the [*Gregg*] opinion concluded, adequately protected against the wanton and freakish imposition of the death penalty. This conclusion rested, of course, on the fundamental requirement that each statutory aggravating circumstance must satisfy a constitutional standard derived from the principles of *Furman* itself. For a system "could have standards so vague that they would fail adequately to channel the sentencing decision patterns of juries, with the result that a pattern of arbitrary and capricious sentencing like that found unconstitutional in *Furman* could occur." To avoid this constitutional flaw, an aggravating circumstance must genuinely narrow the class of persons eligible for the death penalty, and must reasonably justify the imposition of a more severe sentence on the defendant compared to others found guilty of murder. (*Zant v. Stephens*, 876–877, citations omitted)

Thus, "narrow targeting" and proportionality review are essential safeguards against caprice. As discussed in chapter 1, Justice White wrote in *Gregg* that Georgia's law was acceptable because it combined "narrow targeting" with an expectation that a "substantial proportion" of eligible offenders would be sentenced to death. But the Court and indeed the US legal tradition have always had another idea: that some things are so complicated and nuanced that they cannot be precisely enumerated. This is the reason for the "individualized judgment" in the Court's rulings, particularly as it relates to the exercise of mercy, or recognizing mitigating factors that may make a particular inmate not deserving of death, perhaps in spite of a crime for which another inmate would deserve it. Further, since *McGautha* (1971), the Court has held it impossible to state the line that divides life from death, leaving it to the discretion (unguided in *McGautha*, guided since *Gregg*) of the capital sentencer. The concept of mercy, or reducing punishment (even though punishment of some sort may be merited), has a long tradition and is at the base of the executive power of clemency. The Court has used this idea to rule that states may not enumerate an exhaustive list of mitigating factors, nor must mitigating factors be proven beyond a reasonable doubt.

As we will see in this chapter, the states have certainly not succeeded in narrowly targeting only certain crimes as eligible for death. Further, there are few standards by which juries would know how to weigh mitigators and aggravators. Finally, the Court accepted in 1976 not only *Gregg v. Georgia* but also *Jurek v. Texas*, in which Texas did not list any mitigators at all. That state's consideration of "future dangerousness" as a "special issue" tending toward the imposition of a death sentence in fact could easily cause a jury to conclude that an individual who suffered horrific abuse as a child, suffers from mental illness, and perhaps deserves mercy is in fact at increased risk of "future dangerousness" and by law therefore may be sentenced to death.

The State of Texas consistently has argued that jurors may give weight to any mitigators in their assessment of future dangerousness, and in *Jurek* the Court affirmed that approach. However, it is clear that some elements that should be considered mitigators (and are in other states) may be seen by jurors to actually increase future dangerousness; therefore, in practice, a supposed mitigator can become an aggravator or can play that role. The Court ruled this unacceptable for Texas inmates suffering from abuse and intellectual disability in *Penry v. Lynaugh* (1989). According to Steiker and Steiker (2016, 124–125), although the state revised its law, it did not invalidate the hundreds of sentences previously obtained. In a similar circumstance, Oregon invalidated all the death sentences obtained under the law found by the Court to be unconstitutional. Texas, in contrast, went ahead with hundreds of executions. The Steikers continue:

> Ultimately, though belatedly, the Supreme Court again intervened, declaring in 2007 that the Texas and lower federal courts had been wrong all along in viewing the statute as generally adequate for the consideration of mitigating evidence. In fact, the Court declared that the Texas courts' treatment of these claims was not simply wrong, but unreasonably so. By then, however, most of the Texas defendants sentenced under the unconstitutional scheme had been executed. (125)

Texas executed 405 inmates from 1976 through 2007. These inmates' cases were never reviewed, nor were the cases of those inmates on Texas's death row afforded review. In chapter 11 on mental health, we consider more generally the problem of mental illness, abuse, and other theoretical mitigating factors that sometimes effectively increase rather than decrease the chances of death.

In *Gregg v. Georgia*, the Court cited the following elements of sentencing review called for in the Georgia procedures:

a) [I]f the death penalty is only rarely imposed for an act or it is substantially out of line with sentences imposed for other acts it will be set aside as excessive. (205)

b) [W]e view it to be our duty under the similarity standard to assume that no death sentence is affirmed unless in similar cases throughout the state the death penalty has been imposed generally. (205)

Thus, the Court concluded, "It is apparent that the Supreme Court of Georgia has taken its review responsibilities seriously" (205). The Court further noted that the legislature had successfully "channeled" the discretion of the jury, thus avoiding "the basic concern of *Furman* [which] centered on those defendants who were being condemned to death capriciously and arbitrarily" (206). Not only did the legislature guide the discretion of the jury, and the courts' appellate review reassure the Court that Georgia would avoid capricious or "freakish" death sentences, but it also noted the possibility for evolving standards:

> If a time comes when juries generally do not impose the death sentence in a certain kind of murder case, the appellate review procedures assure that no defendant convicted under such circumstances will suffer a sentence of death. (206)

Throughout the decision, the Court laid out explicitly its expectation that if death was not "generally" the penalty for a certain class of crimes, then it could not be the penalty for any such crimes. Juries could not pick and choose; they had to be guided by some rules about how to use their discretion. Further, appellate courts had to review each death sentence to assure that it was not "imposed under the influence of passion, prejudice, or any other arbitrary factor, whether the evidence supports the findings of a statutory aggravating circumstance, and whether the sentence of death is excessive or disproportionate to the penalty imposed in similar cases, considering both the crime and the defendant" (204). In this chapter, we assess whether the modern death penalty system has met the proportionality challenge of *Gregg*. We begin by focusing on previous studies, then provide a review of state laws, showing consistent and widespread problems in "narrowly targeting" capital punishment only to the worst crimes and criminals.

Academic and Legal Studies of Proportionality

The issue of proportionality has been widely studied in the years since *Gregg*, with extremely consistent results. While heinousness and torture tend to make a death sentence more likely, the tendency is very weak. That is, many heinous crimes do not lead to death, and many crimes leading to death were not among the state's most heinous. This literature has also typically attempted to measure race, gender, geography, and other effects, essentially examining every death-eligible homicide and attempting to explain statistically which ones lead to a death sentence and which ones do not. These careful studies are extremely time-consuming and have been done only a few times, since they require a review of not only the cases leading to death sentences but also those that did not. In sum, they require a review of every crime that *could have* led to death, and an assessment of which ones did and which ones did not. The courts have sometimes accepted but very often denied the applicability of these studies. But from a statistical perspective their results are highly robust, and the social science community has seen them as definitive.

A host of studies has shown that nearly *all* homicides in a given state are death-eligible. In California, Steven Shatz and Nina Rivkind (1997) found that 87 percent of all first-degree murders between 1988 and 1992 were factually death-eligible, largely a result of two particularly overbroad aggravators in the state: the "lay in wait" and "felony was committed during the course of murder" statutes. According to Shatz and Rivkind, one or more of the "felony and murder" aggravating circumstances was found in 74 percent of all death judgment cases during the course of their study (1997, 1330). From this large group of death-eligible homicides, they found just 9.6 percent of the offenders were sentenced to death (1328). In *Furman*, the Court had found a 20 percent rate to be unacceptable because it opened the door to too much discretion.

Studies across different states have been able to replicate the findings of Shatz and Rivkind. For example, research on Georgia's death penalty conducted by David Baldus, George Woodworth, and Charles Pulaski (1990) found that 86 percent of all murder and nonnegligent manslaughter cases were death-eligible. However, prosecutors sought the death penalty in only 41 percent of these death-eligible cases (72). And only 17 percent of the death-eligible crimes led to a sentence of death (269). Conducting similar analysis in other states, Baldus and colleagues found that only 6 percent of those who committed death-eligible crimes in New Jersey actually received a death sentence, with that number increasing to only 19 percent in cases where the prosecutor filed a statement of intent to seek a death sentence (245).

In Colorado, Marceau, Kamin, and Foglia (2013) studied death eligibility and found similar results. They determined that 92 percent of all first-degree murders were capital-eligible (1069), while the death penalty was sought by the prosecution in only 3 percent of those murders, was pursued all the way through trial in only 1 percent of these cases, and was successfully obtained in only 0.6 percent of death-eligible cases (1072). As the study points out, in the aftermath of *Furman*, Colorado's death penalty statute has moved from 8 aggravating factors to 17—widening the possible circumstances under which a murder is capital-eligible.

Within the state of Missouri, Katherine Barnes, David L. Sloss, and Stephen C. Thaman (2009) conducted research on death-eligible homicides. They found that 76 percent of all homicides are death-eligible, but only 2.5 percent of homicides resulted in a death sentence. The researchers also estimated that the statutory aggravators narrow the class of death-eligible offenses by between 8.3 percent and 9.5 percent, determining that 91.6 percent of all first-degree murders were capital-eligible under the aggravating circumstance "murder was outrageously or wantonly vile, horrible or inhumane" (322–323).

Other studies on this topic from the initial years post-*Gregg* include one by Vito and Keil (1988), finding 64.5 percent of Kentucky murders from 1976 to 1986 were eligible for death; one by Bienen et al. (1988), finding 57.5 percent of homicides in New Jersey from 1982 to 1986 were theoretically death-eligible, though prosecutors served notice to seek death in less than 20 percent; one by Murphy (1984), finding 52.5 percent of murder indictments in Cook County, Illinois, from 1977 through 1980 led to a guilty verdict with one or more aggravating factors, but just 8 percent led to a death sentence; one by Sharma et al. (2013), finding capital prosecutions in 33.8 percent of all first-degree murder convictions in Tennessee from 1977 through 2007; and one by Paternoster (1983), finding that 19 percent of all nonnegligent homicides in South Carolina from 1977 through 1981 were death-eligible.

Table 5.1 summarizes these studies. While those in Tennessee and South Carolina found that fewer than half of the homicides studied were death-eligible, those in other states showed a very high percentage of murders being death-eligible, and where available, each study showed a low percentage actually leading to a death sentence.

While the studies just reviewed make it clear that *Gregg* has not ushered in the type of "guided discretion" that the justices may have envisioned, they do not answer the question of whether these small numbers of cases are in some way worse than the others—that is, whether the death penalty is reserved for the "worst" or the most heinous crimes. John Donohue of Stanford Law School conducted research on capital punishment in Connecticut, following the Baldus model and designed to study exactly this question. Donohue (2014) analyzed all 205 death-eligible crimes in Connecticut and found that there is no meaningful basis for differentiation between the crimes for which prosecutors seek death and those for which they do not. Donohue also found almost no difference in egregiousness between cases that were charged as capital felonies and those that were not. The same patterns are present with egregiousness and sentencing. Donohue found that the 9 cases in Connecticut that resulted in a death sentence were *not* the 9 most egregious crimes. In fact, he found that 23 percent of all non-death cases scored higher than the average death case. When excluding Michael Ross, who volunteered to be executed, 33 non-death cases scored higher in egregiousness than the highest-ranked death case (679).[2]

Table 5.1 **Summary of Selected State Studies on Death Eligibility and Sentencing**

Article	State	Percent Death-Eligible	Percent Receiving Death Sentence
Marceau, Kamin, and Foglia 2013	Colorado	92	0.6
Shatz and Rivkind 1997	California	87	9.6
Baldus, Woodworth, and Pulaski 1990	Georgia	86	17
Baldus, Woodworth, and Pulaski 1990	New Jersey	—	6
Barnes, Sloss, and Thaman 2009	Missouri	76	2.5
Vito and Kiel 1988	Kentucky	65	—
Bienen et al. 1988	New Jersey	58	—
Murphy 1984	Cook County, IL	53	—
Sharma et al. 2013	Tennessee	34	—
Paternoster 1983	South Carolina	19	—

Source: See chapter text.

We noted earlier that, in contrast to many other states, Connecticut actually targets a relatively small percentage of murder offenses for possible use of the death penalty. In his comprehensive study, Donohue identified more than 4,700 homicides but found just 205 death-eligible convictions. His focus was on whether the 9 individuals who were sentenced to death had committed more heinous or aggravated crimes than the 197 who were convicted of death-eligible homicides but not sentenced to death. He found there was little relation. Thus, even in a state with relative success in targeting death eligibility to a narrow group of all homicide offenders still failed with respect to ensuring proportionality in which of those death-eligible offenders were sentenced to death.

Finally, Sherod Thaxton published work in 2016 reviewing 1,238 homicides committed in Georgia from 1993 to 2000. Applying a method similar to that of Baldus and colleagues, and essentially updating their earlier study, Thaxton documented dramatic variation in the probability of a factually similar case receiving a death notice. Looking across all the judicial districts in the state, and statistically modeling the probability of seeking death in a factually similar case, he found some districts with close to a 10 percent chance and others ranging as high as 50 percent or more. Extrapolating to the entire state, he indicated that if the entire state followed the same practices as the district at the 5th percentile in proclivity to seek death (Cobb Circuit), there would be 274 death notices; if the entire state followed the practices of the district in the 95th percentile (Griffin Circuit), there would be 681 (Thaxton 2016, 181, Table 3). That is, two murders with the same underlying facts but occurring in different areas of the state would see vast differences in the likelihood that the state would seek death. The crime in Griffin Circuit is 2.5 times as likely to lead to a death notice as the crime in Cobb Circuit.

Aggravators

In *Furman*, the Court concluded that the death penalty was imposed too infrequently, since only 15 to 20 percent of death-eligible cases actually led to death sentences (see Liebman and Marshall 2006). Justice Stewart found that statistic to be unacceptable, as it left too much room for the play of arbitrary factors or outright discrimination. A better system, the justices thought, would be one in which the legislature would narrow the eligibility for the death penalty to those who commit only certain, particularly heinous, crimes, and then apply the punishment to more of those who are convicted of such crimes. If, for example, killing a police officer in the line of duty were death-eligible, and (say) 95 percent of all those who were convicted of doing so reliably faced the death penalty, then the arbitrary and capricious nature of the pre-*Furman* death penalty would have been satisfactorily addressed. There should be both a "quantitative" element to the narrowing that the justices wanted, and a "qualitative" one. Quantitatively, the death penalty should be narrowly focused so that only a small percentage of all murders fit the definition. Qualitatively, those eligible should be the "worst" or "most deserving" (see Rosen 1990).

This "individualized consideration" would include assessment of both the crime and the individual. Aggravating factors would have to be proven, but sentencers (typically, juries) could consider any mitigators they chose. Note the ambiguity: if mercy was afforded to a large proportion of those convicted of otherwise death-eligible crimes, it would raise the question of whether arbitrary and capricious (or possibly discriminatory and biased) factors were being used to excuse most from the sentence of death, but reserve it still for a capriciously chosen few. So the Court wanted to maintain individualized sentencing and consistently ruled that the full set of appropriate mitigating circumstances could never be listed (e.g., "beyond present human capability" in *McGautha*; "diverse frailties of humankind" in *Woodson*), but it also wanted "narrow targeting" to be accompanied by death for a "substantial portion" of those convicted. One could wonder if this is a logic akin to attempting to pass a camel through the eye of a needle.

The states understood *Furman* would require them to revise their existing laws. In successive rulings early in the modern period, the Court ruled in *Woodson v. North Carolina* that a mandatory death penalty for first-degree murder could not be the solution to the arbitrariness problem: the states would have to list the narrow range of acts that define particularly aggravated murders and limit their use of the death penalty to these carefully specified acts. Shortly after *Woodson*, *Coker v. Georgia* (1977) invalidated the death penalty for the crime of rape of an adult woman. Eventually the Court ruled that the death penalty for the rape of a child was disproportionate (see *Kennedy v. Louisiana*, 2008). The states could impose the death penalty only for first-degree murder and crimes committed against the state. As we will see, however, the focus of the death penalty on only the "most deserving" crimes left significant room for interpretation and has never led to the type of narrowing that the justices may have been expecting. Further, as time progressed, the states added new aggravators, to a point where in many states the vast majority of murders are now death-eligible, directly contravening the spirit and motivation of *Gregg* and reverting to the pre-*Furman* situation that the justices had rejected. We will demonstrate this in the pages to come. But let us first look at how the modern system developed.

The process included a set of model guidelines from the American Law Institute (ALI). Table 5.2 lays out the eight aggravators identified in the ALI recommendations.[3]

Some of the categories listed in the model code are objective facts: Was the offender already in prison, attempting to escape, or a previous murderer? Were there

Table 5.2 **Eight Aggravators Listed in Model Penal Code**

Number	Aggravator
1	The murder was committed by a convict under sentence of imprisonment.
2	The defendant was previously convicted of another murder or of a felony involving the use or threat of violence to the person.
3	At the time the murder was committed the defendant also committed another murder.
4	The defendant knowingly created a great risk of death to many persons.
5	The murder was committed while the defendant was engaged or was an accomplice in the commission of, or an attempt to commit, or flight after committing or attempting to commit robbery, rape, or deviate sexual intercourse by force or threat of force, arson, burglary or kidnapping.
6	The murder was committed for the purpose of avoiding or preventing a lawful arrest or effecting an escape from lawful custody.
7	The murder was committed for pecuniary gain.
8	The murder was especially heinous, atrocious, or cruel, manifesting exceptional depravity.

Source: ALI 1962 (Model Penal Code § 210.6(3)).

multiple victims? Was the murder committed during the commission of another serious crime? But some of the elements may be surprisingly elusive. Pecuniary gain seems clear, but are all robberies therefore among the "worst of the worst" crimes? The last element, of course, exceptional depravity, seems clear. But in the hands of a prosecutor, which intentional homicide could not be made to seem exceptionally depraved? The eight categories in the model penal code presage a more important problem: state legislatures determine the laws of death eligibility, and the elected officials who make up these bodies have little political incentive either to limit the number of death-eligible crimes or to tie the hands of prosecutors who may find that overly explicit or limiting language errs on the side of precluding their use of the death penalty in cases that seem truly to merit it. Table 5.3 summarizes which crimes are death-eligible across all the US jurisdictions with the death penalty. The table lists "aggravators" that a prosecutor can use to determine that the crime is death-eligible or a jury can use in deciding whether the aggravators outweigh the mitigators, leading to a sentence of death.[4]

Table 5.3 presents an aggregated summary of aggravating circumstances and eligibility criteria found within individual state codes. Because of differences in the language used by states, multiple statutes are placed under a single category. For example, the category "victim on public duty" encompasses situations in which the victim was a peace officer, a penal officer, a prosecutor, a state or federal official, a subpoenaed witness, a schoolteacher, a news reporter, and so forth, who was acting in the line of duty at the time of the murder, or situations in which the murder was a response to or retaliation for an action the victim made while on public duty. The category "criminal sexual conduct" encompasses rape, sexual assault, sexual abuse of a minor, sodomy, oral copulation, and rape by instrument. "Victim vulnerability" includes statutes concerning the victim's youth or old age or situations in which the victim was unborn, was known to be pregnant, was mentally or physically disabled, was incarcerated, or had a protective order. A comprehensive list of underlying statutes can be found in Appendix A, listing aggravators and eligibility factors, and Appendix B, listing mitigators, on our website.

Because each state has its own statute, semantic differences are common. For example, California's capital punishment statute considers a murder carried out for "financial gain" as an aggravating factor, while Delaware's statute refers to "pecuniary gain." These statutes differ only in form, and the table allows the two statutes to be identified under the same category. Also note that totals for the number of states with any category of eligibility characteristics may be larger than the number of states that share any single statute within that category. For example, in the case of "victim on public duty," 24 states include "victim is a peace officer" (the most common statute in this category), and 10 states specify "victim is a subpoenaed witness" (the next most common) or "victim is a jail or prison official," but combining all statutes related to a victim's public service results in 29 states having at least one related specification in their codes.

Table 5.3 **Death-Eligible Crimes/Aggravating Factors**

Aggravating Circumstance	Number of States	States
Defendant criminal history	31	AL, AZ, AR, CA, CO, DE, FL, GA, ID, IN, KS, KY, LA, MS, MO, MT, NV, NH, NC, OH, OK, OR, PA, SC, SD, TN, TX, UT, VA, WA, WY
Victim on public duty/peace officer	29	AZ, CA, CO, DE, FL, GA, ID, IN, KS, KY, LA, MS, MO, MT, NV, NH, NC, OH, OK, OR, PA, SC, SD, TN, TX, UT, VA, WA, WY
Interfere with justice/avoid arrest/while under conviction	27	AL, AZ, AR, CO, DE, FL, GA, ID, KS, LA, MS, MO, MT, NV, NH, NC, OH, OK, OR, PA, SC, SD, TN, TX, UT, WA, WY
For gain	27	AL, AZ, AR, CA, CO, DE, FL, GA, KY, LA, MS, MO, NV, NH, NC, OH, OK, OR, PA, SC, SD, TN, TX, UT, VA, WA, WY
Criminal sexual conduct	26	AL, CA, DE, FL, GA, ID, IN, KS, KY, LA, MS, MO, MT, NV, NH, NC, OH, OK, PA, SC, SD, TN, TX, UT, VA, WA
Kidnapping	25	AL, CO, DE, FL, GA, ID, IN, KS, KY, LA, MS, MO, MT, NV, NH, NC, OH, OK, PA, SC, SD, TN, TX, UT, WA
Risk to many	24	AL, AZ, AR, CO, FL, GA, ID, KS, KY, LA, MS, MO, MT, NV, NH, NC, OH, OK, PA, SC, SD, TN, UT, WY
Robbery	22	AL, DE, FL, GA, ID, IN, KY, LA, MS, MO, NV, NC, OH, OK, PA, SC, SD, TN, TX, UT, VA, WA
Heinousness/cruelty	21	AL, AZ, AR, CA, CO, DE, FL, GA, ID, IN, KS, LA, MO, NH, NC, OK, SD, TN, UT, VA, WY

(continued)

Table 5.3 **Continued**

Aggravating Circumstance	Number of States	States
Burglary	21	DE, FL, GA, ID, IN, KY, LA, MS, MO, NV, NH, NC, OH, OK, PA, SC, SD, TN, TX, UT, WA
Victim vulnerability	20	AZ, AR, CO, DE, FL, KS, KY, LA, NV, NH, OH, OR, PA, SC, SD, TN, TX, UT, VA, WY
Type of weapon (i.e., bomb)	17	AZ, CO, DE, FL, GA, IN, KY, MS, MO, NV, NC, OR, SD, TN, UT, WA, WY
Multiple victims	17	AL, AR, CA, CO, DE, KS, KY, LA, MT, NV, OH, OR, SC, TN, TX, UT, VA
Torture/dismemberment	16	AL, AR, DE, IN, KS, LA, MO, MT, NV, NH, PA, SC, TN, UT, VA, WY
Arson	15	AL, DE, FL, ID, IN, MS, MO, NV, NC, OH, SC, SD, TN, UT, WA
Piracy/wrecking/hijacking	10	AL, FL, GA, MS, MO, NC, PA, TN, UT, WY
Location/proximity of weapon or victim	10	GA, ID, KY, MS, NV, NC, SD, TN, UT, WA
Directed another	9	DE, GA, IN, KS, MO, OR, PA, SD, VA
Drug charges	6	AL, IN, LA, PA, SC, SD
Terrorism	6	LA, MS, NV, OH, TN, VA
Defendant is future danger	5	ID, OK, OR, TX, VA
Interfering with victim's free speech	5	DE, OH, OR, SC, UT
Gang activity	4	AL, FL, IN, MO,
Lying in wait/stalking	4	CA, IN, KS, MT
Poisoning	3	CA, DE, SC
Hate crime	2	CA, CO

Note: Delaware's death penalty was ruled unconstitutional in August 2016.

Some important elements emerge from Table 5.3. Five of the 10 most frequent aggravating factors involve committing a homicide during the course of a felony; the second most frequent eligibility characteristic is the defendant's criminal history. The most frequently listed conceptual category to be present in the statutes of all 31 states was that the victim was serving on public duty. The vulnerability of the victim is another recurrent theme across the states. Victim vulnerability is an eligibility characteristic for 20 states, with the elderly, the young, the pregnant, and the disabled being designated as protected groups in various states.

The goal of *Furman* and *Gregg* was to limit the death penalty to a narrow category of particularly heinous crimes. But we see in Table 5.3 that states wrote laws that are often quite broad: "risk to many," "in the commission of a felony," or even "defendant previous history" could potentially include many crimes that neutral observers might not classify as among the "worst of the worst." Limiting the reach of the death penalty only to certain narrowly defined crimes, then applying it in the vast majority of the cases that meet those definitions, was seen as the solution to the arbitrary and capricious nature of the penalty in the pre-*Furman* years. We saw in chapter 4 that extensive racial and gender targeting characterizes the modern death penalty system. The race and gender of the victim are important factors, statistically speaking, in determining whether an individual is executed. Race and gender, of course, are never listed in the law; they enter the process through practice and norms.

Jurek v. Texas (1976) and the Texas Rules of Death Eligibility

When the Court affirmed Georgia's new procedures in *Gregg*, it also affirmed in two other cases: *Proffitt v. Florida* and *Jurek v. Texas*. (It rejected North Carolina's and Louisiana's systems, which involved mandatory death sentences.) The Florida system was similar to Georgia's with regard to aggravating and mitigating circumstances, though there were two differences. First, Florida juries were asked specifically to weigh the mitigating evidence against the proven aggravators. (In Georgia the law required that the jury find at least one aggravator to be legally demonstrated beyond a reasonable doubt and then allowed—but did not require—juries to consider other factors, including aggravators not proven as well as mitigators.) Further and more important, the jury's determination in Florida was only advisory to the judge, who was free to overrule. (This aspect, judge overrule, was also present in Alabama and Delaware and was overturned by the Court in *Hurst v. Florida* in 2016; in any case, it was considered constitutional for the first 40 years of the application of the modern system.)

Texas had a different approach, which was also approved by the Court on the same day as *Gregg*. The Texas system did not use aggravators and mitigators at all. Rather, it narrowed the list of death-eligible crimes to just five specific types of murders: (1) of a police officer or fireman; (2) committed during a kidnapping, burglary, robbery, rape, or arson; (3) for hire; (4) while attempting to escape from incarceration; or (5) by a prisoner against a prison employee. Then, if an individual is convicted of a capital crime as laid out in the preceding list, and the prosecution seeks the death penalty (which is optional), the jury considers "special issues": (1) whether the conduct of the defendant causing the death was committed deliberately and with the reasonable expectation that the death would result; (2) whether it is probable that the defendant would commit criminal acts of violence constituting a continuing threat to society; and (3) if raised by the evidence, whether the defendant's conduct was an unreasonable response to the provocation, if any, by the deceased (*Jurek v. Texas*, 428). If the jury answers yes to all the questions in the penalty phase, then a death sentence is imposed. The Court wrote: "While Texas has not adopted a list of statutory aggravating circumstances the existence of which can justify the imposition of the death penalty, as have Georgia and Florida, its action in narrowing the categories of murders for which a death sentence may ever be imposed serves much the same purpose" (*Jurek v. Texas*, 427).

Because the Texas law delimited eligible crimes to a narrow list and required that the individual circumstances of the crime and the defendant be assessed, the Court affirmed, arguing that this sufficiently narrowed the use of the death penalty in a manner substantially similar to the Georgia law. Concerns raised by the petitioner that the "future dangerousness" clause essentially required the jury to predict the future were rejected by the Court, which held that the clause would allow defendants to present evidence having the substantive effect as mitigating evidence. Thus, while the language and approach of the Texas law are different, we list "future dangerousness" as an aggravator in Table 5.3. The Court's affirmation of a system that allows prosecutors complete discretion to seek death in any robbery-murder and that requires the jury to impose death if it finds that the defendant will "probably" be a "future danger" gives some insight into the range of systems the Court was willing to accept. Texas's position as the leading death state in the modern era of course is likely related to the difference in its system from those of all the states that use some form consideration of mitigating and aggravating circumstances.

Mitigators

If capital punishment is to be reserved for the "worst," then it should not be given to those for whom there are strong vulnerabilities. Therefore, the law allows "aggravators" to be weighed against "mitigators" in the penalty phase. Mitigating circumstances serve as explanations of the defendant's behavior in ways that may be relevant to a sentencing decision (Haney 2005). Note, however, that the Court ruled in *Skipper v. South Carolina* (1986) that juries should "not be precluded from considering, as a mitigating factor, any aspect of a defendant's character or record and any of the circumstances of the offense that the defendant proffers as a basis for a sentence less than death," thus affirming previous rulings from *Locket v. Ohio* (1978), refusing to accept a statutory list of eligible mitigating factors, to *Woodson v. North Carolina* (1976) and *McGautha* (1971). Jurors can consider any mitigating factors that they choose, and they can assign them any amount of weight. Table 5.4 lists eight general mitigating circumstances, as recommended by the ALI model penal code, and which continues to provide the basis of much of the law.

Table 5.4 provides insight into the circumstances that lessen the gravity of offense for a defendant facing the possibility of death. Many of these mitigating circumstances are the reciprocates of common aggravating circumstances. For example, while having a criminal history is an aggravating circumstance that will increase a defendant's likelihood of being sentenced to death, lacking a criminal history can reduce a defendant's chances. While aggravating circumstances tend to focus on the defendant's criminal actions and victims, mitigating circumstances focus primarily on the personal details of the defendant and court evaluations of his or her character. For example, until 2005, when the Supreme Court ruled in *Roper* v. *Simmons*, states could execute minors under the age of 18. This may explain why a plurality of states with the death penalty consider the defendant's age when determining whether the death penalty should be imposed.

Table 5.5 summarizes mitigating circumstances that can be found in state legal codes. The purpose of categorizing mitigating circumstances is to represent conceptual themes in a comprehensive manner. As iterated earlier for Table 5.3, states use

Table 5.4 **Mitigators Listed in Model Penal Code**

Number	Mitigator
1	The defendant has no significant history of prior criminal activity.
2	The murder was committed while the defendant was under the influence of extreme mental or emotional disturbance.
3	The victim was a participant in the defendant's homicidal conduct or consented to the homicidal act
4	The murder was committed under circumstances which the defendant believed to provide a moral justification or extenuation for his conduct.
5	The defendant was an accomplice in a murder committed by another person and his participation in the homicidal act was relatively minor.
6	The defendant acted under duress or under the domination of another person.
7	At the time of the murder, the capacity of the defendant to appreciate the criminality [wrongfulness] of his conduct or to conform his conduct to the requirements of law was impaired as a result of mental disease or defect or intoxication.
8	The youth of the defendant at the time of the crime.

Source: ALI 1962 (Model Penal Code § 210.6(3)).

Table 5.5 **Mitigating Circumstances**

Mitigating Circumstance	Number of States	States
Age of defendant	25	AL, AR, CA, CO, DE, FL, IN, KS, KY, LA, MS, MO, MT, NV, NH, NC, OH, OR PA, SC, TN, UT, VA. WA, WY
Capacity to conform conduct compromised	23	AL, AR, CA, CO, DE, FL, IN, KS, KY, LA, MS, MO, MT, NH, NC, OH, PA, SC, TN, UT, VA, WA, WY
Defendant had a minor role	23	AL, AZ, AR, CA, CO, FL, IN, KS, KY, LA, MS, MO, MT, NV, NH, NC, OH, PA, SC, TN, UT, WA, WY
No significant criminal record	23	AL, AZ, CA, FL, IN, KS, KY, LA, MS, MO, MT, NV, NH, NC, OH, OR, PA, SC, TN, UT, VA, WA, WY
Victim was participant/ consented/induced	21	AL, AZ, AR, CA, FL, IN, KS, KY, MS, MO, MT, NV, NH, NC, OH, PA, SC, TN, VA, WA, WY
Under extreme duress/ domination	21	AL, AZ, AR, CO, FL, IN, KS, KY, LA, MS, MO, MT, NV, NH, NC, OH, PA, SC, UT, WA, WY
Extreme mental/physical disturbance	21	AL, AR, CA, FL, IN, KS, KY, LA, MS, MO, MT, NV, NC, OR, PA, SC, TN, UT, VA, WA, WY
Defendant intellect/ intelligence	7	AZ, AR, DE, LA, OH, SC, VA
Defendant believed there was moral justification	5	CA, CO, KY, LA, TN
Defendant not a future danger/ imprisonment is sufficient	3	AZ, CO, WA

Note: All states permit consideration of any nonstatutory mitigating circumstances during the sentencing phase of a capital trial. As a result, some states do not statutorily list *any* mitigating circumstances.

different language in their statutes, but we group similar provisions together here. Recall that following the 1978 *Lockett* decision, jurors can also consider additional mitigators not listed here, reinforcing the Court's logic in *McGautha* (1971) that no list could ever be complete.

Although Table 5.5 is not comprehensive, it can provide some insight into what circumstances are commonly used to mitigate a death-eligible crime. While common aggravating circumstances are centered around characteristics of the victim—including victim vulnerability and whether the victim is a public official—many of the common mitigating circumstances are centered around characteristics of the defendant. For example, the defendant's age, his or her mental state, whether the defendant acted under duress, and the defendant's capacity to conform conduct are among the most frequently statutorily listed mitigating circumstances. The level of participation in the murder is a statutorily enumerated mitigating circumstance in 21 states, which is particularly interesting given the fact that 24 states consider felony murder a capital-eligible crime (see later for more discussion of felony murder).

Intellectual capacity and mental illness are considered mitigators in many states, in particular with where statutes refer to "compromised capacity to conform conduct," which might apply to many cases where the defendant has a severe mental illness or intellectual deficiency. We should note, however, that the Court ruled in *Atkins v. Virginia* (2002) that those with severe intellectual deficiencies are categorically ineligible for the death penalty, so this is no longer a mitigator; it is an exclusion. Milder forms of intellectual deficiency may remain mitigators. Similarly, severe mental illness can also be an exclusion; individuals who cannot understand the severity of their actions, who are not competent to stand trial or aid in their own defense, or who otherwise have very serious mental illness are not eligible for a death sentence. We review these complicated elements in greater detail in chapter 13.

It seems clear from this short review of the most common aggravating and mitigating factors that the goals of *Gregg* have likely not been met. Even in the now-abandoned ALI model penal code guidelines for the death penalty, aggravators include relatively subjective factors that could potentially apply to a large percentage of all homicides, and mitigators are by law unlimited. Further, there is literally no guidance for juries about how to weigh mitigators against aggravators. Rather, if a robbery goes bad, leading to a homicide, and the offender had been abused as a child, one jury might select death as the appropriate punishment, and another jury might not. We reviewed the evidence in chapter 4 that, in virtually every large empirical study of who gets death, the accumulation of aggravating factors is strongly correlated with death, but mitigating factors tend to have less impact. Considering that juries are typically given no guidance on how to weigh aggravators and mitigators, and the tradition of mercy in Anglo-American law which suggests that a penalty can be lessened for any reason, makes it difficult to imagine juries following the kinds of clear guidelines that the justices may have envisioned in *Gregg*. Thus, the goal of standardization and ensuring that the death penalty be reserved only for a single class of offenders, the "worst of the worst," appears elusive. In the next section we explore this in greater detail, looking at the more subjective factors of death eligibility across the states.

Are the Worst of the Worst Being Executed?

We can consider several factors in assessing whether the modern death penalty successfully targets only the worst of the worst. These include whether the statutes in place limit capital punishment only to a narrow class of offenses, as well as practical issues of how the death penalty has in fact been implemented in 40 years of practice. We turn first to the laws.

Vague, Broad, or Ambiguous Aggravators

The Court mandated in *Gregg* that the death penalty be "narrowly targeted," but many states have included aggravators that in practice are vague, broad, or ambiguous. Table 5.6 lists six such categories, some of which are part of the model penal code; the table also shows how common these vague aggravators are by indicating which states have each one. The aggravators are the defendant committed the crime with heinousness/cruelty/depravity of mind; the defendant created a grave risk of life/risk to many; the defendant committed the crime for pecuniary gain; the defendant lay in wait; the defendant is a future danger; and the defendant interfered with justice.

Heinousness

The heinousness or cruelty of the crime is among the most common broad aggravators, statutorily prescribed in 21 of 31 death states. Is this overly broad, or is it narrowly targeted? Justice Potter Stewart, in *Gregg v. Georgia*, acknowledged that "[i]t is, of course, arguable that any murder involves depravity of mind or an aggravated battery" (*Gregg*, 50). Though the ruling was overturned in *Walton v. Arizona* (1990), the Supreme Court in both *Godfrey v. Georgia* (1980) and *Maynard v. Cartwright* (1988) found the "heinousness" aggravating circumstance, without any guidance provided to juries to distinguish the heinous from the "garden variety" homicide, to be unconstitutionally vague. Many legal scholars, such as Richard Rosen (1986) and Jeffrey Kirchmeier (1998), have found that the heinousness statute fails to narrow the capital eligibility of homicides, instead leading to virtually unchecked prosecutorial discretion. Many scholars have labeled the "heinousness" statute, and others like it, as "catch-alls"—broad aggravators meant to allow prosecutors to charge individuals with capital crimes when the more specific categories laid out in the statute fail to include a particularly "bad" crime. While the legislative intention

Table 5.6 Vague Aggravating Circumstances

State	Number	Heinousness	Risk to Many	For Gain	Lying in Wait	Future Danger	Interfere with Justice
Oklahoma	5	Yes	Yes	Yes		Yes	Yes
Alabama	4	Yes		Yes		Yes	Yes
Arizona	4	Yes	Yes	Yes			Yes
Arkansas	4	Yes	Yes	Yes			Yes
Colorado	4	Yes	Yes	Yes			Yes
Florida	4	Yes	Yes	Yes			Yes
Georgia	4	Yes	Yes	Yes			Yes
Idaho	4	Yes	Yes			Yes	Yes
Kansas	4	Yes	Yes		Yes		Yes
Louisiana	4	Yes	Yes	Yes			Yes
Missouri	4	Yes	Yes	Yes			Yes
New Hampshire	4	Yes	Yes	Yes			Yes
North Carolina	4	Yes	Yes	Yes			Yes
South Dakota	4	Yes	Yes	Yes			Yes
Tennessee	4	Yes	Yes	Yes			Yes
Utah	4	Yes	Yes	Yes			Yes
Wyoming	4	Yes	Yes	Yes			Yes
California	3	Yes		Yes	Yes		
Delaware	3	Yes		Yes			Yes
Mississippi	3		Yes	Yes			Yes
Montana	3		Yes		Yes		Yes
Nevada	3		Yes	Yes			Yes
Ohio	3		Yes	Yes			Yes
Oregon	3			Yes		Yes	Yes
Pennsylvania	3		Yes	Yes			Yes
South Carolina	3		Yes	Yes			Yes
Texas	3			Yes		Yes	Yes
Virginia	3			Yes			
Indiana	2	Yes			Yes		
Kentucky	2		Yes	Yes			
Washington	2			Yes			Yes

Source: Compiled from state codes.

may be to provide a fail-safe, the effect may be to give very wide discretion to prosecutors, recreating the pre-*Furman* problem rather than providing "narrow targeting" (see also Sharon 2011).

While the court seems to have found that these "heinousness" statutes are no longer unconstitutionally vague, in practice it is unclear how exactly these aggravating
circumstances narrow the pool of death-eligible crimes. As Kirchmeier points out,
the Arizona Supreme Court found "depravity" based on a defendant's bragging that
the killing showed his "machismo," but it found no "depravity" in another case in
which a defendant bragged that the victim "squealed like a rabbit." Kirchmeier adds:

> Courts have found the [heinousness] aggravator present both where the
> victim died slowly—because the victim suffered—and where the defendant
> used excessive force in killing the victim quickly. Such reasoning leads one to
> conclude that unless a defendant uses exactly the proper amount of force to
> kill, then the "heinousness" aggravator is satisfied. In those cases, however,
> the aggravator often is found to be present where the victim anticipated his
> or her fate. Such applications are consistent with common sense—because
> all murders are heinous—but such applications are not consistent with the
> Eighth Amendment objectives of eliminating arbitrariness and narrowing
> the group of defendants eligible for the death penalty. (1998, 368)

Thus, we may have not only a failure to target the death penalty narrowly but also
something that comes close to being arbitrary, as heinousness or depravity clauses
may be found in some cases but not in others for reasons that are difficult to explain.

Future Dangerousness

Another aggravating circumstance with a particularly wide breadth is when the
"defendant is a future danger." Though it is on the books in only five states, it is a
broad and vague aggravator that yet again fails to narrow death-eligible crimes. In
fact, an argument can be made that just as all murders or homicides are heinous, all
individuals who commit a death-eligible crime are a future danger. Because states
do not define what constitutes a future danger, juries are left largely in the dark,
using intuition and judgment to decide whether an individual constitutes a future
danger. To alleviate this problem, some states, such as Texas, use the testimony of
psychiatrists to attest to an individual's likelihood of committing a future crime.
One of these psychiatrists is Dr. James Grigson, who by 1989 had testified about
the future dangerousness of one-third of the Texas death row population. However,
it is clear that the reliability of psychological testimony on future dangerousness is
tenuous.[5]

Texas law requires that jurors consider "whether there is a probability that
the defendant would commit criminal acts of violence that would constitute a

continuing threat to society." In the case of Duane Buck, heard by the US Supreme Court in its fall 2016 term, the defense brought forward a psychologist who, in response to questioning, told jurors that as a black man, Buck was statistically more prone to violence than a white, and Buck was sentenced to death. Had this been an expert for the state, the defense could have objected. However, this expert was for the defense, and therefore the state did not object to this evidence. Numerous appeals on behalf of Buck failed to remove him from death row, where he has been since 1997 (see Chummah 2016). In February 2017, the Court granted relief to Buck, with Chief Justice Roberts writing for a 6–2 majority that it is unacceptable to argue that the color of his skin made Buck more appropriate for the death penalty (see Liptak 2017).

It is, of course, difficult to predict whether a person will commit murder in the future. While professionals may offer expert testimony, and jurors may reach their own assessments, none of these should be seen as perfectly accurate. Referring to the American Psychological Association (APA), Justice Blackmun summarized: "The APA's best estimates are that two out of three predictions of long term future violence made by psychiatrists are wrong" (*Barefoot v. Estelle* (1983), 921).

Lying in Wait

Another aggravating circumstance that opens the door to wide discretion is the "defendant lay in wait" statute that four death states have on their books. In *People v. Morales* (1989), a California case that clarified the definition of the term, the state found three elements necessary for a murder to involve the defendant "lying in wait": "1) [a] concealment of purpose; 2) a substantial period of watching and waiting for an opportune time to act; and 3) immediately thereafter, a surprise attack on an unsuspecting victim from a position of advantage." This definition seems to fit the court mandate of narrowing the crimes eligible for capital punishment. In application, however, it has become clear that the statute has become so broad it does not serve that function. For example, in *People v. Edwards* (1991), the California Supreme Court ruled that "[s]ince more than a quarter of a mile separated the spot where defendant first saw the girls and where he shot them, and they were on foot, the jury could reasonably infer that a matter of minutes elapsed from the time defendant first saw them until he shot them. This was substantial" (821). In addition, "[T]he jury now has vast discretion in deciding which activities are designed to gain a position of advantage" (826). With rulings like these, the boundaries of what constitutes lying in wait become unclear. As legal scholar H. Mitchell Caldwell puts it, "[A] concealment of purpose, or taking the victim by surprise, has become the failure to immediately indicate to the victim that you intend to kill him outright. A substantial period of watching and waiting has diminished to a few minutes" (2003, 371). In fact, it is unclear how exactly an individual can *fail* to meet the criteria to be lying in wait.

Financial Gain, Public Officer, Risk to Many

Though on their face most other aggravators may appear to be clear and objective, a closer look at many of these aggravators indicates that they are not clear. Among the most common aggravators, the "for financial gain" factor appears to be rather objective, serving the purpose of making murder-for-hire situations death-eligible. But the aggravator applies in any situation in which something of value is taken as part of the crime where the murder occurs, making a broad swath of homicides capital-eligible. Note that the item taken does not have to be of high value, just any value: taking a bracelet, a ring, or $20 constitutes "financial gain" according to the law. Similarly, the "victim is peace officer" or "victim on public duty" aggravator appears in nearly every state. While it appears to narrow the pool of capital-eligible crimes, it too is vague—as some states do not specify whether the peace officer or public official must be engaged in an act of peace or public office for the aggravating circumstance to be present.[6] The aggravator "risk to multiple victims/risk to many," which is found in 22 of 31 death states and the model penal code, also appears to be vague. Many states fail to specify what type of conduct, location, or weapon constitutes a risk to many—leaving the prosecutor with wide discretion about whether to seek death, and juries with equally wide discretion about whether to impose it.

Estimates of the Percentage of Homicides That Are Death-Eligible

A host of studies has shown that nearly *all* homicides in a given state are death-eligible as a result of aggravators such as those listed in Table 5.6. Steven Shatz and Nina Rivkind (1997) found that 87 percent of all first-degree murders in the state of California from 1988 to 1992 were death-eligible. Research on Georgia's death penalty found that 86 percent of all murder and nonnegligent manslaughter cases were death-eligible (Baldus, Pulaski, and Woodworth 1983). In Colorado that number sits at 92 percent (Marceau, Kamin, and Foglia 2013), while in Missouri 76 percent of all homicides are death-eligible (Barnes, Sloss, and Thaman 2009).

Not all studies have found such high percentages, as some states have more restrictive laws. In a review of 504,475 homicides from 1976 to 2003, Fagan, Zimring, and Geller (2006) coded each for common aggravating factors, finding that 24.5 percent were capital-eligible nationwide (1819, Table 1); the percentage was 21.1 for Texas (1821). In his review of Connecticut homicides discussed earlier in this chapter, Donohue found just 4.4 percent of homicides led to death sentences (2014, 641). Note that unsolved murders were not included in Donohue's study, as his team looked only at murder convictions. Still, the numbers are much lower than average. Clearly, the states vary widely in the degree to which they "narrowly target" only a small subset of homicides.

Finally, we should note that Table 5.6 includes almost every death state. That is, each state with the death penalty has at least one "catch-all" category, whether by design or oversight. Texas, which has three vague aggravating circumstances, has a death sentence rate between 3 and 6 percent of all eligible homicides. Given that the Supreme Court, in *Furman*, found a death sentence rate of only 20 percent to be arbitrary, and insufficiently narrow, the presence of these vague and overbroad aggravating circumstances across *all* states makes it unlikely that these states sufficiently narrow the pool of death-eligible crimes. In sum, the promise of *Gregg* has never come close to being fulfilled with regard to the concept of narrowing.

Felony Murder

In the United States, 46 of the 50 states have felony murder statutes. "Felony murder" is a confusing phrase to those who are not lawyers. Of course, all murders are felonies. But a felony murder is when an individual is killed during or as a result of the commission of another felony. While this difference may seem only semantic, it is very meaningful legally. It means that the perpetrator of a statutorily defined set of dangerous crimes is liable for any death or deaths that occur during the offense, even if the perpetrator does not have the intent or purpose of killing.

Several elements are of concern with regard to using felony murder as a death eligibility criterion or as an aggravator. First, many states use felony murder as part of their definition of first-degree murder. But if capital crimes are supposed to "narrowly target" the set of first-degree murders that merit the ultimate punishment, this simply elevates such a murder from below first degree all the way to capital. Second, as we discuss in the following, an individual may participate in a felony but not be the murderer; nevertheless, he or she remains eligible for death. Finally, a murder committed during a felony may not have been planned or even purposeful. Does an accidental murder committed during a robbery qualify as among the "worst"? Certainly robbery and other felonies should be punished, but the felony murder concept generates a great number of problems with regard to "narrow targeting" and disproportionality.

Felony murder is sometimes referred to as the "law of parties"—any party to a crime is guilty of all of its aspects. To put it simply, consider the getaway driver, who never enters the store but knowingly participates in a robbery (e.g., a felony). Then imagine that the accomplice inside the store panics and pulls the trigger, killing the cashier. Both the killer and the getaway driver are guilty of felony murder. The law of parties treats both of them the same. Even further afield, an accomplice who helped plan the robbery, but was not even there, could hypothetically be charged under the doctrine of felony murder for whatever ensued during the commission of the crime. Not only is a murder committed during a robbery treated more harshly than a murder committed outside the circumstance of an underlying felony, but the "law of

parties" means that all those who participate in the robbery are potentially eligible
for death even if they did not individually participate in a murder.

The US Supreme Court has addressed felony murder on a few occasions. The
Court ruled 5–4 in 1982 (*Enmund v. Florida*) in favor of the driver of a getaway car
whose accomplices had committed a robbery and two murders that, because he had
neither committed the murder nor intended for it to occur, the death penalty was
disproportionate for that crime. Mr. Enmund was resentenced, therefore, to life in
prison. Five years later, in *Tison v. Arizona* (1987), the Court ruled (again, 5–4) that
death was appropriate where the defendant was a "major participant" in the underlying felony and had shown "reckless indifference" to human life. Brothers Raymond
and Ricky Tison had participated in breaking their father out of an Arizona prison
and then participated in a crime and killing spree during their efforts to flee. Their
father died of exposure in the Arizona desert while attempting to avoid capture. The
brothers argued that *Enmund* required their death sentences be struck down, but
they lost at the Supreme Court.

Also note from Table 5.5 that "defendant had a minor role" is a mitigating circumstance in many states. But the nontriggerman accomplice remains eligible for
the death penalty in any felony murder situation. The jury may or may not consider such an accomplice's role to be minor, and the prosecutor is authorized to seek
death in such cases. Even if the jury does recognize the participation to be minor,
the inmate remains eligible for death if convicted of the crime, and there are no
guidelines for how heavily the jury may weigh "minor participation" as a mitigating factor. Further, many defendants wrongly believe they could not possibly be
sentenced to death when they did not pull the trigger, and therefore refuse to accept
a plea bargain; at the same time, their triggerman accomplice may know that the
possibility is all too real and thus may cooperate with the authorities in exchange for
a reduced sentence. The United States has executed 10 nontriggerman accomplices
while sparing the lives of the actual murderers.[7]

Beauford White is one example. White, a Florida resident, stood guard while
two men went into a house and killed six occupants during the course of a robbery.
Unlike his two accomplices, White never attempted to kill anyone. In fact, all indications are that he never intended that anyone be killed. Despite the fact that White
himself played no role in any of the six killings, the trial court used the "especially
heinous, cruel, and atrocious" nature of the homicides as the necessary aggravating
circumstance to justify White's death sentence. Neither the Florida Supreme Court
nor the trial court in White's case considered the fact that he was not the triggerman
to be a mitigating circumstance, and he was executed in 1987.[8]

In some cases, individuals convicted of felony murder can receive harsher sentences than those who actually caused the death(s). In 1996, Steven Hatch was
executed in Oklahoma on a felony murder charge.[9] Hatch and his accomplice, Glen
Ake, invaded a home, raping a child and tormenting the family. Ake shot and killed
the parents, while Hatch waited in the car. Ake was initially sentenced to death but

later had the sentence reduced to life without parole. As a result, Hatch, who killed no one, received a harsher sentence than his accomplice. Hatch, who waited in the car, has been executed, while Ake, who committed rape and multiple murders, is off death row.

Texas scheduled an execution in July 2016 for a getaway driver, Jeff Wood, for a 1996 crime for which the triggerman, Daniel Reneau, was executed in 2002. Many questioned the value and appropriateness of killing the accomplice after 20 years on death row for a crime in which he was an accomplice, not the true killer. However, under Texas's "law of parties," Wood is considered equally culpable as Reneau, and the state plans to add Wood to the list of just a dozen individuals who have been executed in modern times for participating in a crime leading to murder, though they were not the actual murderer (see Hedayati 2016; McCullough 2016). Five days before the scheduled execution, the Texas Court of Criminal Appeals sent the case back to the lower court, not to review whether Wood was eligible but to review testimony by a discredited psychiatrist that the defendant "would certainly pose a future risk" (Associated Press 2016). We will review evidence in chapter 13 that shows that very few Americans support the death penalty for nontriggerman accomplices.

Idiosyncratic Death-Eligible Circumstances

In Mississippi and Nevada, committing a homicide on educational property is a capital offense. In Alabama and Arkansas, killing someone inside a car or truck triggers death eligibility. In Arizona, if the murder weapon is a remote stun gun, capital punishment is an option. One can certainly imagine particular crimes, for example, in a school, that are particularly heinous and merit placement in the category of worst of the worst. However, as state lawmakers debate and pass legislation, they can be tempted to add categories of crimes, perhaps in response to a recent or notable tragedy, that do not precisely target only the most serious crimes. Table 5.7 lists a number of idiosyncratic aggravating circumstances across death states.

Certainly the murder of a schoolteacher is a terrible thing, or that of a custodian or other school employee. Certainly the lawmakers in Arkansas who made it a capital offense to kill a teacher or school employee, or a person inside a vehicle, had in mind certain crimes such as those that may have occurred before a classroom full of schoolchildren. But when the law was passed with that language, prosecutors were given permission to seek death in all such crimes, not only the most heinous of that category.

Nonhomicide Capital Offenses

The Court has made clear that death for any crime short of intentional homicide is excessive, even the rape of a child (see *Kennedy v. Louisiana* (2008)). However, states still list within their statutes certain crimes that are eligible for death sentences even

Table 5.7 **Idiosyncratic Aggravating Circumstances**

Aggravating Circumstances	*Number of States*	*States*
Perpetrated on educational property.	2	MS, NV
Victim in a vehicle.	2	AL, AR
Victim is conservation officer.	2	NH, MS
Victim is liquor enforcement inspector.	2	MS, OR
Defendant had familial or custodial authority of victim.	1	FL
Interfering with victim's First Amendment right.	1	DE
Murder to increase position in hierarchical organization.	1	WA
Perjury causing execution of an innocent person.	1	CA
Possession of the weapon was felony.	1	CO
Weapon was a remote stun gun.	1	AZ
Victim is family member of defendant.	1	WA
Victim is news reporter.	1	WA
Victim is teacher or school employee.	1	AR

Source: Compiled from state codes.

though they are not related to first-degree murder. Table 5.8 lists all nonmurder capital-eligible crimes. Currently, no state has executed an inmate on one of these charges during the post-*Gregg* era. However, it is not clear what would happen if a state attempted to carry out a sentence of death for one of these crimes.

None of the crimes in Table 5.8 are minor. However, none necessarily involve killing. Aggravated assault by a persistent felon may fall far short of murder, and the accused may never have committed murder. Placing a bomb near a bus terminal is not necessarily more heinous than placing a bomb near an airport, train station, or subway entrance, in a school, or in any other high-traffic area. It is not clear what would happen if a state attempted to carry out a sentence of death for one of these crimes, and it seems likely that if the crime did not also involve murder, it would be rejected by the Court as disproportionate. But these laws remain on the books.

Multiple Victims

Killing multiple victims is typically considered to be a significant aggravator, one that narrows the pool of death-eligible crimes and differentiates the worst of the

Table 5.8 **Nonmurder Capital-Eligible Crimes**

Crime	Number of States	States
Treason	9	AR, CA, CO, GA, IL, LA, MS, MI, WA
Aggravated kidnapping	5	CO, ID, IL, MO, MT
Drug trafficking	2	FL, MO
Aircraft hijacking	2	GA, MO
Placing a bomb near a bus terminal	1	MO
Espionage	1	MO
Aggravated assault by incarcerated, persistent felons or murderers	1	MT

Source: Compiled from state codes.

worst. Still, most executed inmates had just one victim. Further, 78 percent of all executed inmates had at least one white victim, whereas just 15 percent and 10 percent, respectively, had black or other-race victims. Table 5.9 shows how many victims were associated with each of the 1,422 inmates executed in the modern period. These inmates had a total of 2,222 victims.

Of the total number of 2,222 victims, three-quarters are white, 15 percent are black, and 9 percent are of another race. The vast majority of inmates executed had at least one white victim, and 73 percent had a single victim. Fewer than 10 percent of all those executed had more than two victims; fewer than 1 percent had five or more victims. Whatever we might say about the crimes for which executions follow, the death penalty is clearly not focused on multiple murderers; the vast majority involve just a single victim. Note, however, that because a previous record of homicide may be an aggravator, some serial killers may have received the death penalty for a single homicide after having received a lesser sentence for a previous homicide. For example, Donald Henry Gaskins was executed in South Carolina for killing another inmate in prison.[10] Gaskins had committed many previous homicides and was known as one of America's most prolific serial killers. The crime for which he was executed, however, was a single homicide, and he would therefore be listed as such in Table 5.9. There are a number of such cases, but not enough to alter the general pattern that is apparent in the table. An individual such as Timothy McVeigh, with multiple victims in a single murderous episode, is clearly the exception to the rule. Most of those executed had just a single victim. And that victim was very likely to be white.

Table 5.9 **Number of Victims among Executed Inmates**

Number of Inmates with *n* Victims	Number of Victims							
	White		Black		Other		Total	
	N	Cum %	N	Cum %	N	Cum %	N	Cum %
0	317	22.3	1,210	85.1	1,280	90.0		0.0
1	831	80.7	151	95.7	110	97.8	1,044	73.4
2	176	93.1	36	98.2	17	99.0	231	89.7
3	57	97.1	17	99.4	11	99.7	89	95.9
4	28	99.1	2	99.6	2	99.9	35	98.4
5	7	99.6	2	99.7	0	99.9	12	99.2
6	2	99.7	3	99.9	0	99.9	6	99.7
7	0	99.7	0	99.9	1	99.9	0	99.7
8	1	99.8	0	99.9	0	99.9	1	99.7
9	0	99.8	0	99.9	1	100.0	1	99.8
10	0	99.8	0	99.9	0	100.0	0	99.8
12	1	99.9	0	99.9	0	100.0	1	99.9
16	1	99.9	0	99.9	0	100.0	1	99.9
More	1	100.0	1	100.0	0	100.0	1	100.0
Total victims	1,678		342		201		2,222	
Percent of victims	75.5		15.4		9.0		100.0	

Note: The table shows that 1,044 inmates had 1 victim, 231 had 2 victims, and so on. Most inmates had at least 1 white victim, but 85 percent had no black victim, and 90 percent had no victims of another race, including Hispanic. Timothy McVeigh had 168 victims, including 129 whites, 32 blacks, and 7 of another race.

Conclusion

In his concurring opinion in *Furman v. Georgia*, Justice White wrote that "capital sentencing scheme[s] must, in short, provide a meaningful basis for distinguishing the few cases in which [the death penalty] is imposed from the many cases in which it is not." In the post-*Gregg* era, states have moved toward guided discretion statutes in sentencing, in an effort to identify specific aggravating circumstances that meaningfully narrow the pool of death-eligible crimes. Implicit in this court-mandated narrowing is an understanding that the crimes that remain death-eligible are those that are the "worst of the worst." Evidence presented in this chapter shows that the states have not been able to live up to this demand. Almost every state with the death penalty includes at least one "catch-all" category of crime that is designed to allow prosecutors to use it against a heinous criminal but that opens the door for use against others as well. Further, the list of death-eligible crimes cannot be said to be particularly narrow. Rather, certain classes of victims are singled out, with the others presumably covered by a general "heinousness" category. In any rational assessment, it must be concluded that the "modern" and "guided" death penalty has been no better than the one rejected in *Furman* in limiting death only to those who deserve it the most.

Two fundamental problems may plague our search for "narrow targeting" combined with use in a "substantial proportion" of those specified types of crimes. First is what was described earlier in this chapter: the Court's desire to combine guarantees of reliability with its desire for individualized assessments. Given what Justice Harlan wrote about the difficulties of laying out exactly what we mean by heinous, depraved, or "worst of the worst," then, inevitably juries and judges will have to use their judgment, and that inevitably will vary from case to case. This may or may not be acceptable. But we also know that race, class, and various social conditions may render many if not most actors involved in the criminal justice system more outraged at some crimes than at others. So a lack of reliability may be combined with systematic social, religious, gender, and racial biases.

A second fundamental issue with targeting is understanding the difference between the "worst crime" and the "most deserving defendant." Some crimes may be unspeakably horrific, but the defendant driven to that action may have powerful mitigating factors that explain (not excuse) how he or she could have done such a thing, when another person would not have. If we seek to target the death penalty on the most deserving criminals, we have to look beyond only which ones committed the most terrible crimes. Mitigating evidence, however, is treated as mercy is in an executive commutation. It, too, can seem arbitrary, and even the Court has said it cannot enumerate the precise list of mitigators that should be considered; indeed, it has barred the states from attempting to do so. If a system must rely on something it cannot explain, it will always be difficult to eliminate arbitrary and capricious distinctions from being made.

Further Readings

Baldus, David C., Charles A. Pulaski, and George F. Woodworth. 1983. Comparative Review of Death sentences: An Empirical Study of the Georgia Experience. *Journal of Criminal Law and Criminology* 74 (3): 661–753.

Baldus, David C., George G. Woodworth, and Charles A. Pulaski. 1990. *Equal Justice and the Death Penalty: A Legal and Empirical Analysis.* Boston: Northeastern University Press.

Donohue, John J., III. 2014. An Empirical Evaluation of the Connecticut Death Penalty System since 1973: Are There Unlawful Racial, Gender, and Geographic Disparities? *Journal of Empirical Legal Studies* 11 (4): 637–696.

Kirchmeier, Jeffrey L. 1998. Aggravating and Mitigating Factors: The Paradox of Today's Arbitrary and Mandatory Capital Punishment Scheme. *William and Mary Bill of Rights Journal* 6 (2): 345–459.

Phillips, Scott, and Alena Simon. 2014. Is the Modern American Death Penalty a Fatal Lottery? Texas as a Conservative Test. *Laws* 3 (1): 85–105.

6

Which Jurisdictions Execute
and Which Ones Don't?

The death penalty in the United States has become an overwhelmingly geographi-
cally concentrated punishment.[1] As of 2015, 19 states and Washington, DC, have
abolished the death penalty, leaving 31 states with active death penalty statutes.
Discounting the 3 federal executions that have taken place, there have been 1,419
executions in the modern death penalty era, spanning from 1976 to 2015. Sixteen
states and the District of Columbia have not executed a single person. When we
focus on county-level data, we see that only 474 counties, or 15 percent of all US
counties, have carried out an execution. Even among those counties that have carried out an execution, frequency of usage is highly skewed. A report by the Death
Penalty Information Center shows that the majority of executions carried out in
the United States are attributable to only 2 percent of counties (Dieter 2013). In
previous chapters, we have explored the unequal application in capital punishment
that arises from factors such as race and gender. Here, we will move on to look at the
geographical disparities in its application.

The Most Active Jurisdictions

Whether we look at states, counties, or the counties within the most active death
penalty states, we find that a small share of the jurisdictions account for the vast bulk
of the executions. Here we look at states.[2]

State Level

Figure 6.1 shows the distribution of executions by state. As seen in the graph, the
distribution of executions is extremely skewed. The Lone Star State dominates US
death penalty usage, accounting for more than a third of the executions in the modern period, executing a total of 531 inmates, which is greater than the next six states

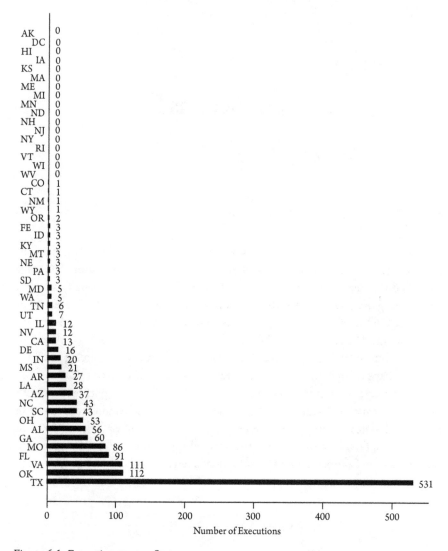

Figure 6.1 Executions across States

combined. The second-highest executing state is Oklahoma, which has carried out 112 executions, or around 21 percent of the number in Texas. Virginia follows close behind with 111 executions, followed by Florida with 91 executions and Missouri with 86. Considering that there has now been 40 years of experience with the modern death penalty, the states just listed are the only ones to average more than 2 executions per year. In fact, while Texas shows an average of 13 executions per year, 42 states or jurisdictions have fewer than 1 per year; just 20 states have more than 1 execution per year; 5 states have more than 2 per year. Of course, there are thousands of homicides, as we saw in chapter 3.

Many states, such as California, Florida, Illinois, Georgia, and Pennsylvania, have had tens of thousands of homicides in the 40 years since the modern death penalty began, but their executions are numbered in one or two digits. Even in Texas, the 531 executions we see represent just 1.11 executions per 100 homicides. Thus, executions are very rare compared with homicides, but they are highly skewed to just a few states (and these are not the states with the highest homicide rates). What we see in comparing the 50 states is also apparent when we look at a lower level of aggregation, namely, counties.

County Level

Previous research has established county-level disparities in the use of capital punishment (see Donohue 2014). The skewed distribution of executions becomes even more apparent when analyzed at the county level. Of the 3,143 counties in the United States only 474, or 15 percent, have carried out a single execution in the modern era. Figure 6.2 shows these data, restricted only to those counties that have had one or more executions.

The horizontal axis (x-axis) shows the number of executions, ranging from 1 to 125. The vertical axis (y-axis) shows the frequency of counties carrying out at least that number of executions. A total of 474 counties have had at least 1 execution, 223 have had 2 or more, 6 have had 25 or more, and only 1 county, Harris County, Texas, has had 125 executions. The shape of the distribution shows that there are only a handful of counties that account for the majority of the execution in the United

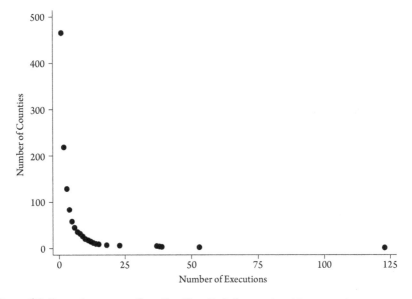

Figure 6.2 Executions across Counties. Note: Excludes counties with no executions.

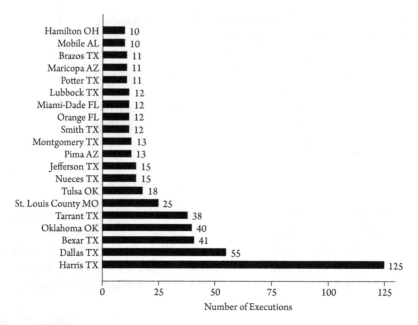

Figure 6.3 Top Executing Counties

States. The top executing counties are displayed in Figure 6.3, including those counties that have executed 10 or more individuals in the modern era.

Several points stand out here. First, only 20 counties have executed 10 or more inmates in 40 years. Second is the high concentration in Texas, which is home to 11 of the 20 top executing counties. If Harris County, Texas (Houston), were classified as its own state, it would be second only to the rest of Texas in terms of executions. Third is that the use of the death penalty is an overwhelming southern phenomenon; the only nonsouthern county that appears on the list is Hamilton, Ohio (Cincinnati).

Even within states there are drastic differences in the practice. Figure 6.4 illustrates these trends for Texas and Oklahoma. In Texas, the top executing state, a large percentage of executions are concentrated in only a few counties. Of the 246 counties in Texas, only 84 have carried out a single execution; 31 have had as many as 5 executions over 40 years; 11 have had 10 or more; and 1 county was accountable for 125, or almost 24 percent of all executions in the state of Texas. Similarly, of the 77 counties in Oklahoma, only 31 have carried out a single execution, 16 have executed more than 1 person, and only 2 have executed 10 or more.

Texas and Oklahoma are the nation's most active execution states. Even in these states, however, executions are rare. Considering the 40 years that have passed since *Gregg*, no county in Oklahoma has averaged even a single execution per year, and just three have reached that threshold in Texas. Eighteen counties in Texas saw

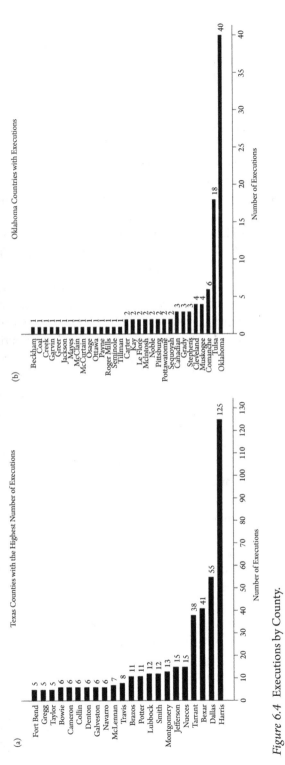

Figure 6.4 Executions by County.

A. Texas

B. Oklahoma

400 or more homicides from 1984 to 2012, and the number of executions in these counties ranges from none (in Webb County, despite 459 homicides) to 123 in Harris (with more than 12,000 homicides). In the next section, we explore the links between homicides and executions.

Homicides and Executions

Table 6.1 shows the US states sorted by their cumulative numbers of executions in the modern period, the number of homicides in the 1984 to 2012 period, the states' 2010 population, and the rates of homicide per population and execution per homicide. For states with no executions, cumulative homicide totals and rates per population are listed in the last row. Nonexecuting and executing states differ only slightly in homicide rates (1.53 per 1,000 population for the states with no executions, compared with 1.68 overall). The table shows that individual states that have seen executions show great variation in homicide rates per population, however. Similarly, executions per 100 homicides range widely around the national average of 0.27. Delaware, Texas, and Oklahoma are the only states that surpass a rate of 1 execution per 100 homicides, and just four more states (Virginia, Missouri, Alabama, and Montana)[3] have rates above 0.50 executions per 100. Clearly, executions are not a widely used punishment for homicide, as the overall rate of application is on the order of one-quarter of 1 percent. Note that the table lists more than 500,000 homicides in the United States over the period of study. Thus, while homicides are extremely common across all the states, there is little difference in the rate of homicide per population across executing and nonexecuting states, and among executing states the rates of homicides per 1,000 population and the rates of executions per 100 homicides show great variability. Executions are extremely rare compared with homicides and appear to follow no pattern related to homicides.

Figure 6.5 shows the relation between homicides and executions from Table 6.1, including only those states with any executions. Figure 6.5A shows the raw numbers, and Figure 6.5B shows the rates.

Florida, Texas, and California stand out with the largest cumulative numbers of homicides from 1984 through 2012 (the most recent year available), but they differ dramatically in the number of executions. Figure 6.5B shows how the *rate* of homicide (per population) compares to the *rate* of execution (per homicide). Here, we see that Louisiana is by far the most violent state per capita, but it has a relatively low rate of executing. In fact, the correlation between homicide rates and execution rates is zero, even slightly negative. In sum, it is hard to make sense of the linkages between homicides and executions; there is no clear connection, though of course there cannot be an execution without an underlying homicide. This is largely because the rate of execution, even in states that use the death penalty relatively frequently, is extremely low. Even in Houston, the epicenter of America's

Table 6.1 **Executions and Homicides across the States**

State	Population (2010)	Homicides (1984–2012)	Executions (1976–2015)	Homicides per 1,000 Population	Executions per 100 Homicides
Texas	25,145,561	47,918	531	1.91	1.11
Oklahoma	3,751,351	6,532	112	1.74	1.71
Virginia	8,053,257	12,773	111	1.59	0.87
Florida	18,801,310	29,877	91	1.59	0.30
Missouri	5,988,927	11,489	86	1.92	0.75
Alabama	4,779,736	10,489	56	2.19	0.53
Georgia	9,687,653	18,465	60	1.91	0.32
Ohio	11,536,504	14,924	53	1.29	0.36
North Carolina	9,535,483	16,488	43	1.73	0.26
South Carolina	4,625,364	9,320	43	2.01	0.46
Arizona	6,392,017	10,283	37	1.61	0.36
Louisiana	4,533,372	16,538	28	3.65	0.17
Arkansas	2,915,918	5,708	27	1.96	0.47
Mississippi	2,967,297	5,512	21	1.86	0.38
Indiana	6,483,802	9,391	20	1.45	0.21
Delaware	897,934	950	16	1.06	1.68
California	37,253,956	77,292	13	2.07	0.02
Illinois	12,830,632	23,561	12	1.84	0.05
Nevada	2,700,551	4,327	12	1.60	0.28
Utah	2,763,885	1,557	7	0.56	0.45
Tennessee	6,346,105	12,119	6	1.91	0.05
Maryland	5,773,552	14,132	5	2.45	0.04
Washington	6,724,540	6,123	5	0.91	0.08
Idaho	1,567,582	868	3	0.55	0.35
Kentucky	4,339,367	5,127	3	1.18	0.06
Montana	989,415	538	3	0.54	0.56
Nebraska	1,826,341	1,488	3	0.81	0.20
Pennsylvania	12,702,379	19,503	3	1.54	0.02
South Dakota	814,180	333	3	0.41	0.90
Oregon	3,831,074	3,117	2	0.81	0.06
Colorado	5,029,196	4,984	1	0.99	0.02

(*continued*)

Table 6.1 **Continued**

State	Population (2010)	Homicides (1984–2012)	Executions (1976–2015)	Homicides per 1,000 Population	Executions per 100 Homicides
Connecticut	3,574,097	3,837	1	1.07	0.03
New Mexico	2,059,179	3,547	1	1.72	0.03
Wyoming	563,626	415	1	0.74	0.24
States with no Executions	71,012,628	108,904	—	1.53	—
Total	308,797,771	518,429	1,419	1.68	0.27

Sources: Population, 2010 US Census; homicides, BJS statistics as compiled by Gram 2015; executions, DPIC.

death penalty, the number of executions (125) is small compared with the number of homicides (more than 12,000). With executions following only on average from one-quarter of 1 percent of all homicides, where the two occur is not tightly linked. In fact, homicides and executions follow almost completely distinct patterns across the United States. We examine at this geographical distribution by looking at some maps similar to those we presented in chapter 3 on homicides. In that chapter, we saw that homicides are centered in Los Angeles, Chicago, Detroit, and the Northeast Corridor (see Figure 3.10), and we saw that the highest homicide rates are in New Orleans, St. Louis, and the mid-Atlantic region (see Figure 3.11). In Figure 6.6, we replicate those same two maps in parts A and C, then show where the executions occur in parts B and D.

Figure 6.6B shows the total number of executions from 1977 to 2015, and Figure 6.6D shows the rates of execution per homicide. Executions are centered in Texas and Oklahoma, with scattered centers in other states, including Arizona, Missouri, and Florida (see Figure 6.3 for the list of high-execution counties). Execution rates per homicide are high in some of these same regions, as well as in the mid-Atlantic region.

The maps in Figure 6.6 clearly show a lack of correlation between high homicide and high execution hubs. The correlations among the four variables shown in the maps are very low: homicides to executions, 0.31; homicide rates to executions, 0.06; homicide rates to execution rates, −0.26. It is quite clear that there are no strong causal or statistical links tying homicides to executions, even in the high-use death penalty states.

Table 6.2 provides three paired comparisons to illustrate the low correlation between homicides and executions, and the arbitrary nature of these differences. It shows the same data as in Table 6.1 and Figure 6.6 for three pairs of adjacent counties.

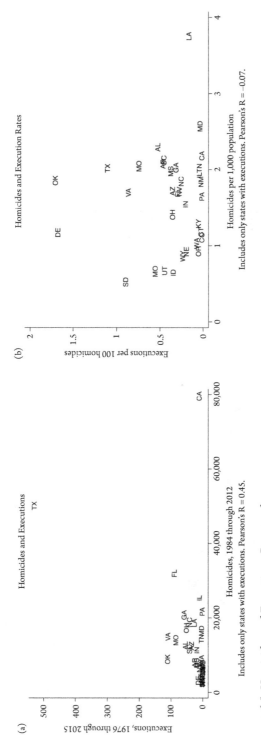

Figure 6.5 Homicides and Executions Compared.

A. Numbers. Source: See Table 6.1.

B. Rates. Source: See Table 6.1.

(a)

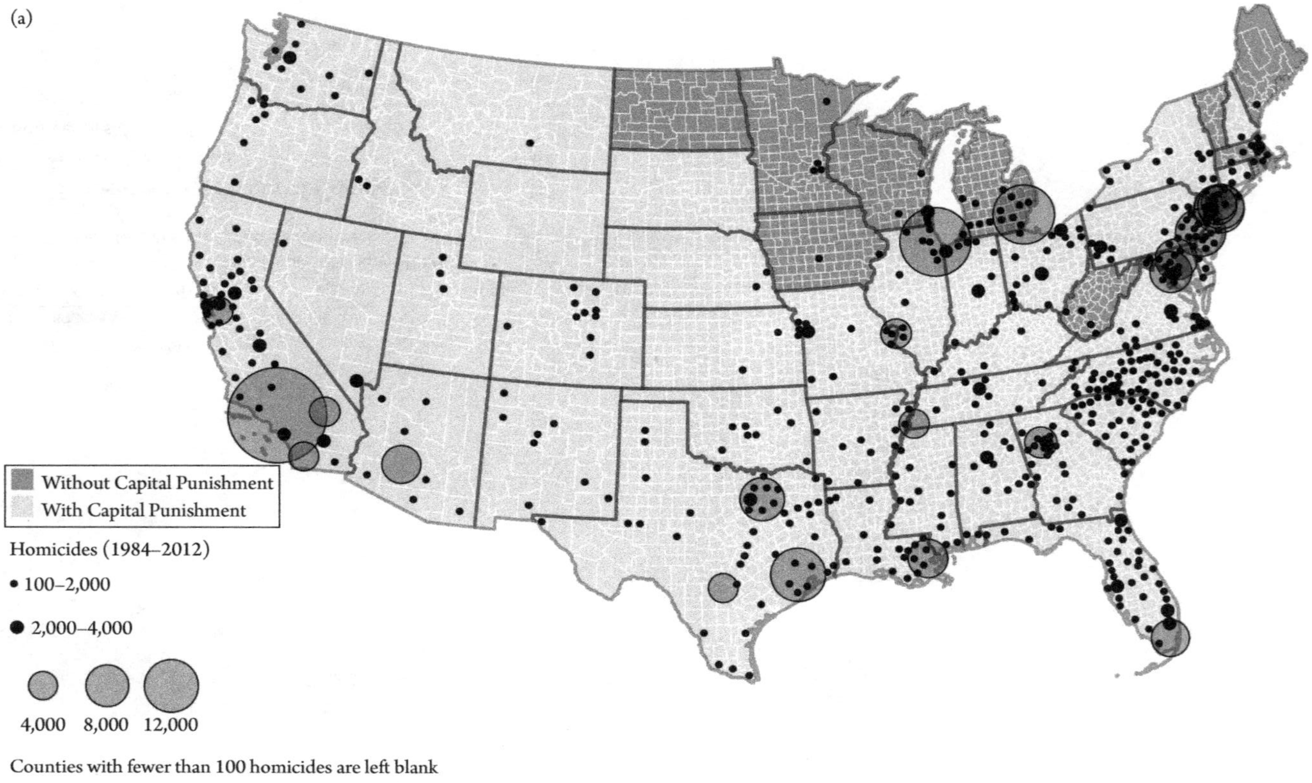

Without Capital Punishment
With Capital Punishment

Homicides (1984–2012)

· 100–2,000
● 2,000–4,000

4,000   8,000   12,000

Counties with fewer than 100 homicides are left blank

Figure 6.6 Homicides and Executions Mapped

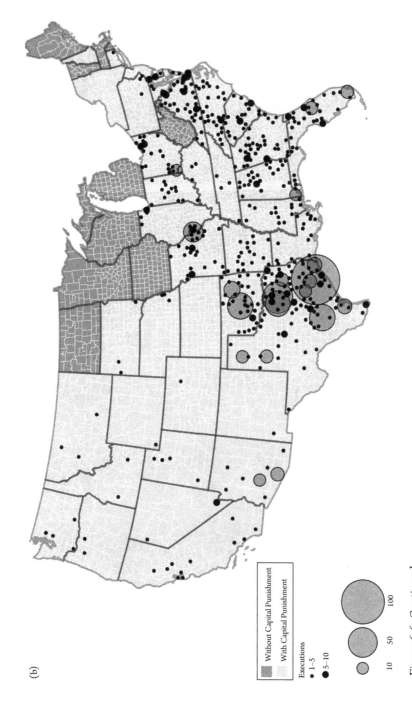

(b)

Without Capital Punishment

With Capital Punishment

Executions

• 1–5

● 5–10

10   50   100

Figure 6.6 Continued

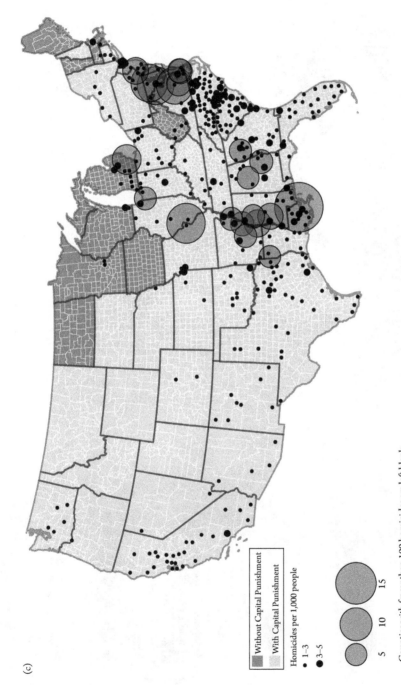

(c)

Without Capital Punishment

With Capital Punishment

Homicides per 1,000 people

· 1–3
● 3–5

5 10 15

Counties with fewer than 100 homicides are left blank

Figure 6.6 Continued

(d)

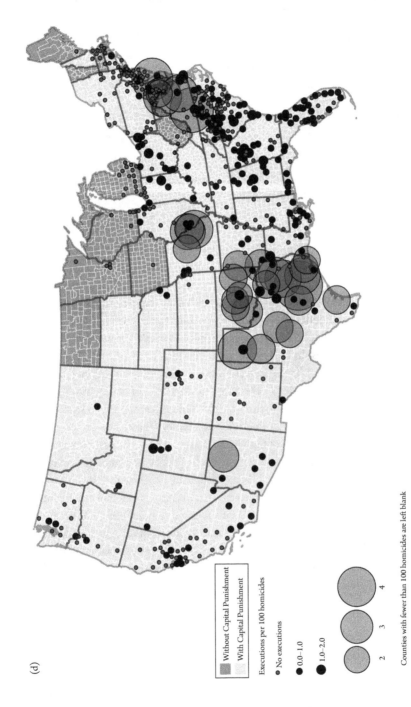

Without Capital Punishment

With Capital Punishment

Executions per 100 homicides

· No executions

• 0.0–1.0

● 1.0–2.0

2   3   4

Counties with fewer than 100 homicides are left blank

Figure 6.6 Continued

Table 6.2 **Paired Comparisons of Homicides and Executions in Six Jurisdictions**

County	Population (2010)	Homicides (1984–2012)	Executions (1976–2015)	Homicides per 1,000 Population	Executions per 100 Homicides
St. Louis County	998,954	1,008	25	1.01	2.480
St. Louis city	319,294	4,462	8	13.97	0.179
Jefferson Parish	432,552	1,340	4	3.10	0.299
Orleans Parish	343,829	7,040	4	20.48	0.057
Baltimore County	805,029	864	4	1.07	0.463
Baltimore city	620,961	7,846	0	12.64	0.000

Source: See Table 6.1.

New Orleans, Baltimore, and St. Louis are some of the most violent places in the nation, with extraordinarily high homicide rates, as shown in the table. In each case, neighboring counties have much lower homicide rates but much higher rates of execution. In Orleans Parish, Louisiana, 4 executions have resulted from more than 7,000 homicides; in Jefferson Parish (which abuts the city of New Orleans and extends south to the Gulf of Mexico), the same number of executions have followed from only 1,340 homicides. In Baltimore, no executions have followed from more than 7,800 homicides, but 4 have come from the surrounding county in spite of it seeing fewer than 900 homicides in the same period. St. Louis displays a similar pattern: just 8 executions from more than 4,000 homicides in the city, but 25 executions from just 1,008 homicides in the outlying county. These data underline the lack of connection between areas of high homicides and high execution rates.

They also call into question the issue of race. Each of the central cities has a majority nonwhite population, whereas the suburban counties are largely white. That is, in each case, the suburban area, with the higher execution rate, has a much higher percentage of white residents. In each case, the central city, with more homicides but few executions, is majority nonwhite. Before exploring these racial dynamics in greater detail, let us review the concept of prosecutorial discretion. After all, as many have argued, juries and locally elected district attorneys may reflect not random or arbitrary application of the law but differences in what people want (see, e.g., Scheidegger 2011).

Prosecutorial Discretion

Some variation in the use of the death penalty may be attributable to the discretion of US prosecutors, and possibly to electoral incentives. In the United States, only three states have appointed prosecutors; typically they are elected officials (Wright 2008; Ellis 2012). While prosecutors are supposed to make sentencing decisions based on heinousness and other relevant characteristcs of a crime, the fact that they must stand for re-election naturally makes them concerned about the state of public opinion, particularly that of likely voters. Recently, a large study showed significant effects on judicial review of death penalty cases, with state appellate judges subject to retention or nonpartisan elections particularly susceptible to public opinion effects, especially in recent years (see Canes-Wrone, Clark, and Kelly 2014). That is, judges subject to electoral review were more likely to turn down appeals from inmates facing execution. We will explore the dynamics of public opinion in considerable detail in a later chapter; in fact, given the extreme skew in the geography of the death penalty, we will see that public opinion cannot be a good explanation of this, since it does not vary as much, by orders of magnitude, as executions across the states or localities. In any case, prosecutors typically play a key role in deciding whether to seek death when a death-eligible crime occurs, so we look at that process here. Whereas our analysis suggests there is little correlation between local public opinion and the use of the death penalty, we do find huge variation in levels of usage. Because prosecutors are the first actors to be involved in the decision of whether to seek death, and typically have considerable discretion, variation across prosecutorial offices may be the most likely explanation for the extreme geographical disparities that are apparent in the use of the death penalty. Some prosecutors simply "go for death" in great numbers, whereas others do not. (For a recent in-depth study of Pennsylvania prosecutors, see Brambila 2016.)

Whereas local district attorneys are typically elected, we can compare them to federal prosecutors, who are appointed. US attorneys, in contrast to district attorneys, not only have no electoral incentives to differ based on local opinion but are part of a single bureaucratic structure and report to the US attorney general. One might therefore expect that US attorneys would seek death in relatively similar proportions nationally, but in fact they do not. As part of their duties, US attorneys must submit all death-eligible cases to the US attorney general for death authorizations. Out of the 94 federal judicial districts, only 6 account for one-third of death authorizations. More than half of all death authorizations are requested from only 14 federal judicial districts; two-thirds of the districts have not sentenced anyone to death. This wide variation could not exist if there were a consistent application of the death penalty by prosecutors nationwide. There appears to be a wide disparity between county-by-county usage of prosecutorial resources and sentencing decisions that is unexplainable by crime rates, murder rates, or the heinousness of crimes prosecuted capitally (Cohen and Smith 2010). Suprisingly, perhaps, variation across the federal system is almost as great as that across the states. What drives this high level of geographical disparity?

Local Control, Self-Reinforcement, and the Power Law of Death

The distributions of executions across geographical units shown in Figures 6.1 and 6.2 are obviously extremely skewed; just a few states or counties account for the vast bulk of the observations. Such distributions belong to a class called "fat-tailed" distributions, of which a particular form is a power-law distribution, the significance of which we explain in this section. Intuitively, we understand that many things in life differ randomly, as in the familiar bell curve. We observe a bell curve (or a normal distribution) in some circumstances, but we observe power-law or fat-tailed distributions in others. What is the difference?

A power-law distribution stems from a process of self-reinforcement. If "the rich get richer," then such a process will never generate differences that can be described by a bell curve. This explains why wealth, in fact, was observed to follow a power-law distribution more than 100 years ago by Italian sociologist Vilfredo Pareto (1965 [1896]). Processes that generate normal curves have some kind of error correction or self-canceling elements: When one throws dice, sometimes they are high, sometimes low. But throwing high one time does not increase the chance of throwing high the next time: successive throws usually average out to something close to a common expected value no matter how many times the process is repeated. In fact, for uncorrelated events (i.e., where the outcome of the second event is independent from the outcome of first event), the central limit theorem (CLT) guarantees that the distribution will be a bell curve (for an explanation of the CLT, see Blalock 1979 or any standard statistics book). The key element is whether or not the events are uncorrelated. Executions are, in fact, highly correlated at the local level. Having carried out an execution in one case increased the odds of carrying out another one quite dramatically. Thus, the process by which executions are carried out corresponds to a power-law distribution, not a random one. This helps explain the extremely skewed distribution of so many executions in such a small number of jurisdictions. But it also calls into question the equal protection clause of the US Constitution, since executions are supposed to be reserved for the most heinous murders, not those that happen to occur here rather than there.

Examples of "rich-get-richer" processes (and therefore power-law distributions) include such things as the structure of links in the World Wide Web. Sites with many links generate more and more links, as new site developers want to link to those sites that are likely to be of interest to more, rather than few, users. Academic and legal citations show a power-law distribution: scholars seeking to link their work to the work that has come before them naturally link to the most prominent works. Therefore, as time goes by, those citations that were more prominent than others become progressively ever-more prominent. Popular music follows a power-law: some bands or artists become so popular that radio disc jockeys feel they should play them, making them more widely known than others, in a cycle of self-perpetuation that is common to all these processes (see Adler 1985). Personal wealth has already been mentioned: great wealth makes it easier to generate even greater wealth as time goes by. The size of cities follows a power-law; already-large cities become larger because growth in population is in proportion to the previous size (see Bak 1996 for a good discussion of these effects across many settings.

One could understand that across states or counties, executions would not follow perfectly a clear mathematical formula linking them to homicides: one could not expect, for example, that executions would equal exactly one-quarter of 1 percent of homicides. Some homicides are more heinous than others, some jurisdictions might have randomly had a few more egregious ones, some juries may inexplicably have reached a verdict of death in a case that might surprise, or some may have done the opposite. All these are reasons to expect that any relation between homicides and executions should not be a perfect one. But random fluctuation would suggest that a normal curve would explain the imperfections in any relation between homicides and executions.

If the distribution of executions across jurisdictions follows a power-law, it suggests that there must be some kind of self-reinforcing, rich-get-richer process generating the distribution. Such a distribution simply cannot occur as a result of a process of uncorrelated decision-making. On the other hand, it could easily be the case if local legal cultures develop separately, each focusing on its own history rather than how it relates to surrounding or other jurisdictions, even within the same state.

Imagine the prosecutor's decision-making process when faced with a horrific murder in a jurisdiction where 25 executions have already been carried out. A number of factors suggest seeking death again: previous homicides where executions occurred may not have been as horrendous as this one; the prosecutor knows that juries will support it, that he or she has the staff to follow through, and that judges and appellate courts will condone it; and so forth. Compare this to the same homicide in a jurisdiction that has yet to carry out a single execution. Was this the single most horrendous murder ever in the history of that jurisdiction? Will a jury return a verdict of death? Will a judge and appellate courts, for the first time in history, allow the verdict to stand? The two jurisdictions self-separate into high and low users of the death penalty. In any case, what we observe in the distribution of executions across jurisdictions is consistent with this "rich-get-richer" phenomenon of self-reinforcement.

Figure 6.1 shows the extremely sharp gap between Texas and every other death penalty state, and the high concentration of executions in just a few states. A power-law distribution fits the following equation:

$$N(s) = s^{-k} \qquad (1)$$

where $N(s)$ is the cumulative frequency of an event with size s, and k is a constant to be estimated (Bak 1996).

Taking the log of each side of that equation leaves:

$$\log N(s) = -k \log(s) \qquad (2)$$

If the relationship is a power-law, the relation between the log of the cumulative frequency of the event will be a linear function of the log of the size of the event. Thus, a simple test of a power-law distribution is to plot the size of the event against the cumulative frequency of events of that size, using a logarithmic scale for both the x-axis and the y-axis in the figure. If the data array on a straight line, it is a power-law distribution.

Figure 6.7 depicts a log-log presentation of the same distribution that is presented in Figure 6.1: executions across the 50 states. Figure 6.8 shows the same across the counties of the United States. Figure 6.9 shows similar data within the top two death states, Texas and Oklahoma. In every case, the vast majority of jurisdictions abstain completely, but a few generate very high values indeed. And in every case, the logged data array on a straight line. Executions follow a power-law distribution.

The fact that executions are skewed so sharply to a very small set of jurisdictions, and that we can see a similar distribution consistently no matter if we look at counties within a state, counties across states, or states in the United States, strongly suggests that the process is not driven by factors that might cancel each other out. Rather, it is driven by factors that reinforce each other. Earlier in the chapter, we demonstrated that executions are not correlated with homicide rates and are only weakly correlated with homicides. We have now shown why this could be the case. Over time, local jurisdictions have separated out into those areas that never execute, in spite of significant numbers of homicides, and those that much more often carry out executions. These differences are more related to the number of executions

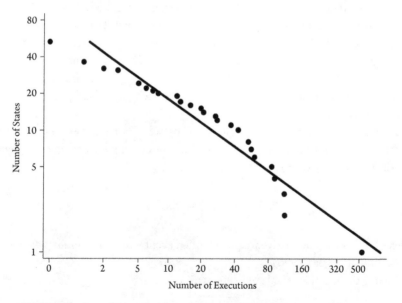

Figure 6.7 Distribution of Executions across States, 1976–2015. Note: Ln(number of executions + 1) = 6.65 – 1.47 (ln(frequency)); R2 = .9163.

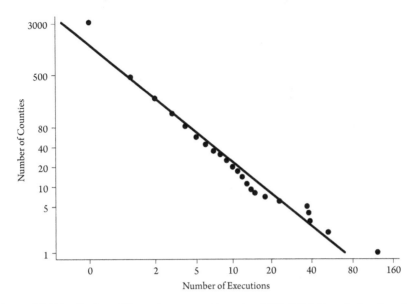

Figure 6.8 Distribution of Executions across Counties, 1976–2015. Note: Ln(number of executions + 1) = 4.32 – .596 (ln(frequency)); R^2 = .965.

previously carried out in the same jurisdiction, leading to shared expectations by all the decision makers involved, than they are related to the egregiousness of the underlying crime. It is not reasonable to think that Houston has had so many more egregious murders than Chicago or New Orleans. So the difference in execution rates per homicide cannot be due to legally relevant factors such as egregiousness. They are self-reinforcing.

Conclusion

The death penalty is used so rarely in the United States that it cannot be seen as a usual punishment for capital-eligible crimes. This chapter has presented evidence showing how concentrated its use is across the country, and that the current system cannot be seen as having fair and equal application of the punishment. Rather, its use is centered in certain hubs across the country, and even within those states that have high usage there are geographical inconsistencies throughout. The geographical concentration of the death penalty has often been thought to be a simple reflection of different local norms and cultures. Citizens in Vermont do not support the death penalty as much as those in Georgia, or so the traditional understanding has been. But the evidence we have shown here goes strongly against any such argument. Consider Richmond, Baltimore, Charlotte, Tallahassee, Atlanta, New Orleans, and Houston; none would be considered a hotbed of criminal justice

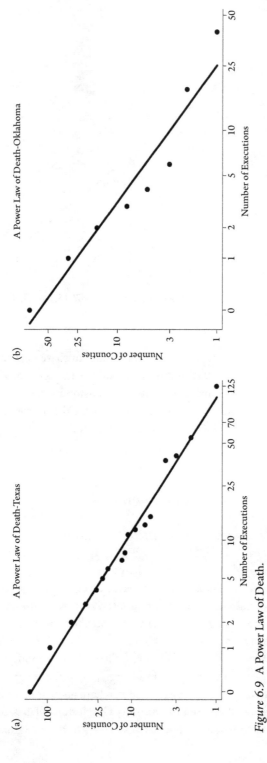

Figure 6.9 A Power Law of Death.

A. Texas. Note: Ln(number of executions + 1) = 4.450 − .771 (ln(frequency)); R^2 = .954.

B. Oklahoma. Note: Ln(number of executions + 1) = 3.225 − .649 (ln(frequency)); R^2 = .885.

liberalism. Each sees large numbers of homicides each year. Each is within a state that has executed. But the likelihood of the same crime leading to execution differs dramatically across these cities. Even within the same state, these differences persist. Our review of the geography of the death penalty creates a number of puzzles. One of those is public opinion, which we will explore in a later chapter. Like other factors, however, we find that this cannot explain the vast disparities this chapter has uncovered.

Of course, many observers defend "local control" and the variations in criminal justice outcomes, chalking them up to elected prosecutors reflecting the will of the local community, and to juries exercising their judgment. Justice Lewis Powell, for example, defended any disparities that come from juries: " 'The inherent lack of predictability of jury decisions does not justify their condemnation,' Powell wrote, adding that 'discretion in the criminal justice system offers substantial benefits to the criminal defendant' " (quoted in Mandery 2013, 429). Where juries offer mercy, of course, one can say that there are benefits to the defendant. But the evidence in this chapter has clearly demonstrated much greater variability in the application of the death penalty than can be attributed only to differences across norms and practices associated with public opinion and local culture. Rather, it comes from practices within the legal profession, in particular the district attorney's offices and the courts. In fact, as we will discuss in greater detail in chapter 13, it cannot be attributed to variability in public opinion. This makes sense, as Americans who do not believe in the death penalty are often struck from capital juries.

Further Readings

Baumgartner, Frank R., Woody Gram, Kaneesha R. Johnson, Arvind Krishnamurthy, and Colin P. Wilson. 2016. The Geographic Distribution of US Executions. *Duke Journal of Constitutional Law and Public Policy* 11 (1–2): 1–33.

Bazelon, Emily. 2016. Where the Death Penalty Still Lives. *New York Times Magazine*. August 23.

Cohen, G. Ben, and Robert J. Smith. 2010. The Racial Geography of the Federal Death Penalty. *Washington Law Review* 85 (3): 425–492.

Dieter, Richard. 2013. *The 2% Death Penalty: How a Minority of Counties Produce Most Death Cases at Enormous Costs to All*. October. Washington, DC: Death Penalty Information Center. http://www.deathpenaltyinfo.org/documents/TwoPercentReport.pdf.

Donohue, John J., III. 2014. An Empirical Evaluation of the Connecticut Death Penalty System since 1973: Are There Unlawful Racial, Gender, and Geographic Disparities? *Journal of Empirical Legal Studies* 11 (4): 637–696.

Fair Punishment Project. 2016a. *America's Top Five Deadliest Prosecutors: How Overzealous Personalities Drive the Death Penalty*. June. Cambridge, MA: Harvard University Law School.

———.2016b. *Too Broken to Fix: Part I. An In-Depth Look at America's Outlier Death Penalty Counties*. August. Cambridge, MA: Harvard University Law School.

———. 2016c. *Too Broken to Fix: Part II. An In-Depth Look at America's Outlier Death Penalty Counties*. September. Cambridge, MA: Harvard University Law School.

Smith, Robert. 2011. The Geography of the Death Penalty and Its Ramifications. *Boston University Law Review* 92 (1): 227–289.

7

How Often Are Death Sentences Overturned?

As we discussed in chapter 2, two of the characteristics that separate the "modern" death penalty from its historical counterpart are proportionality and direct review.[1] These reviews provide the opportunity to ensure that the death penalty is reserved for the "worst of the worst." Condemned inmates may avail themselves of direct review, and they may also seek further review from the courts "for cause," once their direct appeals have been heard. These safeguards are designed to ensure that executions follow only from procedures that have been reviewed and confirmed by superior courts and, if necessary, by the federal courts. In this chapter we review how often these appeals are successful. We make use of the most recent report of the US Department of Justice, which reviews the outcome of each death sentence from 1973 through 2013 and shows how many inmates have been executed, remain on death row, or have had another outcome (Snell 2014). Perhaps surprisingly, the vast majority of death sentences have been overturned.

Of the 8,466 inmates sentenced to die between 1973 and 2013, a total of 3,586 had their sentences overturned or commuted, compared with 1,359 inmates who were executed.[2] These numbers speak for themselves: 1,359 executions based on 8,466 death sentences is just 16 percent. Apparently, being solemnly condemned to death does not really mean that one will be executed. In fact, by far the most common outcome following a death sentence is that the sentence is vacated on appeal, and the inmate is removed from death row. Just 16 percent of US death sentences have been carried out. To be clear, vacating a death sentence does not set an inmate free; exonerations following a death sentence are the focus of chapter 9. (Exonerations represent a small proportion of all death sentence reversals: just 156 of more than 3,500.) Reversal of a death sentence typically results in the sentence of life in prison without the possibility of parole, a very harsh alternative indeed. But the threat of death by execution is removed. In this chapter we review what may be very surprising facts and describe how these trends have developed over time and differ from state to state.

Capital Sentence Dispositions

To the uninitiated, it would seem obvious that a death sentence, once duly and solemnly handed down, would be carried out. After all, the sentence is the most severe any state can enact, and it comes after a lengthy two-stage trial in which there is a separate phase solely to consider whether the penalty is warranted. In most states, judges must clearly instruct the jury about the mitigating and aggravating factors, and death is not even an option unless the crime met certain specific requirements, as discussed in other chapters. Invariably, the pronouncement of the sentence of death is a solemn act, with the judge often intoning from the bench a phrase that has no legal meaning in American courts but is often used, following long-standing tradition: "May God have mercy on your soul." One would think that, with life and death literally in the balance, the courts would typically get it right. Of course, perhaps a small percentage of cases might be recognized as flawed, but surely the courts would not take lightly their responsibility to be careful in such a serious matter.

Table 7.1 shows the dispositions (final outcomes) of every death sentence handed down since 1973, as of December 31, 2013.[3] As shown in the table, of all death-sentenced individuals, 35 percent remain on death row, 16 percent have been executed, 6 percent have died while awaiting execution, and 43 percent have had their death

Table 7.1 **Capital Sentence Dispositions, 1973–2013**

Disposition	Number	Percent of Death Sentences	Percent of Finalized Cases
Total	8,466	100.00	
Remaining on death Row as of December 31, 2013	2,979	35.19	
Subtotal: finalized cases	5,487	64.81	100.00
Death sentence reversed	3,619	42.75	65.96
Penalty overturned	1,781	21.04	32.46
Conviction overturned	890	10.51	16.22
Statute overturned	523	6.18	9.53
Commutation	392	4.63	7.14
Other removal	33	0.39	0.60
Death by suicide or natural causes	509	6.01	9.28
Execution	1,359	16.05	24.77

sentence overturned for one reason or another. Because appeals are likely to be in progress for those inmates who remain on death row, we distinguish here between "finalized dispositions" and others. Inmates currently on death row are not considered "finalized." Fully two-thirds of all finalized dispositions are reversed.

Finalized Dispositions

A finalized sentence is one where the inmate has been removed from death row; this includes removal by means of execution, by death, or by having the sentence reversed on appeal. As long as the inmate remains on death row, there is some uncertainty about what the final disposition may be. But once inmates are permanently removed, by either execution or reversal, we can solidly estimate the proportions seeing each outcome. We count natural death and suicide as final dispositions because these terminate any further legal review; this serves to underestimate, if anything, the reversal rate, since we do not count deaths as reversals, but some inmates who die may have seen their sentence reversed on appeal if they had lived longer. Table 7.1 shows that about 65 percent of death sentences can be considered finalized; there are no longer any judicial appeals pending. This number is greater, naturally, for death sentences that were issued some time ago. Figure 7.1 shows the percent of death sentences that are finalized, based on the year of the sentence. For those sentenced to death before 1983, for example, well over 80 percent have seen

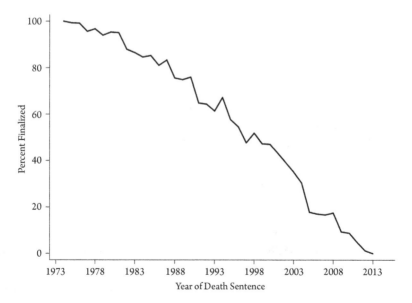

Figure 7.1 Finalized Sentences 1973–2013

the final decision. For those sentenced since 2000, in contrast, less than 20 percent have seen the final outcome of their death sentence. The others remain on death row.

Unfinalized Dispositions

Large portions of death sentences are unfinalized, which refers to any inmate who remains on death row either waiting for execution or making his or her way through the appeals process. As of 2013, there were 2,979 inmates on death row—roughly 35 percent of all inmates sentenced in the modern death penalty era. The number of unfinalized cases is the obverse of the number of finalized ones. Figure 7.1 therefore shows the very high percentage of unfinalized cases for those inmates sentenced to death in recent years.

In the following analysis, we look at finalized dispositions. For example, Table 7.1 shows that execution was the final result in 16 percent of all death sentences; however, executions represent almost 25 percent of all finalized cases. This last percentage can be more instructive because it shows the likelihood of each outcome, based on all the cases where the final outcome is known. Typically, full judicial review of a death sentence takes many years. That means that for a case to be finalized before, say, 15 years, one of two things most likely happened: the inmate's sentence may have been reversed very quickly, perhaps on the first appellate review, or the inmate may have died. In the analysis here, we typically review trends in reversals only through 2001 so that we do not inadvertently attribute to a trend what is really a selection effect. That is, finalized death sentences that stem from cases less than 15 years old are not reflective of the general trends, so we exclude them from the following analysis.

Why Are Sentences Overturned?

Condemned inmates may be removed from death row for many reasons. The Bureau of Justice Statistics (BJS) report we use distinguishes between several types of reversals, which we review here in turn based on their relative frequency.

Penalty Overturned

Across all capital cases tried in the modern era, the most common form of reversal is penalty overturn, in which the defendant's guilty verdict is sustained, but his or her death sentence is successfully challenged. During this 40-year span, 1,781 defendants, making up 50 percent of those who were granted reversals, had their conviction of guilt upheld but their sentence of death overturned. A death sentence may be overturned for a variety of reasons, including discovery of potential errors made during the sentencing phase of the trial (e.g., improper or incomplete instructions to the jury, ineffective assistance of counsel in presenting full mitigation evidence) or as a result of proportionality review. If a sentence is determined to be inappropriate or disproportionate on this ground, or if mitigating factors or other cause for appeal is found, the appeals court vacates the sentence and returns it to trial court for resentencing. At that point the inmate may be sentenced to death again, may seek a plea agreement with the prosecutor to take a lesser sentence, or may go to trial and receive a lesser sentence by the judge or jury.

The most common sentences following a reversal of the penalty are life in prison without the possibility of parole (especially for cases since the mid-1990s) or life in prison with the possibility of parole in 25 or 30 years (for older cases). Table 7.1 shows that the single most common outcome of all finalized death sentences since 1973 has been to see the sentence of death vacated and replaced with a lesser punishment. Nearly one-third of all finalized cases have later been reduced in such a manner.

Conviction Overturned

The second most common type of reversal is when the finding of guilt is overturned. Between 1973 and 2013, a total of 890 capital defendants had their conviction overturned by an appellate judge, accounting for 25 percent of all overturned sentences during the review period. As established by the Supreme Court in *Gregg v. Georgia*, capital cases are subject to bifurcated proceedings in which there are separate trials for the guilt and penalty phases. Potential errors in the initial guilt phase can result in the reversal of a defendant's conviction, should he or she be able to prove that an error or errors occurred and that those errors significantly contributed to the conviction. However, it is important to note that conviction overturn is not the same as exoneration and that those who receive such verdicts most commonly return to court for a new trial, one that results in a reduced or alternative sentence.

Reversed convictions are about half as common as reversed penalties of death, as Table 7.1 shows. Still, it is remarkable that 16 percent of all finalized death sentences are based, after judicial review, on a flawed trial of guilt. To vacate a finding of guilt means that an appellate court found errors of such consequence that they could have changed the outcome of the trial. These might relate to withheld evidence, perjured testimony, or other serious flaws; they cannot be errors deemed "inconsequential" to the outcome of the trial. Almost 900 condemned inmates have had their findings of guilt vacated by a court. As in the previous situation, these inmates then face a new trial of guilt. There is some chance that they will be found guilty again and sentenced to death a second time; however, in such cases BJS would list them according to the final disposition of their case as of the end of calendar year 2013. So, these cases with a reversed conviction can be understood as ones where the conviction was overturned and where at a subsequent trial the inmate was not sentenced to death. These 890 cases would also include approximately 156 cases where the charges were then dropped or where the inmate was found not guilty at the second trial. We focus on exonerations in chapter 9.

Statute Overturned

The overturn of a statute occurs when the Court finds that the statute under which defendants were sentenced to death is invalid. When such findings occur, all individuals sentenced to death under such statutes are removed from death row, and their sentences are reduced to the most severe punishment available at the time of their trial (typically LWOP, for cases since the mid-1990s). Almost 10 percent of finalized death sentences have been reversed en masse in this manner, when the Court finds that the death sentence may not be applied, for example, to juveniles, or when the death penalty for crimes less than homicide was invalidated. When the US Supreme Court invalidated the death penalty in its 1972 *Furman* decision, it invalidated every existing statute. Such a decision does not render any inmate not guilty of his or her crime; rather, it invalidates the death sentence and causes the inmate to be resentenced to the next most severe punishment available. For example, in 2005 the Supreme Court ruled in *Roper v. Simmons* that capital punishment may not be applied to minors, sparing 72 death row inmates in 20 states. Overturning underlying death penalty laws has led to more than 500 inmates being removed from death row in the modern period, though we will see that this was particularly common for those sentenced before 1976, when the *Gregg* decision provided greater clarity to the states about exactly what the Court considered to be acceptable death-sentencing statutes.

Commutation and Other Outcomes

Though it was more widely used in previous periods (see Banner 2002), commutation of death sentences is relatively rare today, with only 392 granted between 1973 and 2013, or fewer than 10 per year, nationwide. When a defendant is granted a commutation, his or her guilt is sustained but the sentence is reduced to life imprisonment, either with or without the possibility of parole. A form of executive clemency, commutations are typically granted by the governor following an exhausted appeals process or, in some states, at the recommendation from the state parole board. Commutations do not technically represent a judicial finding of error, but the decision to commute a death sentence is often based on arguments that the penalty was excessive. The vast majority of clemency requests are denied.

Clemency is rare, but in one recent instance many inmates were granted clemency at the same time. Just before leaving office in 2003, and after a series of scandals had rocked the Chicago Police Department, Illinois governor George Ryan commuted the death sentences of all 163 inmates on that state's death row, also pardoning 4 of them who were deemed to be innocent. The governor said: "Our capital system is haunted by the demon of error: error in determining guilt and error in determining who among the guilty deserves to die" (quoted in Wilgoren 2003). This is the largest state commutation that the United States has ever seen in the modern period. While Governor Ryan was profoundly shaken in his faith in the death penalty and decided to empty his state's death row completely (Illinois eventually abolished the death penalty in 2011), no other governor has commuted such a large number of inmates at any given time, and we typically see just a handful of commutations across the country in any given year.[4]

A small number of reversals could not be classified, and we do not analyze these, as they represent less than 1 percent of all the finalized cases, and less than one-half of 1 percent of all modern death sentences.

What Percent of the Condemned Are Executed?

Table 7.1 shows that just 16, or 25 percent, of death sentences are carried out, depending on if we compare to all death sentences or only to those that have been finalized. Figure 7.2 shows these trends.

With more than 8,000 death sentences, of which almost 6,000 have been finalized, there have been only 1,359 executions through 2013. Comparing executions to all death sentences, which shows a rate of 16 percent implementation of the punishment, is perhaps misleading as some inmates may have just recently been sentenced, and once their mandatory appeals are complete, they will indeed be executed. That is why the comparison to finalized death sentences is instructive. Essentially, this eliminates the relatively recent cases; indeed, it eliminates all of those currently on death row. Between 16 percent and 25 percent is therefore the most reasonable figure for the likelihood of execution. No matter which number we choose, it is a low one.

Likelihood of Capital Sentence Reversal
General Trends

The most likely outcome of a death sentence given in the United States is for the sentence to be reversed. In the modern death penalty era 3,586 of the 5,487 finalized sentences, around 65 percent, or roughly 42 percent of total sentences, have resulted in some form of removal from death row. Figure 7.3 shows the percentage of death sentences that have resulted in an overturn from 1973 to 2001.

Sentences that were given at the beginning of the modern death penalty period were reversed at close to 100 percent—many of these because the underlying statutes were overturned, effectively emptying death row one state at a time. These issues were generally resolved by 1976 or so, and reversal rates declined. By about the early 1980s, reversal rates stabilized at about 60 percent, where they have remained relatively steady. We stop our analysis at 2001 simply because the

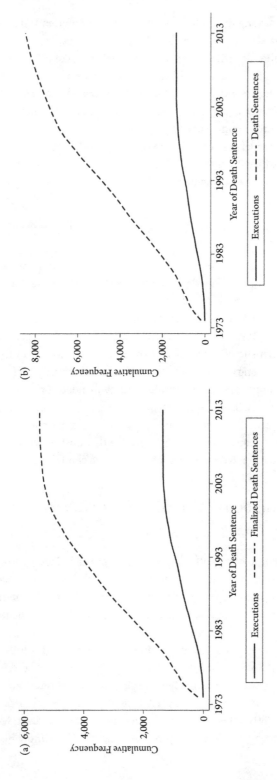

Figure 7.2 Executions as a Share of Death Sentences.

A. Finalized Dispositions. Note: Executions: 1,359; finalized dispositions: 5,487; odds of execution: 25 percent.

B. All Death Sentences. Note: Executions: 1,359; death sentences: 8,466; odds of execution: 16 percent.

Figure 7.3 Percent of Finalized Sentences Resulting in Overturn, 1973–2001

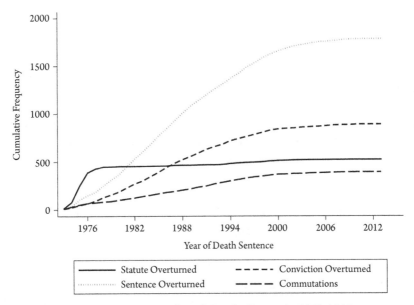

Figure 7.4 Cumulative Frequencies of Death Penalty Reversals, 1973–2013

percentage of cases finalized declines below 40 percent at that point. Most likely, many of these cases will be reversed in future years.

Figure 7.4 shows the cumulative outcome of all death sentences given from 1973 through 2013. The lines indicate the cumulative number of inmates reversed for the reason indicated, since 1973. So, for example, the solid black line increases sharply from 1973 to 1977 and then remains relatively flat. This reflects the fact that statute reversals occurred commonly in the early period, then were more rare. As time goes on, that line flattens out as there are fewer statutes overturned, and the other types of reversals become more common. Commutations are rare throughout the period; reversals of guilt occur much more commonly that commutations, but at about half the rate of reversals in the penalty phase of the trial. These trends are relatively consistent over the entire period of study. Note that all the years refer to the year of the initial death sentence, not the reversal.

Death sentences have typically been overturned. At first, this was because the underlying statutes under which the inmate was sentenced were ruled unconstitutional. Consistently since the mid-1970s, however, individual death sentences have been reversed. More rarely, findings of guilt were reversed, requiring a new trial resulting in a penalty less than death. Rarely, inmates have been commuted by their state's governor. In all, Figure 7.4 documents the trends resulting in more than 3,600 inmates having their sentence overturned. This is more than the number (2,979) remaining on death row as of December 31, 2013, and much more than the number (1,359) whose death sentences have been carried out.

A Glimpse at Sentence Reductions and Reversals in Particular States

Because the national figures from the BJS do not break down sentence reversals in great detail, we do not know what kind of sentence condemned inmates eventually receive. Two state-level reports indicate that it is typically life in prison. Baumgartner (2015) analyzed all North Carolina death sentences and found that 401 inmates were sentenced between 1977 and 2014; 249 of these sentences were finalized (i.e., 152 were on death row as of the end of 2014). Of those with finalized dispositions, 5 were commuted, 8 were exonerated, 10 were sentenced to a term of less than life, 153 were sentenced to life in prison, 24 died of natural causes, 6 committed suicide, and 43 were executed. These North Carolina figures are in line with the national figures just reviewed (but with slightly higher rates of reversal: 71 percent, and a lower rate of execution, just 17 percent of finalized cases). And they indicate that is it quite rare for an inmate to be resentenced to anything other than life when his or her death sentence is vacated: just 10 cases. But note that eight individuals were completely exonerated, set free, after their initial death sentence was found to be in error. The ratio of exonerations (8) to executions (42) is also highly troubling: about 20 percent, or one exoneration for every five executions.

A similar study conducted by Baumgartner and Lyman (2016) for the state of Louisiana documented 241 death sentences and 155 finalized cases. Of these, 9 individuals were exonerated, 127 had their sentence reversed, and 28 were executed. Thus, for Louisiana, execution was the result in just 18 percent of finalized death sentences, whereas 82 percent were reversed. These authors also reviewed the causes of the reversals: the most common was judicial error, followed by prosecu-torial misconduct, constitutionally excessive penalty, ineffective assistance of coun-sel, plea agreements, and general review (68). Louisiana also showed an even more troubling ratio of exonerations (9) to executions (28): almost one for three.

Typically, when a death sentence is reversed, the inmate's attorneys negotiate a plea with the district attorney to accept a sentence of life in prison. Occasionally, evidence suggests that a lesser charge, even manslaughter or second-degree mur-der, is appropriate, and if so the eventual sentence may be less than life. And, rarely, the inmate is fully exonerated either because the DA agrees to drop the charges, or because, in a second trial for guilt, the inmate previously sentenced to death in a trial that was later reversed is found not guilty in the subsequent trial. Statistically, the most common outcome of death penalty reversals, however, is LWOP.

Systematic Comparison of Sentence Outcomes by State

We have previously noted the dramatic differences across the states in the rates at which they impose death and execute. Strikingly, some states such as California and Pennsylvania seem to have a "virtual" or a purely symbolic death penalty in the sense that they have sentenced many to die but executed very few. At the same time, Texas, Oklahoma, and Virginia clearly lead the country with executions, so there may be large differences in the rates at which condemned inmates see their sentences reversed, have their sentences carried out, or linger on death row with no finalized decision. Steiker and Steiker (2016, 118) write that the United States now has four types of states with respect to the death penalty: (1) fully abolitionist ones where the death penalty has been legally abolished, (2) de facto abolitionist ones where the death penalty remains on the books but is virtually never imposed, (3) symbolic states where death sen-tences are imposed but rarely carried out, and (4) executing states. These categories can clearly be seen in the data. Our focus here is on the last two categories.

Figure 7.5 shows the outcomes of sentences in those states that have executed 20 or more inmates. The black portion of the bar indicates the percent of inmates whose sentences that have resulted in a reversal, which includes penalty, statute, and conviction overturns, commutations, and other forms of removal. The next lighter shade, just above the bottom, represents the percent of condemned inmates who remain on death row. Next are those who died while awaiting execution, and finally, the lightest shade represents those who were executed. Note that all the bars add up to 100 percent, but the states differ dramatically in how many death sentences they have imposed. This presentation allows a clear comparison of the likelihood of reversal, however. It can be easily read by looking at the height of the darkest bar along the bottom of the graph.

Of the highest executing states, Indiana has the highest percentage of death sen-tences resulting in reversals, at just over 60 percent, or 63 reversals of the 103 sen-tences from 1973 to 2013. The states are ordered from left to right according to this

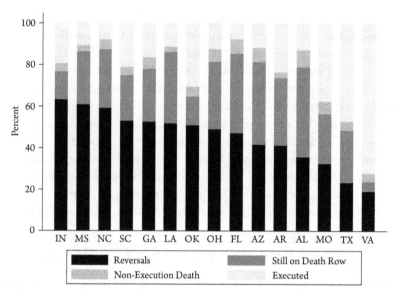

Figure 7.5 Sentencing Outcomes by High-Execution States. Note: Includes states with 20 or more executions.

variable, with Virginia at the far end with a reversal rate of only 18 percent (i.e., just 29 of the 152 sentences given).

The figure also shows the likelihood of execution; looking across the top of the figure from left to right, we see that Virginia has carried out the vast majority of death sentences it has imposed (110 execution from 152 death sentences); in fact, it is the only state to have carried out more than half of its death sentences. Other states with high execution rates include Texas (508 executions/1,075 death sentences), Missouri (70/186), and Oklahoma (108/353). The 15 states listed in Figure 7.5 include only the most active executing states. Even here, however, it is notable that just one state has executed as many as half of those it has condemned to die. In fact, the average reversal rate for these active death penalty states is about 50 percent. Just one state stands out in carrying out its death sentences: Virginia.

Figure 7.6 shows another group of states: those that have executed relatively few, but have sentenced 40 or more to die. These states have active death-sentencing systems but a very low likelihood of carrying out executions. (We exclude 12 states with fewer than 40 death sentences cumulatively from 1973 through 2014, as percentages based on such small baseline numbers can be misleading. New Hampshire, for example, had just 1 death sentence; Rhode Island just 2; and Massachusetts only 4.)

There are two ways in which a death sentence might not be carried out: reversal and warehousing. Looking at the bottom, black-shaded part of Figure 7.6, it is clear, for example, that New Jersey, Illinois, and Maryland reverse, whereas Oregon,

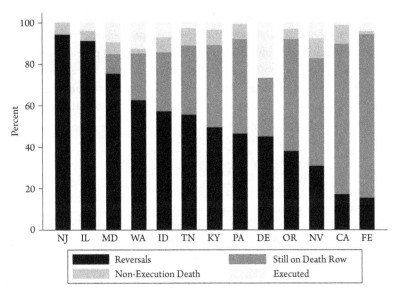

Figure 7.6 Sentencing Outcomes in Death Penalty States Executing Fewer Than 20
Inmates. Note: Includes only states with 40 or more death sentences and fewer than 20 executions.

Nevada, California, and the federal government (FE in the graph) warehouse. New
Jersey sentenced 52 individuals to die and executed none before it abolished the
death penalty in 2007. Illinois executed 12 of 307 condemned before Governor
Ryan emptied death row by commuting all the sentences in 2003 and later repealing
in 2011. At the other extreme, the federal government has sentenced 71 individuals to die, and 56 of them remain on death row as of 2013. Similarly, California has
meted out 1,013 death sentences, executed just 13 individuals, and had 735 remaining on death row as of the end of 2013. Pennsylvania merits attention here as well;
it has seen 194 reversals and 30 deaths, has 190 individuals still on death row, and
has executed just 3. Its system, then, is relatively equally divided between reversal
and warehousing. California and the federal system, on the other hand, define the
warehousing system. The extremely high reversal rates in New Jersey, Illinois, and
Maryland may be part of the reason these states abolished the death penalty altogether in 2007, 2011, and 2013, respectively.

The states that have been left out of the preceding analyses include Colorado,
Connecticut, Kansas, Massachusetts, Montana, Nebraska, New Hampshire, New
Mexico, New York, Rhode Island, South Dakota, Utah, and Wyoming. Because
these states have very low sentencing and execution rates, not much can be drawn
from their trends. Colorado has given out only 22 sentences and executed only 1
person. Connecticut abolished the death penalty in 2012, having executed 1 individual out of 17 sentenced to die. In 2015, the state supreme court commuted the
sentences of 11 inmates remaining on death row after abolition. Kansas has given

out 13 sentences and has not executed any inmate in the modern death penalty period. New York had 10 sentences and no executions before abolishing in 2007. Montana has handed out only 15 sentences and executed 3 people. South Dakota has also only executed 3 people out of the 7 sentences it had given. Wyoming has executed only 1 person in the modern period, and handed out only 12 sentences. Of these low usage states, Utah has given out sentences and executed at the highest rate, with 27 and 7, respectively.

A Broken System?

The numbers we have laid out in this chapter should shock. And they did when results of the first major study on the topic were published to wide media attention in 2000, during a period when the media was greatly focused on flaws in the death penalty system. The "broken system" study by James Liebman and colleagues was certainly a prime reason why attention to innocence, errors, and unreliability in the death penalty system came to dominate news coverage of the death penalty in the first decade of the twenty-first century (see Baumgartner, De Boef, and Boydstun 2008). In the largest study of its kind, Liebman, Fagan, West, and Lloyd (2000) systematically reviewed the outcomes of 5,760 death sentences imposed from 1973 through 1995. The results were sobering: 68 percent of the cases were reversed. Further, the researchers pointed out how each stage of the process filtered the cases, suggesting that each stage also allowed faulty cases to be affirmed. In percentage terms, state direct appeal reversed 41 percent of the original capital judgments. State postconviction review then reversed another 10 percent. Federal habeas review then reversed 40 percent of the remaining cases. Just 32 percent of the cases were affirmed. Among the 68 percent of inmates whose sentence was reversed due to serious error, just 12 individuals were resentenced to death, beginning the process again. Half of the cases led to subsequent sentences less than death, and 5 percent were acquitted completely of the crime (see Liebman, Fagan, West, and Lloyd 2000, 7).

Liebman and colleagues' careful study gained a lot of attention, as it deserved. Their results were initially published in an article in the June 2000 issue of *Texas Law Review*, with a longer report released in June 2000 and an important and extensive second report in 2002 (see Liebman, Fagan, and West 2000; see also Liebman et al. 2002; Gelman et al. 2014). The study noted trends similar to those reported here but identified the source of reversal in each case. In the 2002 update, Liebman and colleagues give more sobering detail:

> Analyses presented for the first time here reveal that 76% of the reversals at the two appeal stages where data are available for study were because defense lawyers had been egregiously incompetent, police and prosecutors

had suppressed exculpatory evidence or committed other professional misconduct, jurors had been misinformed about the law, or judges and jurors had been biased. (Liebman et al. 2002, i)

The authors note that error rates appear to be correlated with the rate at which death sentences are imposed. A lower percentage of cases are reversed in those jurisdictions that impose death sentences relatively rarely. By contrast, those that issue a higher number of death sentences per 100 homicides have higher reversal rates. They suggest that wide use of the death penalty is associated with consistently high error rates, and that we should not have confidence that all the errors are subsequently uncovered (Liebman et al. 2002, i–iv). As they conclude:

> Over decades and across dozens of states, large numbers and proportions of capital verdicts have been reversed because of serious error. The capital system is collapsing under the weight of that error, and the risk of executing the innocent is high. Now that explanations for the problem have been identified and a range of options for responding to it are available, the time is ripe to fix the death penalty, or if it can't be fixed, to end it. (vi)

Conclusion

The persistence and extraordinarily high rates of capital punishment reversals should shock the reader. Capital trials have at their heart a horrific crime, and emotions are high during all phases of the trial. But they are also solemn affairs. They represent the single most powerful act that a government can take against one of its citizens: the decision to put him or her to death. Therefore, we might expect that these decisions would never be taken lightly. But in fact, on review, most of these sentences are thrown out. To be clear, death sentences occur for the most part in states and localities where there is broad support for the punishment, including in various levels of the judicial system. The Texas Court of Criminal Appeals (CCA), for example, is no enemy to the death penalty, and Texas sits within the Fifth Circuit, often considered the most conservative of the federal courts. But even in Texas, hundreds of death sentences have been reversed by the CCA or federal courts. In other states, such as New Jersey, no executions have taken place in spite of more than 50 death sentences. The numbers should be upsetting. They represent a broken and dysfunctional system.

Two things are important to consider when interpreting the numbers we have presented in this chapter. First, reversals do not occur lightly. They cannot come because of a misplaced paper clip in a court document, so to speak. Rather, they must result from the determination by an appellate court either in the same state that issued the penalty or by a federal court that the initial trial of guilt or the penalty phase of that same trial was so flawed as to render its conclusion meaning-less. Only such flaws as significant judicial error, withheld evidence, or other items that are deemed to be "material" (i.e., which may have affected the result of the case, as opposed to "harmless error") can justify rendering moot a penalty so costly to achieve. And yet, reversal is the typical outcome; executions follow death sentences only 16 percent of the time.

A second point of reference is how capital punishment might compare with other decision-making processes within government. Would we expect the Internal Revenue Service to send tax refund checks for the wrong amounts, only to correct the problem on review? Certainly, such errors probably occur. But if this occurred even 5 percent of the time, voters and citizens would be outraged. Imagine if the US Postal Service failed to deliver even 1 percent of its first-class mail. People would be outraged, and elected officials would look into the matter forcefully. And yet here we have the single most solemn act that a government may take, and in the *majority of the cases* it is deemed to have been improperly arrived at, on review.

Perhaps we can understand why this astronomical level of error is unknown to most Americans when we consider the people who are affected by it. More than 3,500 individuals have been sentenced to death, only later to see that solemn decla-ration rendered moot. With the exception of 156 individuals who were exonerated, the vast majority of these men and women remain in prison, convicted murderers. But the cost of reversing death sentences is enormous. Family members of the crime victim are given false promise of "closure" only to find out years later that the perpe-trator in their family's case will not, in fact, receive the death sentence he or she was so solemnly promised that day in court. Family members of the condemned also suffer the needless trauma of being told that their loved one would be executed, only to find out later that the threat of death has been removed. Condemned inmates themselves have to endure the process of being condemned, often being held in soli-tary confinement on death row, only to be told later that it was all a judicial error and that their penalty will instead be life in prison. The threat of death is removed, but why was it put there in the first place if it was so likely to be removed? Untold bil-lions of dollars go into a system that generates the outcome it promises only 16 per-cent of the time.

In many states, and within the federal system, only minute percentages of those sentenced to death are executed. As Steiker and Steiker point out (2016, 152–153), the extremely low rates of execution in these "symbolic" states raise the same ques-tions of arbitrariness and caprice that were so troubling to the justices in *Furman*. What distinguishes the vast majority of inmates in California who have been ware-housed from the 13 who have been executed? If it is random chance, then the system fails the *Furman* test of reliability. Ironically, the generally higher levels of concern with inmates' due process rights in some of the symbolic states compared with the high-execution states may protect the symbolic states from certain constitutional pitfalls but make them open to a different flaw: capricious and arbitrary separation of the small numbers selected for execution compared with the large numbers not chosen.

We saw in the previous chapter that executions depend considerably on the jurisdiction in which the crime occurs. This chapter has reinforced our understanding of that process by explaining that this high degree of geographical variability is related not only to the odds of being charged with a capital crime but to dramatic differences in the likely outcome of a death sentence once handed down. Just one state is statistically likely to carry out a death sentence: Virginia. Even in Virginia, however, 40 percent of the condemned escape death. States reverse improperly imposed death sentences at extremely high rates, and many, like the federal government, typically warehouse inmates for decades at a time, neither executing nor reversing the sentence. In the next chapter, we turn to the issue of how long the typical inmate spends on death row awaiting execution. If the numbers in this chapter were quite surprising, those will be as well.

Further Readings

Gelman, Andrew, James S. Liebman, Valerie West, and Alexander Kiss. 2014. A Broken System: The Persistent Patterns of Reversals of Death Sentences in the United States. *Journal of Empirical Legal Studies* 1 (2): 209–261.

Liebman, S. James S., Jeffrey Fagan, Andrew Gelman, Valerie West, Garth Davies, and Alexander Kiss. 2002. *A Broken System, Part II: Why There Is So Much Error in Capital Cases, and What Can Be Done about It.* February 11. Columbia University Law School. http://www2.law.columbia.edu/brokensystem2/index2.html.

Liebman, James S., Jeffrey Fagan, and Valerie West. 2000. *Error Rates in Capital Cases, 1973–1995.* June 12. Columbia University Law School. http://www2.law.columbia.edu/instructionalservices/liebman/liebman_final.pdf.

Liebman, James S., Jeffrey Fagan, Valerie West, and Jonathan Lloyd. 2000. Capital Attrition: Error Rates in Capital Cases, 1973–1995. *Texas Law Review* 78:1839–1865.

Snell, Tracy L. 2014. *Capital Punishment, 2013—Statistical Tables.* Washington, DC: Bureau of Justice Statistics.

8

How Long Does It Take?

The right to a speedy trial as guaranteed by the Sixth Amendment does not imply that one has the right to speedy appeals.[1] In fact, states often do not even appoint appellate attorneys for inmates having been sentenced to death for a number of years following conviction and sentencing (see *Jones v. Chappell* (2014)). Executions typically take place more than 15 years after the trial at which the death sentence is pronounced, and with each year these average delays increase substantially. A new norm is emerging in which inmates are housed on death row for long periods of time, usually never to be executed at all. Most see their death sentences overturned, as we saw in the previous chapter. Others linger, often for more than two decades in the rare cases in which they are executed. With the exception of those who "volunteer" for execution by instructing their attorneys to abandon all appeals, it is rare to see an execution carried out less than 10 years after the crime; as of 2015 the average delay from crime to execution was more than 18 years, and delays of 30 years or more are not unusual. Executions are rare, even among the condemned, and they are extremely slow in coming. Further, the trends are clear: delays increase every year, on average, and have done so throughout the past 40 years.

The issue of how long it can take to carry out an execution originally raised concerns of constitutionality in *Lackey v. Texas* (1995) and more recently in *Jones v. Chappell* (2014). These cases raised the question of whether there is any additional penological value in an execution that follows what amounts to life in prison. Of course, no state has purposefully designed a system that generates, first, a very high rate of reversal, followed by decades of delay and then the long-belated execution of only a small percentage of those condemned. But this is increasingly what we see in practice. It seems likely that the US Supreme Court will be faced with deciding whether these practices, surely unintentional, amount to cruelty and are therefore unconstitutional. However, up to now the Court has never so ruled.

The question of how long a delay is constitutionally permissible has never been directly adjudicated by the US Supreme Court, and historically the Court has not been friendly to demands that appeals be handled quickly; the constitutional right to a speedy trial does not extend to speedy consideration of demands by convicted inmates in prison. Once the trial is over, inmates are presumed to be guilty, and therefore there is no logic on protecting them from punishments they may not deserve based on their presumption of innocence, as in an original trial. The Court unanimously rejected, in 2016, the claim that a 14-month delay before an inmate received his sentence after a guilty plea violated the speedy trial clause of the Constitution. In this case, *Betterman v. Montana* (2016), the inmate complained of the "emotional roller coaster due to the anxiety and depression caused by the uncertainty" in not knowing his sentence, which eventually was set at seven years in prison, with four years suspended (see Liptak 2016b). The state's argument had been that the protections due to the presumptively innocent defendant in a trial end at the moment of conviction: "[A]t the moment of conviction, a defendant's liberty is justly deprived" (quoted in Liptak 2016c). The Court agreed. Some justices held open the possibility, however, that the due process clause could potentially be used to seek a remedy for excessive delay. Because this claim was not raised in that case, however, the Court did not rule on it.

While the Court firmly rejected Mr. Betterman's complaint about the anxiety and depression stemming from being in prison for 14 months without knowing how long his sentence would be, what about 15 or more years on death row? What about multiple execution dates, later canceled? What about watching some death row inmates see their sentences reversed, with others being executed and still others simply waiting? On these matters, the Court has been unwilling to rule in favor of any death row inmate. It rejected Mr. Lackey's claim, as we discuss in the following. But it has never indicated whether a 40-year delay, for example, might be acceptable. Nor has it ruled on the difference between delays that are due to dilatory tactics by the inmate's attorneys and those that result from delays caused by the state. In *Jones v. Chappell* (2014), a federal judge ruled that because the State of California generates extremely long delays by its process of appointing attorneys only after long delay, and by providing hearings only after even longer delays, the responsibility for the delays falls on the state, not the inmates, and that this is unacceptable. Because that decision was overturned on procedural grounds (ironically, perhaps, on the basis that the state courts had not completed their own review of the case, some 20 years after it started), there is no final judicial statement on how much delay is too much. This issue may eventually reach the Supreme Court because, as we will show here, delays are enormous and have been growing steadily over the years.

On April 18, 1978, Clarence Allen Lackey was sentenced to death by the State of Texas for the 1977 murder of Diane Kumph. In 1994, Lackey filed his first federal habeas petition, in which he argued that executing him after such a lengthy delay (16 years at the time) should be considered cruel and unusual and therefore a violation of the Eighth Amendment. He argued that a punishment coming after such a long delay cannot be said to have a deterrent value, and its retributive value is low as well. In 1995, Lackey filed his second petition, adding to his claim that it was necessary to consider who was to blame for such a lengthy delay. He brought up the paradox that by exercising his legitimate right to obtain review of his case, a petitioner would be adding more of a delay, and that much of the delay time was caused by negligent or purposeful action of the state itself. Although his claim was denied, his case was the first that raised the lengthy delays between sentencing and execution as a constitutional issue. Mr. Lackey was executed in May 1997. In 1997, the State of Texas executed 37 inmates, with an average time from crime to execution of 12.2 years. Mr. Lackey's delay of 19.8 years put him at the higher end of the range, but his was not the longest delay from crime to execution even in his own state (two other inmates had waited slightly longer). Today, a delay of 20 years would be utterly unremarkable, even in Texas, as we show later. A number of inmates have raised "Lackey claims" following his case, but none have been successful.

The Lackey case was of interest for many reasons, one of which was a memo written by Justice Stevens raising a number of concerns about the case (see Flynn 1997, 291ff.). Did the framers envision a death penalty imposed decades after the condemnation? Clearly not. Is there an additional retribution value in execution as opposed to life in prison, once the inmate has already served 17 years or more? Justice Stevens thought not. Is there a deterrent value to executing inmates many years after the death sentence, and after reversing most other death sentences? No. In fact, the Court has considered a number of issues about the pre-execution conditions of confinement to constitute substantial punishments in themselves, if not cruel and unusual ones: What about protracted solitary confinement, not an unusual condition on the nation's various death rows? Is that not already a powerful punishment?

Stevens also raised a three-point test about the causes of delay; these, he wrote, could be due to (1) abuse of the right of appeal by the prisoner, (2) the legitimate use of appeal by the prisoner, and (3) intentionally dilatory tactics by the state (see Flynn 1997, 326). Only the first type of delay can be put at the feet of the inmate; with regard to the second type, clearly prisoners cannot be granted a right to appeal and then be punished for using it. Of course, the third type is not the fault of the inmate in any case.

Flynn (1997) reviews the emotional toll of excessive waiting on death row inmates. This results not only from delay itself but also from the often harsh conditions of death row (e.g., years of solitary confinement) and the uncertainty associated with not knowing whether or when the death sentence will actually be carried out. (Justice Breyer, in his *Glossip* dissent, mentioned Stevens's opinion in *Lackey* and common in other cases, referring to the "dehumanizing conditions of confinement" but also adding: "The dehumanizing effect of solitary confinement is aggravated by uncertainty as to whether a death sentence will in fact be carried out." Breyer notes that the Court had previously expressed its concern about the psychological suffering related to a four-week delay from trial to execution, but that today we measure these delays "not in weeks, but in decades.") We discuss last-minute stays of execution in more detail in chapter 11; chapter 7 already demonstrated that the odds of execution, given a death sentence, are surprisingly low. All this would add to a great deal of uncertainty about one's own fate, an extremely stressful situation. Many of these issues were raised in a 2014 case in California in which the inmate alleged, and a federal district court ruled, that the California death penalty was unconstitutional because of delays and inefficiencies.

Ernest Dewayne Jones was sentenced to death by the State of California on April 7, 1995; however, 20 years later he still awaited his execution. Although this may seem like a rare case, it is actually the norm in California. On average, those who exhaust the appeals process in that state wait on death row for 25 years or more. Of the 700-plus inmates on death row in California as of 2014, 40 percent had been there longer than 19 years (*Jones v. Chappell*). In this particular case, Mr. Jones raised the question of the constitutionality of the death penalty on Eighth Amendment grounds. A federal district judge agreed with Jones, issuing a ruling that read as a scathing indictment of the California death penalty system and noting, as Lackey had argued, that much of the reason for the delay was due to actions of the state, not the inmate. The judge ruled that if a legislature passed a law specifying first a 20-year wait on death row, and second a small percentage of inmates to be selected randomly for execution, this would clearly be ruled unconstitutional on its face. But what if that process is the unintentional consequence of policies and procedures put in place? The judge wrote of such a quiet transformation, and found it unconstitutional:

> [T]he death sentence carefully and deliberately imposed by the jury has been quietly transformed into one no rational jury or legislature could ever impose: *life in prison, with the remote possibility of death*. As for the random few for whom execution does become a reality, they will have languished for so long on Death Row that their execution will serve no retributive or deterrent purpose and will be arbitrary. (*Jones v. Chappell*, 1–2 (2014), emphasis in original)

Judge Carney's ruling in 2014 was overturned on procedural grounds, and therefore his indictment of a system with long delays was never evaluated. Therefore, we can only speculate about what the US Supreme Court might do if faced with such a case. But we can assess whether the trends rejected so firmly by Judge Carney are peculiar to California or instead might be reflected, even if to a lesser degree, in other states. It is clear that in states like California or Pennsylvania, which rarely carry out an execution, with each passing year, the average time elapsed from crime to execution would have to be growing. But the fact that we also see such a trend in Texas, with its very active execution chamber, suggests that increasing delays may be a national problem, not an isolated one. Here we take all those inmates who have been executed since 1976 and assess the time elapsed from their crime to their death sentence to their execution. Of course, we know from the previous chapter that the vast bulk of death sentences are later reversed, so it is important to keep in mind that this chapter is dealing with the "successful" cases where the death sentence is finally carried out. As we will see, delays are enormous, growing, and ubiquitous. How the Supreme Court might rule on these issues is not clear. So far, the Court has never held that there is a right to a speedy execution, and in fact the concept may seem at first glance to be absurd. But is a delay of 40 years, with continued uncertainty about whether the penalty will ever be carried out, acceptable? It seems likely that the Court will be faced with a need to address the issue, as the numbers we turn to now suggest a growing national crisis.

From Crime to Execution

The vast majority of executions today span years of delay between the date of a crime and the date of an execution. Figure 8.1 illustrates this point. Since 1976, the United States has executed 1,422 inmates. Using publicly available sources, we compiled the dates of the crimes, sentencing, and execution for all of these cases.[2] Figure 8.1 shows the correspondence between the date when an individual was executed and the years elapsed since the crime. Each dot in the figure represents an executed inmate. The vertical placement of each dot shows how many years elapsed from the crime to the execution, and the horizontal placement indicates when the execution took place. The figure illustrates at a glance how delays have steadily increased over time, with the straight line indicating the average increase: 125 days per year.

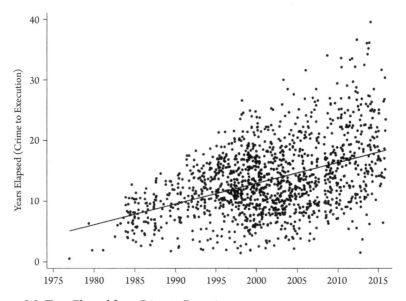

Figure 8.1 Time Elapsed from Crime to Execution

Figure 8.1 shows a number of things. First, obviously, there has been a dramatic increase in the average time on death row before execution. There is no significant increase in the *minimum* time served; volunteers can still drop their appeals, and they occasionally do so. On the other hand, the maximum time served, the average time served, and the spread between the minimum and the maximum have all increased substantially. Of course, no one can be executed based on laws predating the *Furman* ruling, as all existing state laws were invalidated. Therefore, 1973 (but more realistically 1975, by which time the new laws were mostly in place) is the earliest time from which an inmate could be executed under the current system. In every period since 1976, we have been executing people for crimes that occurred in the middle to late 1970s. Some are executed more quickly, of course, but the average delays are increasing steadily, and the maximum delays are consistently close to the maximum possible delay. Let us illustrate these points by comparing two inmates, Gary Gilmore and Thomas Knight.

Gary Gilmore is represented by the dot at the bottom-left corner of the figure. He was first sentenced to death for a crime he committed in 1976[3] and was the first inmate to be executed after the reinstatement of the death penalty, dying by a firing squad in Utah in 1977. His execution ushered in the "modern" death penalty. Gilmore waived his right to appeal his sentence and subsequently volunteered to be executed. Gilmore's crime occurred on July 19, 1976 (just days after the *Gregg v. Georgia* decision by the Supreme Court); his death sentence came on October 7 of that same year, and his execution took place on January 17, 1977. The total elapsed time from crime to execution was just 182 days. No other inmate has been executed with such little time delay.

Thomas Knight is represented by the dot at the top-right corner of the figure. Knight was executed in early 2014 for crimes he committed beginning in 1974. While awaiting trial for a double homicide, he and several other inmates escaped the Miami–Dade County jail. While traveling through Georgia, he participated in an armed robbery at a liquor store that resulted in the deaths of two clerks. After Georgia returned Knight to Florida and he was sentenced to death for the original crime, he murdered a death row prison guard. Even though Knight was arrested immediately after committing the 1974 double homicide, he was not executed for another 39 years, the longest delay before execution in US history.[4] Moreover, Knight's crime (July 17, 1974) and death sentence (April 21, 1975) came before Gilmore's crime (July 19, 1976) and death sentence (October 7, 1976). This means that on the day that Gary Gilmore was executed in 1977, Thomas Knight was settling into his second full year on death row; he would serve 37 more years before being executed.

Volunteers and Others

The stories of Gilmore and Knight, who, respectively, had the shortest and longest stays on death row before being executed, illustrate another common theme: those who volunteer are executed more quickly. This is intuitive, as long stays on death row are mostly caused by appeals, and volunteers instruct their legal teams to cease all appeals. Overall, using the DPIC definition, we classify 137 inmates as "volunteers" and 1,285 as "nonvolunteers." Figure 8.2 shows the same data as Figure 8.1, but it highlights the volunteers by representing them as black dots, with the nonvolunteers represented by a lighter shade of gray.

Along the bottom of Figure 8.2 we see a number of volunteers. In fact, 23 inmates experienced a delay of less than 3 years from crime to execution, all of whom were "volunteers." While these dots are located in various places throughout the graph, the majority are clustered in a line along the bottom, under the 5-year mark for years on death row. For volunteers, the median wait is almost 6 years, but many who volunteer apparently do so only after waiting a long time. Four "volunteers" were executed after more than 20 years on death row; 10 more after more than 15 years; and 20 more after more than 10 years of waiting. Many inmates, like Gary Gilmore or Timothy McVeigh (the Oklahoma City bomber), immediately instruct their attorneys to file no appeals and seek to expedite their execution, right from the beginning. However, judging from the fact that 34 inmates served more than a decade on death row before execution (about one-quarter of all those who have "volunteered"), it would appear that a sizable number of inmates volunteers as a result of their time on death row, not at the beginning of it. We will return to this issue of volunteers, or suicide by the state, in chapter 12, on mental illness.

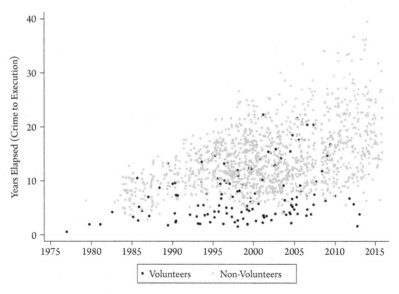

Figure 8.2 Volunteers and Others

Lengthier Trials or Longer Appeals?

We can distinguish between delays in the initial investigation of a crime, apprehension of the accused offender, trial, and death sentence, on the one hand, and those associated with postsentencing appeals, on the other. This analysis shows clearly that the delays have little to do with an increase in the time from crime to sentencing. Rather, they result from appeals.

Figure 8.3 breaks down the data from Figure 8.1 into two periods: from the crime to the death sentence, and from the death sentence to execution. This makes very clear that there has been no particular increase in the first, and that virtually all the increased delay associated with carrying out the death penalty relates to appeals.

Occasionally, a long time elapses between a crime and a death sentence. Figure 8.3A shows 1 inmate with a 20-year delay, and 14 inmates altogether with more than 10 years' delay before their initial death sentence. However, on average, the delay between crime and execution is just 18 months, and this number has not changed much over time: just 10 additional days per year. Figure 8.3B shows where the delays occur: after the sentence; these average 12 years and have increased by 116 days per year over 40 years. For inmates executed before 1990, their average delay from death sentence to execution was 6.8 years, but this number grew to 16.6 years for those executed since 2010. For these same groups of inmates, delays from crime to sentencing increased from only 1.3 to 1.8 years. Thus, delays have not resulted from slower investigations, lengthier trials, or greater difficulties in apprehending suspects. They stem from appeals.

A New Dynamic of Warehousing

In 1984, there were roughly 1,400 individuals under the sentence of death across the nation, 11 individuals had been executed in the modern period, and the average execution delay for those inmates was around 7 years. By the end of 2015, more than 2,900 individuals were under the sentence of death across the nation, 1,422 had been executed, and the average execution delay had increased to almost 19 years. Figure 8.4 shows these evolving dynamics.

For the first 25 years after *Gregg*, the size of the US death row population increased rapidly. It peaked in 2000 and has since been falling. During the period of growth, execution delays also increased; however, after 2000, delays in execution and the size of the death row population have become inversely related. That is, in the first years following *Gregg*, one could have imagined that delays were due to the increasing numbers of individuals in the system. Over the past 15 years, however, the dynamic has reversed. Fewer inmates are being sentenced to death, increasing numbers of reversals are occurring, and the average delay on death row is rapidly increasing. The average execution in 2014 or 2015 was of an inmate who had already served 19 or 20 years. Reducing the number of new death sentences, and

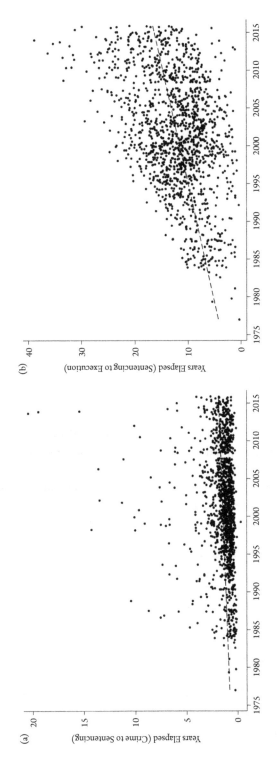

Figure 8.3 Delays Related to Trial and Appeals.
A. Crime to Sentencing.
B. Sentencing to Execution.

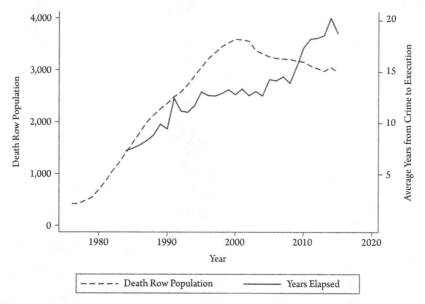

Figure 8.4 Increasing Delays Even as Death Row Shrinks. Note: Death row population from Snell 2014 (updated for 2013 and 2014 from Fins 2015); average delay from our own calculations. No estimate for years elapsed is given until 1984 because of low numbers of observations. Average years from crime to execution is calculated annually for all inmates executed in that year.

the number of inmates on death row, has been associated with no net decline in the average wait before execution; indeed, these delays have only increased, as Figure 8.4 shows.

Delays have affected almost every state, with one exception, though not equally. In the following section we explore state-level variation in delays.

State-Level Variation

Inmates Clarence Lackey and Ernest Jones contended that their waits on death row in Texas and California, respectively, were unconstitutionally long. At the time when Mr. Lackey's case was heard, in 1995, the average time a Texas inmate waited for execution after being sentenced to death was approximately 9.7 years. Between 1995 and 2015, this had increased to 12.7 years. Clearly, for Texas, the issue of execution delays has not resolved itself since the Supreme Court denied Lackey's writ. In California, of course, delays are much longer than in Texas, and Mr. Jones had waited more than 20 years at the time of his appeal, denied on the basis that the state review of his case was not yet complete.

We can compare average execution delays for each state that has executed enough inmates to provide reliable estimates. Of course, our analysis excludes those inmates who are not executed, and who may have waited many years before seeing their death sentence overturned. Henry McCollum, a North Carolina inmate, was fully exonerated in 2014 after 30 years on death row;[5] Anthony Ray Hinton similarly served 30 years on Alabama's death row before his 2015 exoneration.[6] So we

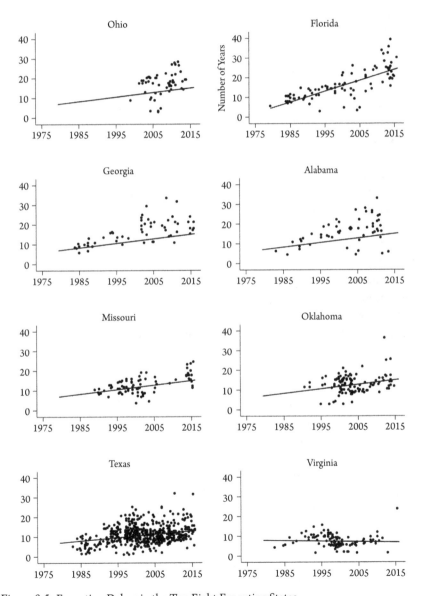

Figure 8.5 Execution Delays in the Top Eight Executing States

know that exoneration or the reversal of a death sentence can sometimes come after decades of delay.

Figure 8.1 shows that, nationally, each passing year is associated with approximately 125 additional days of delay from crime to execution. Figure 8.5 shows data identical to those in Figure 8.1 for the top eight executing states.

Increased delays in execution affect almost every state, including those that are the most active in executing. Virginia is the only state that has not seen a dramatic increase in the average time from crime to execution over the 40 years since *Gregg*. Even in Texas, delays increase, on average, by 60 days per year. This is less than the national average as indicated in Figure 8.1, but it is substantial nonetheless. Of course, among active death states, these two are not only among the most rapid to execute but also among those with the slowest rate of increase over time. Ohio and Florida have more than twice the national average increase, and this number is likely to continue to expand in the future. Ohio suspended all executions in October 2015 because of a shortage of lethal injection materials,[7] and Florida saw its entire death sentencing structure called into question by a US Supreme Court decision in January 2016.[8]

We saw in chapter 6 that executions are highly and increasingly concentrated in just a few states. Figure 8.5 gives some idea of this process in more detail, showing how delays vary by state. Virginia stands alone in avoiding any kind of increase in the delay between crime and execution. It also has the lowest reversal rate of any state, by far, as we saw in chapter 7. In fact, the four states with the lowest increased delays, Missouri, Oklahoma, Texas, and Virginia, are also in the top five for cumulative executions and among those with the lowest reversal rates. The nation may be separating out into two death penalty systems: a few states have relatively low reversal rates, shorter elapsed times on death row, less increase in these elapsed times, and higher use of the death penalty. Another, larger, group of states have more reversals, more and increasing delay, and fewer executions.

The United States has seen 156 exonerations during the same period it has seen 1,422 executions: a rate of 10.97 exonerations per 100 executions. The rate for Virginia is just 1 for 111, or 0.90 percent. Texas has seen 13 exonerations and 531 executions: 2.44 percent. Missouri (4.65 percent) and Oklahoma (8.93 percent) are also below the national average. Florida, with its rapidly increasing delays, has seen 26 exonerations for 91 executions: 28.57 percent. The rates of exoneration in other states are even higher, but none of these are high death use states, nor are they among the most rapid to move from crime to execution.[9]

We have seen that delays from crime to execution are huge and increasing, but that all states are not equally affected by these trends. Because our analysis has focused on those cases where executions have actually been carried out, we have not discussed Pennsylvania, which like California has a death penalty system that is reserved almost exclusively for volunteers. Such states have reached a system where their large death rows are really not waiting rooms for a death chamber at all. Rather, they are long-term warehouses for the condemned, who in fact are more likely to die of natural causes than to be executed by the state. At what point, if any, the Court would find that such a situation amounts to cruelty remains an open question.

Conclusion

Timothy Kaufman-Osborn (2002) notes that the US Supreme Court advised as early as 1890 (when instructing the State of New York on the permissibility of the electric chair) that "punishments are cruel when they involve torture or a lingering death" (*in re Kemmler*, 136 U.S. 436 (1890), 447, quoted in Kaufman-Osborn 2002, 39). Clearly, the Court was referring to the final act of execution, not the lingering process that so characterizes the US death penalty of sentencing many to death, reversing a large portion of those death sentences, then carrying out a small number of executions after many years of delay. We will see in the next chapter that approximately one inmate is exonerated from death row for every nine who are executed. And we will see in subsequent chapters that when executions are carried out, there is often uncertainty right to the last minute; stays are routinely granted, and many inmates have seen their sentences reversed after previously having received a death warrant (i.e., a scheduled execution date). The Court will eventually be faced with deciding whether these false promises of death, and the extremely long delays in carrying out the punishment, constitute torture.

Further Reading

Flynn, Kathleen M. 1997. The "Agony of Suspense": How Protracted Death Row Confinement Gives Rise to an Eighth Amendment Claim of Cruel and Unusual Punishment. *Washington and Lee Law Review* 54 (1): 291–333.

9

How Often Are People Exonerated
from Death Row?

The death penalty stands alone in the criminal justice system because of its finality.[1] Once an individual is executed, there is no recourse to free the inmate or reverse and remand his or her sentence. As a result, protections are provided, such as the bifurcated trial and lengthy appeals process, to ensure that those who are sentenced to death have received a fair trial (see chapter 2). However, false convictions remain a serious problem for capital punishment. Exonerations are one indication of how pervasive false convictions are within a state's criminal justice system. No one condones executing the factually innocent, but individuals differ on how likely they think this may be and whether it has ever occurred in the past.

We saw in chapter 7 that the vast majority of death sentences are overturned on appeals. This chapter focuses on a small subset of all those cases: inmates whose original conviction is thrown out, and who are released from prison with no further legal action to follow. The innocent constitute only a small proportion of those whose death sentences are reversed, but a particularly important one because of the risk they faced of wrongful execution.

Reversed sentences or convictions occur when an appellate court determines the original court's ruling or procedures were seriously flawed. Factors contributing to a reversed sentence or conviction might include evidence that was available but was improperly excluded from consideration, official misconduct, ineffective assistance of counsel, or other matters. While direct review focuses on procedural flaws, new evidence not available at the time of the original trial may sometimes be presented during collateral or habeas review. When an appellate court reverses the original sentence, the prosecutor must make the decision again on whether to pursue death. As we saw, many individuals are sentenced to death a second or even a third time after their original trial finding of guilt or the penalty phase is reversed. *Commuted sentences* are not reversals at all; the inmate remains guilty, but the governor grants mercy in the form of reducing the death sentence in favor of a lesser sentence, usually life without parole.

Exonerations are different from the preceding cases: with exonerations, all charges are dropped, or a previously condemned individual is acquitted at a second trial, and that individual walks out of prison a free man or woman. For an exoneration to occur, the original trial's finding of guilt must be reversed, and the district attorney must decide not to retry the individual; or if the DA does retry, the defendant is found not guilty. On rare occasions, governors issue pardons, another form of exoneration. Once a conviction is thrown out and a new trial occurs, the defendant may get a different lawyer; or, having seen the potential outcomes, the defendant may cooperate more with his or her attorney; or any number of other differences may ensue. The prosecution may have trouble using the same witnesses (depending on timing, some may have passed away, for example). If there was a finding of error in the trial (the only reason for a new trial, after all), then the error obviously cannot be repeated, and this can work to the benefit of the defendant. (For instance, if the error is that the prosecution withheld evidence, and that evidence really is helpful to the defense, then either the state may drop the charges or, if a trial ensues, the defendant may be acquitted.) The point is that any number of factors may lead to a new trial, and once there is a new trial, an acquittal is always possible. Exactly what is *the* cause of the exoneration is therefore hard to say; in this chapter we review a number of the leading contributing factors.

Although all Americans start out with a presumption of innocence, once we are found guilty, it is hard to re-establish innocence. Further, there are few judicial processes by which innocence is established; the system is designed to establish guilt. Just recently, some states have established procedures leading to a certificate of innocence in the form of either a governor's "pardon of innocence" or a decision by a judicial body; however, these are rare and recent innovations. For these reasons, most of those who have been exonerated have not been "proven" to be innocent. Rather, the state's proof of their guilt has disappeared. There is no single or widely available legal mechanism in the United States to prove innocence, as all Americans are presumed to be innocent until proven otherwise.

Two major organizations provide lists of exonerations, the Death Penalty Information Center (DPIC) and the National Registry of Exonerations. The DPIC list, of course, includes only those exonerations associated with previous sentences of death (156 individuals exonerated from 1973 through 2015). The DPIC makes clear its criteria for inclusion:

> Defendants must have been convicted, sentenced to death and subsequently either:
> a. Been acquitted of all charges related to the crime that placed them on death row, or
> b. Had all charges related to the crime that placed them on death row dismissed by the prosecution, or

c. Been granted a complete pardon based on evidence of innocence. (https:// deathpenaltyinfo.org/innocence-list-those-freed-death-row)

The National Registry of Exonerations is more complete, as it has no specific focus on death row. As of February 2017, it lists 1,994 exonerations, with its time coverage beginning in 1989. Its definitions are as follows:

> Exoneration—A person has been exonerated if he or she was convicted of a crime and later was either: (1) declared to be factually innocent by a government official or agency with the authority to make that declaration; or (2) relieved of all the consequences of the criminal conviction by a government official or body with the authority to take that action. The official action may be: (i) a complete pardon by a governor or other competent authority, whether or not the pardon is designated as based on innocence; (ii) an acquittal of all charges factually related to the crime for which the person was originally convicted; or (iii) a dismissal of all charges related to the crime for which the person was originally convicted, by a court or by a prosecutor with the authority to enter that dismissal. The pardon, acquittal, or dismissal must have been the result, at least in part, of evidence of innocence that either (i) was not presented at the trial at which the person was convicted; or (ii) if the person pled guilty, was not known to the defendant, the defense attorney and the court at the time the plea was entered. The evidence of innocence need not be an explicit basis for the official action that exonerated the person.

> Exoneree—A person who was convicted of a crime and later officially declared innocent of that crime, or relieved of all legal consequences of the conviction because evidence of innocence that was not presented at trial required reconsideration of the case.

Note that the DPIC and National Registry of Exonerations definitions are slightly different. First, DPIC goes back to 1973 and focuses only on death row cases whereas the registry begins in 1989 and includes non-capital cases as well. Second, the registry includes in its definition that the exoneration must be, at least in part, based on new evidence of innocence that was not part of the original proceedings.

It is possible, of course, that some inmates may have had their charges dropped only because the district attorney decided there was not enough evidence against them to prove their guilt beyond a reasonable doubt. Note that these are all individuals whose guilt not only was proven in a previous trial but who also were sentenced to death. Judges are loath to throw out death sentences for anything other than important violations of constitutional rights, procedural errors, or powerful evidence of a mistake. While it may sometimes occur that a person who truly committed the crime later sees the charges dropped or is acquitted on retrial, far more often an innocent person is wrongfully convicted for reasons that we explore in greater detail in the pages to come.

Some states do allow for "pardons of innocence" in which the governor formally recognizes the factual innocence of the individual concerned. Sometimes, judges recognize the innocence of the person when that person is released. More commonly, however, charges are simply dropped, and the individual is free to go. Typically, there is no apology, no compensation, and even no recognition of innocence. Often, the inmate does not receive even a bus ticket and after being freed is not eligible for those services such as job training that the guilty would be eligible to receive if they had served their time or were released on parole.

Factors Contributing to Wrongful Convictions

The National Registry of Exonerations has identified several legal factors associated with wrongful convictions. These include official misconduct, perjury or false accusation, false or misleading forensic evidence, ineffective legal defense, mistaken witness identification, DNA evidence, and false confessions. Table 9.1 summarizes the factors that contributed to all exonerations, including death row exonerations. Often, these factors exist simultaneously as it is rare for a wrongful conviction to be based solely on one factor. DNA evidence, for example, may be associated with a

Table 9.1 **Contributing Factors in Exonerations, 1989–2015**

Contributing Factors	All Exonerations		Death Row Exonerations	
	N	%	N	%
Official misconduct	1,007	50.8	90	77.6
Perjury or false accusation	1,192	60.1	85	73.3
False or misleading forensic evidence	469	23.7	32	27.6
Ineffective legal defense	460	23.2	31	26.7
Mistaken witness identification	582	29.3	25	21.6
DNA evidence	434	21.9	25	21.6
False confession	236	11.9	22	19.0
Total	1,983	—	116	—

Note: Percentages do not sum to 100 because multiple factors may be present in any case. DPIC lists 156 death row exonerations, and the registry lists just 116 because the DPIC list goes back to 1973 and the registry covers only the period since 1989, and because the two organizations use different criteria to determine which cases qualify as exonerations.

Source: University of Michigan Law School National Registry of Exonerations (1989–2016).

case that also involves official misconduct; the categories are not mutually exclusive. We should point out the obvious: many wrongful convictions are never discovered, and the National Registry of Exonerations is a registry of cases where exonerations occurred; these are a subset of wrongful convictions, and perhaps a small one. No one knows how many innocents are in jail or on death row.

Reasons for Exonerations (Excluding DNA Evidence)

Official Misconduct

Official misconduct occurs when officials such as law enforcement officers, prosecutors, or other government officials abuse the power of their positions in a way that is proven to influence the conviction. For example, a "Brady violation" occurs when a prosecutor's office refuses to share with the defense evidence that it uncovers during its investigation of the crime that would tend to be exculpatory. The US Supreme Court ruled in *Brady v. Maryland* (1963) that such evidence must be shared. Official misconduct plays a role in 78 percent of all death row exonerations.

Perjury or False Accusation

Perjury or false accusation describes a situation where a person was convicted of a crime because of a false accusation made by another person. There is much documentation of plea bargains being given to other defendants or prisoners in exchange for information regarding the crime. This is a common contributing factor in two-criminal crimes where one of the prisoners flips and gives a false account of the story in exchange for a lesser sentence. In death row exonerations, false accusations are part of the explanation in almost three-quarters of the cases. The registry distinguishes between false accusations and perjury because in cases were an individual pleads guilty, the false accuser may never have had to testify in court and is therefore not guilty of perjury. But the false accusation may nonetheless have contributed to the wrongful guilty plea. False accusations can be thought of as statements that would have been perjury if they had been made under oath in court. More than 70 percent of death row exonerations have been associated with false accusations.

False or Misleading Forensic Evidence

False or misleading forensic evidence refers to a situation in which forensic evidence was used to convict a defendant during trial and then this same evidence was found to be false or misleading. This can happen in one of four ways. First, the exoneree's conviction was based on forensic information that was caused by errors in forensic testing. Second, the conviction was based on unreliable or unproven methods, including testing methods that are later proven to be inadequate. Third, the forensic evidence was presented to the judge or jury with exaggerated and misleading confidence. Fourth, the conviction was based on fraudulent forensic information, possibly also linked to official misconduct. These factors are apparent in about 28 percent of all death row exonerations.

Many previously accepted forms of forensic evidence have fallen into disrepute as scientific methods have advanced and DNA cases have demonstrated conclusively that previous testimony was erroneous. In April 2015, the FBI released the results of a comprehensive analysis of previous "microscopic hair analysis" and concluded that the testimony of its own experts had been erroneous in "at least 90 percent" of the cases (see FBI 2015; Hsu 2016). Needless to say, such a conclusion throws into doubt a great number of convictions and calls into question what is "scientific" about the evidence presented. Wrongful convictions are replete with "experts" testifying on such topics as human bite marks, dog trainers arguing that their dog can sniff under water, and other individuals asserting things that in retrospect have been shown to be fanciful or simply wrong. In Arizona, Ray Krone, known as the "snaggletooth killer," was convicted in large part on the basis of testimony from a dentist who swore under oath that only Krone's teeth (which had been damaged in a car accident earlier in life) could have produced the injuries found on a victim's body. (Krone served 10 years on Arizona's death row before being exonerated.) William Dillon, wrongfully convicted in Florida, faced testimony from a "dog scent expert" supposedly linking him to a crime; Dillon served 27 years (for the Krone and Dillon cases, see the National Registry of Exonerations).

Ineffective Legal Defense

Ineffective legal defense describes situations where the exoneree's legal defense provided ineffective representation. The legal standard for asserting ineffective defense is very difficult to meet, but such findings are apparent in more than one-quarter of all death row exonerations. This is likely to be a vast underestimate of how many wrongful convictions actually involve poor lawyering. In fact, Samuel Gross and Michael Shaffer suggest that poor lawyering may be associated with more than half of all wrongful convictions, though they cannot document this number. In the first major report from the registry in 2012, they wrote:

> For 104 exonerations [460 cases in Table 9.1, based on updated data], our information includes clear evidence of severely inadequate legal defense, but we believe that many more of the exonerated defendants—perhaps a clear majority—would not have been convicted in the first instance if their lawyers had done good work. The failures of defense counsel are overwhelmingly sins of omission, especially the failure to investigate. Unless those failures are actually litigated, they are likely to go unmentioned, and in many cases there is no occasion to question the competence of the defense attorney. (Gross and Shaffer 2012, 42)

We may never know how many individuals are sentenced to death because of poor legal assistance, and as we discussed in chapter 1, the courts have not been very receptive to claims of inadequate assistance. The numbers in Table 9.1, more than one-quarter, are certainly underestimated.

Mistaken Witness Identification

Mistaken witness identification occurs when at least one witness wrongfully identifies the exoneree as the person who committed the crime. These are true errors; if the misidentification was a deliberate lie, then it is instead included as false testimony or perjury, described earlier. Mistaken identifications occur in more than 20 percent of death row cases. According to the registry, these are particularly common in robbery and sexual assault crimes. Just 27 percent of homicides have such witness mistakes (see Gross and Shaffer 2012, Table 13). Mistakes, as opposed to lies, may come from many sources, including suggestive police investigations (e.g., improperly conducted photographic or in-person lineups). These may occur even when there are multiple eyewitnesses, may be based on the initial police suspicion of an individual suspect, and may be more common when the eyewitness and the suspect are of different races. During the stress of a violent crime, victims and survivors of the crime may not always be able to identify key details. Further, the desire to close a case and put a violent criminal away may lead to mistakes; human memory is imperfect.

False Confession

False confession may occur in more circumstances than many readers would expect. First, confessions may be coerced through police interrogation techniques ranging from subtle pressure to outright torture. Many who have given such false confessions have been young or intellectually impaired, susceptible to agree with a police investigator who proposes a confession. Henry McCollum and Leon Brown were 15 and 19 years old, respectively, when they were held by police without parental or legal representation until they confessed to crimes in which they were completely uninvolved. Second, authorities may take a statement made by the suspect out of context and present it in court as a confession; because it is in the defendant's own words, it can be hard to rebut or explain. Third, authorities may falsely claim that the exoneree confessed, but the exoneree may deny this same confession. Fourth, the authorities may misinterpret a statement made by the defendant as an admission of guilt. False confessions make up about 19 percent of all death row exonerations. As Gross and Shaffer explain, these are more common in homicide cases. In their estimation, the majority of false confessions were coerced. Defendants were "frightened, tricked, exhausted, or all three" when they made their wrongful statements of guilt (2012, 57).

Exonerations and DNA Evidence

DNA evidence has contributed to demonstrating the innocence of 25 death row inmates and more than 400 in the more general records of the National Registry of Exonerations. It has also confirmed the guilt of many individuals whose DNA evidence matched that found at a crime scene. Conventional wisdom largely suggests that the gradual rise in exonerations during the post-*Furman* period resulted from the increased availability of DNA evidence (see Olney and Bohn, 2014). However, most exonerations occurred due to other factors, such as official misconduct, perjury or false accusation, and the other contributing elements presented in Table 9.1. In death row cases, as shown in the table, DNA is a factor in only 21 percent of the cases.

DNA can only be used to convict or exonerate an individual in cases where biological evidence is available for review; typically this involves sexual crimes or violent crimes where blood evidence is available, either that of the perpetrator at the scene of the crime or that of the victim associated with the perpetrator. Where a killer shoots a victim from across a distance, DNA may not be of any use. In addition, DNA is simply irrelevant in many criminal cases. The rise of exonerations cannot be explained by the greater availability of DNA testing; in fact, official misconduct is a much more important element, as Table 9.1 makes clear.

DNA evidence exonerated Kirk Bloodsworth in 1993 after it proved his semen did not match the evidence found at the crime scene, corroborating his long-standing claims of wrongful conviction (Junkin 2004). This marked the first time DNA evidence was ever used in a death row case; it occurred four years after DNA evidence aided in establishing the innocence of two criminal defendants (Gross et al. 2004). Including Bloodsworth's exoneration, 25 death row inmates have had their innocence established because of DNA evidence. Further research conducted on the use of DNA evidence for all capital-eligible murder-rapes during the 1980s found that 3.3 percent of those convicted would have been found not guilty had DNA evidence been available at that time (Risinger 2007).

Prevalence of Death Row Exonerations

The National Registry of Exonerations lists 1,983 exonerations from 1989 through December 31, 2016. Within this population, 116 exonerations, or 5.8 percent, involved individuals previously sentenced to death. Figure 9.1 displays the total number of exonerations and exonerations for death row inmates of each year since 1989.

The number of exonerations listed in the registry has reached the point where an inmate is exonerated almost every business day, somewhere across the country; 157 exonerations were listed in 2015 and 165 in 2016. These numbers may be rising

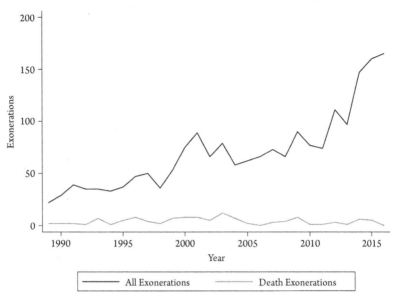

Figure 9.1 Exonerations and Death Row Exonerations. Source: National Registry of Exonerations.

because the registry is doing a better job of recording exonerations for later years than in earlier years. (There is no central location such as FBI crime reports where such things are automatically recorded, so the numbers in general may be considerably under-reported, especially for earlier time periods.) No matter what the trends are with exonerations overall, death row exonerations remain stable and never represent a large proportion of all exonerations. Figure 9.2 makes use of the DPIC list of exonerations and shows the number each year during the post-*Furman* era. In total, 156 individuals on death row have been exonerated since 1973, an average of fewer than 5 per year.

Exonerations from death row are steady but relatively low in numbers. Figure 9.1 shows, on the other hand, that there are significant increases in exonerations overall. In the next section we note dramatic increases in the time served on death row before exoneration.

Time from Conviction to Exoneration

Some exonerees have spent as little as a year on death row before being exonerated, while others have spent more than 39 years. Figure 9.3 shows the elapsed time between conviction and exoneration for each exonerated inmate, according to year of exoneration. On average, death row exonerees have spent 11.9 years in prison prior to being exonerated. Over time, however, delays have increased. For

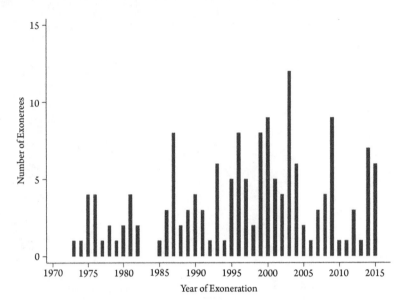

Figure 9.2 Death Row Exonerations by Year, post-*Furman*. Source: DPIC list of exonerations.

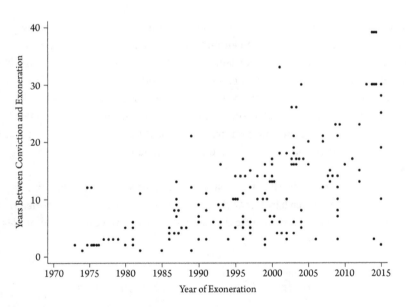

Figure 9.3 Time from Wrongful Death Sentence to Exoneration. Note: More than 50 cases have exactly the same year of exoneration and years on death row. These appear as a row of adjacent dots on the graph.

example, between 1973 and 1978, the average exoneree spent 3.7 years on death row. Between 2010 and 2015, the average exoneree spent 24 years on death row before release.[2]

Cumulatively, the 156 inmates represented in Figure 9.3 spent 1,923 years in prison after being wrongfully condemned to die. Thus, while the number of individuals exonerated may not be huge in any given year, the accumulated time wrongly served under threat of death is large and dramatically growing. Ricky Jackson, for example, who was exonerated in 2015, served more than 39 years; he had three co-defendants who collectively served more than 100 years in prison for a crime they did not commit.

Who Is Exonerated from Death Row?

Race and Exonerations

Table 9.2 compares the racial composition of those exonerated while on death row with the racial composition of all persons who have served on death row since *Furman*.[3] Blacks are more highly represented among the exonerees than on death row. Since *Furman*, blacks have made up more than half of those exonerated, but according to BJS statistics (as of 2013), they constitute just 41 percent of those condemned to die. Whites have made up 39 percent of those exonerated, but 48 percent of those sentenced to death.

It is unclear why black inmates would be over-represented among exonerees. One reason might be greater prosecutorial zeal in convicting them, or less jury empathy in considering their cases. In a study of Philadelphia death sentence decisions, Jennifer Eberhardt and colleagues (2006) found that facial features of black defendants with white victims had a significant impact on the likelihood that they would be sentenced to death rather than to prison. If there is less empathy and

Table 9.2 **Race and Ethnicity of Those Sentenced to Death and Those Exonerated, 1973–2015**

Race	*Death Sentences*		*Exonerations*	
	N	*%*	*N*	*%*
White	3,907	48.1	61	39.1
Black	3,334	41.0	81	51.9
Hispanic	755	9.3	12	7.7
Other	128	1.6	2	1.3
Total	8,124	100.0	156	100.0

Note: Death sentence data from Snell 2014, Table 12; exonerations from DPIC.

greater willingness to condemn, this might extend even to individuals for whom there may be doubts about guilt.

A 2004 study by Talia Harmon comparing 82 exoneration cases with matched cases from the same states resulting in executions raised troubling concerns about the impact of race. Harmon found that nonwhites convicted of killing whites were more than twice as likely to be exonerated as white offenders with white victims (2004, 88, Table 2). The author notes that while it is encouraging that these individuals were eventually exonerated, their original wrongful conviction may have been tainted by racial bias (92–93). She notes chillingly that "capital reversals *because of* 'doubts about guilt' could be compared with capital executions *despite* 'doubts about guilt' in order to explore potential racial differences between these groups" (93). That is, where a black offender kills a white victim, perhaps the juries are not quite as careful in ensuring fairness for the defendant but are more focused on ensuring closure for the victim.

State-Level Variation in Exonerations

Figure 9.4 displays the number of exonerations for each state with the death penalty. The top eight states in terms of number of exonerated death row inmates

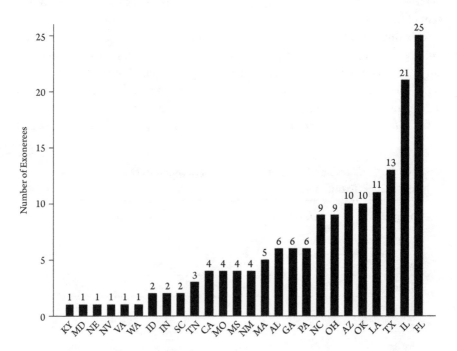

Figure 9.4 Death Row Exonerations by State. Source: DPIC list of exonerations.

also have the highest death row populations. Illinois and Florida account for 47 of the 156 exonerated death row inmates, or 30.1 percent. The example of Illinois shows the close connections between demonstrated innocence claims and support for the death penalty. Following scandals in the Chicago Police Department, which was found to have used torture to extract false confessions from a number of individuals who later were exonerated, Republican governor George Ryan commuted the sentences of 167 death row inmates and pardoned 4 other inmates during his last days in office. At the time, 13 inmates had been exonerated from death row; Ryan's review of the cases convinced him that the system was dangerously prone to error. He declared a moratorium on the use of the death penalty in 2000, and the state abolished the penalty in 2011 (see Wilgoren 2003, Table 1.1).

Gender and Exonerations

Women make up only 1.9 percent of all death row inmates (Snell 2014) and a similarly small percentage of all death row exonerees, 1.3 percent. There are some important differences between the cases that lead to a wrongful conviction of a woman as compared with a man. First, women are much more likely to have been falsely convicted of a crime that never took place. In fact, 63 percent of all exonerated women were convicted and sentenced to death for a crime that had never occurred. The corresponding rate for men is just 21 percent (Redden 2015). In many of these cases involving women, a woman has been convicted of killing her child when the child in fact died of natural causes or an accident. One such example is Sabrina Butler in Mississippi, who served five years on death row for the death of her infant child before being acquitted in a subsequent trial. Beverly Monroe, while not a death penalty case, was wrongfully convicted of killing her long-term partner when in fact he had committed suicide; Monroe served 11 years of a 22-year sentence.[4] Rather than being allowed to grieve the loss of their loved ones, these women have been wrongfully sent to prison or to death row. Such cases, where an accident or a suicide is turned into a crime, are not limited to female defendants, of course, but they have disproportionately involved women.

Compared with men, women are also less likely to be able to use DNA evidence to prevent or reverse a wrongful conviction. Since 1989, 27 percent of exonerated men have presented DNA evidence as a justification for their release, while only 7.6 percent of women have done so (Redden 2015). This may of course be related to the nature of the crimes men and women are alleged to have committed. Sexual crimes and violent murders often leave a DNA trace, but such evidence might be unavailable where the case involves an infant who fell from a crib or succumbed to a disease but where the mother was charged with murder.

Is the Exoneration Rate a Valid Measure
of False Convictions?

Given that the United States has executed 1,422 individuals since 1973 but has exonerated 156, many have commented that one exoneration for every nine executions is not a high rate of accuracy. Others, however, have strongly condemned such comparisons, asserting that convicted murderers have ample opportunity to defend themselves in court and that the odds of executing an innocent person are minuscule. These arguments range from suggesting that 1,422 is not the proper denominator but that 8,000 death sentences is more appropriate. This would suggest that rather than one exoneration per nine executions, it is merely one per 50 death sentences. Of course, we saw in chapter 7 that the vast majority of death sentences are in fact never carried out. But one can point to these reversals, and to the exonerations, as signs that the system "works"—after all, the inmate was not executed. Justice Scalia was well known for his strong defense of capital punishment, and in his concurring opinion in *Kansas v. Marsh* (2006) he stated that there has not been "a single case—not one—in which it is clear that a person was executed for a crime he did not commit. If such an event had occurred in recent years, we would not have to hunt for it; the innocent's name would be shouted from the rooftops" (7–8).

One reason it may not be clear that a person was executed for a crime he or she did not commit is that once the execution occurs, there is no longer any legal remedy or standing to seek an official inquiry, a topic we cover in the next section. One implication of this lack of standing is that evidence can be discarded or destroyed after an execution occurs. This precludes us from ever knowing the truth.

It is difficult to measure false convictions, but exoneration rates help provide key information on the prevalence of false convictions within the criminal justice system. The most complete and definitive study on this topic was done by Samuel Gross and colleagues, who found that, between 1973 and 2004, 1.16 percent of all death sentences later resulted in exoneration (Gross et al. 2014, 7231). However, this proportion may be lower than the actual rate of false convictions because exoneration rates do not take into account (1) individuals already on death row who will be proven innocent in the future; (2) individuals removed from death row because their sentence was reduced on appeal, but who were in fact innocent; (3) individuals who were falsely convicted and will never be proven innocent (i.e., executed); and (4) inmates remaining on death row who are innocent but who cannot prove it. Studies have attempted to compensate for this loss of information by using statistical analyses to determine the actual false conviction rate. Gross et al. concluded that 4.1 percent of individuals sentenced to death between 1973 and 2004 were falsely convicted (7235). Their methodology took into account inmates who had been executed and who committed suicide or died of natural causes while under the threat of death, and it focused on comparing the rates of exoneration for those on death row with rates for those no longer on death row. This change in "threat of execution" increases the likelihood that an innocent person will never be exonerated (7234). That is to say, once an inmate leaves death row, he or she loses a number of legal protections, and the case may fall in the list of priorities where attorneys allocate their attention to those individuals still under the threat of death. Although it can happen (as it did for Kirk Bloodsworth and Leon Brown), it is rare for an exoneration to come years after an inmate's death sentence has been reversed and that person is serving a life term in prison. An inmate is more likely to be exonerated while on death row.

If roughly 4 percent of those sentenced to death were innocent, and 8,000 have been so sentenced, this would be 320 individuals. Given that 156 have been exonerated, this means that more than half have not. We do not know how many may have been executed, how many may have had their sentence reversed and now languish in prison, or how many remain on death row, innocent but unable to prove it.

Postexecution Innocence

Research on postexecution innocence is difficult because government documentation is sparse. Once a state executes an inmate, his or her case becomes moot within the criminal court system; there is no more legal issue to determine, so appeals and reviews come to a halt.

While a majority of Americans believe that an innocent person has been executed in the United States (Liebman and Marshall 2006), there are precious few legal incentives to pursue innocence claims posthumously. Some researchers have attempted to calculate numbers. Bedau and Radelet (1987) conducted research on twentieth-century executions and found 23 cases where a defendant had been wrongfully convicted and executed, and Kirchmeier (2006) identified 6 cases of wrongful executions during the post-*Gregg* era. Although it is rare to find concrete examples of innocent executed inmates, there are several examples where the defendant may well have been innocent. Of course, there are many historical examples as well, including the Salem witch trials. Baumgartner, De Boef, and Boydstun (2008, 53) reviewed several previous studies, including books published on the topic going back as far as 1932 (see Borchard 1932; Bedau and Radelet 1987; Radelet, Bedau, and Putnam 1992).

The DPIC lists 13 executed individuals for whom there is significant evidence of their innocence, as of August 2016, though there is generally no legal proof of it. The National Registry of Exonerations lists 19 cases of posthumous exoneration, including for 3 individuals who were previously sentenced to death. Two illustrative cases are those of Cameron Todd Willingham and Carlos DeLuna.

On December 23, 1991, a fire burned down Willingham's home, killing his three daughters. As a result, the Texas resident was charged with arson and capital murder. At his trial, the prosecution claimed that he intentionally set the fire, despite

Willingham's statement that he had been asleep when the fire started. The prosecution's case centered on the testimony of an arson specialist and on information from a jailhouse informant who claimed that Willingham had confessed to the crime. On October 29, 1992, Willingham was sentenced to death. Twelve years later, Willingham's attorneys sent the governor a report from Gerald Hurst, a nationally recognized arson expert, stating that Willingham's conviction was based on faulty forensics. Unfortunately, the Board of Pardon and Parole did not act upon the report, and Willingham was executed days later, on February 17. His last words were a steadfast maintenance of his innocence: "The only statement I want to make is that I am an innocent man convicted of a crime I did not commit. I have been persecuted for twelve years for something I did not do. From God's dust I came and to dust I will return, so the Earth shall become my throne."[5] The most powerful evidence for his innocence may be in new developments in how arson specialists understand how fires work within structures. Arson testimony at the core of Willingham's convictions does not seem valid by modern standards. Was he the victim of a tragedy in which his children died in an accidental fire, or was he a ruthless murderer who killed his own children by setting the house on fire? The State of Texas concluded he was the latter. However, much of its case rested on the testimony of an arson specialist whose work has since been discredited (see Grann 2009).

Carlos DeLuna was sentenced to death for killing a 24-year-old gas station attendant on February 4, 1983. The victim, Wanda Lopez, was stabbed multiple times and was on the phone with the police when she died. There were two eyewitnesses to the crime: Kevan Baker and George Aguirre. Baker had stopped for gas and claimed to have seen a man dragging Lopez's body to the back of the gas station. Aguirre had also stopped for gas, and he claimed to have seen a man standing outside the gas station, drinking a beer and playing with a knife. The man asked Aguirre for a ride, but Aguirre declined and drove away. When he looked back, he saw the man and Lopez struggling inside the store. Police found DeLuna 30 to 40 minutes after the crime, hiding underneath a parked truck. Although the crime scene was very bloody, no blood was found on DeLuna, who was convicted entirely on the basis of the eyewitness accounts of Baker and Aguirre. According to later investigations, guilt points not to Carlos DeLuna but to another man, Carlos Hernandez; DeLuna maintained his innocence throughout his trial and up to the date of his execution. In 2014 Columbia University Press published *The Wrong Carlos: Anatomy of a Wrongful Execution* by law professor James Liebman and his team of researchers, documenting this tragedy (see Liebman and the Columbia DeLuna Project 2014).

Occasionally, officials have recognized the innocence of individuals who were executed in previous historical periods.[6] Colorado pardoned Joe Arridy in 2011 for a crime that occurred in 1936; South Carolina pardoned Thomas Griffin and Keeks Griffen in 2009 for a crime from 1913. In 2014, a South Carolina judge vacated the 1944 murder conviction of George Stinney, who was 14 years old at the time of the crime. A *New York Times* article on the posthumous exoneration features a photo of a cherubic Stinney in prison garb (see Robertson 2014). In the rare instances where a court or a governor takes the initiative officially to recognize a miscarriage of justice from the past, it has generally been because of the mobilization and passion of a small group of supporters and has involved a decision from the distant past.

In 2009 a Texas judge officially exonerated Timothy Cole for a 1985 crime, though Cole had died in prison in 1999. Frank Lee Smith was exonerated in Florida in 2000 for a 1986 conviction; he had died of cancer on death row. DNA evidence cleared Smith and identified the true perpetrator of the crime. Testing had come about through the case of another inmate, Jerry Townsend, who had served 22 years for crimes committed by Eddie Lee Mosley. Both Townsend and Smith had been convicted of crimes actually committed by Mosley. The rarity of judicial recognition of posthumous innocence does not mean, of course, that no innocents have been executed. We simply do not know how often this may occur.

Postexoneration Compensation

There is a common belief that upon release from prison, naturally the newly freed would be compensated by the government, perhaps automatically given hundreds of thousands of dollars to pay them back for lost years, lost family connections, and suffering. However, this is not the case. In fact, only about one-third of the people exonerated due to proof of innocence have been compensated. There are statutes providing for some type of compensation in 30 states and Washington, DC, but many of these statutes have surprising gaps. Among these 30 states, only 15 provide a monetary amount based on time served. Fourteen have a cap on the maximum amount of compensation, which ranges from $20,000 to $2 million (Mandery et al. 2013). On average, exonerees spend around 11.87 years on death row before their conviction is overturned, yet inmates are often released and left without money, housing, transportation, or insurance. Additionally, many prisoners are left with a lasting criminal record. Only four states even begin to address the issue of record expungement, three provide immediate expungement, and one requires a separate hearing to address the issue.

There are three main ways that exonerees receive compensation: private compensation bills, litigation, and compensation statutes. The first option requires the exoneree to obtain a private compensation bill from the state legislature, something that is quite difficult (such bills typically fail; just 9 percent successfully pass the legislature). Litigation takes large amounts of time and money, and only 28 percent of Innocence Project exonerees have received compensation through this method.[7] When they were successful, these procedures took an average of four years to complete; in other words, even when this approach is successful, it is not quick. Thirteen of the 30 states with compensation statues have requirements for the type of crime the exoneree had to have been convicted of to be eligible for compensation. Four states require a pardon for eligibility. Twenty statutes have at least one stated disqualification, the most common being "serving a concurring sentence for a crime of which he or she is presumably guilty." Five states also disqualify exonerees from receiving compensation if they are convicted of a felony following their exoneration. (Many drug possession convictions are felonies.) Some states bar compensation from exonerees who falsely confessed or initially pleaded guilty; the logic here is that they participated in their own wrongful conviction and deserve no compensation (ignoring pressure, torture, or other vulnerabilities that might make one confess under duress, even falsely). Other disqualifications involve time limits, previous failure to pay back taxes, and so on. These disqualifications only create additional battles for wrongfully convicted prisoners once they are released (see Norris 2012). The bottom line, according to Norris, who has done the most extensive survey on the issue, is that compensation is slow, rare, difficult, and subject to many and sometimes arbitrary restrictions. This contrasts sharply with the popular conception that inmates are routinely, quickly, and generously compensated. They are not.

Official Misconduct and Immunity

The single most common cause of wrongful conviction for death row in Table 9.1 was official misconduct, which was present in three-quarters of all such cases. Official misconduct is actually more common proportionately in death row cases than overall, being present in half of cases overall but in 78 percent of death row cases. This may be because it is more common for murder cases in general; the stakes are highest there, and prosecutors are naturally keen to get a conviction. The most common form of misconduct is withholding favorable (or "exculpatory") evidence from the defense. The US Supreme Court ruled in *Brady v. Maryland* (1963) that such requirement applied to all prosecutors: during their investigations, any evidence favorable to the defense, such as a confession from a different perpetrator, or a witness statement that the defendant was not involved, or a lab test that excludes the defendant, must be turned over to the defense before trial. Of course, not all such evidence, if turned over, would necessarily change the outcome of the trial, but some might. Thus, courts must review *Brady* violations to determine if they are "harmless" (i.e., they would not have changed the outcome, given other evidence) or "material." A material *Brady* violation would be withholding evidence that was so powerfully in favor of the defendant that it could have changed the outcome of the trial.

The Supreme Court's decision in *Connick v. Thompson* (2011) suggests just how high the bar is set to demonstrate a material *Brady* violation. John Thompson was wrongly convicted of murder and sentenced to death, serving 14 years on death row and receiving seven different execution dates. Days before the last date, in 1999, his lawyers received exculpatory information from a former prosecutor. Thompson was eventually exonerated and awarded a settlement in a civil suit against the DA's office, led by

Harry Connick Sr., the long-time prosecutor in Orleans Parish, Louisiana. Thompson had sued Connick's office for failing to train its staff of prosecutors sufficiently on their need to avoid *Brady* violations. Thompson was not the only victim of such misconduct; several others had had their cases overturned for similar violation in what appeared to be a pattern of disregard for *Brady* (see Robertson and Liptak 2011). The US Supreme Court ruled in a divided opinion, with the other four conservative justices following Justice Thomas in arguing that the entire case boiled down to a single violation, and that, in the words of Justice Scalia, "*Brady* mistakes are inevitable" (Scalia, concurring opinion, 2). Four liberal justices (Ginsburg, Breyer, Sotomayor, and Kagan), led by Ginsburg, argued in their dissent that a string of errors had generated the wrongful conviction and that the "prosecutorial transgressions were neither isolated nor atypical" (Ginsburg, dissenting opinion, 1). For the dissenters, the Orleans Parish DA's office had a long-established practice of ignoring or "giving short shrift to *Brady*'s requirements" (1), and such a pattern cannot be held acceptable. However, they had only four votes. Five justices found a way to overturn the jury's award to Thompson and find that the entire matter boiled down to a single "aberrant" violation, something that cannot be avoided in any large bureaucracy. Mistakes will happen.

This 2011 decision was highly contentious as it suggested that the Supreme Court would not be vigilant in protecting its own ruling in *Brady*. The Orleans Parish DA's office was again in the news in June 2016 when the same issues were raised in another case: persistent violations, with the Louisiana Supreme Court routinely dismissing challenges to them as immaterial to the outcome of the case (see Hasselle and Simerman 2016). Baumgartner and Lyman (2016) reviewed all Louisiana death sentences, noting the high rate at which they are reversed, even compared with national standards. Nine reversals were for *Brady* violations, but almost all of these were found acceptable to the Louisiana Supreme Court; they were reversed by federal courts instead (see Lyman quoted in Hasselle and Simerman 2016). If the DA's office routinely violates *Brady*, but the local courts consistently find that these violations were "inconsequential" or "harmless" (i.e., they would not have affected the outcome of the trial), then the DA's office may rightly conclude that it can continue with such a practice. New Orleans and the State of Louisiana in general seem to be the epicenter for issues of lax state court review of prosecutorial misconduct. But the Court has made clear, particularly in *Connick v. Thompson*, that the bar to prove such misconduct is set very high indeed.

Does the Constitution Allow the Execution of an Innocent Person?

One might think that the Constitution would clearly bar the execution of an innocent, but according to the justices, it does not. In 1993 the Supreme Court was presented with the question of whether an inmate duly sentenced to death and having had the case affirmed by appellate courts could argue that newly discovered evidence not available at the time of the earlier proceedings demonstrated that he was "actually innocent" and that the Constitution's prohibition of cruel and unusual punishment and guarantee of due process forbade execution in such a situation. The Court's ruling was succinct: "*Held*: Herrera's claim of actual innocence does not entitle him to federal habeas relief" (*Herrera v. Collins*, 390). The court then explained:

> In criminal cases, the trial is the paramount event for determining the defendant's guilt or innocence. Where, as here, a defendant has been afforded a fair trial and convicted of the offense for which he was charged, the constitutional presumption of innocence disappears. Federal habeas courts do not sit to correct errors of fact, but to ensure that individuals are not imprisoned in violation of the Constitution. (390)

As Carol Steiker and Jordan Steiker (2016) point out, the key issue in *Herrera* was not how the Court came to its conclusion but that it refused clearly to answer "yes" to the question of whether or not the Constitution prohibits executing the innocent. In fact, the Court has not so ruled to this day. Considerations of finality, expectations that executive clemency might be more appropriate, an unwillingness to retry the facts of a case, and skepticism about claims of those found guilty in a fair trial appear to have motivated the justices. The prospect of inmates simply arguing that the system "got it wrong" seems unacceptable.

In *Herrera*, the Court went further than simply refusing to agree to an absolute ban on executing the innocent, as explained in the majority opinion by Chief Justice Rehnquist, joined by Justices O'Connor, Scalia, Kennedy, and Thomas. After reviewing the presumption of innocence and the various constitutional protections that "make it more difficult for the State to rebut and finally overturn the presumption of innocence" (399), he continued:

> But we have also observed that "[d]ue process does not require that every conceivable step be taken, at whatever cost, to eliminate the possibility of convicting an innocent person." (. . .) To conclude otherwise would all but paralyze our system for enforcement of the criminal law.
>
> Once a defendant has been afforded a fair trial and convicted of the offense for which he was charged, the presumption of innocence disappears. (. . .) Here, it is not disputed that the State met its burden of proving at trial that petitioner was guilty of the capital murder of Officer Carrisalez beyond a reasonable doubt. Thus, in the eyes of the law, petitioner does not come before the Court as one who is "innocent," but, on the contrary, as one who has been convicted by due process of law of two brutal murders. (399–400, citations and passages within parentheses omitted)

In summary, the Court in *Herrera* had the opportunity to rule that one has a right to avoid execution if one is innocent and can prove it, but refused to do so by a margin of 6–3. Appellate review exists to consider whether constitutional violations occurred in trial, not to consider new facts or evidence. Mr. Herrera failed to convince the justices because he made a pure argument of innocence. The majority opinion noted that they are sensitive to innocence, but that "factually incorrect" findings of lower courts are not enough (404). Rather, factual innocence claims, to be heard, must also be accompanied with a constitutional claim based on procedural flaws. "Freestanding claims of actual innocence" (405) are not enough.

The Court did allow the possibility, "for the sake of argument," that "a truly persuasive demonstration of 'actual innocence'" would render unconstitutional a subsequent execution, but it ruled that the bar for such relief would have to be "extraordinarily high" because of the need for "finality" in judicial proceedings and the "disruptive effect" that considering such claims would have on state courts (417). Herrera, the Court argued, had not come close to this extraordinary threshold. No one else has since then, either.

Justice Blackmun dissented in this case, in an opinion partially joined by Justices Stevens and Souter. His two brethren did not, however, join in his last section, just one paragraph in length. Blackmun ended his argument as follows:

> Of one thing, however, I am certain. Just as an execution without adequate safeguards is unacceptable, so too is an execution when the condemned prisoner can prove that he is innocent. The execution of a person who can show that he is innocent comes perilously close to simple murder. (446)

For a consistent majority of the justices of the Supreme Court, the most appropriate safeguard against executing the innocent would be the power of the executive to grant a pardon or a commutation (see, e.g., O'Connor's concurring opinion in *Herrera*). While willing to recognize for the sake of argument that it would be unacceptable to execute the innocent, the justices have been unwilling to recognize that it may ever have happened. That is, if the procedures are fair and constitutional rules of due process are followed, then "freestanding" claims of innocence simply should not be there. In any case, Justice Scalia's summary of the law in a 2009 dissent remains a good summary of the law today:

> This Court has never held that the Constitution forbids the execution of a convicted defendant who has had a full and fair trial but is later able to convince a habeas court that he is "actually" innocent. Quite to the contrary, we have repeatedly left that question unresolved, while expressing considerable doubt that any claim based on alleged "actual innocence" is constitutionally cognizable. (Justice Scalia, dissenting, *In re Troy Anthony Davis*, 3)

Conclusion

In his concurring opinion in *Kansas v. Marsh* (2006), Justice Antonin Scalia claimed the death penalty system had an "error rate of [0].027 percent" (182). The evidence presented in this chapter indicates that this error rate is far too low of an approximation—especially for those sentenced to death. With 156 death row inmates already exonerated, and an error rate that has been estimated at around 4 percent, it is clear that the death penalty harbors serious flaws. Perhaps it is inevitable or not surprising that with the high emotion evoked in a capital trial, and with the adversarial nature of our justice system, corners would be cut. But it is worth serious questioning why we collectively accept the level of error that we have seen in this chapter.

In chapter 7 we focused on how often death sentences are overturned and showed that this occurred in more than 60 percent of the cases. With only 16 percent of condemned inmates executed, once a final disposition of their case has been made, we could say that the vast majority of death sentences are done in error, or at least that the sentence does not withstand review. Of course, typically it is the death sentence, not the guilt, that is overturned. Still, it makes a difference whether one is sentenced to death or to life in prison; if it did not, we would not have the death penalty. If the majority of death sentences are overturned on appeal, it seems fair to conclude that the judicial system has determined that they were reached in error. In this chapter we have focused not on faulty sentences of death but on faulty findings of guilt. Here, thankfully, the error rate is much lower. Some suggest that it is "vanishingly low" (see Justice Scalia in *Kansas v. March* (2006)); others suggest that perhaps it is 0.5 to 1.0 percent of all criminal convictions (see Zalman 2012); others that perhaps it is about 4 percent of all death cases (see Gross et al. 2014). The latter estimate is the only one based on a large-scale scientific approach; Scalia's low estimate is simply a personal opinion; Zalman's is based on a survey, or an average of responses by judicial actors about their own estimates; Gross's estimate is based on a careful and large-scale study. Of course, no one knows how many executed individuals may have been innocent, or how many innnocents remain in prison or on the nation's death rows. The 4 percent estimate carefully arrived at by Gross and his collaborators was derived from conservative estimation techniques, suggesting, if anything, that the true but unknown number is most likely higher. Exactly what it is, of course, we will never know.

There are many areas where we expect extremely high reliability in government activities. For example, while most Americans do not associate the US Postal Service with models of efficiency, we also do not expect significant proportions of the mail to be delivered to the wrong address or lost, yet we send over 100 billion pieces of mail each year. The Internal Revenue Service certainly is not considered by most to be efficient. But when their inspector general evaluated performance in sending or receiving tax payments through electronic "lockboxes" in 2001, it found 78,000 payments lost from a total of 67 million received. The error rate was therefore 0.12 percent. In the face of that, the inspector's report was entitled "Additional Enhancements Could be Made to Strengthen Lockbox Security" (see IRS 2008a). When the inspector general looked at how many packets of information the IRS had sent to taxpayers containing personal information in 2007, it found that 181 of the packages were reported to be lost or damaged (by the United Parcel Service), out of a total of 3 million packets. Facing an error rate of 181/3,000,000 or 0.006 percent, the inspector wrote "Program to Protect Hardcopy Personally Identifiable Information is a Work-in-Progress" (see IRS 2008b). More familiar may be the terrible tragedy of the Challenger and Columbia space shuttle disasters. NASA had 127 manned space shuttles, with these two disasters: A 1.6 percent failure rate (see NASA n.d.). Of course, NASA ended the shuttle and was roundly criticized throughout government for these failures.

We expect government institutions in many areas to work virtually without error, or with truly marginal error rates. But one death-row inmate has been exonerated for every nine individuals we have executed. These innocents have collectively spent hundreds of years in the desolate environment of death row, wrongly condemned to die. Among the guilty, more death sentences are reversed than sustained: most condemned killers see their sentenced eventually reduced to LWOP. Why do we accept these rates of error in the single area of the criminal justice where the stakes are the highest? Why do we not demand better? If the US Postal Service delivered 4 percent of all first-class mail to the wrong address, or discarded it as unimportant to the recipient, our elected officials would certainly demand better. But those wrongfully condemned to die do not generate this level of public concern.

Further Readings

Aronson, Jay D., and Simon A. Cole. 2009. Science and the Death Penalty: DNA, Innocence, and the Debate over Capital Punishment in the United States. *Law and Social Inquiry* 34 (3): 603–633.

Baumgartner, Frank R., Suzanna L. De Boef, and Amber E. Boydstun. 2008. *The Decline of the Death Penalty and the Discovery of Innocence.* New York: Cambridge University Press.

Bedau, Adam Hugo, and Michael L. Radelet. 1987. Miscarriages of Justice in Potentially Capital Cases. *Stanford Law Review* 40 (1): 21–179

Borchard, Edwin M. 1932. *Convicting the Innocent.* New Haven, CT: Yale University Press.

Christianson, Scott. 2004. *Innocent: Inside Wrongful Conviction Cases.* New York: New York University Press.

Doyle, James M. 2005. *True Witness: Cops, Courts, Science, and the Battle against Misidentification.* New York: Palgrave.

Forst, Brian. 2004. *Errors of Justice.* New York: Cambridge University Press.

Garrett, Brandon. 2011. *Convicting the Innocent: Where Criminal Prosecutions Go Wrong.* Cambridge, MA: Harvard University Press.

Gould, Jon B., and Richard A. Leo. 2010. One Hundred Years Later: Wrongful Convictions after a Century of Research. *Journal of Criminal Law and Criminology* 100 (3): 825–868.

Grisham, John. 2006. *The Innocent Man*. New York: Doubleday.

Gross, Samuel R., Barbara O.Brien, Chen Hu, and Edward H. Kennedy. 2014. Rate of False Conviction of Criminal Defendants Who Are Sentenced to Death. *Proceedings of the National Academy of Sciences* 111 (20): 7230–7235.

Norris, Robert J. 2012. Assessing Compensation Statutes for the Wrongfully Convicted. *Criminal Justice Policy Review* 23 (3): 352–374.

Ogletree, Charles J., Jr., and Austin Sarat, eds. 2009. *When Law Fails: Making Sense of Miscarriages of Justice*. New York: New York University Press.

Radelet, Michael L., Hugo Adam Bedau, and Constance E. Putnam. 1992. *In Spite of Innocence*. Boston: Northeastern University Press.

Redlich, Allison D., James R. Acker, Robert J. Norris, and Catherine L. Bonventre, eds. 2005. *Examining Wrongful Convictions: Stepping Back, Moving Forward*. Durham, NC: Carolina Academic Press.

Risinger, D. Michael. 2007. Innocents Convicted: An Empirically Justified Factual Wrongful Conviction Rate. *Journal of Criminal Law and Criminology* 97 (3): 761–806.

Zalman, Marvin. 2012. Qualitatively Estimating the Incidence of Wrongful Convictions. *Criminal Law Bulletin* 48 (2): 221–279.

Methods of Execution

Consistently over US history, hanging was by far the most common form of execution.[1] Indeed, until 1900, 96 percent of all executions since colonial times were by that method. But times change, and in recent decades American justice officials have searched for better methods, literally attempting to "perfect the mechanism" of death. Each new method was portrayed by its promoters and widely adopted by state corrections officials as a cleaner and more humane innovation that would professionalize the process, making use of the latest scientific and technological advances to avoid needless pain to the inmate and advance civilization by avoiding some of the barbarism of previous times.[2]

Electrocution was the first widely adopted solution to the problem of hangings gone wrong, beginning just as electric lights came to America's streets around the turn of the twentieth century. It would make use of the awe-inspiring new power of electricity instantaneously to put a killer to death, unlike the sometimes gruesome and certainly old-fashioned system of the gallows. By 1925, electrocution was the dominant method. Lethal gas was promoted by many in the 1930s and beyond; by 1939, more than 100 inmates had been killed in the gas chamber, and it was regularly used much more than hanging. It, too, was said to be painless. Firing squads had periodically been used throughout US history, including in modern times. But lethal injection became the predominant method in the modern period of the death penalty. Like those methods that preceded it, lethal injection was promoted as a scientifically advanced and more civilized method of killing. Since 1976, 87 percent of all executions have been by lethal injection. In this chapter, we explore why the United States has shifted from one method of execution to the next. We pay special attention to controversies surrounding the medicalization of executions in modern times. Neither hanging, shooting, nor electrocution requires the presence or participation of a doctor or other medical professional. This peculiarity of lethal injection has led to a number of paradoxes, constitutional challenges, and dilemmas.[3]

The US Supreme Court has addressed controversies about methods on several occasions, in particular as they relate to "evolving standards of decency" and what level of suffering or pain may be constitutionally acceptable during an execution.

Further, it has had to grapple with issues of whether "botched" executions reflect isolated and therefore permissible errors or whether they may reflect a pattern and practice of behavior on the part of corrections officials whose training may not include medical procedures, who may have little practice or experience in the activities, and sometimes may not be particularly sympathetic to the needs of the convicted murderers they are charged with putting to death. Further, while inserting a needle may sound simple, and many of us have seen it done routinely during a doctor's appointment, many inmates are former drug abusers whose veins may not be so easily tapped. Thus, the medical nature of lethal injection poses particular challenges and new paradoxes that hanging, firing squads, and other techniques did not.

While any method may work well if carried out properly, each method can also go wrong. This issue is particularly compounded with lethal injections, for two reasons. First, medical professionals have pulled away from participation, as their oath requires them to save lives, not end them. This has often left the task of administering lethal drugs to corrections officials with relatively little training in such procedures. Second, certain pharmaceutical companies have rejected the use of their life-saving products in executions, so states have had to find other sources of drugs or else substitute new drugs that have not previously been tried. This, naturally, has led to legal challenges and charges of human experimentation.

The paradoxes of medicalizing the process of killing are enormous. Not least of these is the widely shared public perception that our courts may be spending too much time concerned about the possible suffering of people who have often been convicted of horrific crimes, including torturing their own victims. Many members of the public would be comfortable with battery acid as the lethal injection of choice, and if the inmate suffers, so be it. In his opinion in *Callins v. Collins* (1994), Justice Scalia compared death by lethal injection to the suffering that the victim, Sabrina Buie, suffered: "For example, the case of the 11-year old girl raped by four men and then killed by stuffing her panties down her throat . . . . How enviable a quiet death by lethal injection compared with that!" (quoted in Beutler 2014). Of course, a significant concern in the Buie case that the justice referenced was that Henry McCollum had not committed the crime and was later exonerated of it after having spent almost 30 years on death row. But Justice Scalia touches, as he often did, on a visceral point: So what if the inmate suffers a little bit? But if the state is to kill, the state is not supposed to torture. How exactly to carry out a judicially sanctioned execution, it turns out, is not that easy to resolve.

A Quick Historical Overview of Methods in Use

Figure 10.1 shows selected execution methods over the full course of US history, dating back to colonial times.[4] Hangings dominated throughout the course of

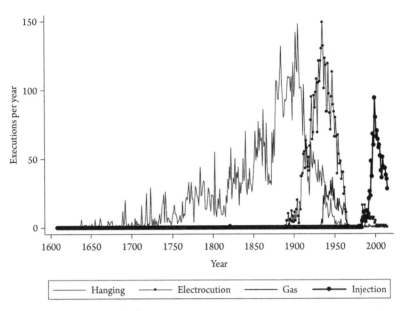

Figure 10.1 Execution Methods over Time. Note: Excludes 144 firing squads and 119 other methods, including burning, pressing, gibbeting, hanging in chains, bludgeoning, and breaking on the wheel. Source: For the modern era, the Carolina Execution Database; for the historic period through 1972, Espy and Smykla 2005.

history until declining rapidly at the turn of the twentieth century. Electrocutions replaced hangings, then gas chambers had some moderate use for a time, and finally lethal injection became the preferred method.

Figure 10.2 focuses on the period from 1900 through the present and clearly shows differences between the pre- and post-*Gregg* systems. The first modern execution, in 1977, was by firing squad, and the electric chair was first brought back into use before lethal injection came to dominate; most of the first modern executions were by the electric chair. By the mid-1990s, however, lethal injections were dominant. By 1995, lethal injections accounted for 87 percent of all annual executions, and that number declined below 90 on only two occasions in any year through 2015. We now review each execution method in greater detail.

Hanging

As mentioned earlier, hangings were "the nearly universal form of execution in the United States" from early colonial times until the end of the nineteenth century. During this time, the only available alternatives were punishments passed down from the Dark Ages—breaking on the wheel, burning alive, hanging in chains, bludgeoning, and so forth. (Indeed, the note to Figure 10.1 indicates that 119 individuals

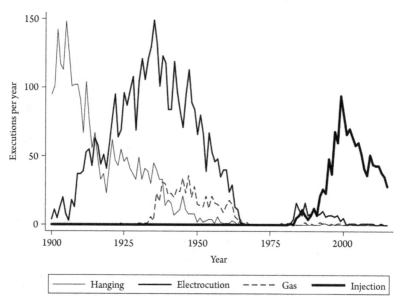

Figure 10.2 Executions since 1900. Note: Excludes 34 inmates killed by firing squad.

were killed by such relatively unusual methods, a small percentage of the total, but still an indicator of social acceptance in the United States during the early years.)

When discussing the death penalty, and hangings in particular, it is difficult not to mention the legacy of lynchings because "the administration of criminal justice" has been "tangled with the history of lynching in profound and important ways that continue to contaminate the integrity and fairness of the justice system" (Equal Justice Initiative 2015, 3). Unlike electrocutions, gas executions, and lethal injections, for which states had the sole responsibility, hangings have populist-based origins and have been used as a measure of social control since before our nation's founding. Throughout American history, the fury of lynch mobs has affected all groups, including blacks, whites, Chinese Americans (Johnson 2011), Native Americans (Baker 2007), Mexican Americans (Carrigan and Webb 2015), and other marginalized groups. However, for blacks in particular, lynchings and state-sanctioned executions have been inextricably linked, often acting as complementary tools of oppression (Beck, Massey, and Tolnay 1989; C. Phillips 1987). Indeed, much of the justification for the death penalty in the pre-*Furman* period was that if populist mobs were not certain that the accused would be executed by the state, they would take matters into their own hands; this was particularly true for those accused of the crime of interracial rape of white women. From about 1900 through the 1930s, the Court reviewed a number of cases where death sentences were hastily imposed, often on scant evidence, in the face of the threat of mob violence (see Steiker and Steiker 2016, 32–37). In a 1906 case out of Chattanooga, Tennessee, the Court actually granted habeas, and the inmate was almost immediately removed from his cell and killed by a mob. A local deputy left a note on the body directly addressing Justice Harlan (33–34). Thus, lynching and the death penalty are powerfully linked in US history, particularly for black defendants. Figure 10.3 compares the number of lynchings of blacks and whites with the number of executions.

Figure 10.3A shows that, for example, Georgia saw almost 600 lynchings of blacks during the period of 1877 through 1972, and that it had about the same number of executions of blacks during the period of 1900 through 1972.[5] Figure 10.3B shows that about 50 whites were lynched in Georgia during that time, whereas almost 150 were executed. There is a strong correlation between numbers of lynchings and executions for blacks (0.62) but not for whites (0.26). The history of lynching blacks in the South is closely related to their legal executions, in the pre-*Furman* period. Indeed, as Steiker and Steiker (2016) make clear, the Supreme Court was forced on numerous occasions to confront the reality that if executions were not duly authorized (and in a timely manner!), mobs would take the law into their own hands. Historically, lynching and the death penalty were tightly connected, but much more so for black or minorities accused of crimes against whites, particularly against women.

Hanging an inmate involves tying a noose around the neck and dropping the inmate's body from an elevated platform. The rapid downward acceleration of the body's weight creates tension in the noose, causing it to tighten, which dislocates the neck. In theory, this should immediately render the inmate insensitive to pain by snapping the spinal cord; death should follow quickly (see Hillman 1993; Pierrepoint 1974). However, several things can go wrong. If the drop is too long, and the body therefore picks up velocity as it drops through space, the result can be decapitation. This is problematic because beheadings are no longer acceptable. If, on the other hand, the drop is too short, the inmate's neck simply settles slowly into the noose, and the inmate dangles until finally suffocating. Asphyxiation after surviving the initial drop can take up to 45 minutes. During this time, the inmate's face will begin to swell and turn blue due to a lack of oxygen reaching the head region (Hillman 1993, 746). Botched public hangings have been horrific affairs (see Sarat 2014).[6]

Only three inmates have been hanged in the post-*Gregg* period, two in Washington (1993 and 1994) and one in Delaware (1996). Washington was the last state in the nation to change its method from hanging to lethal injection following adverse publicity and legal challenges in 1994, subsequently executing three individuals by lethal injection. Delaware regularly made use of lethal injection before and after Billy Bailey was hanged in 1996. Although hangings are no longer as widely practiced today as they once were, several states, including New Hampshire and Washington, currently include hangings as a secondary alternative to lethal injections (Snell 2014).

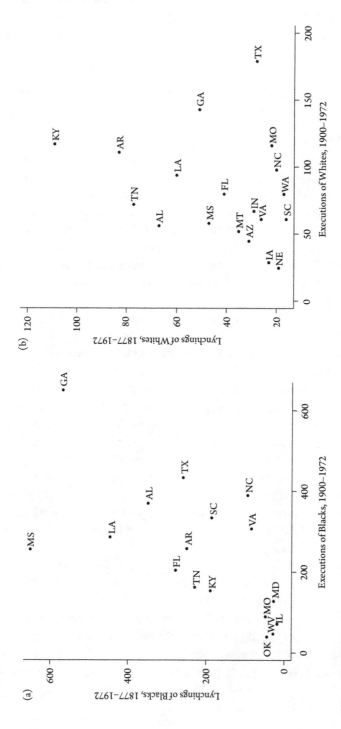

Figure 10.3 Lynchings and Executions by State, pre-*Furman.*

A. Blacks. Note: Lynching data from www.thiscruelwar.com/the-long-list. Excludes states with fewer than 15 lynchings or 15 executions. Pearson's R = .62.
B. Whites. Note: Lynching data from www.thiscruelwar.com/the-long-list. Excludes states with fewer than 15 lynchings or 15 executions. Pearson's R = .26.

Firing Squad

Firing squads have never been a widespread method for executing inmates; however, the practice has remained relevant because of periodic interest during the twentieth century. For example, Utah reauthorized its use of the firing squad in a 2015 amendment to the state law. This was in response to the growing threat of federal courts striking down the use of lethal injection and to shrinking supplies of lethal injection drugs. Many state lawmakers have responded to this with the adage that bullets are cheap. No matter the occasional appeal of the firing squad in some circles, it has never been common. Just 34 inmates have died by firing squad since 1900, as shown in Figure 10.2.

Although firing squads are uncommon, Utah used a firing squad to execute Gary Gilmore, in what was arguably America's most visible and highly publicized public execution, and the first of the modern era (on January 17, 1977). Since then, John Albert Taylor (1996) and Ronnie Lee Gardner (2010) have been the only other Americans executed by firing squad. All three took place in Utah.

Execution by firing squad first requires fastening the inmate to a chair and covering his or her head with a hood. Next, a doctor identifies vital locations on the inmate's body—such as the heart, the lungs, or the head—with a visible target (Weisberg 1991). Following this, several shooters—usually three to five trained shooters—are given a single round of ammunition and are instructed to shoot the targeted area on the inmate's body. The high impact of the bullet should cause the vital organs to rupture, which will cause rapid hemorrhaging and death (Hillman 1993); however, if the shooters miss the vital locations, the inmate may die slowly due to blood loss, trauma, and shock.[7] For example, if not firmly strapped into the chair, the inmate may squirm, causing the shooters to miss the heart, with the result that death by loss of blood comes slowly rather than immediately.

Oklahoma and Utah are the only two states that currently maintain the use of firing squads as a secondary alternative to lethal injections. Oklahoma will approve the use of firing squads only if both lethal injections and electrocutions are deemed unconstitutional by a court with appropriate jurisdiction. Utah authorizes the use of firing squads for those inmates sentenced to death before May 3, 2004, who chose the method (Snell 2014).

Electrocution

On August 6, 1890, New York was the first state to execute a person using the electric chair. Speaking of its creation, the governor at the time wrote: "The present mode of executing criminals by hanging has come down to us from the dark ages, and it may well be questioned whether the science of the present day cannot provide a means for taking the life of such as are condemned to die in a less barbarous manner" (Hill and State of New York 1885, 39). Once the execution had taken place, however, the *New York Times* (1890) called it "a disgrace to civilization." Nonetheless, other states quickly followed New York's lead.

New York shifted toward electrocution after a series of botched hangings prompted the legislature to explore more humane alternatives for executing its inmates. The state legislature adopted electrocution after a state commission's proposal highlighted the practice's "quick and painless" form of death (Nathan and Green 2007, 8). William Kemmler was the unlucky inmate first in line for death by electric chair for murdering his common-law wife shortly after passage of the new law; he would come to be the nation's first citizen executed by electricity (Lumer and Tenney 1995).

Even before it was used, the electric chair was a polarizing execution method. Two of the most visible actors in the debate were none other than Thomas Edison and George Westinghouse (see King 2011; the following paragraphs rely on this source; for fuller accounts of the electric chair, see Brandon 1999; Galvin 2015). Edison and Westinghouse were promoting rival electrical systems for widespread use throughout the country; Edison promoted direct current, and Westinghouse was the champion of alternating current. Today, we see alternating current in virtually all household uses, but at the turn of the twentieth century, competition was rampant, and neither system was clearly poised to dominate; in fact, Edison's direct current system had an early lead in many urban areas. The competition between Edison and Westinghouse ("the battle of the currents") was unlike any in modern time, as each knew that the country could not simultaneously adopt both electrical systems. In the wild and unregulated world of the beginnings of the electrical age, different companies strung electrical lines throughout the nation's largest cities, and it was not uncommon to see industrial accidents where linemen were killed in full view of appalled but helpless bystanders.

Edison set about to destroy the reputation of Westinghouse's system by associating it with mortal danger.[8] He staged electrocutions of various animals, from a dog up to an elephant, to show that alternating current was inherently dangerous. Thousands of New Yorkers watched the publicly staged electrocution of Topsy the elephant at Coney Island in 1903.[9] When the State of New York began to consider the electric chair, Edison, opposed to capital punishment but sensing an opportunity to destroy his rival, promoted the idea that alternating current was the surest way to kill. Westinghouse donated $100,000 to the defense of the inmate, not wanting the electrocution to take place at all, and certainly not wanting to promote the idea that alternating current was inherently dangerous. Edison, meanwhile, was promoting the idea that a significant bolt of alternating current could kill a man in "in the ten-thousandth part of a second."

When New York scheduled William Kemmler to be executed by the electric chair, his attorneys petitioned to the New York Court of Appeals, claiming the use of the electric chair violated New York State's constitutional prohibition on cruel and unusual punishments (Lumer and Tenney 1995; *People ex. rel. Kemmler v. Durston* (1890)). Although electrocution was an untested method, the appellate court rejected this claim, ruling that it was a more humane alternative to conventional hangings.

With the financial support of Westinghouse, Kemmler took his case all the way to the US Supreme Court, but the Court agreed with Edison that the new technology would certainly not cause suffering; death would be nearly instantaneous. Writing the opinion for *In re: Kemmler* (1890), Justice Melville Fuller rejected the petitioner's claims and echoed similar arguments as the New York Court of Appeals. The Court deferred to the soundness of the New York legislature's logic in adopting the electric chair as a better alternative to hangings. After winning this appeal, the State of New York finally executed Kemmler on August 6, 1890. Westinghouse eventually won "the battle of the currents," but Edison helped usher in the age of judicial electrocution.

Executing an inmate through electrocution first requires strapping "a metal skullcap-shaped electrode . . . to the scalp and forehead," which is placed on top of "a sponge moistened with saline . . . . [Next,] curved electrodes are moistened with conductive jelly and bound to the prisoner's legs . . . . [Finally, the inmate] is strapped into the electric chair and blindfolded" (Hillman 1993, 747). After the apparatus is assembled, an electric jolt of up to 3,000 volts is sent through the inmate's body, which paralyzes the respiratory system, causing asphyxiation (Hillman 1993; Bernstein 1973, 1975); however, if the apparatus is misassembled or if not enough electricity is sent through the inmate's body, it may take several attempts for the inmate to die. For example, if the conductors are not moist, the full dose of electrical current may not be transferred to the body.

New York first learned this lesson when it electrocuted William Kemmler in 1890. Although the US Supreme Court and the New York State Court of Appeals were convinced of the electric chair's humaneness and were certain that Kemmler's electrocution would be errorless, witnesses at the execution experienced a truly horrifying spectacle. Edison had promised near instantaneous death, but things did not work out that way in practice. After the first jolt, the lead promoter of the electric chair proclaimed: "This is the culmination of ten years work and study. We live in a higher civilization today" (King 2011). But the first jolt did not kill Mr. Kemmler, who began to gasp for air. While the dynamo ramped up its alternating current for the next jolt, Mr. Kemmler's jacket caught fire; he wheezed and gasped, seeming to be regaining consciousness, and finally the electricity resumed. After a couple of minutes passed, and he went rigid, he was declared dead. The attending physician predicted: "There will never be another execution" (King 2011). The *New York Times*, which published an article on the event titled "Far Worse Than Hanging," lambasted the botched execution as a disgrace to the State of New York and to all civilization. The newspaper's horror at the first electrocution is worth reading in some detail. The story begins as follows:

A sacrifice to the whims and theories of the coterie of cranks and politicians who induced the Legislature of this State to pass a law supplanting hanging by electrical execution was offered to-day in the person of William Kemmler, the Buffalo murderer. He died this morning under the most revolting circumstances, and with his death there was placed to the discredit of the State of New-York an execution that was a disgrace to civilization.

Probably no convicted murderer of modern times has been made to suffer as Kemmler suffered. Unfortunate enough to be the first man convicted after the passage of the new execution law, his life has been used as the bone of contention between the alleged humanitarians who supported the law, on one side, and the electric-light interests, who hated to see the commodity in which they deal reduced to such a use as that. For fifteen months they have been fighting as to whether he should be killed or not, and the question has been dragged through every court. He has been sentenced and resentenced to death, only to be dragged back from the abyss by some intricacy of the law.

The uncertainty in which he has so long lived would have driven any ordinary man insane. That suffering has culminated in a death so fearful that people throughout the country will read of it with horror and disgust.

The execution cannot merely be characterized as unsuccessful. It was so terrible that the word fails to convey the idea. It was, as those who advocated it desired that it should be, attended by men eminent in science and in medicine, and they almost unanimously say that this single experiment warrants the prompt repeal of the law. (*New York Times* 1890, 1)

Even with Kemmler's botched execution fresh in the public's memory, the use of electrocutions rapidly expanded to other states; as shown in Figure 10.2, electrocution was the predominant method of execution throughout much of the twentieth century. Apparently the promise of a "more humane" method, especially a newly discovered and "high-tech" one, was more compelling than the horrific experience of its first use. Florida executed 44 inmates in its now infamous electric chair through 1999 before switching to lethal injection in 2000. The decision to retire "old sparky" came after the horrifically botched execution of Jesse Tafero. The sponge that was supposed to conduct electricity to Tafero's body instead caught fire, burning off the top of his head (see McGarrahan 1999).[10] Although the state later switched to another method, the "flaming electric chair" story dates from 1990, and the switch to lethal injection came 10 years later. Several other botches had ensued, including flames emerging from the head of inmate Pedro Medina in 1997, and the execution of Bud Davis in 1999, where the electricity caused massive bleeding (McGarrahan 1999). Other states also moved away from the electric chair after continued frustration with malfunctions. Indeed, it was in reaction to problems with use of the electric chair and following the death by firing squad of Gary Gilmore that Dr. Jay Chapman, the Oklahoma state medical examiner at the time, developed the idea of using lethal injection. It was designed as a more humane means of killing than the electric chair or the firing squad. Thus, as we will discuss in greater length later, lethal injection, like the electric chair, was said to be the next method in the march toward a more civilized and humane method of execution.

As of 2016, eight states—Alabama, Arkansas, Florida, Kentucky, Oklahoma, South Carolina, Tennessee, and Virginia—listed electrocutions as a possible method for execution (Snell 2014). Most have moved completely away from the electric chair. Alabama, for example, conducted its last electrocution in May 2002 and has conducted 32 lethal injections since then through the end of 2015. Tennessee last conducted an electrocution in 2007; South Carolina in 2008; Florida in 1999; and Texas and Oklahoma have never used the electric chair in the modern period. Virginia, on the other hand, introduced lethal injection in 1995 but has continued with a handful of electrocutions, most recently when Robert Gleason was executed on January 11, 2013. Gleason was the last inmate to be electrocuted in the United States.

Gas Chamber

Nevada became the first state to adopt the use of lethal gas in 1921 (Denno 2002, 83). At the time, the state legislature "sought to provide a method of inflicting the death penalty in the most humane manner known to modern science" (*State v. Gee Jon*, 676, 682, quoted in Nathan and Green 2007, 11). This solution came after the state failed in its attempts at executing Gee Jon—a condemned inmate waiting on death row—by pumping cyanide gas through his cell walls in the middle of the night (DPIC 2016a; Bohm 2012).

Execution through gas asphyxiation requires strapping an inmate into a chair situated in an airtight gas chamber. In this chamber, a pail of sulfuric acid is placed directly in front of the inmate. After the officers leave the chamber interior, "a lever on the outside . . . is used to drop crystals of sodium cyanide into the pail" (Hillman 1993, 748), which produces the lethal gas. To speed up the execution process, officers instruct the inmate to take in a deep breath and to avoid holding his or her breath.

Jacob Weisberg gathered medical expert advice about the possible physical sensations experienced by inmates condemned to the gas chambers for an article in the *New Republic* titled "This Is Your Death." Quoting Dr. Richard Traystman of Johns Hopkins School of Medicine, Weisberg described the beginning sensation of gas asphyxiation as a pain "in the arms, shoulders, back, and chest" similar in experience "to the pain felt by a person during a heart attack" (1991, 25). Because the brain and other vital organs are starved of oxygen, the inmate will die from hypoxia.

Once the execution is completed, the gas is removed from the chamber with an exhaust fan, the inmate's corpse is sprayed with ammonia to remove remaining gases, and corrections officers ruffle the inmate's hair to release any gas that may have been trapped there (Weisberg 1991, 25). States moved away from using the gas chamber for many reasons. One was its association with the death camps of Nazi Germany; gas chambers, not surprisingly, have a bad connotation. Another was more practical. At the death chamber in Raleigh, North Carolina, still available for use with lethal injections as of 2016 and also available for educational tours, small glass cylinders stand between the panes of a double-glass window. These are designed to bubble if exposed to the lethal gas, warning spectators and staff that the gas is escaping from the chamber. In other words, it is not so easy to seal a chamber hermetically and to vent the lethal gas from inside the building once its work has been done. In the modern period, just 11 inmates have been killed by gas, most recently in 1998 (North Carolina) and 1999 (Arizona).

As of 2016, Arizona, Missouri, and Wyoming retained lethal gas as a secondary execution method to lethal injections. Arizona provides the option for a lethal gas execution only to inmates who were sentenced before November 15, 1992, while Wyoming retains the use of lethal gas in the event lethal injection is declared unconstitutional (Snell 2014). In 2015, Oklahoma governor Mary Fallin signed House Bill 1879, which introduced the use of execution by nitrogen gas. As described in an Oklahoma newspaper, "HB 1879 says that if lethal injection is held unconstitutional or is unavailable, an execution shall be carried out by nitrogen hypoxia. Electrocution and firing squad are also other alternatives should nitrogen gas not be available or held unconstitutional" (Hoberock 2016). Nitrogen gas has never been used as a method of execution, but state experts assure that it should be painless. The same article quotes a local critic, who points out that nitrogen would be "highly experimental" and "has been banned in many jurisdictions for the euthanasia of animals" (Hoberock 2016). With three backup plans, Oklahoma legislators clearly wanted to send a signal of their willingness to carry out executions after the terribly botched ordeals of Clayton Lockett and others, described in the next section. HB 1879 passed the two chambers of the Oklahoma legislature by votes of 85 to 10 and 41 to 0.

Lethal Injection

The first modern use of lethal injection occurred in 1982 when Texas executed Charles Brooks Jr., but the practice has been considered by state legislators since as early as 1888 (Denno 2007, 64).[11] New York's Death Penalty Commission was the first to propose the method as an alternative to hangings but rejected it due to ethical concerns over the practice's close resemblance to the field of medicine, favoring electrocution (see Denno 2007). Oklahoma was the first state to develop a lethal injection system, adopting it in May 1977, in legislation that would be widely adopted in other states shortly thereafter.

Oklahoma's legislation was based primarily on the advice of Dr. Jay Chapman, at the time the acting chief medical examiner for the state. Chapman, who has been described as the "father of lethal injection," devised what would become Oklahoma's three-drug protocol (Sanburn 2014). However, it was Oklahoma state senator Bill Dawson and state House representative Bill Wiseman who proposed the capital punishment amendment that most states would replicate (see Denno 2002, 2007). Their bill used Chapman's general vision for lethal injection, but it incorporated vague language with respect to such details as the exact drugs to be used or the quantities required for execution. In addition, "no historical evidence suggests that" the two "consulted any other doctors or scientists, conducted any studies, or considered any of the available evidence concerning the risks and dangers of lethal injection" beyond the advice of Dr. Jay Chapman and Stanley Deutsch, an anesthesiologist at the University of Oklahoma (Nathan and Green 2007, 20). Because of this, "all critical decisions regarding the implementation of lethal injection" were delegated to Oklahoma prison officials, who had neither the medical training nor the expertise to develop a lethal injection protocol (19).

Oklahoma's lethal injection protocol begins by strapping an inmate to a gurney. Next, a needle is inserted into the arm right below the inside of the elbow; if the inmate was an intravenous drug user—as many state and federal inmates disproportionately are (BJS 2007)—and the veins in the arm are not usable, then officers search for alternative needle insertion sites (Hillman 1993; Weisberg 1991). A benign saline solution is then injected into the vein, followed by sodium thiopental, which acts as an anesthetic, sending the inmate into an unconscious state (DPIC 2016a). Immediately following the sodium thiopental, pancuronium bromide is administered, which paralyzes the muscles. Finally, potassium chloride is injected into the veins, which "interferes with the electrical signals that stimulate the contractions of the heart, inducing cardiac arrest" (*Baze v. Rees* (2008), quoting Justice Scalia's concurring opinion, 44).

A peculiar element of the "three-drug cocktail" devised by Dr. Chapman is the second drug. While the purpose of the first drug is clear and medically advisable, to render the inmate unconscious and therefore unable to feel pain (or any other sensation), the purpose of the second drug appears to be completely cosmetic, for the sake of the onlookers, not the inmate. Because this drug is a paralytic, it renders all voluntary muscles inoperable. Though the heart and the lungs continue to function, the inmate literally cannot move a muscle. The face cannot grimace, the mouth cannot gasp, the finger cannot wave, the head cannot lift up. This masks the physical effects of the third drug, which induces cardiac arrest.

Litigation has stemmed from the misadministration of wrong dosages for the first drug, sodium thiopental, which is supposed to numb the patient. Prosecutors have argued their defendants were given the wrong dosage of sodium thiopental, but since they were paralyzed, they could not communicate with onlookers. No one knows for sure whether this has actually occurred.

Our understanding of what may be happening in many lethal injections was greatly enhanced by a large study conducted by a remarkable team consisting of Dr. Leonidas Koniaris (chair in surgical oncology at the Comprehensive Cancer Center at the University of Miami Medical School), with Teresa Zimmers (PhD, Department of Anesthesiology), Dr. David Lubarsky (MD, Department of Anesthesiology and Pain Management), and attorney Jonathan Sheldon, a postconviction capital attorney from Virginia, author of "Virginia Law and Practice: Postconviction Remedies in Virginia" and a practicing attorney in Virginia who focuses on capital appeals. This team sought information on execution protocols from Texas and Virginia, revealing that executioners in neither state had training in anesthesia, that there was no direct observation or monitoring of the level of anesthesia during the executions, and that there was no data collection or documentation of the amounts of anesthesia administered. Koniaris et al. noted that "no assessment of depth or anaesthesia or loss of consciousness was done" (2005, 1412). With no documentation of levels of anesthetic available, the team sought records of postmortem levels of thiopental. The authors continued, "Texas and Virginia refused to provide such data, but we obtained autopsy toxicology results from 49 executions in Arizona, Georgia, North Carolina, and South Carolina" (1412–1413). These reports were either publicly available or came through court records, which the team obtained and analyzed. While the researchers note that the method is not perfect (one would need to know the rate at which the drugs were administered during the procedure, which can last many minutes), they also note that "thiopental concentrations did not fall with increased time between execution and blood sample collection . . . , consistent with data showing that thiopental is quite stable in stored human plasma" (1413); see also Martens-Lobenhoffer 1999). In sum, they looked at autopsies to see how much thiopental was in the bloodstream. What they discovered was very troubling. Almost half of inmates (21) had concentrations of sodium thiopental levels consistent with consciousness (1413). Another large group, 45 percent of the total, had levels lower than what would typically be used in surgery. Just 6 inmates, 12 percent of the total, had levels of thiopental greater than 33 milligrams per liter, which the authors note is typical for surgery. Figure 10.4 illustrates the distribution of sodium thiopental levels among the 49 inmates studied, placing them in three categories: lower than what is required to induce loss of consciousness, lower than surgical levels, and at or above surgical levels. The authors also note that in a hospital setting not only would an initial dose of the drug be given, but it would also be monitored over time and steadily dripped at a lower dose to maintain the needed levels.

Among 49 inmates, this evidence suggests that more than 20 had levels of thiopental insufficient to induce loss of consciousness. Forty-three of the 49 inmates had levels below 38.9 milligrams per liter, the level above which one would be expected not to feel a skin incision. In sum, this team showed that the typical outcome of an execution in the states where they were able to gather data is that the inmate is not, in fact, fully sedated. They further showed that there was a great deal of variation in levels of thiopental observed even in the same state, which "is probably due to differences in drug administration in individual executions" rather than to differences in protocols between states (Koniaris et al. 2005, 1413). If the written protocols are similar across the states, but the results are highly variable, one reason could be that the corrections officials charged with these medical procedures simply do not have the skills, training, and experience reliably to ensure that the proper dosages are, in fact, delivered to the patient. Figure 10.4 suggests that they often fail.

If an insufficient dose of the first drug is given, but the second drug renders the inmate unable to move a single muscle, there is no way to know if or how much suffering may occur when the third drug induces cardiac arrest. Much litigation has followed about the possibility of excruciating pain, completely invisible to those witnessing it. In her *Glossip* dissent, Justice Sotomayor referred to this possibility of an "excruciatingly painful death" as "hidden behind a veneer of medication." We discuss this litigation in a later section of this chapter.

The Spread of Lethal Injection

Oklahoma's relatively simple procedure rapidly spread throughout the nation because it came at a time when state legislators wanted to improve the image of

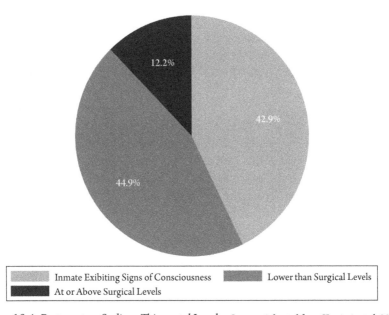

Figure 10.4 Postmortem Sodium Thiopental Levels. Source: Adapted from Koniaris et al. 2005.

capital punishment. No state had carried out an execution since 1965, and when the first execution occurred in the modern period, it was that of Gary Gilmore in 1977, by firing squad. But as the nation's death rows began to fill again following *Gregg*, Oklahoma's new method was very attractive. Dr. Chapman himself had been motivated to develop it as a result of his involvement in the often ugly process of electrocution, and he appears to have been sincerely motivated by a desire to improve what appeared to be a horrific process (see Sanburn 2014). When compared with prior execution methods, lethal injection has a more aesthetically pleasing appearance; there is limited worry of excessive blood (firing squads) or burning flesh (electrocutions), and no historical stigmas are associated with the practice (lethal gas). In addition, the relative cost of implementing a lethal injection execution is minuscule when compared with the maintenance and construction costs of prior methods other than the firing squad; only a clean room and an easily available medical gurney are required. So, many state legislatures "simply mirrored Oklahoma's vague legislative approach and drug combination choices without conducting any independent studies or research" (Nathan and Green 2007, 24).

Across the nation, states developed their lethal injection protocols through a trial-and-error process. For example, when Kentucky adopted Oklahoma's lethal injection three-drug protocol in 1998, it lacked trained personnel to carry out the trainings. Phillip Parker, warden of Kentucky State Penitentiary, was appointed to oversee the implementation of his state's protocol. To practice, Warden Parker permitted his personnel to operate on staff volunteers. During one training exercise, Parker allowed trainees to inject a saline solution into his arm, which was accidentally injected into his muscle tissue, causing pain in his arm for several days (Nathan and Green 2007, 31–32).

Many states hired consultants to help them develop their protocols. However, in the small marketplace for lethal injections, few consultants had expertise, and none had significant experience; the nation had not executed anyone by lethal injection before Texas in 1982. For the immediate years following the Supreme Court's ruling in *Gregg*, Fred Leuchter's company, Fred A. Leuchter Associates, was "the only commercial provider of execution equipment and training in the country." During this time, state legislatures were unaware that Leuchter had fabricated his training credentials (Nathan and Green 2007, 26). In sum, while lethal injection was promoted as the next level of humanity and civilization just as previous methods had been, trouble was brewing from the very beginning.

Legal Challenges to the Use of Lethal Injection

Since the inception of lethal injection, opponents have challenged state protocols within the state and federal court systems. By exposing the risk of cruel and unusual punishment, medical and legal professionals have attempted to challenge the notion of lethal injection being a "widely tolerated" practice (*Baze v. Rees*, quoting

ChiefJustice Roberts, 14). However, so far their attempts to stop its use have proven unsuccessful. The US Supreme Court has upheld lethal injection's constitutionality under the logic expressed best by Justice Scalia's opening remarks in *Glossip v. Gross*: "[B]ecause capital punishment is constitutional, then there must be a constitutional means of carrying it out" (1).

After almost 30 years of experience with the process, the Court faced head-on the fundamental acceptability of the lethal injection process in 2008. In *Baze v. Rees*, Chief Justice Roberts opined that if it is "administered as intended," lethal injection would "result in a painless death" (*Baze v. Rees*, quoting Chief Justice Roberts, 23). Although *Baze v. Rees*, the most prominent case considering the use of lethal injection, did not invalidate the practice, neither did it permanently settle the question. Continued problems in acquiring drugs, refusal of medical professionals to participate in executions, refusal of pharmaceutical companies to sell their drugs to corrections departments, and other procedural issues have created a continually changing legal and logistical landscape. According to Austin Sarat's (2014) historical review of botched executions, over a 120-year period, lethal injection had a greater likelihood of being wrongly administered than did methods considered "less humane": 7 percent of lethal injections were botched, compared with approximately 2 percent of electrocutions and 3 percent of hangings.

Multiple reasons help explain the relatively high rate of botched lethal injections as compared with other methods of execution. Fundamentally, it is a medical procedure administered by corrections officers. In addition, states with lethal injection executions do not keep detailed records on their procedures that are made available to the public. Currently, no standard system exists throughout the nation. Oklahoma's original three-drug protocol is now one variant among many different lethal injection protocols across the nation. And since *Baze v. Rees* the variation in procedures has only increased as legally obtainable supplies of key drugs have become scarce. State corrections departments, unable to procure supplies of the drugs listed in their protocols, could not follow them. The lack of supplies pushed many state legislatures to adapt or replace Oklahoma's sequence with readily available alternatives. These include alternative anesthetics (pentobarbital or midazolam) when sodium thiopental became unavailable; replacement of the three-drug protocol with a single massive dose of an anesthetic; and the use of poorly regulated compounding pharmacies to mix drugs when they are not available prefabricated by the manufacturer. Naturally, each of these innovations and changes has led to litigation, and often to charges of human experimentation. After all, it is hard to say what the effect might be on an inmate when a drug designed for and used in hospitals at relatively low dosages is instead used "off label" and in massive doses. As with electrocution, experts may suggest lethal injection will produce instantaneous and painless death, but again, in reality, it may not.

Oklahoma inmate Richard Glossip challenged the use of midazolam when he sued the State of Oklahoma after the botched execution of Clayton Lockett in

April 2014. Glossip's main argument against the use of midazolam highlighted the drug's failure to render inmates completely unconscious during execution. During Lockett's execution, Oklahoma administered 100 milligrams of midazolam, which failed to leave him fully unconscious. Because of this, "Lockett began to move and speak," causing the lethal injection team to cancel the execution (*Glossip v. Gross*, quoting Justice Scalia, 7). After 40 chaotic minutes, Lockett died on the gurney from cardiac arrest.

Glossip's legal challenge threatened to upend the nation's entire lethal injection system; however, the Supreme Court rejected his claim. The Court noted that if Lockett had been administered the appropriate 500 milligrams of midazolam, as required by Oklahoma's lethal injection protocol, the execution would have proceeded without a hitch (*Glossip v. Gross*, quoting Justice Scalia, 6). Thus, rather than illustrating a systemic problem, the Lockett case was a mere isolated incident. Of course, other justices disagreed, and the *Glossip* decision generated a strongly argued dissent from Justice Breyer in which he called for a full examination of the basic question of the constitutionality of capital punishment itself. Oklahoma's death penalty system came to a grinding halt as a grand jury investigation found widespread failure to follow procedures, incompetence, and errors; several top personnel were forced to resign, including the state's secretary of corrections (see Berman 2016). Charles Warner's botched execution on January 15, 2015, which used the wrong drugs, was the last in Oklahoma at least through 2017, as the state investigates the problems with its system (see Cross 2016). In April 2017 a statewide commission issued a scathing report citing a lack of confidence in Oklahoma's death penalty system and calling for a continuation of the moratorium (see Oklahoma Death Penalty Review Commission 2017).

The degree to which lethal injection has become mired in seemingly endless legal fights can be illustrated further with a recent case from Missouri. There, a drugmaker argued that it has a constitutional right to anonymity based on its First Amendment right to free speech. The pharmacy that provided drugs to the state department of corrections argued that doing so was an expression of its right to make political speech and is therefore protected under the First Amendment. Being identified would infringe its rights. Therefore, like the executioners of old, drug suppliers argued in court that they should be able to be anonymous, shrouded not by a hood but by a cloak of legal secrecy (see Feldman 2016; McDaniel and Geidner 2016).

Arizona corrections officials faced lawsuits from seven death row inmates based on previous botched executions there and reached a settlement mandating extensive reforms in execution procedures, including reduced discretion in determining dosages and procedures to be followed during an exectution and replacing the three-drug cocktail with a single massive dose of either pentobarbital or sodium pentothal (see Campbell 2017). Dale Baich, attorney for the inmates, commented that the state is "now taking appropriate steps to decrease the risk that prisoners will be tortured to death." Litigation will likely continue for some time even if the settlement is approved by a federal judge, as the state has no supply of the needed drugs, has no immediate plans to issue a death warrant, and faces separate legal challenges from news agencies seeking information on the source of drugs and the qualifications of those on the execution team (Christie 2017).

The Judicial Paradox

In confronting issues of lethal injection in *Baze* and then in *Glossip*, the Court has had to deal with the question of how much pain is too much. Justice Scalia, for example, noted that "the Constitution does not require the avoidance of all risk of pain" (*Glossip v. Gross*, 4). The Court has come to distinguish between "isolated errors" (e.g., when a corrections official makes a mistake or fails to follow the protocol, leading to a botched execution) and systematic patterns by which errors occur in a predictable or repetitive manner. It has distinguished between unnecessary pain and suffering (which is not acceptable under the Constitution) and pain that is the "inescapable consequence of death" (*Baze v. Rees*, quoting Chief Justice Roberts, 11). Finally it has asked whether "any risk of harm was substantial when compared to a known and available alternative method of execution" (*Glossip v. Gross*, 2), causing some to infer that the petitioners are being asked to suggest a better execution method.

Gregg prohibited the "unnecessary and wanton infliction of pain" (quoting Justices Stewart, Powell, and Stevens, 173); indeed, the first case to consider electrocution, that involving William Kemmler, stated that the Eighth Amendment forbade all forms of execution that go beyond "the mere extinguishment of life" or which involve "torture or a lingering death" (*In re Kemmler*, 447).

The years between *Baze* and *Glossip* have seen waves of litigation against lethal injection. Between April 2008 and May 2013, approximately 333 cases cited *Baze*. These citations are applied to a variety of concerns such as the adequacy of the state's protocol, executioner qualifications, drug procurement, and drug choices. Furthermore, the Court has regularly rejected these various claims, typically ruling that the petitioners failed to prove substantial risks or failed to provide tenable alternatives. Most defense attorneys are loath to suggest to the government how best to kill their clients; they only object to those methods that are proposed. The Court has said the punishment need not be perfect but must be the "best available" solution to the problem. Defense attorneys refuse to tell the Court which alternatives would be acceptable. The result is a paradox.

Lethal injection is a medical procedure. The drugs required are the same as those used for therapeutic purposes. This creates an association between capital punishment and healthcare that pharmaceutical companies and other medical professionals repudiate. The administration of those drugs requires skills such as IV access and consciousness monitoring. Lethal injection demands the participation of a profession that now rejects it. Whenever the Court, a legislature, or an attorney delves into the details of anesthesiology, but those with medical training stay away, we should have a consensus that neither a law degree, nor judicial appointment, nor elective office constitutes relevant qualifications for judgment. And yet, since *Baze*, the courts have constantly been embroiled in exactly these kinds of questions. The stakes are high. As Justice Sotomayor wrote in her dissent in *Glossip*, the states' lethal injection protocols create at least the possibility of an "excruciatingly painful death hidden behind a veneer of medication" (*Glossip v. Gross*, 31).

Conclusion

Firing squads, hangings, electrocution, and lethal gas were replaced as primary execution methods when growing societal concerns began to mount pressure on state legislatures, and innovators proclaimed they had discovered a new and improved, more humane and civilized method of execution. Today, the ultimate result of that process, lethal injection, is in deep question. But without declaring the death penalty unconstitutional, the Supreme Court has so far refused to rule that any of these methods is, in itself, torture. In the absence of a Court finding that lethal injection protocols are inherently unreliable, any botched execution can be said to be an isolated case. Of course, states could move to other forms of execution, such as the firing squad or hanging, removing the medical professional entirely from the process. However, in US history we have never gone back to a previously rejected form of execution. Rather, we have consistently "progressed" from the "barbaric" and "inhumane" practices of the past to a higher level of enlightenment and civilization. Such are the demands of evolving standards of decency.

Further Readings

Brandon, Craig. 1999. *The Electric Chair: An Unnatural American History.* Jefferson, NC: McFarland.

Dieter, Richard C. 2008. Methods of Execution and Their Effect on the Use of the Death Penalty in the United States. *Fordham Urban Law Journal* 35 (4): 789–816.

Drimmer, Frederick. 2014. *Executions in America.* New York: Skyhorse.

Galvin, Anthony. 2015. *Old Sparky: The Electric Chair and the History of the Death Penalty.* New York: Skyhorse.

King, Gilbert. 2011. Edison vs. Westinghouse: A Shocking Rivalry. *Smithsonian.com*, October 11.

Nathan, Alison J., and Bruce A. Green. 2007. Brief for the Fordham University School of Law, Louis Stein Center for Law and Ethics as *Amicus Curiae* in Support of Petitioners. *Baze v. Rees* 07-5439. November 13.

Sarat, Austin. 2014. *Gruesome Spectacles: Botched Executions and America's Death Penalty.* Stanford, CA: Stanford University Press.

11

How Often Are Executions Delayed or Canceled?

The execution of Troy Davis on September 20, 2011, was a worldwide news event followed by millions.[1] Mr. Davis, a black man from Savannah, Georgia, was accused of killing a white police officer, Mark MacPhail. The case of Troy Davis had come to encapsulate many of the issues associated with the death penalty: violence, poverty, race, southern culture, arbitrariness, claims of innocence, a sympathetic victim, and redemption. But it also was typical in another way that is less widely understood and discussed: it was uncertain right to the last minute. Further, this was not Davis's first appointment with the death chamber; it was his fourth. Three previous dates had been canceled (July 17, 2007, canceled one day before; September 23, 2008; canceled hours before, as he was strapped to the gurney; and October 27, 2008, canceled a few days before). The day before Mr. Davis was actually executed, he was considered and denied for clemency. His last day alive was a frenzy of legal appeals, including a "hail Mary" appeal to the US president, who had no authority over the matter in Davis's case. The US Supreme Court agreed to review Davis's petition for a stay of execution an hour *after* the execution was scheduled to occur. After some hours of deliberation, the Court denied the request, and Davis was executed at approximately 11:00 p.m. that night; the execution had been scheduled for 7:00 p.m. (see Marlowe, Davis-Correia and Davis 2013). In this chapter, we show that such "dances with death" are not uncommon, surprising as that may seem.

In chapter 7 we showed some surprising facts about how common it is for death sentences to be reversed on appeal. In fact, this is the typical scenario: more than half are eventually reversed. In this chapter we document the similarly poorly known fact that it is not uncommon for scheduled death dates to be canceled, often at the last moment. The emotional toll of these "almost" executions is excruciating for all involved, whether they be associated with the inmate or the original crime victim. No one in the criminal justice system particularly likes to publicize or focus on the frenzied and unpredictable atmosphere that often accompanies state efforts to carry out executions. But we do so here.

While most Americans may not realize the likelihood that scheduled executions can be canceled or delayed at the last minute, those with experience in the system are well aware. David Dow (2005), who has represented death row inmates in Texas since the 1980s, describes numerous examples of his last-minute efforts to save his clients. Of course, working in Houston, he often fails and then has to turn his attention immediately to the client with the nearest approaching execution date. A strange but logical process of triage implies that legal attention and firepower be directed at the client in the most imminent danger of death, and an impending death warrant certainly focuses attention. The same appears true not only for defense attorneys, often desperately filing appeals when time is literally running out, but also for judges, governors, and members of the Supreme Court. With death imminent unless they act, the decision to delay or to allow the process to continue is literally one of life or death. Therefore, stays are often granted even if only for the purpose of allowing a fuller hearing of a particular matter, eventually to be decided against the interest of the inmate. We have, then, a process that appears to be back-weighted with numerous legal maneuvers occurring in the weeks, days, and even the hours before the appointed time arrives. Many of these are, in fact, successful, as we will see in this chapter. And when they are not, they are very often still in play until the last minute. That is, death remains uncertain until it occurs. Many inmates have had their last meals, or even been strapped to the gurney, before seeing their appointment with death called off.

During a trial and throughout the appellate process, the US system is one of adversarial justice: each side seeks a particular outcome, and the court is the venue through which each side should have a fair opportunity to make its case. As we noted in chapter 2, however, the state has the opportunity to set a death date at any time after direct appeals are exhausted. In many cases, collateral appeals are ongoing. That is to say, an inmate's attorneys may still be following state postconviction or federal habeas litigation even as the governor or other state official sets an execution date. Defense attorneys must then ask for these death warrants to be stayed while they file appeals. These requests for stays, we shall see, are most often successful, particularly in some states. In fact, the adversarial contest between the state attempting to carry out the death sentence and the defense attorney trying to protect his or her client generally continues to the very last minute. "Finality" (for the legal process) comes only at the moment of execution, not a minute before.

In her book *The Death of Innocents*, Sister Helen Prejean, like David Dow, describes a number of cases of canceled executions, in all of which there was significant evidence of innocence. Dobie Gillis Williams had 11 death dates, including 2 that were stayed only at the last minute, before he was executed in Louisiana in 1999 (see Prejean 2005, 3). For Prejean, a Catholic nun, the process is akin to torture (involving the warning of a punishment, then withdrawing it, re-establishing the threat, withdrawing, and re-establishing without any certainty on the part of the inmate if any one of those times will be real) or an involuntary Russian roulette.

It is shocking and surprising to most Americans that duly imposed death sentences, solemnly chosen by the jury and ceremoniously called out in court by a black-robed judge, would be overturned as often on appeal as we documented in chapter 7. Just the fact of hearing a judge intone, "May God have mercy on your soul" and perhaps some details about the manner in which the state will put one to death, on order of the jury sitting only a few feet away, would be enough to give most individuals traumatic fits. But to know that it is typically a false promise, that the vast majority of death sentences are not in fact carried out, has to make one question why it is done in this manner. In this chapter, we add to these concerning facts by focusing not on the initial stage of the death sentence but on the final stages of scheduling, then carrying out, the actual execution.

Justice Breyer explicitly raises these issues, in particular uncertainty, in his dissent in *Glossip*. It is worth quoting at some length:

> The dehumanizing effect of solitary confinement is aggravated by uncertainty as to whether a death sentence will in fact be carried out. In 1890, this Court recognized that, "when a prisoner sentenced by a court to death is confined in the penitentiary awaiting the execution of the sentence, one of the most horrible feelings to which he can be subjected during that time is the uncertainty during the whole of it." *Medley, supra*, at 172. The Court was there *describing a delay of a mere four weeks*. In the past century and a quarter, little has changed in this respect—except for duration. Today we must describe delays measured, not in weeks, but in decades. (Breyer, in *Glossip*, 20)

At least three concerns are relevant to Justice Breyer's use of the 1890 *Medley* decision: solitary confinement, the length of confinement, and the anticipation of an uncertain execution. We know that solitary confinement, especially for prolonged periods, is a particularly harsh punishment; is it reasonable to *accumulate* the death penalty with solitary confinement? Second, as discussed in chapter 8, and following the *Lackey* controversy, is there any allowable time limit to the pre-execution confinement of an inmate? Whereas Lackey's case was rejected after 16 years on death row, Thomas Knight was executed after 39 years. Is there any constitutional time limit to this question? Finally, there is the question of uncertainty, our focus here.

Death Warrants

Although the process differs by state, typically the governor, attorney general, or director of corrections has the authority (but not the requirement) to set a date of execution for any inmate who has exhausted all "direct appeals" following his or her death sentence. However, as we know from chapter 2, direct appeals can be followed by years of collateral or habeas litigation. The state, however, does not have to wait for these to be complete. Indeed, because the inmate never loses the right to allege a violation of due process, and new evidence could emerge decades after the original trial, any execution date will necessarily be set before "finality" emerges. And in the adversarial system that we have, there is no incentive whatsoever for the inmate to forgo his or her rightful appeals. For those who do, many are "volunteers," often profoundly depressed or mentally ill inmates seeking "suicide by state" (see chapter 8).

As mentioned in chapter 2, the execution process begins with the issuance of a death warrant. Table 11.1 indicates which state official has the authority to issue death warrants, as the process differs substantially from state to state. All have in common, however, that the state has the option either to set the death date or simply to wait. Different states are more or less aggressive in this behavior. Some might set a date knowing full well that it has a high likelihood of being rejected by a court once the inmate's attorneys file such a request. Others might not set a date in such a case, preferring to wait until all legal avenues have been exhausted. The state is the first mover in a game that may have several moves and countermoves.

Though the timeline varies by state protocol, typically, once a death warrant has been issued, the Department of Corrections or the otherwise responsible office must set an execution date no less than 30 days but no more than 90 days after notification. For example, in the state of Arizona the warrant requires an execution date to be set between "thirty-five and sixty days following the issuance of a warrant" (A.R.S. §7.1-13-759), while protocol in Oklahoma requires a minimum of 60 and maximum of 90 days between issuance of the warrant and the potential execution date (22 O.S. §22-1001). The warrant typically specifies a window of time for the

Table 11.1 **Power to Issue Death Warrant, by State**

Actor	States
Governor	Arkansas, Florida, Kentucky, New Hampshire, Pennsylvania
State supreme court	Alabama, Arizona, Indiana, Mississippi, Missouri, Ohio, South Carolina, Tennessee
Trial Court Judge	California, Colorado, Delaware, Georgia, Idaho, Kansas, Louisiana, Montana, Nevada, Oregon, South Dakota, Texas, Utah, Virginia, Washington, Wyoming
State attorney general	North Carolina
State court of criminal appeals	Oklahoma

Note: Death warrants in federal capital cases are issue by trial court judges; in military cases, the secretary of the army, following affirmation of the sentence by the president, does so.

Source: Compiled from DPIC and state sources.

execution to take place. In Texas, it is typically "after 6:00 p.m. on June X, 2016" or something similar. Such wording means that the warrant expires at midnight.

The issuance of a death warrant is determined by individual state protocols, but it may be signed at any time following the conclusion of an inmate's direct appeals or when the period in which the opportunity to file such petitions has expired. In many states, the issuance of a death warrant is largely determined by the appellate actions taken by the defendant within the time frame for collateral review set forth by the state; should the defendant not meet the deadlines to pursue continued postconviction relief, a warrant and subsequent execution date may be issued. What all this means is that nothing can happen until direct appeals are done, a process that is often successful, and which typically takes many years. After that, the states differ with regard to deadlines for their own postconviction review. Virginia, as we saw in chapter 7, has strict deadlines and the highest execution rate for its condemned inmates. Other states have slower processes. Ohio has announced execution dates for inmates out through 2019, though as of the beginning of 2016 it had suspended all executions through 2017 because it had no supply of drugs. As of June 2017, however, James Frazier sits on Ohio's death row, with the date of October 17, 2019, set for his execution.[2] Dozens of other inmates similarly know their "date." In sum, each state does things differently, and some are more aggressive while others are more passive. No matter the process, when the period for appeals has been exhausted, the state then has the *option* to set an execution date.

When a death warrant is issued, this often prompts a new wave of emergency appeals and requests for executive clemency on behalf of the defendant. The inmate's attorneys may seek clemency from the governor, which would permanently remove the inmate from the threat of death, and separately seek a stay from the courts. A stay is simply a temporary cancellation of the scheduled execution date so that a further legal proceeding may take place. Stays of execution can be granted by a state or federal court and, like any decision, may be appealed. Stays are sometimes issued almost immediately after a warrant is signed, and at other times only minutes before an inmate is scheduled to die. They are often appealed immediately by the other side, and the stay can be vacated as quickly as it was put in place. As noted at the beginning of this chapter, on the day he was executed, Troy Davis actually received a stay, coming one hour into the execution time window. The stay was reversed a few hours later, however, and the execution was carried out. Had there been a longer delay, the death warrant would have expired and a new one would have been needed, leading to another delay depending on Georgia law; typically 30 days is the minimum.

Stays, by definition, are not permanent resolutions of the underlying legal issue; they are simply delays of death so that the legal process can proceed. If successful, the stay grants time for legal review, and that review either may lead to the reversal of the death sentence, making any future death warrant a moot question, or it may not. In that case, the process continues, and the state may set another date for execution.

While stays of execution are common, the process of attaining one is by no means simple. Inmates requesting a stay must pass a four-part test: (1) whether it is likely that the inmate will prevail in his or her petition; (2) whether the prisoner will sustain some kind of irremediable harm if the stay is denied; (3) what potential harm the stay could cause to third parties (e.g., the families of the victims); and (4) whether granting the stay would offer a benefit to the public interest (Swallows 1993). Because of the first of these requirements, courts do not grant frivolous stays—there must be some chance that the inmate has a legitimate legal issue that deserves a fuller hearing than can be done in the time remaining. In the event that an inmate has already had a previous execution date stayed, and is petitioning for further stays, additional burdens must be met, including the presentation of new grounds for relief (Swallows 1993). Thus, an inmate cannot continually make the same argument just to gain more time. In sum, while stays are common, they are by no means automatic. If nothing else, we know this from the fact that 1,422 executions have been carried out through 2015.

Reasons for Stays

The Death Penalty Information Center provides short descriptions of stays granted from 2010 through 2015; no other full database is available. Table 11.2 summarizes the reasons that stays are given.

The table shows a total of 285 stays; there were 234 executions during this period. The greatest number of stays are categorized as "other," which includes simply "allowing time for appellate review" or similar explanations, but without explaining what the legal issue was. Controversies over lethal injection procedures

Table 11.2 **Reasons for Stays, by Year**

Year	Supreme Court	Commutation	Evidence Review	Lethal Injection Protocol	Mental Capacity	Flawed Trial	State Moratorium	Other
2010	2	6	1	12	4	1	0	17
2011	6	3	4	14	1	0	1	14
2012	2	2	4	6	9	4	0	27
2013	0	1	4	5	4	1	0	18
2014	3	1	0	17	3	0	5	29
2015	2	0	4	11	2	2	7	26
Total	15	13	17	65	23	8	13	131

Source: Compiled from DPIC reports.

of course have been particularly prominent in recent executions, and these are the second most common justification for stays. Mental capacity or *Atkins* claims are common as well. Appellate review of new or contested evidence has occurred 17 times; Supreme Court acceptance of cert occurred just 15 times; 13 executions have been stayed by state moratoria. (In these cases, all executions in a state were put on hold.) Governors' commutations also occurred 13 times in this period.

Reasons for stays range from "clerical error in setting the execution date" to constitutional challenges, with lethal injection being the most common cause in the past six years. Because a stay is typically a judicial act, it can be appealed and reversed. In contrast to the glacial pace of most appeals (sometimes taking years just to schedule a hearing), successive last-minute appeals, stays, and reversals can take place within hours.

State moratoria are a more important category than suggested in the table because they result in a stay for any executions where a death warrant has already been issued but also prohibit the issuance of any new warrants. A number of states have recently instituted these moratoria, generally citing broad reviews of their capital punishment protocol. Other states have halted executions based on the moral scruples of state leadership regarding the death penalty itself. In 2013, Governor John Hickenlooper of Colorado issued a stay for inmate Nathan Dunlap, citing what he saw as a need for reconsideration of the death penalty. Because this indefinite stay was not made on the basis of facts particular to Dunlap's case, it is likely that this moratorium will remain in place for all scheduled death row inmates while Hickenlooper remains in office (*Denver Post* 2013). Similarly, in February 2015, Governor Tom Wolf of Pennsylvania issued a reprieve for all inmates on death row, citing a need for a broad evaluation of the state's capital punishment system (Office of the Governor 2015). A legislatively mandated study is currently being conducted, and the stays remain in place. Controversy surrounds the order, as district attorneys complained that the governor had overstepped his powers. However, in a state where no inmate has involuntarily been executed in modern times, Wolf's call for a broad review is not surprising. As we will see later in this chapter, Pennsylvania had been routinely issuing death warrants only to see them routinely set aside.

Supreme Court review often involves a stay. As a court of last recourse, the Supreme Court does not get involved in issues until they have been fully considered by lower courts. However, in the matter of immediately pending executions, this is not always possible. In order to attain a writ of certiorari from the Supreme Court, a petitioner must show that there is a reasonable chance that at least four justices on the Court would regard the underlying issues in question to be legitimate, that there is a significant probability of reversal, and again that there is a risk of irreparable harm if cert is not granted. Although it only takes the votes of four justices to grant cert, it takes five votes to grant a stay. It is not uncommon for a fifth justice to vote for a stay simply to allow more time for consideration of the petitioner's claim before the decision is rendered moot by the inmate's execution (Swallows 1993). These peculiarities help explain why the Court is often involved in last-minute decisions, often in the middle of the night, as executions loom as in the case of Troy Davis described at the beginning of this chapter.

The most common reason, accounting for almost half of all recent stays, is litigation regarding lethal injection protocols. A number of high-profile cases have argued that a state's use of particular drugs constitute cruel and unusual punishment given that they do not protect an inmate from unnecessary pain. These cases are often brought to court following high-profile instances of botched lethal injection procedures during executions, as discussed in chapter 10, and later in this chapter in the case of Richard Glossip.

In fact, the longest recent period of a national moratorium on executions related to the litigation surrounding the 2008 case of *Baze v. Rees*, on the question of the constitutionality of a three-drug lethal injection procedure. No executions took place between September 26, 2007, and the Court's ruling on April 16, 2008, more than six months. Following the *Baze* ruling, executions resumed apace. However, botched executions were not uncommon, as we saw in chapter 10. And when previously available drugs were no longer available, inmates argued that the substitute drug was or might be unsafe. Issues relating to the availability of approved drugs have led to statewide moratoria. For instance, in April 2015, Ohio governor John Kasich granted a reprieve to 11 death row inmates scheduled for execution, delaying all executions in Ohio until at least 2017 due to an inability to attain the proper drugs needed to conduct the procedures (Welsh-Huggins 2015). In sum, litigation surrounding lethal injection has been tying the system in knots for almost a decade now.

Individual Case Studies

With 285 stays in six years during which 234 executions were carried out, it is clear that stays are quite common. Some inmates are executed on the first date set, but other cases seem so legally complex and murky that attorneys continue to argue to the last minute, and stay after stay occurs. Sister Helen's example of Dobie Gillis Williams, who had 10 stays (but 11 death warrants), serves to illustrate this dramatic difference. There is no national database that we can use to document each case fully. Here, instead, we provide a few illustrations of what can lead to a stay.

Charles Warner

Charles Warner was convicted in 2003 of the 1997 rape and murder of an 11-month-old infant girl and was scheduled to die by lethal injection in the Oklahoma death chamber on April 29, 2014. Warner shared this execution date with fellow inmate Clayton D. Lockett. Lockett was to be executed first, followed immediately by Warner. Having received his last meal and final visitation, Warner awaited his escort to the execution chamber. However, his trip to the death chamber never occurred that night. Warner's execution was canceled following the botched execution of Lockett, a debacle that lasted 43 minutes, resulting in Lockett's death by heart attack. The tremendous public outcry surrounding Lockett's execution resulted in a six-month stay of Warner's execution. Others were granted stays, as well. On November 13, Warner's execution was again stayed to allow the state to obtain drugs and train staff on a new protocol, with a new execution date set for January 15, 2015 (Connor 2015b).

Despite challenges to the constitutionality of Oklahoma's drug cocktail, The US Supreme Court rejected another stay of execution. Despite pleas, even from the victim's mother (Connor 2015b), Warner was ultimately executed on January 15, 2015, making him the first inmate executed by the State of Oklahoma since the Clayton Lockett execution. Warner's final words were "My body is on fire." An investigation into the autopsy report revealed that officials used potassium acetate rather than potassium chloride to stop Warner's heart (Peralta 2015). The use of the wrong drug in an execution, especially following Lockett's execution, raised many questions. Was the botched execution an isolated mishap or part of a systematic pattern? The state attorney general eventually empaneled a grand jury to look into how the department handled executions, and the director of the Department of Corrections resigned (see Brewer 2015).

To summarize, Warner, saw his date with death canceled only after Clayton Lockett's execution was severely botched. Investigations revealed that Lockett had had several doses of lethal drugs injected not into his veins but into muscle and eventually died of a heart attack after the execution had been called off as a failure. Warner, the next inmate executed, was killed by the wrong drug. The grand jury investigation led to discovery of widespread failure to follow the written protocols in any case. The Lockett and Warner executions were deep embarrassments to those involved, leading to the resignation of the leader of the department and to extensive continued litigation on the topic of whether the State of Oklahoma (which, as we saw in chapter 6, has had more experience with execution than any state but Texas) is capable of carrying out its execution protocol.

Oklahoma's execution protocol, not surprisingly, was subject to Supreme Court review shortly after the Warner execution; this time it related to Richard Glossip (Richinick 2015). Glossip is well known because his case calling into question the state's lethal injection protocol reached the Supreme Court; the case was originally *Warner v. Gross* but was renamed only after Warner was executed and no longer had legal standing to sue.

Richard Glossip

Richard Glossip has received four separate stays of execution (Connor 2015c) and remains on death row as of June 2017. Glossip was sentenced to death for paying co-worker Justin Sneed to murder his boss, Barry Van Treese, in 1997. Sneed pleaded guilty and testified against Glossip, receiving a sentence of life without parole (LWOP) (Berman 2015b). Much of the controversy surrounding Glossip's numerous stays of execution has been related to Oklahoma's lethal injection protocol. Glossip's first stay of execution was granted on October 13, 2014, when the state attorney general announced that the state lacked an adequate amount of drugs needed for the execution of Glossip and two other inmates (Lucero 2015). Glossip was granted yet another stay on January 28, 2015, one day prior to his scheduled execution (Lucero 2015). In a 5–4 decision, the Court held the Oklahoma lethal injection protocol and the usage of midazolam to be constitutional. The state then moved quickly to set a new execution date of September 16, 2015, for Glossip (Berman 2015b).

This latest execution date, however, would be pushed back yet again when the Oklahoma Court of Criminal Appeals granted Glossip another stay, this time only eight hours prior to his scheduled execution (Ford 2015). This latest stay, unlike the previous two, was not related to lethal injection protocol but rather dealt with a new challenge regarding Glossip's possible innocence, in particular, the potential inaccuracy of Justin Sneed's testimony on which the case for Glossip's guilt hinges (Ford 2015). The appeals court granted him a stay of two weeks, only eventually to rule against him (Lucero 2015). Following this latest attempt at reprieve, Glossip was scheduled to be executed on September 30, 2015 (Lucero 2015).

Once again, however, Glossip's execution was stayed in the eleventh hour by Oklahoma governor Mary Fallin. Her unexpected stay came despite the fact that the US Supreme Court denied Glossip's simultaneous petition. Fallin stated that her decision to stay the execution was to ensure that the drugs used in the execution complied with Oklahoma execution protocol. According to Fallin's order, the drug meant to be used for stopping Glossip's heart was potassium acetate, but the drug allowed for by the Oklahoma execution protocol is potassium chloride. Glossip was assigned a new execution date of November 6, 2015. After an investigation in October 2015 revealed that the January 2015 execution of Charles Warner had used the wrong drug, all executions were suspended, and a grand jury was empaneled to investigate the situation. Glossip remains on death row after having had dates with death set for October 13, 2014, and for January 28, September 16, and September 30, 2015; finally, in October 2015, a state moratorium was imposed (see Berman 2015b).

Manuel Valle

Manuel Valle, a Cuban national, was executed by the State of Florida on September 27, 2011, just a week after the execution of Troy Davis in neighboring Georgia. Valle had been convicted of killing a police officer in 1978. While Valle had had two previous execution dates stayed, his third request for a stay went to the US Supreme

Court and focused on the use of pentobarbital. A June 2011 execution using the drug had led Georgia inmate Roy Blankenship to "lurch," "grimace," and "keep his eyes open even into death" (Pilkington 2011).

Controversy surrounding the use of pentobarbital intensified when Staffan Schuberg, head of the Danish drug company responsible for the manufacture and distribution of the drug, wrote to Florida governor Rick Scott. Schuberg urged Scott not to allow the company's drug to be used in executions, citing the fact that it is untested for such a purpose and could cause intense suffering (Pilkington 2011). Despite the delays in execution granted to Valle, the courts eventually rejected his claims. In the end, the Court considered the stay for approximately three hours before allowing the execution to go ahead. Valle's lawyers also argued that administrative hurdles had stopped them from being able to make a final plea to the governor for clemency. Valle was executed after several hours' delay on September 27, 2011. Valle's time on death row was among the longest, with more than 33 years in solitary confinement.

Warren Lee Hill

Warren Lee Hill faced the execution chamber four times in the course of one year prior to his eventual execution in Georgia on January 27, 2015. Hill was already serving a life sentence for the 1986 murder of his girlfriend when he beat a fellow inmate to death using a nail-studded board. Upon his conviction in 1991, he was sentenced to death. Hill endured a rigorous appeals process, with his lawyers asserting strong claims of intellectual disability. The case of *Atkins v. Georgia* (2002) gave some hope to Hill's attorneys that they could demonstrate his intellectual disability, but Georgia insisted that they had not proven this "beyond a reasonable doubt" though Hill's IQ was tested to be 70. Warren Hill received two stays within minutes of the scheduled execution times. Hill was first set to be executed in July 2012. After he ate his last meal and said goodbye to his family, the execution was stayed 90 minutes before it was to begin. His subsequent execution date, set for February 2013, was once again stayed, this time only 30 minutes prior to the scheduled time after Hill had been strapped to a gurney and injected with a sedative. His third execution date, set for July 2013, was stayed only four hours prior to the scheduled time. The mental distress inflicted by these last-minute stays was exacerbated by Hill's intellectual disability, which left him unable to make sense of his circumstances (Khalek 2013).

Warren Hill received enormous support for clemency, including support from the victim's family. Furthermore, former jurors expressed remorse, indicating they were not given the option of LWOP during the sentencing phase (Gallman 2015). Brian Kammer, Hill's lawyer of 20 years, deemed his execution a "grotesque miscarriage of justice" and one that will continue to live on as a "moral stain" on the State of Georgia and the court system (Connor 2015a).

John Balentine

John Balentine was sentenced to death on April 19, 1999, for murdering his ex-girlfriend's brother and two other teenage boys as they slept. He remains on death row as of June 2017 but has made three trips to the execution chamber. The first was on September 30, 2009, when the US Court of Appeals for the Fifth Circuit granted a stay one day before he was scheduled to die. The second came two years later, on June 15, 2011, when the US Supreme Court granted a stay within an hour of the scheduled execution. The third was on August 22, 2012, when the US Supreme Court granted another stay, again about an hour before he was to be executed. This time, the Court granted the stay to allow Ballantine time to bring claims that his court-appointed trial counsel had been ineffective for neglecting to present mitigating factors, such as emotional problems and a difficult childhood. This was Balentine's third last-minute stay and was presumably for a legal problem that had occurred well before the first execution date had been set and canceled. The trip between the Texas death row unit in Polunsky and the execution chamber, which is 100 miles away in Huntsville, is designed to be one-way. Balentine has made the round-trip voyage three times; as of January 2017, he continues to await execution (see Forsyth 2012; updated status from the Texas Department of Criminal Justice website, https://www.tdcj.state.tx.us/death_row/dr_offenders_on_dr.html).

Kelly Gissendaner

Kelly Gissendaner was convicted of murder on November 18, 1998, for recruiting her boyfriend to kill her husband and was sentenced to death. On February 9, 2015, the Gwinnett County Superior Court issued an order for the Georgia Department of Corrections to execute Gissendaner. On February 25, 2015, her execution was temporarily stayed due to inclement winter weather. On March 2, while they were waiting for a response from the US Supreme Court, correctional officials postponed the 7:00 p.m. execution because the lethal injection drugs appeared cloudy. (State officials later reported that the drugs were cloudy because they had been stored at the wrong temperature.) Gissendaner had already been removed from her cell and was in a holding area near the prison's death chamber. The execution was stayed at 11:00 p.m. due to this issue, four hours after it had been scheduled to occur. The next day, corrections officials announced that all executions would be put on hold until further drug analysis took place. On September 29, 2015, Gissendaner's execution, scheduled for 7:00 p.m., was put on hold due to pending appeals, and these appeals were denied by the US Supreme Court at 8:30, 10:45, and 11:30 p.m., successively. Gissendaner was finally executed around 12:30 a.m. on September 30, 2015. She was the first woman executed in Georgia in 70 years. The state kept her on death row for more than 20 years, canceled one death date because of the weather, another because it had mishandled the drugs, and then carried out the third date only after pending appeals were handled at the last second, pushing into the window of death and maintaining uncertainty for more than three hours before eventually killing her (see Berman 2015a).

Jeffrey Wood

Texas stayed the August 24, 2016, execution of Jeffrey Wood after a national outcry about killing a man who was essentially uninvolved in the murder. Under the "law of parties," Wood was responsible for the crime of Daniel Reneau, even though Wood was in a car while Reneau killed a convenience store clerk. Reneau was executed in 2002. A federal judge reversed a 2008 execution date for Wood, mandating further state review of Wood's mental competency and eligibility for the death penalty, given his intellectual disability. The state reviewed and affirmed its plan to execute him. As the 2016 execution date approached, objections came from many sources, including Texas Republican lawmakers, and on August 19 the Texas Court of Criminal Appeals remanded the case back to lower courts because of the involvement of Dr. James Grigson (see chapter 5), who testified in Wood's case that he "would certainly" post a future risk. Wood had been in the car at the time of the murder, not in the store, had no previous criminal history, and was intellectually disabled (see Associated Press 2016).

This small number of illustrations should make clear what those familiar with the death penalty already know: the adversarial process continues up to the end. Unless the inmate gives instructions to attorneys to cease all litigation on his or her behalf (and the inmate is found competent to make this decision), state efforts to schedule and carry out an execution will be met with every legal option; defense attorneys are under an ethical obligation to save the life of their client, and setting a death date focuses attention on that case. Courts follow strict rules on when to grant a stay, but stays are nonetheless common. In the next section we review more systematic evidence that shows just how common these can be.

Pennsylvania Case Study

We cannot say how often executions are delayed at the last minute, to be rescheduled for an hour, a month, or a year later, or to be canceled altogether; no one gathers this information. Pennsylvania, however, provides the opportunity for a full assessment of what happens following a death warrant, since its death warrants, and the outcomes stemming from them, are public records. In this section we review the results of every death warrant in the commonwealth during the modern period. In fact, no death warrant has ever been carried out in Pennsylvania except for three where the inmates volunteered. But more than 400 executions have been scheduled.

Tom Wolf became governor of Pennsylvania on January 20, 2015; on February 13
he was faced with a death warrant for Terrence Williams. Williams had been on death
row for nearly three decades and had received his third death warrant four weeks prior.
Wolf not only granted Williams temporary relief but also pledged to "grant a reprieve
in each future instance in which an execution is scheduled," effectively enacting a moratorium on executions until the state's Capital Punishment Task Force completes its
review of the system and its recommendations are "sufficiently" put into effect (Office
of the Governor 2015). Governor Wolf's decision came after many called into question the deeply flawed elements of the state's efforts to put inmates to death.

Home to the fifth-largest death row population in the country, Pennsylvania has
imposed a sentence of death on 417 individuals since reinstating capital punishment in 1978. As shown in Table 11.3, Pennsylvania's death sentence outcomes
reflect an extremely inefficient system, with 188 individuals' sentences having been
overturned, 190 inmates remaining on death row as they continue their appeals
process, and only 3 inmates executed, all of whom were volunteers.

In chapter 7 we noted that, along with the US federal government, Pennsylvania
is an example of "warehousing." While many inmates see their sentences overturned, many others simply languish on death row. But while they are on death row,
they routinely are issued death warrants, which later are dismissed. While a scholar
or analyst may understand the history and trends associated with the Pennsylvania
death penalty system, the inmate is under serious threat of death, or so it would
appear from the wording of the death warrant. The process also involves notifying
victim and inmate families and loved ones of the date and instructing the inmate's
families on how to retrieve the body (see Dunham 2015).

Since August 1, 1985, Pennsylvania governors have signed 448 death warrants
for 259 inmates, with several inmates being the recipient of more than 1 warrant,

Table 11.3 **Pennsylvania Capital Sentence Dispositions, 1973–2013**

Disposition	Number of Sentences	Percentage of All Sentences
On death row	190	45.6
Sentence overturned	188	45.1
Executed	3	0.7
Commutation	6	1.4
Natural death or suicide	30	7.2
Total	417	100.00

Note: Compiled from annual reports from the Pennsylvania
Department of Corrections. "Sentence overturned" includes six individuals who were exonerated.

and only 3 warrants resulting in an execution. The remaining 445 death warrants could be classified as legally premature, meaning they were "directed at individuals who had not had an opportunity to obtain at least one level of judicial review to which they were legally entitled" (Dunham 2015). As a result, except for the three inmates who instructed their attorneys to let the process run its course, each and every death warrant has been rescinded. But hundreds of inmates have endured a false threat of death at a particular moment, sometimes many times; similarly, the surviving family members of the victims of crime have falsely been told to expect an execution that in fact would never come.

Pennsylvania changed its policies in 1995 at the urging of newly elected Governor Tom Ridge (later US secretary of Homeland Security under President George W. Bush). At a time of heightened concern with crime, and at the peak use of the death penalty, Governor Ridge was concerned that Pennsylvania was not carrying out its death sentences, and he convened a special session of the state legislature to deal with various crime issues. In this special session, the legislature expanded the range of crimes for which the death penalty was possible but also mandated that the governor be officially informed of every death sentence once it was confirmed by the state supreme court, and that within 90 days his office either pardon the inmate, commute the sentence, or issue a death warrant. Upon failure of the governor to act, the secretary of corrections was to issue the warrant at the expiry of the deadline. Readers will recall from chapter 2 that all condemned inmates have a right of direct appeal through the state and federal court system. In Pennsylvania, the law was set up to require a death warrant well before this process could possibly have been completed, as federal appeals typically take years and the federal government typically does not intervene until state review has been completed.

Pennsylvania's reforms in 1995, along with the federal Antiterrorism and Effective Death Penalty Act of 1996, give a sense of the political winds at the time. They were blowing strongly in the direction of getting on with more executions. In retrospect, they came right at the moment of peak usage; since these reforms, counterintuitively, death sentences have declined, reversals have continued, and executions have not been restarted in the commonwealth. But, as we will see, this is not for a lack of effort, at least by some actors in Pennsylvania.

Based on annual reports from the Pennsylvania Department of Corrections, we compiled a complete list of all death warrants and their outcomes. Our database includes the inmate name, death sentence date, county of origin, and the date and outcome of the warrant; note that the same inmate may have multiple warrants. We can analyze the 448 death warrants in various ways, and we do so in several tables here. Table 11.4 shows how long after a death sentence that the warrants are issued; Table 11.5 shows how long inmates live on death row under the threat of an active death warrant; and Table 11.6 shows how close to the execution time it is before the death warrant is canceled. Recall that all these warrants were canceled except for the three volunteers.

Table 11.4 Time from Death Sentence to Death Warrant

	Number	Percent	Cumulative Percent
Less than 2 years	11	4.4	4.4
2 to 4 years	87	34.8	39.2
4 to 6 years	59	23.6	62.8
6 to 10 years	57	22.8	85.6
10 to 15 years	20	8.0	93.6
15 years or more	16	6.4	100.0

Note: Includes 250 death warrants; only the first death warrant is included per inmate.

Table 11.5 Time under Threat of Death

A. By Death Warrant

	Number	Percent	Cumulative Percent
Less than 7 days	55	12.7	12.7
7 to 14 days	86	19.8	32.5
14 to 30 days	181	41.7	74.2
30 to 60 days	86	19.8	94.0
60 to 90 days	17	3.9	97.9
90 days or more	9	2.1	100.0

Note: Includes 434 death warrants, sometimes several per inmate.

B. By Inmate

	Number	Percent	Cumulative Percent
Less than 7 days	26	10.6	10.6
7 to 14 days	31	12.6	23.2
14 to 30 days	62	25.2	48.4
30 to 60 days	75	30.5	78.9
60 to 90 days	37	15.0	93.9
90 days or more	15	6.1	100.0

Note: Includes 246 inmates, across all their death warrants.

Table 11.6 **Time before the Scheduled Execution When the Stay Occurs**

Days	Number	Percent	Cumulative Percent
Less than 1 day	5	1.2	1.2
1 to 7 days	66	15.2	16.4
7 to 14 days	72	16.6	33.0
14 to 28 days	97	22.4	55.4
More than 28 days	193	44.6	100.0

Note: Includes 433 death warrants, sometimes several per inmate.

Death warrants come relatively quickly in Pennsylvania, just as the law is designed to ensure. The average time from death sentence to the first death warrant declined from 7.4 years for the 131 inmates sentenced before 1996 to 4.9 years for the 119 death sentences occurring in 1996 or later. The legislation worked as intended in other ways as well. There were no death warrants from 1979 through 1984; from 1985 to 1994, the number averaged 2.9 per year; but it increased to 31 in 1995 and reached 54 in 1999. Thus the law definitely generated many death warrants, and inmates were not long on death row before they received their first one. More important perhaps than the date of the initial death warrant are two other aspects of the issue: how long the warrants remain in effect, and how close to the scheduled execution date they come before being canceled.

Table 11.5 shows, first for each death warrant and then for each inmate, how long the death warrants remain in effect. Three-quarters are canceled less than 30 days after their issuance. But because an inmate may have several death warrants, in Part B of the table we show that many inmates live with an active death warrant for longer than that. The average total time spent under threat of death, per inmate, is 41 days, although it is not unheard of for inmates to spend a significantly longer period of time under threat of death. One inmate, Hubert Michael, has spent just under a year under the threat of death after being issued five separate death warrants and being granted a total of seven stays. While the lawyers involved may know that it is "only a matter of time" before the warrant will be canceled, certainly the inmates may feel differently. They are forced to cope with an active death warrant for weeks or months at a time. In modern times, Pennsylvania has never carried out a single death warrant against the wishes of the inmate. It is, truly, a hollow promise, but one that has been repeated more than 400 times.

Table 11.6 shows how close the inmates come to their death date before they are informed that the warrant has been canceled. Typically, the executions are canceled routinely and more than a month before the scheduled date of execution. However, 16 percent of the death warrants are still in effect one week before the scheduled date of execution, and five have been canceled only on the last day. Further, Table 11.7 shows that once an inmate survives an initial brush with scheduled death,

Table 11.7 **Total Number of Death Warrants, by Inmate**

Warrants	Inmates	Percent	Cumulative Percent
1	127	50.6	50.6
2	81	32.3	82.9
3	30	12.0	94.8
4	9	3.6	98.4
5	2	0.8	99.2
6	2	0.8	100.0

Note: Includes 251 inmates.

Table 11.8 **Death Warrants Issued to Inmates Later Removed from Death Row**

Warrants	Inmates	Percent	Cumulative Percent
1	32	39.5	39.5
2	39	48.2	87.7
3	6	7.4	95.1
4	4	4.9	100.0

Note: Includes 81 inmates later removed from death row by reversal of their death sentence. Does not include inmates who were executed, committed suicide, died from natural causes, had their sentence commuted by the governor, or have been removed while awaiting a new trial.

chances are about 50/50 that he or she will get another date. And among those who have had two dates, many get a third or fourth.

About half of all inmates who have been sentenced to death in Pennsylvania have later been removed from death row, and 6 have been exonerated. How many of these inmates have had uncomfortably close brushes with death? Table 11.8 shows that 81 inmates later removed from death row have in fact been issued death warrants, and r inmates, later deemed not to have been properly sentenced to death, received four death warrants.

Table 11.7 shows that 251 inmates have received at least one death warrant. In Table 11.8 we see that 81 of those death warrants were issued to individuals who would later be removed from death row. Harold Wilson, a poor black man from Philadelphia, was sentenced to death in October 1989 for a crime in which it was later shown he was completely uninvolved. He was released from prison a free man after being completely exonerated in 2005.[3] During Mr. Wilson's time on death row, however, he was twice scheduled to be executed. The first death warrant, issued on June 17, 1996, called for him to be executed on July 11. This was canceled on July 3, eight days before the death date. On November 20, 1996, another warrant was issued calling for his execution on December 12; this warrant was canceled on November 26. Governor Tom Ridge came very close to executing an innocent man. And then he did it again.

When Governor Ridge brought the legislature into special session in Harrisburg in 1995 to focus on crime, the point was to "get tough" on crime and criminals. As in many other state capitols, officials wanted to show their resolve, passing inarguably tough measures calling for expedited execution procedures, calling for more crimes to be eligible for the death penalty, and pushing to make a broken system work again. What they created, however, was no more effective. Twenty years later, another governor felt compelled by the accumulated evidence to call for a moratorium on executions in a system that provided nothing but false promises.

Similar Data from Florida

We cannot say how typical the extremely inefficient system we found in Pennsylvania may be. The state is, after all, an outlier nationally for its zeal in sentencing to death but its reluctance to carry out the sentences. Florida is different. We saw in chapter 1 that it was the first state in the nation to re-enact its death penalty statute after the *Furman* decision in 1972; its law was already in place by the end of the same calendar year. In chapter 6 we saw that it is the fourth state nationally in number of executions carried out: with 91 executions, it trails only Texas, Oklahoma, and Virginia nationally. The Florida Department of Corrections provides a web page showing information about each executed inmate, including the date of the offense, the death sentence date, the date of execution, the county of conviction, and, uniquely as far as we know, the number of death warrants issued to that individual. Because this is a list of all executed individuals, by definition one of those warrants was indeed carried out. (Our website includes a copy of the Florida web page, as well as a link to the original.) Of the 91 individuals executed, 88 have information listed concerning their death warrants. Of these, 31 were executed on the first warrant (9 of those individuals were volunteers). Twenty-nine inmates had two warrants, meaning they had one "false alarm" or canceled execution date. Sixteen had three warrants; 9 had four warrants, 2 had five warrants, and 1 individual had seven death warrants before being executed. Willie Darden was sentenced to death in January 1974 for a crime committed just four months previously. He served 14 years on Florida's death row before being executed in 1988. During those 14 years, he faced seven dates with death, just one of which was carried out. Thus, the average executed inmate faced one false alarm, and more than 30 percent faced two or more canceled dates with the executioner. Of course, this does not include those individuals who faced canceled execution dates who remain on death row today, who were later resentenced to a penalty other than death, or indeed those who may later have been declared innocent.

Conclusion

In a capital trial, life is on the line. At its conclusion, a judge solemnly intones the verdict: a jury of your peers has sentenced you to die. We saw in chapter 7 that the probability of carrying out such a solemn declaration is 16 percent. At the end of this process, when it is to be carried out, the appropriate authority issues a death warrant, specifying the exact time of death. Even when we get to these last stages of the process, however, a surprising degree of uncertainty remains. The adversarial process continues until the last minute, as lawyers joust, and appellate judges up to the justices of the Supreme Court intervene until the last second, and sometimes beyond the appointed hour as delays push the time of execution back further and further. Many inmates have shared the experience of Troy Davis, seeing several execution dates come and go, often after saying goodbye to their families, eating a last meal, and expecting the end to come. Many families of victims have similarly traveled to the execution chamber to observe the last breath of the killer of their loved one, only to leave without the experience they were told to expect.

Brian Evans of Amnesty International, in an interview related to the Warren Hill case discussed earlier in this chapter, suggests a parallel between a common form of torture, mock executions, and the situation in many US executions. Preparing for death, eating a last meal, saying goodbye to loved ones, being strapped to a gurney, then finding temporary relief bears substantial resemblance to a mock execution. As attorneys grapple with the law, as judges reverse decisions and see their own decisions reversed, and as all this happens at the last minute while an inmate is fully prepared to be put to death, is that torture? Evans notes that mock executions are indeed considered a form of torture under international law (see Khalek 2013). For US courts, there can be little doubt that the situations described in this chapter generate horrible psychological trauma for all those concerned, whether they be associated with the inmates or the original crime victims. The constitutional question may be whether these are inevitable or isolated incidents, or whether they are a systematic and avoidable part of the system. They certainly are not uncommon.

Further Readings

Peel, Diana. 2013. Clutching at Life, Waiting to Die: The Experience of Death Row Incarceration. *Western Criminology Review* 14 (3): 61–72.

Sharp, Susan F. 2005. *Hidden Victims: The Effects of the Death Penalty on Families of the Accused*. New Brunswick, NJ: Rutgers University Press.

Wermiel, Stephen. 2012. SCOTUS for Law Students (Sponsored by Bloomberg Law): Handling Stay Applications. October 26. http://www.scotusblog.com/2012/10/scotus-for-law-students-sponsored-by-bloomberg-law-handling-stay-applications/.

12

Mental Health

(WITH BETSY NEILL)

Throughout history, mental illness and intellectual disabilities (previously referred to as mental retardation) have been associated with a great deal of stigma and misunderstanding.[1] These elements can be heightened in the context of a capital murder trial. To understand the impact of mental illness in this context, we must look at the many factors that can contribute to mental illness and violent behaviors. Further, some elements of mental illness or disability may make the accused appear to lack remorse, respond inappropriately in trial, have difficulty assisting in or refuse to assist in his or her own defense, or appear to pose a heightened risk of future dangerousness. The US Supreme Court, in a long line of cases, has ruled that mental illness and intellectual disability are mitigating factors that render the defendant less culpable and less deserving of the death penalty. In practice, though, if they are not fully explained to a jury or a judge, mental illness and intellectual disability can paradoxically be viewed as aggravating rather than mitigating evidence. In Texas, where future dangerousness is a "special issue," many with mental illness, a history of childhood abuse, or other mental health problems have faced increased, not decreased, chances of a death sentence. In this chapter we explore the complex dynamics of mental illness, child abuse, substance abuse, and intellectual capacity; all are vastly over-represented among executed inmates as compared with the general population. We also look at that subset of inmates who have "volunteered" for death—their rates of mental illness are markedly higher. A central theme here is not only that mental illness and intellectual disabilities are vastly over-represented on the nation's death rows and among those executed, but indeed that these factors, said by the Court to merit leniency, in fact are associated with greater likelihood of a death sentence and execution. Further, with regard to those inmates who have volunteered for execution, many have been suicidal. In the context of death row, dropping appeals and allowing the machinery to go forward without resistance is a means of death not available to the general public: suicide with government assistance.

A mental illness can be caused by biological or environmental factors, but it is almost always a combination of both. However, some mental illnesses can be more attributed to biological factors than others. Schizophrenia, for example, is accompanied by a long list of biological abnormalities, whereas post-traumatic stress disorder (PTSD) is more commonly attributed to environmental factors. This being said, schizophrenia is also influenced by environmental factors, and PTSD is also influenced by biological factors. The disorders that are more heavily attributed to biological factors such as bipolar disorder and psychotic disorders normally develop regardless of whether an individual is imprisoned. The disorders more heavily attributed to environmental factors such as depression and suicidal tendencies can develop before or as a result of an inmate's experience in prison. In this chapter, we explore the prevalence of mental illness among inmates executed between 2000 and 2015, some 824 individuals.[2] Not surprisingly, our review suggests that serious mental illness is very common among those executed.

We must distinguish clearly between mental illness and intellectual disability, which are distinct factors and are treated differently by the courts. Since *Atkins* (2005), no inmate may be subject to the death penalty if he or she shows an IQ of 70 or lower and has adaptive behavioral issues, the court's definition of intellectual disability. States have contested whether the IQ marker of 70 is a firm rule; how to handle the margin of error when one test shows slightly above and another slightly below that number; and what kinds and degree of adaptive behavioral issues can be used to demonstrate that the inmate is on one side or the other of the line. But *Atkins* made clear that an inmate who is determined to have an intellectual disability may not be sentenced to death or executed. Debate centers on whether a given inmate has a disability, not on eligibility for death if he or she does have one. Of course, *Atkins* came only in 2005, some 30 years into the modern period.

Mental illness issues can be raised at many points in a capital trial. Inmates who are clearly insane may be deemed incompetent to stand trial at all. Their potential sentence may be not guilty by reason of insanity, and such an outcome does not allow for a death sentence. (It may lead to a life of confinement in a mental hospital. Or, as for John Hinkley, who attempted to assassinate President Ronald Reagan, it could lead to eventual release if the illness is deemed to have subsided.) Mental health issues such as insanity or diminished capacity may also be presented at the guilt phase of the trial. Juries may find defendants not guilty by reason of insanity or guilty of lesser charges if they believe their mental state at the time of the crime did not allow them, for example, to understand the gravity of their actions. Finally, if a defendant is found guilty in a capital trial, then mental illness may be debated again in the penalty phase: if the death penalty is supposed to be reserved for the worst of the worst, the most culpable offenders, then mental illness can be an effective mitigator. Childhood experiences such as abuse and trauma can be presented not to absolve the defendant from guilt for the crime but to suggest that the criminal behavior may have been influenced by factors such as a lack of remorse or feeling stemming from sometimes horrific abuse during childhood, as many inmates have experienced. The state of mind of the defendant at the time of the crime is supposed to be considered, as is his or her possible level of intoxication. Great numbers of offenders are drunk or high at the time of the commission of their crimes, and according to the law these may be considered by the jury as mitigating factors at the sentencing phase. When intoxication interacts with underlying mental illness, the effects can be exaggerated.

Of course, juries may also interpret "worst of the worst" not with regard to the state of mental capacity or desire to inflict harm but by the actions or events associated with the crime. And here, what is supposed to be a mitigator can sometimes be flipped: those who are high, mentally ill, or otherwise not thinking as others do can commit horrible crimes. Similarly, childhood abuse experiences may suggest to a jury that the inmate is so desensitized that he or she poses a future danger. Our point here is that at the penalty phase, mental health evidence may be presented, but it is not always clear how it will be interpreted by the jury. Most states give little guidance for how to weigh mitigating and aggravating factors at this stage. And, for mental health issues, what is supposed to be a mitigator may in fact not work that way in the minds of the jury. Also, as we mentioned in chapter 2, a jury is called upon to evaluate the culpability of the defendant, but sometimes it may focus on the horror of the crime. If a mentally ill individual commits a particularly terrible crime, a jury may be so sensitive to that that it refuses to show mercy. Juries (or judges in some cases) have extremely wide latitude in evaluating mitigation evidence. One option is to discount it completely.

If mental health evidence can enter the trial at one of many points, its actual presentation is only as good as the defense team makes it. In the 2016–2017 capital defense trial of Dylann Roof, the white supremacist convicted in 2016 of killing nine people in a shooting in a historic black church in Charleston, South Carolina, Roof sought the assistance of counsel during the guilt phase but chose to represent himself at the penalty phase. In Roof's journals that were presented in trial, he wrote: " 'I want to state that I am morally opposed to psychology. It is a Jewish invention, and does nothing but invent diseases and tell people they have problems when they dont [sic].' " Writing to the judge, he indicated: " 'I will not be calling mental health experts or presenting mental health evidence' " (quoted in Sack and Blinder 2017). Journalistic speculation suggested that Roof did not want embarrassing elements of his childhood to be recounted in public. His attorneys would have painted a picture of childhood abuse and family dysfunction. Indeed, his highly qualified defense attorney, David Bruck, did manage to enter into the guilt phase the following argument: " 'On what planet does someone have to be to think that you can advance a political agenda by attacking and murdering these nine people who are among the most kind, upstanding, and I will use the word "noble," people you could possibly find?' " (quoted in Bauerlein 2016).

Where a defense attorney plans to argue that the defendant is crazy, but the defendant has the right to defend him- or herself with no attorney present, it is clear that the system provides no guarantee that information relevant to mental illness will be entered into evidence. The reasons may range from inadequate defense preparation or funding to outright hostility by the defendant him- or herself. Of course, some inmates may see presenting no such evidence, particularly at the penalty phase, as the quickest route to suicide (or martyrdom, in the cases of federal inmates Roof and Timothy McVeigh, the Oklahoma City bomber).

In this chapter we focus on those 824 inmates executed from 2000 through 2015, and we review the prevalence of mental health issues among them, comparing statistics for this group with statistics for other groups where possible. We should make clear before proceeding how conservative our assessments are, since they are based only on what is presented in trial and/or reported in the press. This is certain significantly to underrepresent the true prevalence of each issue we discuss here. At trial, the defense attorney or the prosecutor may request a psychological assessment from a psychiatrist, clinical psychologist, forensic psychologist, social worker, or other mental health expert. This assessment may focus on a variety of factors such as whether or not the defendant has a mental illness or an intellectual disability, is mentally capable of understanding the crimes he or she committed, or is a continued threat to society and whether there is any information about the defendant's childhood or adult past or any other psychological information that the defense or prosecution finds relevant to the case. Some of this information may be relevant to the trial of guilt, and other elements may be presented in the penalty phase.

Once a defendant is sentenced to death, a psychological expert may still assess him or her on death row. Because the *Atkins* decision came only in 2005 but invalidated death sentences for those already on death row, to prove an intellectual disability to the satisfaction of the court is to see a death sentenced reduced to a sentence of life. Many death row inmates sought the opportunity to make this point. But if at the original trial an ineffective defense attorney never hired a psychologist for a test, if the inmate grew up in circumstances of poverty where his or her illness went undiagnosed and untreated, or if no investigator searched for the inmate's school and hospital records, many of these cases would go unreported.

Our data show that at least 48 percent of inmates executed from 2000 to 2015 suffered from a mental illness or substance abuse disorder at some point in their adult life. Some of these individuals may have developed their illness in the harsh conditions of life on death row. However, it is likely that many already suffered from various mental illnesses at the time of their crime and during their trial. In fact, many of the cases we review here suggest that while mental illness is in theory a mitigating factor, in reality it can easily become an aggravating factor in the eyes of the jury. We turn to this issue first.

Constitutional Review in the 1980s and Beyond

In 2002, Daryl Atkins challenged the constitutionality of executing someone who has an intellectual disability. Atkins had an IQ of 59, which is 11 points below the threshold for borderline intellectual functioning. In his case, the Supreme Court ruled 6–3 that executing someone with an intellectual disability was cruel and unusual and was therefore a violation of the Eighth Amendment. The threshold for an intellectual disability is typically understood to mean an IQ score less than or equal to 70. This seemed like an easy, nonarbitrary way of defining intellectual disabilities, but the problem that arose was that not everyone scores exactly the same on every IQ test. If someone scores a 69 on one test and a 71 on another, the jury must make the decision about which score is more accurate. The Court clarified in *Hall v. Florida* (2014) that the margin of error in such testing should be taken into consideration by lower courts.

Atkins v. Virginia was not the first case where the concern of mental health was discussed. In 1986, the Court ruled in *Ford v. Wainwright* that executing someone who was incompetent to understand the punishment is cruel and unusual. However, the decision did not specify a constitutional definition of competency, so later courts had little direction for how to use this ruling. In 1989, *Penry v. Lynaugh* held that the execution of those with intellectual disabilities was constitutionally permissible (this decision was directly reversed in *Atkins*). In 1994, in *Barnard v. Collins*, the Court ruled that the petitioner's awareness at the time of the crime was a separate factor from his mental illness and deemed the petitioner competent to stand trial in spite of his diagnosed psychosis, hallucinations, and delusions.

The Court has also struggled to rule clearly on the issue of mental health treatment with the intention of making someone competent to stand trial. In *Perry v. Louisiana* (1990), the Court ruled against executing someone whose competency status was changed after they received mental health treatment. However, in the same year, *Washington v. Harper* (1990) held that medical officials may forcibly medicate a prisoner, even against his or her will. This decision was reinforced in *Riggins v. Nevada* (1992), holding that individuals with mental illness can be forced to take antipsychotic medication while they are on trial. These decisions were overturned in a landmark case, *Sell v. United States* (2003), in which the Court declared that it is unconstitutional forcibly to medicate someone with a mental illness with the intent of changing their mental status from incompetent to competent. This violates the Fourteenth Amendment, the Court finally held. Throughout the period from the 1980s to the first years of the twenty-first century, mental illness was at the core of the Court's rulings with regard to the death penalty, with *Sell* (2003) and *Atkins* (2005) settling at least some of the most difficult matters on the side of reduced punishment for those who are mentally ill, are incompetent, or have an intellectual disability.

Clearly, the Court has had great difficulty finding a clear standard for how to handle mental illness claims in trial. This may be because jurors have difficulty as well. What may in theory be supposed to mitigate could potentially aggravate if juries interpret mental illnesses as affecting future dangerousness, or even if they simply deprive the defendant of the compassion a jury may have with one who does not suffer from a mental illness, and who may therefore look or behave differently in the courtroom. If jurors are expecting to see remorse and careful meditation in the courtroom demeanor of a defendant charged with a serious crime, those with mental illness or intellectual disability may be denied the jury's sympathy or understanding. Even worse, such a defendant may stimulate fear within the jury that he or she must be executed because of the unpredictability of future outbursts. Of course, prosecutors may seek to exaggerate these fears, and defense attorneys may be at a disadvantage in attempting to suggest not that their client is innocent of the action but that his or her culpability is reduced. If juries commonly misunderstand court instructions, it is not surprising that cases have risen to the Supreme Court and have generated a string of contradictory rulings. As we saw in chapter 5, five states require that juries consider "future dangerousness" in considering the death penalty. Two of those states, Texas and Oklahoma, have generated almost half of the national total of executions. It is certainly possible that a jury's estimate of possible future dangerousness could have put a number of seriously mentally ill inmates into the death chamber.

We can clearly distinguish three key moments at which the mental state of the accused or convicted comes into play. First, if defense attorneys can show that the defendant was insane at the time of the crime, an insanity defense would remove any possibility of a death sentence. Second, at the time of trial, was the defendant competent to understand the charges and able to assist in his or her own defense? Finally, following *Ford v. Wainwright* (1986), at the time of execution, an inmate should be competent to understand the nature of the punishment. Different standards apply to each of these assessments, but there is no question that the mental state of the defendant has long been considered a fundamental concern for the courts. This does not make it easy to make these distinctions, however. And given the context of a capital crime and the passions and emotions raised by the nature of some of the crimes, there is no reason to assume that the legal system always gets it right.

Existing Literature

There is very little systematic information about the prevalence of mental illness or intellectual disability among those on death row. Much of the existing research is limited in scope. In a literature review conducted in 2002, Mark Cunningham and Mark Vigen (2002) found just 13 clinical studies in the published literature. None of these was particularly large in scope, with the number of inmates studied ranging from 8 to 83. However, by analyzing these clinical studies along with government reports on demographics and institutional records, they were able to paint a partial picture of the mental health situation on America's death row. It is not good.

Cunningham and Vigen cite a study by Lewis et al. (1988) of juveniles on death row. Though they note some limitations to the study (such as a small sample size), they write:

> For each of the offenders studied, Lewis and colleagues detailed descriptive findings of head injuries, neurological dysfunction, psychiatric symptoms, neuropsychiatric and psychoeducational scores, and any family history of physical abuse, sexual abuse, family violence, and/or family psychiatric illness. A pattern of multiple significant vulnerabilities was demonstrated among most of these offenders. (2002, 198)

Many of the studies evaluated intellectual capacities, the authors write, and generally found mean IQ scores in the "average to low average range, generally consistent with the intellectual capabilities of general prison population inmates" (199). They continue:

> A significant minority of death row inmates, though, exhibited marked intellectual limitations. For example, 27% of the Mississippi death row sample investigated by Cunningham and Vigen (1999) had WAIS-R Verbal IQ scores below 74. At a standard error of measurement 95% confidence interval, IQ scores of 74 or below may fall in the "mentally retarded" range of intellectual functioning. Similarly, Frierson et al. (1998) reported that 28% of their death row sample obtained IQ scores in the borderline or mentally retarded classifications. (199)

Eleven of the studies reviewed by Cunningham and Vigen assessed the psychological functioning of death row inmates: "All 11 reported a high incidence of psychological symptoms and disorders, ranging from maladaptive defenses to pervasive depression, mood lability, and diminished mental acuity to episodic and chronic psychosis" (200). Studies also documented low levels of formal education (with fewer than half completing high school; 199), high levels of "neurological abnormalities and neuropsychological deficits" (201), substance abuse (201), and "histories of paternal abandonment, foster care and institutionalization, abuse and neglect, and/or parental substance abuse" (202). It is worth quoting their conclusions at some length:

> While much of the research on death row inmates has limitations in specificity, sampling, methodology, and reporting, there are a number

of recurrent findings. To summarize these, death row inmates are over-whelmingly male and disproportionately Southern. Over half of death row inmates are non-whites. A majority did not graduate from high school. Mean IQ scores of death row inmates are in the low-average-to-average range, but a disturbingly large minority exhibits IQ scores in the borderline and mental retardation ranges. Functional literacy capabili-ties are well below what would be expected from the years of schooling attended.... There is also a significant incidence of neurological and neu-ropsychological abnormalities among death row inmates.

Psychological disorders are quite frequent among death row inmates. The particularly adverse conditions of death row confinement in some jurisdictions appear to not only undermine efforts to adaptively cope, but also act to aggravate psychological symptoms. Current prison mental health interventions are insufficient.

Pre-confinement histories of disturbed families of origin, parental alco-holism, childhood abuse and neglect, and/or personal substance depend-ence are disturbingly common. A sizeable percentage of death row inmates reported pre-confinement substance dependence and/or were under the influence of alcohol or drugs at the time of the capital offense. (206)

In sum, to the extent that previous scholars have investigated mental health con-ditions of inmates on death row, the results have been quite concerning. Some of the disorders likely result from preexisting conditions that may have led to the com-mission of the crime. Others may have developed or been exacerbated by the living conditions on death row, which are unpleasant to say the least. Given that there has been so little previous work on this topic, we have collected new data to attempt to assess the prevalence of various mental health issues among those inmates executed in recent years.

Data Collection

We collected statistics on each of the 824 death row inmates executed between the years 2000 and 2015, using as our source the Clark County Prosecutor website[3] and the legal website Justia.com. The Clark County Prosecutor database, which includes information from 2000 to 2014 with the exception of two inmates from 2014, is a compilation of many news articles and law sources pertaining to the cases. Justia is an online database with records from various courts and write-ups of cases. For information for 2015 and the two excluded inmates from 2014, we did a Google search and selected the top five mainstream sources as well as Justia. We repeated this process for each inmate executed from 2000 through 2015. Earlier cases were excluded mostly because less information was available online for each inmate, making any interpretations less reliable. Our analysis of 824 inmates is complete for all those executed from 2000 through 2015; these inmates represent 58 percent of the 1,422 executed in the modern period.

Using these sources, separately for each inmate, we searched for the following: "psych," "mental," "suic," "diagnos," "hospital," "abus," "child," "neglect," "abandon," "retard," "alcohol," "drug," "depend," "addict," and "disorder." These helped us find information on the psychological testimonies and mitigating circumstances related to mental health, including substance abuse, mental illness, intellectual disabilities, suicidal tendencies, hospitalizations, and trauma. For each inmate executed, we recorded whether or not and to what degree he or she had each of these specific serious mental health issues. In compiling our data, we simply coded as a 1 when there was a judicial finding or other significant evidence that the inmate had been professionally diagnosed as having the given disorder, which are detailed in the next section.[4]

Our estimates of mental illness are conservative in two ways. First, we used very strict criteria to ensure that we did not overestimate the numbers; we listed an inmate as having an illness only if we found credible source material that he or she had been diagnosed with it, such as in evidence or testimony presented at trial, or repeated in the media. Second, our numbers likely are underestimates because much psychological evidence may not have been addressed in court or formally assessed by a professional. Because we rely on these publicly available sources, any inmate's illness that was not addressed in court or in news coverage about the case would likely escape our purview, leading to an underestimate of the prevalence of mental illness.

Prevalence of Mental Illness

According to the National Institute of Mental Health (NIMH), about 18.1 percent of the US population, or almost one person in five, suffers from a mental illness. The NIMH compiled the data from a number of sources, but typically sources involve individual self-reports on whether or not an individual had suffered from a mental illness "within the past year." The NIMH distinguishes between "any mental illness" (AMI) and "serious mental illness" (SMI); both of these exclude substance abuse disorders, and SMI is limited to those ailments that result in functional impairment that interferes with at least one major life activity.

The most common form of mental illness is anxiety disorders, which include generalized anxiety disorder, social anxiety disorder, phobias, obsessive-compulsive disorder, trauma-related disorders, and a few others. Many anxiety disorders can be extremely debilitating, but most are not considered an SMI. In the United States, 18.1 percent of the population have an anxiety disorder, and 4.1 percent are considered "serious." There are, of course, many other forms of mental illness. Figure 12.1

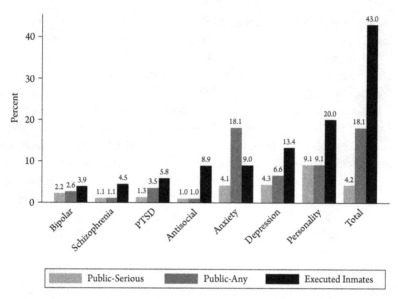

Figure 12.1 Prevalence of Mental Illness among Inmates Executed and in the General Public. Source for general public: National Institute of Mental Health.

compares the prevalence of various forms of mental illness in the US population and in those inmates executed from 2000 through 2015. In each case, we present the general public numbers for "any" and for "serious" forms of the disease compared with the mental illness prevalence numbers of the executed inmates, excluding all substance use disorders. Some of the figures for AMI and SMI are the same because some disorders, such as schizophrenia, are always considered serious.

Figure 12.1 makes clear that executed inmates have much higher rates of every type of mental illness, often by very large margins. For each of the types of mental illness, as well as for overall frequency, the inmates are typically much more likely to exhibit symptoms. Every category of SMI is significantly lower for the general population than among the executed inmates. More than 40 percent of the inmates suffered at some point in their lives from an SMI, according to our review of court records and news accounts, which of course is most likely an understatement. The prevalence of mild anxiety is more common in the general public than among executed inmates. However, serious anxiety, interfering with a major life activity, is more than twice as common among the inmates than in the general population. In every other case but this one, the inmates show much higher rates than the general population, whether we look at mild or serious forms of each illness.

Figure 12.2 shows the ratio between the rates of the same types of mental illness for the two groups. So, for example, 18.1 percent of the general public has "any mental illness" whereas 43.0 percent of the inmates do; this ratio is therefore 2.4. The graph arranges the illnesses in order based on this ratio, making it clear which illnesses are proportionately more common among the inmates. In Figure 12.2A, we

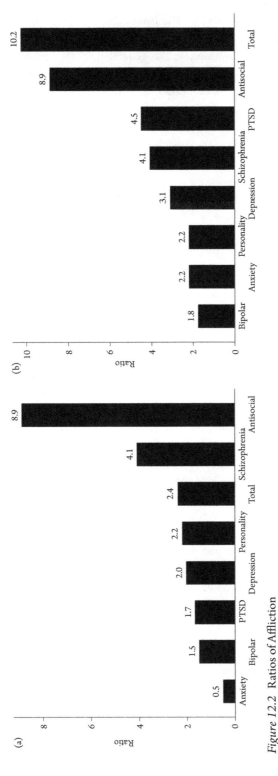

Figure 12.2 Ratios of Affliction

A. Any Mental Illness. Each bar shows the percent of executed inmates with the indicated disorder divided by the percent of the general public with a form of the same illness. 1.0: equal prevalence. 2.0: twice as common among the executed.

B. Serious Mental Illness. Each bar shows the percent of executed inmates with the indicated disorder divided by the percent of the general public with a serious form of the same illness. 1.0: equal prevalence. 2.0: twice as common among the executed.

compare the inmates to the prevalence of "any mental illness" in the general public, and in Figure 12.2B, we use "serious mental illness."

Mild anxiety is twice as common in the general public as among executed inmates. This may be because such things may not be mentioned in a trial or in media coverage of a capital trial. In every other case, the inmates show rates ranging from 50 percent more likely to more than eight times more likely to have any mental illness, with the rates much higher when we look only at those for SMI.

Antisocial personality disorder is a relatively rare phenomenon in the general public, affecting just 1 percent of the US population, but it is not so uncommon on death row; almost 9 percent of the inmates we reviewed had it. This is one disorder that can easily be skewed by the prosecution and thus used as an aggravating factor because it is the technical name for the terms "sociopath" and "psychopath" that are often used in the media. Similarly, schizophrenia occurs in only about 1.1 percent of the general population but in more than 4 percent of the inmate group. Most of the diagnoses are more than twice as likely to occur among the inmates as in the general population, with schizophrenia and antisocial personality disorders sharply more prevalent.

Figures 12.1 and 12.2 point to the extreme differences between the prevalence of mental illnesses among executed inmates and the general public. But the numbers here underestimate the true differences, in part because our review of media and court documents would surely have missed some cases and would most likely be focused on individuals with severe afflictions, not self-diagnosed individuals or possibly marginal cases as in the general public. But there is also another reason: executed inmates are overwhelmingly male (just 13 of the 824 executed inmates were women), whereas mental illness is more common among women than men. Nationally, 5 percent of women suffer from an SMI compared with only 3.1 percent of men.[5] This gender difference is even larger with AMI. About 21.8 percent of women and only 14.1 percent of men suffer from AMI. Among executed inmates, this gap is much smaller, but the rates for both males and females are very high: for the men, 42.4 percent suffered from a non-substance-related mental illness; among executed women, the percentage was 38.5, or about the same. Whereas in the general public mental illness is more common among women, among the executed inmates there is no significant gender difference, and both the men and the women have extremely high rates. Because we compare overall rates for the general public in Figure 12.1 rather than male-specific rates, but the vast majority of executed inmates are male, the increased prevalence of severe mental illness is even greater than the figure suggests.

Schizophrenia Case Example

Whereas PTSD and depression are often attributed to environmental factors, schizophrenia is heavily attributed to biological factors. Schizophrenia is relatively rare in the general US population. Only about 1.1 percent of individuals in the United

States suffer from schizophrenia; however, as mentioned earlier, this number rises to 4.5 percent for executed inmates. This is not to say that schizophrenia is a dangerous disorder because most individuals who have schizophrenia live a nonviolent life. In fact, on the Violence Risk Appraisal Guide, more commonly known as the VRAG, a future dangerousness assessment often used in court, having schizophrenia actually decreased a defendant's likelihood of committing a future violent act. Psychotic disorders, such as schizophrenia, contribute to the difficulty of determining competency to stand trial, and they may affect assessments of whether the defendant was insane at the time of the crime. Thus, different judgments (often using different standards) must be made about the mental state of inmates at specific moments in time: Were they insane at the time of the crime (leading possibly to a different plea, charge, or sentence)? Were they competent to stand trial? Are they competent to be executed? Was their competency changed by medication in prison designed solely for that purpose? Finally, no matter what the medical literature may say, jury members may interpret the fact that a defendant at trial has schizophrenia as a sign that he or she may be violent in the future. Thus an illness that might be thought to be a mitigating factor can become an aggravating one in practice.

Schizophrenia, like all mental illnesses, is the result of an interaction between environmental and biological factors. There are many brain abnormalities associated with schizophrenia. Studies using positron emission tomography (PET) scans have shown that when there is no noise in a room, areas of the brain associated with auditory functions indicate brain activity on the scan at the same time that the individual reports hearing something. That is, schizophrenic individuals actually have auditory hallucinations that others cannot hear—they hear voices (Silbersweig et al., 1995). There are also many genetic factors associated with schizophrenia. In fact, studies have shown that heritability and genes account for about 80 percent of the development of schizophrenia (Castelliani et al. 2015, 438; Cardno and Gottseman 2000, 13).

The medical diagnosis of schizophrenia is not just a seat-of-the-pants assessment by a hired expert. A psychological expert performs multiple tests, but to qualify as having a mental illness, the individual must meet all of the criteria as defined in the latest version of the *Diagnostic and Statistical Manual of Mental Disorders* (*DSM*). This process can take multiple days, and the defendant may spend a few nights in a psychiatric hospital until all the testing is completed. The criteria for schizophrenia are extensive, and it is important to understand the process of a diagnosis in order to understand why different experts may reach such different conclusions about the competency of an individual. Schizophrenia is defined in the *DSM-V* as:

A. Two (or more) of the following, each present for a significant portion of time during a 1-month period (or less if successfully treated). At least one of these must be (1), (2), or (3):
   1. Delusions.
   2. Hallucinations.

3. Disorganized speech (e.g., frequent derailment or incoherence).
4. Grossly disorganized or catatonic behavior.
5. Negative symptoms (i.e., diminished emotional expression or avolition).

B. For a significant portion of the time since the onset of the disturbance, level of functioning in one or more major areas, such as work, interpersonal relations, or self-care, is markedly below the level achieved prior to the onset (or when the onset is in childhood or adolescence, there is failure to achieve expected level of interpersonal, academic, or occupational functioning).

C. Continuous signs of the disturbance persist for at least 6 months. This 6-month period must include at least 1 month of symptoms (or less if successfully treated) that meet Criterion A (i.e., active-phase symptoms) and may include periods of prodromal or residual symptoms. During these prodromal or residual periods, the signs of the disturbance may be manifested by only negative symptoms or by two or more symptoms listed in Criterion A present in an attenuated form (e.g., odd beliefs, unusual perceptual experiences).

D. Schizoaffective disorder and depressive or bipolar disorder with psychotic features have been ruled out because either 1) no major depressive or manic episodes have occurred concurrently with the active-phase symptoms, or 2) if mood episodes have occurred during active-phase symptoms, they have been present for a minority of the total duration of the active and residual periods of the illness

E. The disturbance is not attributable to the physiological effects of a substance (e.g., a drug of abuse, a medication) or another medical condition.

F. If there is a history of autism spectrum disorder or a communication disorder of childhood onset, the additional diagnosis of schizophrenia is made only if prominent delusions or hallucinations, in addition to the other required symptoms of schizophrenia, are also present for at least 1 month (or less if successfully treated). (American Psychiatric Association 2013, 99–100)

One example of an executed inmate who met these criteria for schizophrenia was James Willie Brown.[6] Brown, who was assessed for trial and was diagnosed with paranoid schizophrenia, was born prematurely to a 15-year-old mother and grew up in an extremely abusive household. His alcoholic father regularly beat him with belts, boards, branches, cords, and his fists both at home and in public so that James would feel humiliated. His maternal uncle also regularly molested him. Around second grade James developed a stutter and was consistently picked on at school for it. His troubled childhood most likely was an environmental contribution to the development of his mental illness and his violent behavior, in addition to genetics. Poverty, a family history of mental illness, fetal alcohol syndrome, and other factors can continue for generations, making some individuals particularly susceptible to mental illness from before birth.

Brown was arrested in 1968 but was deemed incompetent to stand trial due to hearing voices and noises, passing out, and having severe headaches. He was sent to a psychiatric hospital, where he attempted suicide by cutting his own throat. He was prescribed antipsychotics and tranquilizers and was in and out of psychiatric hospitals. He started having delusions that he was Jesus Christ and even signed his name that way on documents. He believed that someone was trying to poison him with germs and regularly saw hallucinations of God and the Devil, whom he believed guided his actions. He was diagnosed on 17 different occasions with schizophrenia. In 1981, he was found guilty of brutally raping and suffocating Brenda Watson and was sentenced to death; the crime dated to 1975. Brown's sentence was overturned in 1988 because he was deemed incompetent to stand trial due to his mental capacity. In 1989, he was retried and given the death sentence once again when an expert testified that he was not schizophrenic but instead suffering from flashbacks when he had abused LSD. Brown was deemed competent and was executed by the State of Georgia on November 4, 2003.

This is one of many examples in which an executed inmate's psychological state and competency at the time of death appear arbitrary and subjective. Despite getting the same diagnosis 17 times and previously being deemed incompetent to stand trial, Brown was ultimately determined to be competent based on the testimony of a single expert who disagreed with the other 17. There is no doubt that Brown was a scary and violent individual; there was no claim of innocence for the horrible crime of which he was found guilty; nevertheless, there should be no doubt that he was sick and his crimes were fueled largely by the symptoms of his illness. Indeed, he had spent the greater part of his adult life in mental hospitals until the time of the crime.

Abusive Upbringing

As mentioned earlier, mental illness and violent behavior result from a combination of biological and environmental factors. These environmental factors can date back to childhood, to in utero experiences, and indeed to patterns established in previous generations of abusive families. For children born into families with long histories of poverty, mental illness, substance abuse, and other pathologies, chances are higher that they will also develop similar problems of their own. According to the US Department of Health and Human Services, in the United States, 1 in 10 children are abused. Of those who are abused, about 80 percent suffer from childhood neglect or abandonment (8 percent of the US population), making this the most common type of abuse. The next most common is physical abuse. Of those abused, 18 percent suffer from physical abuse (1.8 percent of the US population); finally, 9 percent suffer from sexual abuse (0.9 percent of the US population).

(These numbers, of course, may be under-reported, and national population data do not report emotional or verbal abuse.)

When we compare executed inmates from 2000 to 2015 to the general population figures just reviewed, the numbers go up significantly: 39.7 percent of executed inmates experienced some type of abuse, 12.6 percent were sexually abused (again, likely under-reported), 26.2 percent were physically abused, 16.1 percent were neglected, and 7.7 percent provided evidence of abuse but did not specify which type. It is important to note that physical abuse is the most common form of abuse among those executed between 2000 and 2015. This suggests that from an early age, more than a quarter of these individuals were taught that punishment was enforced with physical force and violence. Those who were sexually abused during childhood were introduced to sex in a very unhealthy way, contributing to a confused understanding of relationships later in life. Childhood sexual victimization in particular can have a variety of ramifications, including rage, depression, anxiety, eating disorders, and violence. Figure 12.3 summarizes the stark differences in the rates of various forms of childhood abuse between the general population and executed inmates.

The numbers in Figure 12.3 show startling differences in the rates at which executed inmates were abused as children compared with the general public (and, of course, these numbers most likely understate the scope of the problem in both populations, as well as the difference between the two groups, because for the executed inmates we know of the abuse only if it was recorded in court testimony or in newspaper coverage of their cases). The increased rates at which executed inmates

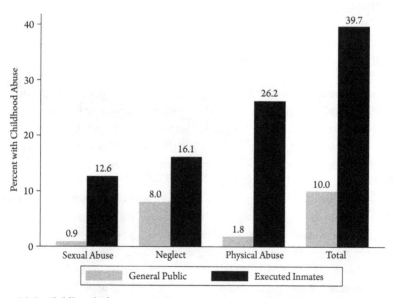

Figure 12.3 Childhood Abuse among Inmates Executed and in the General Public

experienced abuse range from about twice as likely for neglect (16.1 percent compared with 8.0 percent) to more than 10 times as likely for physical or sexual abuse combined. Childhood sexual abuse occurs in less than 1 percent of the general public, according to official statistics, but in more than 12 percent of executed inmates. More than one-quarter of the executed inmates suffered childhood physical abuse, compared with less than 2 percent of the general public, and almost 40 percent experienced some form of childhood abuse, compared with 10 percent among the general public.

Our statistics include abuse that is reported at trial or in the news articles we reviewed. Many cases of abuse are not reported. There were also many mentions of situations such as a traumatic childhood or poverty, as well as cases where the inmate claimed he or she had been molested or beaten, but there was no way of proving these events happened because no one could testify as a witness. Therefore, the numbers about abuse should be viewed as the bare minimum of abuse cases, with consideration of the cases that went unreported or unsupported with evidence. National statistics on child abuse are vastly underreported, as not every child's abuse is brought to the attention of the authorities. Overall, executed inmates grew up in abusive households much more often than the general population of the United States. Some individual stories of abuse are horrific.

Alton Coleman is one example of an inmate who grew up in an abusive environment and later developed a mental illness.[7] Coleman was executed in 2002 for a violent and truly horrific crime spree in the summer of 1984. Moreover, he had committed a series of violent crimes even earlier. His childhood was truly abnormal. His mother was a prostitute who abused drugs and alcohol while she was pregnant with him. When he was young, she threw him into a trash can, and he was saved when someone heard him crying and took him out. He was raised mostly by his grandmother, who ran the brothel and gambling house where his mother worked. His grandmother practiced voodoo rituals in which she forced Coleman to kill animals so that she could use the blood to make potions. In the brothel, he was repeatedly raped and physically abused by the customers. He also witnessed many group sex activities involving his mother and grandmother with men and other prostitutes, and he was exposed to drugs, alcohol, sex, bestiality, gambling, and violence starting from a very young age. As a child he was known as "Pissy" because he routinely wore filthy clothes soiled with his own waste.

Coleman was later diagnosed with pansexual propensities, a personality disorder, and brain dysfunction. The psychologist suggested that he possibly suffered from PTSD as a result of the trauma he endured as a child, but did not present a formal diagnosis of it. A diagnosis of pansexual propensities means that he was willing to have sex with any person or object presented to him. Coleman was arrested on multiple charges of raping adults and children and eventually received a death sentence for raping and brutally killing two women, following a crime spree that generated death sentences for him in Ohio, Indiana, and Illinois. His crimes were horrific, and he was executed on April 26, 2002, by the State of Ohio. Coleman's unhappy story is but one of many among the 800-plus inmates executed from 2000 through 2015 whose cases we have reviewed.

Substance Abuse

Considering the levels of childhood abuse just discussed, it should come as no surprise that substance abuse is common among executed inmates, both in their early years and at the time of their crimes. Those with horrific trauma or mental illness often turn to some kind of "self-medication" or numbing through alcohol or other substances. Abusing substances can affect the brain in ways that can be as detrimental to development as some genes, especially because the brain is still developing even after adolescence. For each executed inmate, we assessed whether there was a record of previous use of an illicit drug or alcohol, whether he or she suffered from a substance abuse disorder, and whether he or she was under the influence of intoxicants at the time of the trial. For the last item, we do not feel confident in our coding beyond noting that intoxication is a very common theme; it was not possible to put hard numbers on that estimate, however, because determining whether someone was under the influence of the substance he or she consumed was often difficult. But for the first two variables, we can clearly see that a higher percentage of executed inmates abused alcohol and drugs than in the general population: among the executed inmates, 52.9 percent presented evidence that they abused a substance, and 15.9 percent of inmates suffered from a substance use disorder, dependency, or addiction; these numbers are much higher than in the general public. The Substance Abuse and Mental Health Services Administration reports that in 2014, for adults aged 18 to 25, 6.6 percent suffered from an illicit drug use disorder and 12.3 percent suffered from an alcohol use disorder. For adults aged 26 or older, 1.9 percent had an illicit drug use disorder and 5.9 percent suffered from an alcohol use disorder (Hedden et al. 2015).

Many of the inmates who were executed between 2000 and 2015 were under the influence of a substance at the time of their crime. One example is Marco Allen Chapman, who suffered from depression, became suicidal, and experienced hallucinations and horrific flashbacks to this abuse.[8] He began using drugs at a very young age, following brutal sexual and physical abuse by his alcoholic parents. Using cocaine originally provided an escape for Chapman but escalated into a dependency that fueled his violent acts and contributed to his aggressive mental state at the time of his crimes. After a night of binging on cocaine, he broke into the home of Carolyn Marksberry to rob her for more money for cocaine. He raped and stabbed her, but she survived the attack. Her three children were awakened by the noise and were then attacked as well. Chapman slit two of their throats and stabbed the third child multiple times. This injured child escaped, however, after playing dead, and ran to a neighbor's home to call the police. Chapman fled the scene but was soon apprehended, partly because he was already well known to the victim, who was a friend of his estranged girlfriend. Chapman's drug addiction contributed heavily to his violent behavior and was his motive for originally robbing the house. Chapman's final words included these: "I don't know why I did the thing that I did" and "I am not a monster even though I did a monstrously evil thing." Chapman was an execution volunteer and died on November 21, 2008, in the Kentucky execution chamber.

Research has shown that cocaine, alcohol, and many other substances increase a person's likelihood of acting violently because the substances inhibit many of the ways we control our impulses. One study concluded: "Because alcohol and drugs are disinhibiting, they increase the likelihood that juveniles will act on their violent impulses. As with adults, the use of stimulants, such as cocaine or methamphetamine, is particularly associated with disinhibition, feelings of grandiosity, and paranoia that may contribute to violent behavior" (Scott and Resnick 2006, 605). According to the Bureau of Justice Statistics, in 1991, 48 percent of males and 65 percent of females who were arrested for a homicide tested positive for marijuana, cocaine, opiates, PCP, methamphetamine, methadone, methaqualone, benzodiazepines, barbiturates, or propoxyphene at the time of their arrest. Unfortunately, such a state of mind can indeed make individuals do things they never would do while sober. As we search for the worst of the worst, sometimes we find the most incapacitated, drunk, or strung out.

Intellectual Disabilities

As mentioned earlier, *Atkins v. Virginia* (2002) barred the execution of those with intellectual disabilities, typically defined as having an IQ of 70 or lower combined with adaptive behavioral problems. As in the case of James Willie Brown's competency, there is also a subjective element that factors into intellectual disabilities. Oftentimes, someone scores differently each time he or she takes an IQ test. Rickey Lynn Lewis is one of 25 inmates between 2003 and 2015 who scored a 70 or lower on an IQ test but was nonetheless executed.[9] In most of these cases, the inmate was tested multiple times, sometimes scoring below 70 and sometimes above. Lewis scored 59, 70, 75, and 79 in various test administrations. Two of these scores deemed him ineligible for execution according to *Atkins v. Virginia*, but the other two deemed him eligible. Courts chose to dismiss the lower scores and to trust the higher scores, and as a result Lewis was executed on April 9, 2013.

Too late for Lewis, the US Supreme Court revised its *Atkins* ruling in *Hall v. Florida* (2014). When tested, Hall was found to have an IQ of 71 and was therefore found competent to be executed according to the ruling in *Atkins*. Hall argued in his case that the 70 cut-off was unconstitutional because, without a margin of error, the state risks executing someone with an intellectual disability. The court ruled that having such a strict cut-off was indeed risky and that those falling within the IQ test's margin of error (this number varies depending on the specific IQ test that is used) must be allowed to present additional evidence about eligibility. It seems as though being tested and having a psychologist do a formal assessment would prove to be much less arbitrary, but just as we see with mental illness assessments, experts do not always agree, especially in the highly charged and conflictual domain of a criminal trial. The experts, after all, do not work for the court but for either the prosecution or the defense.

The Court in *Atkins* ruled that the states could not execute those with intellectual disabilities, but it left to the states the determination of who has such a disability. In late 2016, the Court heard the case of Bobby J. Moore, a Texas death row inmate whose attorneys argued that the State of Texas used outdated and stereotypical definitions, including standards suggesting that the character "Lennie" in John Steinbeck's novel *Of Mice and Men* would be ineligible for a death sentence, based on a general but vague popular understanding and in spite of the fictional character's ability to perform certain everyday functions, such as mow a lawn (see Liptak 2016a). The Court's 2016 arguments made clear (1) that state definitions must go beyond only IQ tests to include tests of "adaptive functioning" but also (2) that these should not be an arbitrary set of factors based on a layperson's understandings rather than the best medical evidence. Clearly, while *Atkins* gave a blanket exemption for those with intellectual disabilities, it opened a Pandora's box in attempting to ascertain who exactly qualifies.

Ironically, intellectual disabilities are relevant to death row not only because of the *Atkins* and *Hall* rulings; having a sufficiently low score can get an inmate off death row, according to these two relatively recent rulings. But intellectual disabilities also make it easier to be sentenced to death. Those with such disabilities are prone to suggestion, may not realize that their "discussion" with a police investigator is actually a criminal investigation, and have often signed false confessions written by the investigator. Once such a confession is signed, even if elements in it are demonstrably false, it is difficult to avoid a guilty verdict. And in trials for those with intellectual disabilities or mental illness, jurors may have reduced empathy or greater fear of future dangerousness. A recent double exoneration in North Carolina illustrates these points.

Nineteen-year-old Henry McCollum and his 15-year-old half-brother, Leon Brown, were falsely convicted of the murder of Sabrina Buie on October 25, 1984, in Robeson County, North Carolina.[10] McCollum had an IQ that tested as low as 56; Brown had scored 49 on one IQ test. The two had been visiting relatives from their home in New Jersey and were identified as suspects partially by a high school student who said that Henry "looked weird." During separate interrogations with no adult present and no legal representation, the police officers fed the confused and scared brothers information about the murder so that they knew facts that later would make them appear guilty. The officers told them that if they signed a piece of paper, they could go home with their mother, who was waiting at the station, demanding unsuccessfully to be allowed to accompany her sons in the interrogation. Once the confessions were signed, the young men's fates were sealed. It would take 30 years before they were exonerated, with McCollum serving the entire time on death row but Brown having his death sentence reversed and serving a life sentence. The brothers' low IQs made them easy targets for the police department, which was anxious to close a terrible case. With no attorney present, McCollum was tricked and intimidated into confessing to a crime that he did not commit. It was not until 30 years later, on September 2, 2014, that McCollum was exonerated. New DNA evidence linked another man to the murder; he not only lived in the house next to the crime scene but also had committed a similar murder just a few weeks later. By the time he was arrested for that crime, however, Brown and McCollum were already in jail awaiting trial, their signed confessions already in place.

Several other exonerated inmates have had low intellectual functioning. Two recent cases from the North Carolina Innocence Inquiry Commission illustrate these problems, though they did not involve death row inmates. Rather, these inmates were innocent men with serious intellectual disabilities who were wrongfully convicted of crimes they did not commit. In 2015, the commission recommended exoneration, and in 2016 a three-judge panel completely exonerated Knolly Brown; commission documents showed that he had scored 72, 67, 67, and 71 on successive IQ tests from 2009 through 2015; further, he had been diagnosed with PTSD, a personality disorder, schizophrenia, impulse control disorder, borderline intellectual functioning, and polysubstance dependence.[11] Such an individual would certainly have a hard time defending him- or herself against false accusations. In another North Carolina Innocence Inquiry Commission case leading to a 2014 exoneration for a crime committed in 1979, Willie Womble's attorney stated: "I recall Mr. Womble being 'very slow' or 'retarded.' There was very little I could do for him."[12] Many exoneration cases involve defendants with an intellectual disability, which is also a significant issue among those condemned to die.

Suicide and Depression

John H. Blume conducted a study of death row volunteers from 1976 through 2003, finding that 88 percent had a mental illness or substance abuse disorder (2005, 962). As a comparison, we have also calculated rates of suicidal tendencies, depression, and mental illness based on our own data. Our numbers are lower, but they result in similar findings—mental illness, suicidal behavior, suicide attempts, and depression are much higher among those who volunteer to skip the appeals process and die than among others on death row. Trauma does not always stem from the world outside of prison. Death row specifically can be a very demeaning and melancholy environment because every inmate faces the constant, harsh inevitability that he or she could be executed at any moment. This is often referred to as "death row syndrome" (Smith 2007, 238). An inmate may enter death row already suffering from depression or may develop it as a side effect of his or her experiences on death row. Suicide is not uncommon, and depression is quite common.

We noted in chapter 8 that roughly 10 percent of all executed inmates have been "volunteers" and that only some of these inmates were executed relatively soon after arriving on death row; others apparently decided to volunteer years after receiving their death sentence. We used the same methodology described earlier for assessing mental illness to assess previous suicide attempts, suicidal ideation, and depression. This analysis shows that of the inmates executed from 2000 to 2015, 10.07 percent had previously attempted suicide in their lifetime, and 14.4 percent had previously exhibited suicidal thoughts or tendencies. In the US general population, the Centers for Disease Control and Prevention report that in 2013, among adults, 3.9 percent had suicidal thoughts or tendencies, 1.1 percent made an actual plan to commit suicide, and 0.6 percent acted on that plan and made a suicide attempt.[13] So, again, the executed individuals have much higher rates of suicidal thoughts and attempts than the general population. Figure 12.4 shows how execution volunteers compare with others who have been executed.

Mental illness is very prevalent on death row, as we have documented throughout this chapter. However, it runs even higher among that subset of executed inmates who have volunteered to cease their legal appeals. Often after periods of depression, previous suicidal thoughts, or previous failed suicide attempts, they can indeed find a way. Execution of condemned inmates who drop their appeals is a form of "suicide

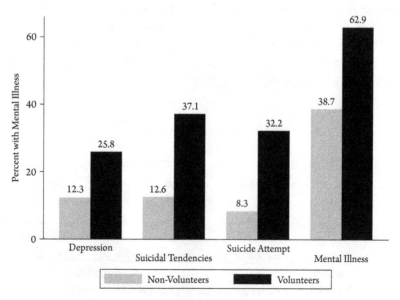

Figure 12.4 Mental Illness among Execution Volunteers

by state." About 10 percent of US executions, 137 individuals, have succeeded in doing so.

In a 2012 article in *Law and Society Review*, Meredith Rountree reviewed a number of Texas cases involving "volunteers" for execution. She begins with the story of Charles Rumbaugh, an inmate with "a history of psychiatric hospitalization and suicide attempts" (589), then continues:

> In an Amarillo, Texas federal district court hearing on whether he was sufficiently mentally competent to drop his legal appeals in order to expedite his execution, Rumbaugh testified:
> "All I really wanted to say is that it doesn't matter to me; that I've already picked my own executioner and I'll just make them kill me. If they don't want to do it . . . if they don't want to take me down there and execute me, I'll make them shoot me.
> I think I'll make them shoot me right now."
> At this point, Rumbaugh charged a deputy U.S. Marshal, who duly shot him. Rumbaugh survived, leaving the court to decide whether to permit Rumbaugh to hasten execution. The court did. (589–590, citation omitted)

Charles Rumbaugh was executed by the State of Texas on September 11, 1985. Rountree's evaluation of the common causes of suicide by execution highlights a number of features, in particular the ethical quandary for an attorney who is defending a client who may or may not be mentally competent to make a decision of this nature, but who is also required to represent the client's wishes (here, suicide). In Texas, she notes, the attorney is under no responsibility whatsoever to obtain professional testing for competency, and the records she reviewed showed no examples of requests for appointment of mental health experts to report to the defense attorney about the competency of the client. Instead, defense attorneys rely on the reports given to the court (Rountree 2012, 611). In sum, the adversarial legal process is in a quandary when one side refuses to fight.

Veterans and Post-traumatic Stress Disorder

Trauma does not always have to be from childhood. It can be physical trauma from a car accident, rape over the age of 18, domestic abuse, the death of a loved one, or another form of adulthood abuse. One type of adulthood trauma is war trauma.

A recent report published by the Death Penalty Information Center (2015) estimates that more than 300 death row inmates are military veterans, amounting to approximately 10 percent of the current death row population across the United States. In 2015, the first person executed was Andrew Brannan, a decorated

Vietnam War veteran. Brannan had previously received full mental disability from the Veterans Administration (DPIC 2015). This raises the crucial issue of the effects of combat on mental illness and diminished emotional capacity. A significant number of veterans who served in combat-intensive conflicts such as those in Vietnam, Afghanistan, and Iraq suffer from PTSD (DPIC 2015). While convicted veterans have indeed committed horrific and tragic crimes, it is questionable whether should they be eligible for execution, given the government's responsibility for the severe psychological trauma they experienced while serving in the US armed forces. An in-depth quantitative survey of veterans on North Carolina's death row and an investigation into a few individuals assist in understanding how an individual transitions from honorable veteran to being judged as the "worst of the worst."

North Carolina Case Study

North Carolina is home to a vast array of military bases, including Fort Bragg and Camp Lejeune, among many others. The state has one of the largest concentrations of military facilities in the United States and larger than average numbers of active duty personnel as well as veterans; more than 775,000 veterans live in North Carolina. Death row is no different; veterans are there as well. Since 1976, 401 inmates have been sentenced to death in North Carolina, and 43 have been executed. Table 12.1 shows how many of these individuals have been veterans.

Table 12.1 provides counts of the number of veterans, categorized by sentence outcome, who are or have been inmates on North Carolina's death row from 1976 through the end of 2014. Out of 401 total inmates, 44 have served in the military. This is approximately 11 percent of the entire death row population of North Carolina, which is close to the national estimate of 10 percent mentioned earlier. The State of North Carolina has executed 43 inmates since 1976, 6 of whom have been veterans. This constitutes about 14 percent of executions, which is a roughly similar proportion as those sentenced to death.

On December 2, 2005, Kenneth Lee Boyd was the 1,000th inmate executed in the United States.[14] As described by members of his community, Boyd was a loving father, shy yet likable, and a hard-working employee. With an IQ of only 77, he suffered a difficult childhood, growing up as an only child with a strict father. He had several learning disabilities, which prevented him from finishing high school despite his best efforts. As a result, Boyd joined the army at the age of 18 in 1966 and was first stationed in Germany. Due to his status as an only child, the army refused to deploy Boyd to Vietnam, but he volunteered to serve. In Vietnam, he witnessed many horrific acts in combat, including the death of many friends and getting trapped in a minefield. As a result, he suffered from several blackouts and was honorably discharged in 1969, receiving a medal for gallantry. He also developed severe alcoholism, and his alcohol abuse remained an issue after the end of his military service, when he also continued to experience blackouts and flashbacks.

Table 12.1 **Veterans on North Carolina's Death Row**

	Veterans
Executed	6
Suicide	0
Natural death	4
Resentenced to life	9
Found not guilty; exonerated	1
Currently on death row	24
Total	44

Note: Survey from consolidated list of 401 inmates who have served on North Carolina's death row from 1976 through December 31, 2014. Categories reflect sentence outcomes. Veterans refers to inmates with prior service in any branch in the US military. Veteran status obtained through the use of court records and news articles.

He married Julie Curry in 1973, and they had three sons; the marriage was often described as "stormy." On March 1988, Boyd entered the home of Curry, then his estranged wife, and shot and killed her and her father with a .357 Magnum pistol he had purchased just days prior. An alcoholic, he was heavily intoxicated at the time of the murder. After the murder he called 911 to report himself and subsequently surrendered to the police, not being able to recall the actions he had just carried out.

Kenneth Boyd did not have a violent past. His hard work, reputation in his community, disabilities, and service to his country suggest that he was not among the "worst of the worst." His marriage with Curry caused him a great deal of pain for which he lacked the adequate emotional coping capacity due to his PTSD. In police questioning, Boyd described the crime as being "similar to being in Vietnam."

A Recent Case from Texas

A recent case has brought attention to the controversy of executing someone who suffers from PTSD as a result of serving time in a war. John Thuesen grew up in rural Texas, playing football and raising turkeys while in high school and enlisting in the US Marines before graduation. A story from the *Dallas Morning News* explains the rest:

> When he returned to his rural Texas home near College Station, his family and friends said, he had changed.
>
> He was depressed and drank too much. A former girlfriend testified at his trial that he was violent with her. After an attempted suicide, Thuesen was briefly hospitalized, but despite his family's concerns that he needed

more treatment, doctors from the Veterans Administration sent him home. (Grissom 2015)

A few months later, in 2009, he shot and killed his girlfriend Rachel, a track star at Texas A&M University, and her brother, also a student. He was sentenced to death. While the jurors in the case were told that he had seen some violence while serving as a marine, they were not given expert testimony about the lasting effects of PTSD. Thuesen today sits on death row in Texas. Although some argue that it is contradictory for the government to subject individuals serving in the military to trauma, then for another arm of the government to sentence them to die for criminal acts they may not have committed if it were not for the PTSD induced by that trauma, others disagree. The prosecutors in Thuesen's case will seek to affirm his death sentence on appeal: PTSD, according to them, should not be a "pass" for horrific acts such as a double homicide of two college students (see Grissom 2015).[15]

Clearly, there are no simple answers in the area of mental competency and culpability for actions when an individual suffers from mental illness. The cases of US veterans bring into sharp relief, however, important questions about whether the death penalty is reserved for the worst criminals, or rather for the most vulnerable. The crimes of John Thuesen, Kenneth Boyd, and Alton Coleman were undoubtedly terrible. But it seems that their mental illnesses may have made them more, rather than less, susceptible to the death penalty. And, for Thuesen and Boyd at least, their status as veterans earned them little mercy.

Conclusion

Individuals with mental illness or intellectual deficits are heavily over-represented among those who have been executed. This may be because they commit more or more heinous crimes, because they make easy targets for prosecutors seeking the most severe punishment the system offers, because they appear very unsympathetic to juries considering their fates, because of traumas experienced during their death row incarceration, or for many other reasons. One thing is clear: modern standards of decency suggest that reduced capacity for reason or understanding right from wrong should be a mitigating factor, suggesting reduced eligibility for the death penalty. In reality, however, it may work in precisely the opposite way. Juries may be unsympathetic to these defendants, and judging from their over-representation among those actually executed from 2000 to 2015, appeals on their behalf are often not successful. We execute those with mental illness and intellectual disabilities at markedly high rates. Further, we actively participate in suicide by allowing the condemned to exercise their right to cease all appeals in spite of demonstrated suicidal tendencies.

Further Readings

Blume, John H. 2005. Killing the Willing: "Volunteers," Suicide and Competency. *Michigan Law Review* 103:939–1009.

Cunningham, Mark D., and Mark P. Vigen. 2002. Death Row Inmate Characteristics, Adjustment, and Confinement: A Critical Review of the Literature. *Behavioral Sciences and the Law* 20 (1–2): 191–210.

Death Penalty Information Center (DPIC). 2015. *Battle Scars: Military Veterans and the Death Penalty*. November 11. Washington, DC: Death Penalty Information Center. http://www.deathpenaltyinfo.org/veterans.

Edens, John F., John Clark, Shannon Toney Smith, Jennifer Cox, and Shannon E. Kelley. 2013. Bold, Smart, Dangerous and Evil: Perceived Correlates of Core Psychopathic Traits among Jury Panel Members. *Personality and Mental Health* 7 (2): 143–153.

Edens, John F., Karen M. Davis, Krissie Fernandez Smith, and Laura S. Guy. 2013. No Sympathy for the Devil: Attributing Psychopathic Traits to Capital Murderers Also Predicts Support for Executing Them. *Personality Disorders: Theory, Research, and Treatment* 4 (2): 175–181.

Perlin, Michael L. 2013. *Mental Disability and the Death Penalty*. Lanham, MD: Rowman and Littlefield.

13

How Deep Is Public Support for the Death Penalty?

To this point, this book has largely focused on the trends present in the *application* of the death penalty.[1] Here we step back and ask how the general public feels about the practice. In our exploration of public opinion, we consider how it depends on the precise question asked in the survey, how it has evolved over time, how it differs from place to place, and how all these factors correlate (or not) with actual use of the punishment.

Public opinion also carries direct legal significance. The US Supreme Court has explicitly stated that public opinion on the death penalty may serve as a factor in determining the constitutionality of the practice. In 1910 the Court directly tied the Eighth Amendment to public opinion, stating: "[I]t is not fastened to the absolute but may acquire meaning as public opinion becomes enlightened by a humane justice" (*Weems v. United States*). In *Furman v. Georgia*, the Court recognized public opinion as an indicator of "contemporary standards of decency." Similar references by the Court in death cases came in *Atkins v. Virginia* (2002), in which the Court invalidated the death penalty for those with intellectual impairments, and in *Roper v. Simmons* (2005), in which the death penalty for juveniles was ruled unconstitutional. Public opinion is important in determining the constitutionality of capital punishment.

Because capital punishment is explicitly referenced in the US Bill of Rights (Fifth Amendment, referring to a "capital, or otherwise infamous, crime," "jeopardy of life," and being "deprived of life"; and later in the Fourteenth Amendment, referring to the possibility that a state may "deprive any person of life"), and since during the time of the ratification, governments commonly executed and tortured individuals convicted of crimes, it is clear that any "original intent" interpretation of the Constitution would have to find, at least in the abstract, that the death penalty meets constitutional standards. Supreme Court majority opinions and dissents have often made this point. On the other hand, the Eighth Amendment bars "cruel and unusual" punishments, and the Fourteenth Amendment requires "equal protection" of the law, so there are at least potential contradictions within the constitution itself. But it is clear that one cannot argue that the framers envisioned a world without capital punishment, since it is explicitly referenced in the Bill of Rights. The constitutional questions associated with the death penalty must involve not abstract questions but particular ones, or relate to such concepts as "evolving standards of decency," a concept to which the Court has referred on a regular basis for more than 100 years. Thus, public opinion on the death penalty is not just an academic question; it has direct constitutional relevance.

This chapter presents an analysis of question wording to show the influence that wording can have on apparent levels of public support for capital punishment. It then develops a comprehensive index of aggregate public opinion over time, covering the entire period from 1976 through 2015, showing the rise and decline in public support for the death penalty. Over time, we show that opinion has closely tracked death sentences; as opinion grew warmer to the death penalty in the 1970s through the 1990s, the number of death sentences increased. As public support has declined since the mid-1990s, so too has the use of capital punishment. This suggests that public opinion truly is part of a broader system of "evolving standards," but it also indicates that standards can evolve in any direction. The growth in support for capital punishment came also at a time when legislatures were expanding its applicability, and during which its use grew. Since the mid-1990s, public opinion has been in concert with many other indicators such as the number of death sentences, legislative actions to restrict or abolish the use of the punishment, the number of executions, and the number of distinct legal jurisdictions (states, counties) carrying out executions, as we explore in chapter 15. We also present new evidence on regional and state-by-state variation in death penalty opinion. Comparing opinion with the number of executions, however, we find that there is almost no correlation whatsoever. Finally, we look in detail at the state of Texas, showing that Houston residents are in fact less supportive of the death penalty than residents of other areas of the state, clearly indicating that Houston's high execution numbers cannot be explained by public opinion. Thus, the data suggest that geographical variability in the use of the death penalty cannot be explained directly by measures of public opinion. This may be because the "death qualification" limits participation on capital juries only to those willing to vote for death at least in some circumstances.

Understanding Public Opinion
on Capital Punishment

Most people know very little about the death penalty, but they nevertheless support it. Thurgood Marshall famously argued in his *Furman* decision that public opinion polls, while interesting, are of only limited use in understanding death penalty opinion. The issue, he wrote, was not so much what people think but more what they *would* think if they knew the facts (see Sarat and Vidmar 1976; Bohm 2012; Bohm, Clark, and Aveni 1991).[2]

The death penalty has traditionally maintained majority support over time, with Gallup poll questions regularly generating average responses in the 60 to 80 percent range in favor. Figure 13.1 traces responses to the most common question that Gallup has asked over the years.[3] The question was first asked in 1936 and, as the figure shows, has been asked regularly throughout the modern period, increasingly so since about 2000.

In response to the question "Are you in favor of or opposed to the death penalty for persons convicted of murder" (hereafter, "Gallup Murder"), anywhere between 42 and 80 percent of Gallup respondents have answered "in favor" over 53 administrations of the survey; the average value is 65 percent support. The low point occurred in 1965, the only time at which opposition surpassed support. Support rose steadily from that time until reaching its peak in 1994. Since then, it has declined substantially, but the series ends in 2015 with values of 61 to 37 in support of the death penalty.

The raw answers to the Gallup Murder question provide important but limited information about the state of public opinion; in this chapter we seek to go much deeper into the meaning of these trends. One key issue is to look at precise question wording. The Gallup Murder question, we will show, generates higher apparent levels of support for the death penalty than almost any other question wording that has commonly been used. Some polling questions, including those posed by

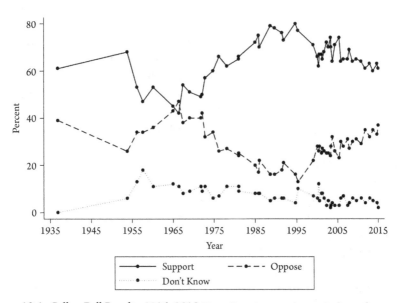

Figure 13.1 Gallup Poll Results, 1936–2015. Note: Question text: Are you in favor of or opposed to the death penalty for persons convicted of murder? Source: Gallup Poll.

Gallup, attempt to measure *why* people support the death penalty, asking: "[I]t is a deterrent, that is fear of such punishment discourages potential murderers ... is this among the best reason to support the death penalty, or not?" The mention of a particular group, such as those with intellectual disabilities or juveniles, often leads to a large decrease in support. Similarly, the presentation of alternate punishments, like life without parole (LWOP), causes a drop in support (sometimes a very substantial one). On occasion, when the death penalty is one option, but LWOP and a penalty of life with the possibility of parole after a long time period are also presented as options, support for the death penalty can be surprisingly low.[4] Question wording must be considered in any evaluation of public support for the death penalty (for examples, see Bowers 1993; Cullen, Fisher, and Applegate 2000; Durham, Elrod, and Kinkade 1996; Ellsworth and Gross 1994; Fox, Radelet, and Bonsteel 1991; Vidmar and Ellsworth 1974).

In studying public opinion, it is important to keep in mind how responding to a survey questionnaire differs from the experience of sitting on a capital jury. To the survey respondent, 45 minutes of questions and answers on a variety of topics may seem interesting, or perhaps not. When a question or two refers to capital punishment, these are considered abstract issues, and people respond accordingly, perhaps based on general, abstract beliefs. The Gallup Murder question does not specify which types of murders it is referring to, for example. Very few might support the death penalty for second-degree homicides or crimes of passion. On the other hand, more respondents typically do express support when the names of particularly infamous criminals are used. But the question is quite vague, asking about general attitudes, not specific applications. While the public is quick to assert their abstract support for the death penalty, the penalty is rare. With more than 700,000 homicides since 1976 but only about 8,000 death sentences and just 1,422 executions, it is clear that death is not, in fact, a very common punishment for murder. So there is a puzzle of how we can have such high apparent levels of support for the death penalty in the abstract, based on public opinion polls, and such relatively rare use of it, given the scope of the homicide problem in the United States. Not only is generalized public opinion relatively high, given the low rates at which juries impose death, but this is even more impressive when we consider that those who are morally opposed to the death penalty are not allowed to sit on capital juries. Clearly, the jury experience is very different from the survey one, judging from the vast disjuncture between expressed opinion in national surveys and the behaviors of juries.

A series of Gallup surveys explores the reasons Americans give for their support for the death penalty.[5] Gallup coded the open-ended responses to the question "Why do you favor the death penalty for persons convicted of murder?" The most common response was always some version of " 'An eye for an eye'/fair punishment/they took a life/fits the crime": 50 percent said this in 1991, 48 percent in 2001, 37 percent in 2003, and 35 percent in 2014. Other prominent answers were deterrence (declining from 19 percent in 1991 to 6 percent in 2014); cost savings (peaking at 20 percent in 2001, down to 11 percent in 2003 and 14 percent in 2014); incapacitation (19 percent in 1991, down to 7 percent in 2014); and deterrence/set an example (13 percent in 1991, down to 6 percent in 2014). No other response category received as much as 10 percent of the answers in any given year.

The same surveys asked for reasons that individuals oppose the death penalty, and here the answers focus on "It is wrong to take a life" (41 percent in 1991, 46 percent in 2003, and 40 percent in 2014); the possibility of convicting the innocent (11 percent in 1991, 25 percent in 2003, and 17 percent in 2014); such punishments should be left to God/religious reasons (17, 13, and 17 percent, respectively, across the three survey administrations); no other categories received more than 10 percent of the responses. So we have retribution/just deserts on the one hand, and a moral opposition to killing on the other.

The abstract nature of public opinion questions about the death penalty, and the highly abstract/moralistic/religious-based reasons that are the most common justifications for support of or opposition to the death penalty make it perhaps surprising that such opinions would change much over time. After all, in the abstract, people are unlikely to waver in their feeling that "it is wrong to take a life" or that some crimes are so heinous that death is the only punishment that "fits the crime." Thus, we have some interesting puzzles to explore.

Question Wording and Support for the Death Penalty over Time

It is worth questioning exactly what the Gallup Murder question, like any other, means. How should one interpret a positive or a negative response? The question refers to "persons convicted of murder." Does that mean all murderers? All first-degree murderers? A select few of the most egregious ones? Those who kill a particular target, such as the president or a child? Those who combine murder with torture? In fact, the question does not specify, so we cannot know. But we do know that the exact question wording makes a difference in generating different levels of apparent support.

Table 13.1 shows five different question wordings and their corresponding level of pro–death penalty responses. Each of these questions was posed to a national sample of American adults during 1995. As mentioned earlier, 1995 was when enthusiasm for the death penalty was near its peak, and in response to the Gallup Murder question, 80 percent gave the pro–death penalty response. However, when asked about sentencing a "young teenager" or someone who was "only an accomplice" to the crime, support drops to 52, then 32 percent. And when asked if any innocent people have been sentenced to death in the past 20 years, only 14 percent of Americans say they do not believe this to be the case. While the last question is not directly related to support for the death penalty, it

---

Table 13.1 **Public Support for the Death Penalty by Question Wording, 1995**

Question Wording	Pro- Response	Percent Pro-
Do you favor or oppose the death penalty for persons convicted of murder?	Favor	80
In a recent case that received a lot of media attention, Susan Smith confessed to drowning her two young sons in her car. If found guilty of murder in this case, do you think Susan Smith should receive the death penalty, or not?	Yes	71
Please tell me whether you would generally favor or oppose the death penalty for murder in each of the following circumstances. If the convicted person was . . . a young teenager at the time of the crime, would you favor or oppose the death penalty?	Favor	52
Please tell me whether you would generally favor or oppose the death penalty for murder in each of the following circumstances. If the convicted person was . . . only an accomplice to the person who actually did the killing, would you favor or oppose the death penalty?	Favor	32
How often do you think a person has been sentenced to the death penalty who was, in fact, innocent of the crime he was charged with? Do you think this has ever happened in the past 20 years, or do you think it has never happened	Never	14

Source: Surveys collected from iPoll, made available through the Roper Center for Public Opinion Research, Cornell University: https://ropercenter.cornell.edu/ipoll-database/.

does reflect an attitude of trust in the system. And, as we will see, trends over time even in such indirect questions can be helpful in constructing an index of aggregate public opinion over time.

Table 13.1 provides insight into how different questions on the death penalty generate vastly different levels of support. The first question, on favoring or opposing the death penalty for murder, is the most commonly asked question on the subject by survey organizations. As we saw earlier, most who respond affirmatively to this question assert an "eye for an eye" reason for doing so. At the abstract level, many feel that way. In contrast, referencing a specific case, even a particularly high-profile one like Susan Smith's, lowered the level of support for the death penalty in 1995.[6] Referring to "young teenagers" or to someone who was "only an accomplice" moves opinion to around 50 percent or even significantly lower, and this is in the same year that the same survey organization found 80 percent support for the death penalty using the "generic" question. We do not interpret the last question in the table as an indicator of support or opposition to the death penalty but include it there to indicate the range of responses that are possible for questions about the death penalty in general.

In response to the questions "How often do you think a person has been sentenced to the death penalty who was, in fact, innocent of the crime he was charged with? Do you think this has ever happened in the past 20 years, or do you think it has never happened?" 86 percent of people agreed that an innocent person has been sentenced. While this question does not directly test whether or not respondents approve of the death penalty, it certainly presents a possible contradiction. A vast majority of individuals agree that an innocent person has been wrongfully condemned in the past 20 years, yet a vast majority of individuals also support the death penalty.

In 2005, CBS News asked the question "What do you think should be the penalty for persons convicted of murder—the death penalty, or life in prison with no chance of parole, or a long prison sentence with a chance of parole?" Only 46 percent of respondents chose the death penalty. In that same year, the Gallup Murder question generated 76 percent support, and the "Gallup Life" question generated 49 percent support. So we can see that listing alternative punishments in the question can significantly move apparent levels of support: from 76 to 46 percent support in this example. But we should recall that in 2005, every state that had the death penalty also offered these lower possible penalties for the crime of murder. But simply reminding the survey respondent of these facts altered their responses dramatically. So question wording matters a lot, and we need to be careful in interpreting responses to any single question. In the following section, we demonstrate that it is possible to generate a single index of public opinion support for the death penalty regardless of the particular questions used.

Constructing an Index of Public Opinion

Table 13.2 shows eight different question wordings that have been posed to national samples of Americans from various reputable survey research organizations such as Gallup, CBS/New York Times, the National Opinion Research Center (NORC), and others. The Gallup Murder question discussed earlier was asked in 26 separate years from 1976 through 2015, the period of our focus here. NORC has asked almost the identical question 24 times in the same time period. The table lists for each question the exact question wording, the number of years it was asked,[7] and the average pro–death penalty response that the question generated.[8]

The different levels of support shown in Table 13.2 should not be taken too seriously because they represent averages across responses at different times. Table 13.3

Table 13.2 **Different Question Wordings**

Question Name	Question Wording	Number of Years Asked	Average Support
A. Gallup Murder	Are you in favor of the death penalty for a person convicted of murder?	26	73
B. NORC Murder	Do you favor or oppose the death penalty for persons convicted of murder?	24	58
C. Gallup Life	If you could choose between the following two approaches, which do you think is the better penalty for murder—the death penalty or life imprisonment, with absolutely no possibility of parole?	16	58
D. Gallup Morally Acceptable	Regardless of whether or not you think it should be legal, for each one, please tell me whether you personally believe that in general it is morally acceptable or morally wrong. How about . . . the death penalty?	15	69
E. Gallup Often	In your opinion, is the death penalty imposed—too often, about the right amount, or not often enough?	13	73
F. PSR Murder	I'd like to read you a list of some programs and proposals that are being discussed in this country today. For each one, please tell me whether you strongly favor, favor, oppose, or strongly oppose it . . . . The death penalty for persons convicted of murder.	10	72
G. Gallup Applied Fairly	Generally speaking, do you believe the death penalty is applied fairly or unfairly in this country today?	10	60
H. ABC News Murder	Do you favor or oppose the death penalty for persons convicted of murder?	8	73

Source: See Table 13.1.

shows how responses for each of the questions presented in Table 13.2 have varied over time. Glancing down the columns, it is clear that support for capital punishment is not static; it goes up and down over time. Glancing across the rows, we see how levels of apparent support differ depending on the question wording; because each row represents the year when the question was asked of a random sample of American adults, these are directly comparable. Glancing down several columns in parallel, we can see that the trends in one question series seem closely reflected in the others. Over time, the different series follow parallel trends; when one goes up over time beyond the margin of error, so too do the others; when one goes down significantly, so do the others. We will take advantage of this shared movement over time across multiple question wordings to develop an overall index of the dynamic movement of public opinion over time. In the far-right column, the table shows the value of an index of public opinion, which we explain later. This index is made up not only of the questions included in this table but from others as well. It can be thought of as a weighted average of every public opinion poll on the topic of the death penalty. But before we explain the construction of the index in detail, let us consider the questions one at a time.

Responses to Question A, the Gallup Murder question, reaches a peak of 86 percent in 1995, declining to a low of 63 in 2013.[9] Question B, which is virtually identical in wording but comes from NORC rather than Gallup, shows very similar levels of support, high in the 1980s and 1990s before declining as well. Question C, which refers to the possibility of LWOP, is consistently lower than the other two questions but also reaches its highest levels in the mid-1990s before declining significantly. The other columns can be read in the same manner.

Table 13.3 makes clear that each individual question may generate different levels of support, but when public opinion tends to move up or down over time, this dynamic trend is reflected in almost any individual survey question. Therefore, we can construct an aggregate index of public opinion over time that reflects the shared movement of all the individual questions, making the best use of all available information and reflecting the best estimate of the dynamics of US public opinion across the entire time period from 1976 through 2015. We explain the construction of the index in greater detail in appendix D on our website; it is an update of that presented in Baumgartner, De Boef, and Boydstun (2008). Figure 13.2 presents the index along with the five questions from Tables 13.2 and 13.3 that were asked the most often.

The Stimson Wcalc algorithm, now standard in the analysis of aggregate dynamics of public opinion, assesses the shared movement over time in survey responses to the same question at two or more time points. If the questions load on the same underlying factor, assessed by shared variance over time, then the overall index can be seen as representative of the underlying public opinion on that topic. Our index on death penalty opinion explains 72.51 percent of the underlying variance in movement across all 66 individual question series.[10]

Table 13.3 **Survey Responses to Different Question Wordings, 1976–2015**

Year	A	B	C	D	E	F	G	H	Index
1976	72	69							59
1977		72							60
1978	70	70							58
1979									55
1980		71							58
1981	73							78	59
1982		78						78	64
1983		77							64
1984		74							63
1985	80	80	62						65
1986	76	75	61						63
1987		74							63
1988	83	76							65
1989	83	79							66
1990		80							67
1991	79	77	60						66
1992			57					80	63
1993		77	67						66
1994	83	79	61						66
1995	86								67
1996						81		80	66
1997			68			76			65
1998		73							64
1999	76				73	77			62
2000	70	68	54		71				59
2001	72	69	55	70		71		69	58
2002	74	69	55	70	76	72	57		58
2003	71		55	67	76	68		67	57
2004	73	68	52	70	76		59		57
2005	72		59	74	79	70	64	68	59
2006	70		49	76	78	71	63	67	59

Table 13.3 **Continued**

Year	A	B	C	D	E	F	G	H	*Index*
2007	70			71			60		55
2008	68	67		67	77		59		56
2009	68			67	78		63		56
2010	69	68	52	70	81	68	62		56
2011	64			70	73	62			55
2012	66	65		63					52
2013	63			67	52		57		52
2014	66		53	69	57		55		53
2015				66					52

Source: Calculated from iPoll; see Table 13.1 for question wordings.

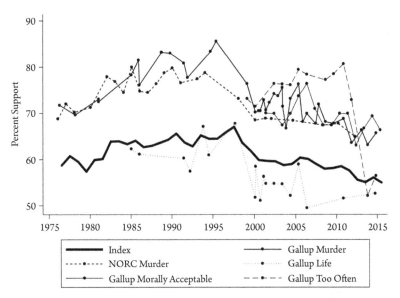

Figure 13.2 Index of Public Opinion with Its Five Largest Component Questions.
Note: The index is based on 66 individual questions, each posed at least twice to a national sample of US adults. A total of 488 national surveys are included. The five most common questions are listed individually (see Table 13.2 for question wordings). The index is generated using Jim Stimson's dyad ratios algorithm and Wcalc software. See appendix D on our website for more detail.

Figure 13.2, considered along with Table 13.3, makes two things clear: responses vary systematically depending on exactly how one asks the question, and there is significant movement in public opinion over time. No matter how we ask the question, opinion moves in the pro–death penalty direction from the beginning of the modern period until the mid-1990s, then begins a long decline.

It is important to recognize that our index of public opinion is sensitive to the mix of national surveys that are available to be included in it. The single most common survey question, the Gallup Murder question, generates some of the highest rates of support for the death penalty. While the resulting index clearly and accurately generates a dynamic index of opinion over time, it is difficult to assess what a particular value on the index means. That is, a score of 55 cannot be interpreted as relative support for or opposition to any particular option with regard to the death penalty, since it is a weighted mixture of responses to many different questions. However, we can compare the values on the index against their own values in previous or subsequent years: we know if the index is going up or down. Figure 13.3 presents a rescaled version of the index, where its value in 1976, the beginning of the modern era, is set at zero. This allows us to say how opinion in any given year compares with that point.

Support for capital punishment reached its peak in 1995. Following *Gregg v. Georgia*, use of and support for the death penalty increased, stemming from the encouragement of tougher punishments and more punitive policies. Support for the death penalty was an all-time high in 1995, at +8.7, and has since fallen to the lowest it has been since the death penalty was reinstated in 1976, at –6.9 in 2015. In the following sections, we explore how this index corresponds to use of the death penalty.

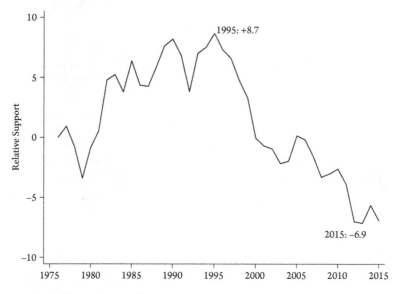

Figure 13.3 Public Opinion Index

Public Opinion and Policy Response

There are strong links between our public opinion index on the death penalty and trends over time in the use of the punishment. In contrast, the links between public opinion and public policy are not complete. We first focus on aggregate trends over time, then note some anomalies in the linkage between public opinion and the death penalty by looking at those categories of crimes that find little public support, but where the death penalty has nonetheless been used. Finally, we assess geographical differences in public opinion, looking cross-sectionally at the entire United States, then in more detail within the state of Texas to see if those jurisdictions with greater use of the penalty are also those with the highest levels of public opinion support. We find little evidence that this may be the case.

Aggregate Trends over Time

Using a similar process to the one we have used here, Peter Enns (2014, 2016) has recently shown that US public opinion grew dramatically more "punitive" with regard to crime in general. His index includes some death penalty questions but covers such things as support for harsh sentencing practices such as "three strikes" laws, mandatory minimum sentences, and many other elements. Figure 13.4 compares our index on capital punishment opinion with Enns's more general "crime punitiveness" index.

Public opinion on the death penalty tracks very closely with crime punitiveness in general among the public. Enns found a close relationship between public

Figure 13.4 Death Penalty Opinion and General Punitiveness. Note: Crime opinion from Enns 2014. Both series set to zero in 1976. Pearson's R = .88.

opinion on crime and policy response. His research showed that when the public's attitude toward crime was more punitive, incarceration rates went up. When public opinion appeared to be less harsh, incarceration rates diminished (Enns 2014). We find the same situation with regard to the death penalty. Figure 13.5 shows the relation between our measure of public opinion and the number of death sentences imposed annually from 1976 through 2015.

As the US Supreme Court has suggested, use of the death penalty strongly reflects "evolving standards of decency." As public opinion drifted upward with regard to support for the death penalty after its historic lows in the 1960s (see Figure 13.1), so too did the number of death sentences. Both death sentences and public opinion reached their peaks in the mid-1990s. Our opinion index reached a peak of +8.7 in 1995, just as the number of death sentences also peaked (averaging more than 310 from 1994 to 1996). At the end of the series, in 2015, there were just 49 death sentences, and the opinion index stood at a value of –6.9. Fifteen points of movement in aggregate public opinion represent a large shift by any measure, and here we show its substantial impact on death sentencing.

Of course, there is no direct causal mechanism that links death sentences to public opinion. After all, death qualification keeps all US juries uniformly accepting or at least tolerant of capital punishment, at least in theory. But public opinion does not evolve in a vacuum; it responds to changing aggregate social understandings, media coverage, and political trends. While opinion was drifting toward more support for the death penalty, so legislatures were expanding the list of crimes that were death-eligible, politicians were learning the political cost of opposing the death penalty or

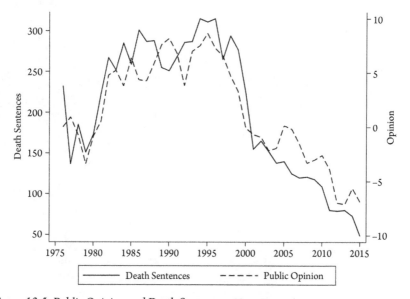

Figure 13.5 Public Opinion and Death Sentences. Note: Pearson's R = .92.

appearing soft on crime, and media coverage was drifting toward more routine coverage of death penalty expansions. For the past 20 years, however, all these trends have moved in the opposite direction, reflecting a broad social and political shift, perhaps most strongly brought on by concerns about the possibility of executing the innocent (see Baumgartner, De Boef, and Boydstun 2008). In any case, we can state with certainty that Figure 13.5 summarizes some very powerful and important social trends.

Lack of Public Opinion Support for Certain Death Penalty Practices

Felony Murder

We noted in chapter 5 that many states make it a capital crime to participate in a felony during which a murder occurs. That is, even a person who was not involved in the murder can be eligible for death if death occurred during the commission of a felony, and he or she participated in that felony. The prototypical example of this is the driver of a getaway car whose accomplice shoots a storekeeper; according to the felony murder doctrine, both the "triggerman" and the driver are eligible for death. According to the Death Penalty Information Center (DPIC), 10 individuals have been executed for such crimes since 1976 (DPIC 2016b).

Public support for the death penalty for accomplices is nearly nonexistent. Two questions in surveys conducted by the Princeton Survey Research Associates in 1995 and 1997 asked respondents about their support for capital punishment for accomplices to murder: "Please tell me whether you would generally favor or oppose the death penalty for murder in each case of the following circumstances. If the convicted person was . . . only an accomplice to the person who actually did the killing . . . would you favor or oppose the death penalty?" In 1995 the question generated only 32 percent support; this dropped to 27 percent support two years later when it was asked again. Note that 1995 and 1997 were near the peak of public opinion support for capital punishment overall, as we saw earlier in this chapter.

With approximately 70 percent of Americans expressing opposition to executing individuals who did not kill, even while participating in a felony during which a murder occurred, and even during a period when more than 80 percent of Americans reported support for the death penalty, one might think that it would never occur. And indeed, many capital defendants apparently gamble that it cannot happen. The "triggermen" in such crimes may know they are in serious trouble and accept a plea agreement whereas accomplices may feel they have good chances of avoiding death at trial; they can be wrong. Three of the triggermen associated with the 10 felony murder accomplices executed were sentenced to lesser terms (see DPIC 2016b). Doyle Skillern was executed by the State of Texas in 1985; his accomplice who pulled the trigger is eligible for parole. Oklahoma executed Steven Hatch in 1996 for crimes committed during a home invasion; his accomplice, Glen Ake, who killed a couple during the crime, is serving a life term. Texas executed Robert Thompson in 2009 but sentenced fatal shooter Sammy Butler to life in prison; Thompson had shot but not killed a clerk during a robbery; Butler's shot was fatal. We discussed in chapter 11 the case of Jeffrey Wood, whose scheduled execution in August 2016 was stayed so that lower courts could reconsider evidence by a psychologist that he "would certainly" pose a future risk to society; Wood is intellectually disabled and was in the car when another man, Daniel Reneau, committed homicide during a robbery; Reneau was executed in 2002 (see chapter 11; Associated Press 2016).

Vulnerable Populations: Those with Intellectual Disabilities, Juveniles, and the Mentally Ill

The public largely opposes the death penalty for various vulnerable populations, including individuals with intellectual disabilities or mental illness and juveniles. While constitutional practice has caught up with public opinion with regard to those who were juveniles at the time of their crimes (see *Roper v. Simmons*, 2005), we see continued litigation even after the Court ruled in *Atkins v. Virginia* (2002) that executing an inmate suffering from an intellectual disability was cruel and unusual. Finally, we saw in chapter 12 that those with mental illness are greatly over-represented on death row. Here, it may be that the abstract concern that the public shows about those with mental illness is counterbalanced by a visceral fear or lack of empathy when a seriously mentally ill defendant appears before a jury. Let us consider the three types of cases in turn.

Surveys on public support for the execution of those with intellectual disabilities were first posed in 1989, resulting in 71 percent opposition. Over time, the level of support has been fairly stable, never exceeding 29 percent. Prior to *Atkins v. Virginia*, however, it was not uncommon to execute those with intellectual disabilities, though exact counts are not known.

When the public has been asked about support for executing juveniles, responses have been relatively negative. In fact, in the earliest recorded survey on the topic, in 1936, Gallup asked a national sample its standard question, getting 61 percent support for the death penalty, and followed it up with a question about whether the respondent supports the penalty for "persons under 21" years of age. Support was cut in half. Table 13.4 shows what data are available.

Support for executing younger offenders was very low in 1936, according to the Gallup poll of the time. This is remarkable because, though it is beyond the scope of our focus on the "modern" death penalty, 1936 was near the peak historic use of the death penalty in the United States, which occurred in 1935, with 197 executions (see Baumgartner, De Boef, and Boydstun 2008, Figure 2.1). We found only two additional surveys specifically asking questions on this topic, from 1991 and 1995; both showed majority support for executing even "a young teenager," but these should also be considered within the context of the very high levels of support

Table 13.4 **Public Opinion Support for the Death Penalty in General and for Young Offenders**

Question Text	Year	Percent Support for the Death Penalty	Percent Support, Gallup Murder
If so, are you in favor of it (the death penalty for murder) for persons under 21?	1936	30	61
If a teenager commits a crime that could carry the death penalty for an adult, do you think he or she should receive a death sentence, or not?	1991	58	81
If the convicted person was . . . a young teenager at the time of the crime, would you favor or oppose the death penalty?	1995	52	86

Note: Percent support is calculated as a percent of those giving a directional response (i.e., it eliminates the "don't know" and "no answer" responses). Gallup Murder refers to responses to the Gallup Murder question during the same year. The Gallup Murder question is not focused on young offenders.

Source: See Table 13.1.

for the death penalty in general. Further, the 1990s were the time of concern with "superpredators"—supposedly dangerous young men with extreme disregard for any social values and immune to the possibility of rehabilitation (see DiIulio 1995). In sum, 52 percent support may seem very high today, but compared with 86 percent support for the death penalty in general in 1995, it was perhaps remarkably low, especially considering the rhetoric at the time associated with youthful crime waves. Jeffrey Fagan and Valerie West (2005) have carefully documented the declining use of the juvenile death penalty that presaged the 2002 decision by the Supreme Court finally to abolish it. "Evolving standards" of practice eventually converged with what the public had long been saying to pollsters.

If the public has never been particularly enthusiastic about the death penalty for youthful offenders, and while it has been ruled unconstitutional to subject a juvenile to the death penalty, in fact, in the modern period we have executed 22 inmates for crimes committed while they were juveniles, according to our analysis. So the public's lack of support in this case certainly did not preclude district attorneys from seeking and judges approving death sentences for youthful offenders.

The *Atkins* and *Roper* examples suggest that the Court may have "caught up" with the public, eliminating the death penalty for two classes of vulnerable defendants. Those with mental illness remain subject to the death penalty, though there is significant litigation on this issue today, as we saw in chapter 12. Further, in the case of mental illness, while the limited survey evidence that is available suggests that people express lower support for the death penalty for these individuals, we saw in chapter 12 that those with mental illness are routinely sentenced to death. Their crimes may be more aggravated; their demeanor in the courtroom may seem less appropriate; and jurors may feel they have enhanced "future dangerousness." So here is another example where it may be difficult to extrapolate from the abstract and general feelings expressed in a public opinion survey and the more visceral and emotional reactions in the jury room.

In sum, we see some significant gaps in the linkage between public opinion and death penalty practice when we look at juveniles, those with intellectual disabilities, those with mental illness, and those who are accomplices to a crime where a murder occurs. The public does not support executions of juveniles, those with mental illness, and those judged less culpable such as accomplices in a crime where another person actually killed the victim. Sometimes, juries and the US Supreme Court have been in line with these standards, and sometimes not. Juvenile executions have been ruled unconstitutional since *Roper* in 2005. Diminished mental capacity has excluded one from the death penalty since *Atkins* in 2002. But the execution of those with mental illness is not at all uncommon. And, although it is rare, we do occasionally execute those who are mere accomplices to a homicide, and many states allow this through their "felony murder" statutes.

State-by-State Variation in Public Opinion and Death Penalty Use

We know from chapter 6 that Texas executes more inmates than any other state. Here we ask whether we can explain that by public opinion. Are Texans much more supportive of capital punishment than, say, Floridians? A strong defense is often made of local variation in the use of the death penalty by arguing that local elections typically determine who is the district attorney and that local norms affect who sits on juries. For example, in a rebuttal to a comprehensive analysis of geographical disparities in Connecticut's death penalty, showing that one city was particularly more prone to use it than the rest of the state, Kent Scheidegger (2011) argued that this is the prerogative of local communities, and indeed the root of the entire jury system. Justices Scalia and Thomas argued similarly in dismissing Richard Glossip's claims and in responding to the arguments of their colleague Justice Breyer in his dissent from the case (*Glossip v. Gross*; Scalia, concurring opinion). They point out that the jury system is a "cornerstone of Anglo-American judicial procedure" (4) and argue that because one jury decided to be merciful in not assigning death cannot mean that another jury was wrong in withholding such mercy.

If juries and elected district attorneys behave differently across different areas of the country, or within different areas of the same state, perhaps this is a simple reflection of their local community norms. If so, we should be able to see this in measures of public opinion, once we pass the hurdle of measuring public opinion at the state or local level. That is what we do here.

As described earlier, Gallup has been asking its standard question for many years. With the cooperation of its staff, we were able to get individual-level survey response data for 24 iterations of the national survey, covering the years 1978 through 2015. Data included demographics and other characteristics of each respondent; the overall sample N was 28,443, or an average of slightly more than 1,000 per survey. This large compilation of data allows us to estimate public opinion for almost every state. (Alaska and Hawaii are excluded, and some states have low numbers of respondents, as we show later.) Of course, we are aggregating public opinion over many years, and we saw in the previous section that opinion has shifted dramatically over the years. However, we do not have sufficient data to see whether yearly trends in death sentences or executions in each state reflect changes in public opinion; in any case, death sentencing and execution use tend to follow national trends in each state. Julianna Pacheco, a leading expert on state-level public opinion, found in a 2014 study that death penalty opinion varies much more over time than it does across states. Looking at General Social Survey data from 1966 to 2002, she found that 85 percent of the variance in death penalty opinion was across time, and just 15 percent was across states. That is, there is strong evidence that states move in rough parallel over time, so that national trends toward or against support of the death penalty should affect each state relatively equally (see Pacheco 2014; see also Shirley and Gelman 2015, who present a more complicated picture based on Bayesian estimation techniques).

Table 13.5 presents our state-by-state estimates of public opinion on the death penalty. We report the number of respondents across all 24 survey administrations from 1978 through 2015 and calculate the percent in support of the death penalty as a percentage of all those expressing an opinion. (That is, we ignore the neutral responses, those who say they don't know, and those who did not answer the question.) The last column indicates the number of executions in that state, from chapter 6. Note that the table includes all 50 states but that the number of respondents from some states (including, for example, Alaska) is very low.

The "directional N" is the number of respondents in each state who, over 24 iterations of the Gallup poll, gave a pro– or anti–death penalty response. For 7 of the largest states, we have more than 1,000 respondents, making our estimates of public opinion in those states most likely very accurate. For a few states, however, the number of respondents dwindles to fewer than 100 (South Dakota, North Dakota, Delaware, Wyoming, Hawaii, and Alaska). Two of these states (Hawaii and Alaska) have never had the death penalty. Figure 13.6 uses the same data as Table 13.5 and shows the correlation between public support for the death penalty and the number of executions carried out in the modern period. The figure includes the 35 states that had the death penalty for the bulk of the period under consideration (i.e., it retains such states as Connecticut and Illinois, which had the death penalty for most

Table 13.5 **Death Penalty Public Opinion Data by State, 1978–2015**

State	Pro-DP N	Anti-DP N	Directional N	Survey N	Pro-DP Percent	Executions 1976–2015
AL	271	95	366	415	74.04	57
AK	10	8	18	20	55.56	0
AR	195	55	250	269	78.00	27
AZ	280	110	390	426	71.79	37
CA	1,880	778	2,658	2,905	70.73	13
CO	328	143	471	529	69.64	1
CT	207	105	312	345	66.35	1
DE	50	21	71	80	70.42	16
FL	1,020	303	1,323	1,439	77.10	92
GA	521	195	721	786	72.77	61
HI	26	5	31	34	83.87	0
IA	246	88	334	365	73.65	0
ID	130	20	150	162	86.67	3
IL	758	282	1,040	1,147	72.88	12
IN	469	153	621	691	75.36	20
KS	210	85	295	324	71.19	0
KY	301	115	416	468	72.36	3
LA	331	85	416	458	79.57	28
MA	350	261	611	683	57.28	0
MD	334	162	496	550	67.34	5
ME	100	56	156	185	64.10	0
MI	582	282	864	967	67.36	0
MN	277	194	471	543	58.81	0
MO	423	114	537	591	78.77	86
MS	193	79	272	301	70.96	21
MT	109	29	138	154	78.99	3
NC	519	210	729	812	71.19	43
ND	50	24	74	78	67.57	0
NE	180	54	234	260	76.92	3
NH	95	35	130	145	73.08	0
NJ	536	215	751	832	71.37	0

Table 13.5 **Continued**

State	Pro-DP N	Anti-DP N	Directional N	Survey N	Pro-DP Percent	Executions 1976–2015
NM	137	54	191	211	71.73	1
NV	117	31	148	159	79.05	12
NY	1,130	597	1,727	1,905	65.43	0
OH	864	247	1,111	1,211	77.77	53
OK	265	64	329	365	80.55	112
OR	228	105	333	369	68.47	2
PA	1,061	352	1,413	1,544	75.09	3
RI	76	50	126	134	60.32	0
SC	252	98	350	398	72.00	43
SD	66	20	86	93	76.74	3
TN	426	133	559	638	76.21	6
TX	1,134	381	1,515	1,655	74.85	533
UT	211	31	242	266	87.19	7
VA	479	218	697	765	68.72	111
WA	522	179	701	758	74.47	5
WI	398	186	584	645	68.15	0
WV	165	59	224	242	73.66	0
WY	35	5	40	48	87.50	1

Note: Pro-DP, anti-DP N = total number of responses pro- or anti-DP; directional N = sum of previous two variables, all respondents who gave a "directional" response; survey N = total number of respondents in that state, across all the surveys (this number may be larger than the directional N because it includes people who did not respond to the question, or who gave neutral responses); pro-DP percent = percentages based on the Ns in the second, third, and fourth columns; executions = number of executions from 1977 to 2015.

Source: Public opinion data are based on 25 surveys conducted by Gallup between 1978 and 2015. Each question asks, "Do you favor or oppose the death penalty for peoples convicted of murder?" These data were graciously made available to us by Gallup.

of the modern period and abolished only in the last 10 years), and it excludes the 3 additional states with low numbers of survey respondents.

The evidence here is quite clear: the number of executions a given state has is almost unrelated to the level of support for capital punishment in that same state. Virginia, the state with the third *most* executions in the post-*Furman* period, has the fifth *lowest* level of public support for the death penalty among states with capital punishment statutes for the majority of the period. Texas, which has nearly five times as many executions as Oklahoma, the state with the second most executions

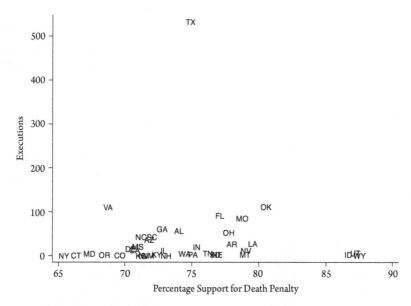

Figure 13.6 Death Penalty Public Opinion and Executions by State. Note: Includes 35 states that had capital punishment statutes for the majority of the modern period and with a minimum of 100 respondents. Pearson's R = .072. Source: Table 13.5

in the post-*Furman* period, is not the state with the highest level of public support for capital punishment. In fact, 17 states with capital punishment statues for the majority of the post-*Furman* period have higher levels of public support for the death penalty than Texas. Among the big users of the death penalty, Virginia, Georgia, Alabama, Texas, Florida, Ohio, Missouri, and Oklahoma, public opinion ranges from the lowest quartile to the highest. The overall correlation, .072, shows that there is virtually no relation between opinion and use of the death penalty.

Texas Public Opinion

We know from chapter 6 and the preceding analysis that Texas stands out as the center of the US capital punishment system. The State of Texas has executed 533 individuals in the post-*Gregg* period, a number that is nearly five times as high as in Oklahoma, the state with the second most executions during this time period. The primary driver of this high execution count is Harris County, the "epicenter" of executions and capital convictions. The county, which overlaps with the city of Houston, has executed 116 individuals since 1976—almost one-quarter of all executions within the state of Texas, and almost one-tenth of all those carried out nationally. We showed earlier that public support in Texas is not particularly high on the death penalty by national standards: Oklahoma, Florida, Missouri, Louisiana, Nevada, and several other states rank higher than Texas with regard to public

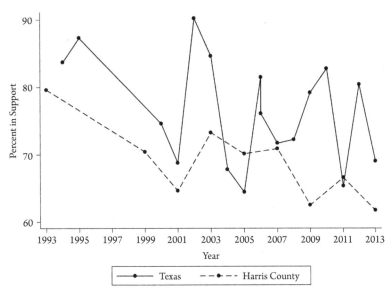

Figure 13.7 Texas and Harris County Public Opinion on the Death Penalty. Note: Question text: Are you in favor of the death penalty for persons convicted of murder? Source: Texas: Gallup Poll. Harris County: Houston Area Survey (Rice University Kinder Institute). Percent support is calculated on the basis of those expressing an opinion.

support for the death penalty. What about within Texas? Is Houston more support-ive of the punishment than, say, Dallas? We exploit another data resource to look at the linkages between public opinion and executions within the state of Texas here.

Figure 13.7 compares Harris County public opinion to that of the State of Texas. For Texas, we used the Gallup poll results from the previous section. For Harris County, we made use of a periodic Rice University/Kinder Institute survey of Houston area residents. The Houston Area Survey has regularly polled samples of 650 or more residents of Harris County, using a random probability design. The sample was expanded beginning in 2012 to include 1,300 residents of the nine-country Houston metropolitan region. But from 1990 to 2011, it has been a random sample of Harris County adults.[11]

While the numbers in Figure 13.7 fluctuate each year, the 17 Texas polls included there show an average level of support of 76 percent; the nine Houston Area Surveys show an average of 69. So, by about 7 points, average public support in Harris County is actually *lower* than that for the state overall. And if we compare surveys conducted in the same year, support in Harris County is almost always lower than the statewide results; in the two cases where it is higher, it is marginally so, within likely sampling variability. This is no anomaly. In fact, Houston residents are not particularly fond of the death penalty (see Price 2015). The area has a large African

Table 13.6 **Death Penalty and Its Alternatives, Houston Area Survey**

Preferred Punishment	2000	2004	2006	2008	2010	2012	2014
Death penalty	40.6	33.6	31.8	39.2	36.9	30.3	28.1
Life without parole	31.0	45.4	46.3	43.1	39.7	38.2	39.1
Life with parole after 25 years	22.3	16.6	17.4	13.1	14.1	26.5	29.4
Refused/don't know	6.1	4.4	4.5	4.6	9.3	4.9	3.4
Total	100.0	100.0	100.0	100.0	100.0	99.9	100.0
Total responses	650	650	765	702	750	1266	959

Note: Cell entries are percent of respondents giving each answer. Ns are indicated in the last row. Question text: What do you think should generally be the penalty for persons convicted of first-degree murder: the death penalty, life imprisonment with no chance for parole, or life imprisonment with a chance for parole after 25 years?

Source: Houston Area Survey. https://kinder.rice.edu/KHAS/Death_Penalty/.

American population and a large and rapidly growing Hispanic population; both of these groups are less likely than whites to support the death penalty in general.

For the past 15 years, the Houston Area Survey has asked about alternative punishments to the death penalty. Table 13.6 lays out these results. In 2014 the death penalty came in third out of the three options provided. It is hard to use public opinion as the explanation for why Houston is the epicenter of the US death penalty.

Since 2010, the University of Texas and the *Texas Tribune* have regularly surveyed samples of the adult population throughout Texas and have reported levels of death penalty support for the major urban areas: Houston metro, Dallas–Fort Worth area, San Antonio area, Austin area, and other parts of the state. We know that these areas can be ranked in order as Houston, Dallas–Fort Worth, San Antonio, the rest of Texas, and Austin in terms of use of the death penalty. Do they rank the same way in terms of public opinion? Figure 13.8 shows that they do not.

Figure 13.8 indicates that differing local norms do not account for geographical variation in the application of the death penalty across the regions of Texas. The data come from responses to a question asked by the *Texas Tribune* that read, "Do you strongly support, somewhat support, somewhat oppose or strongly oppose the death penalty?" This survey was repeated nine times from 2010 to 2015, and the figure shows the percent of respondents expressing an opinion who were supportive. While there is some variation from survey to survey, overall the levels of support are as follows: other areas, 80.6; San Antonio, 79.0; Dallas–Fort Worth, 74.3; Houston, 72.5; and Austin, 65.0. In other words, public opinion cannot be used as the explanation for why Harris County has so many executions.

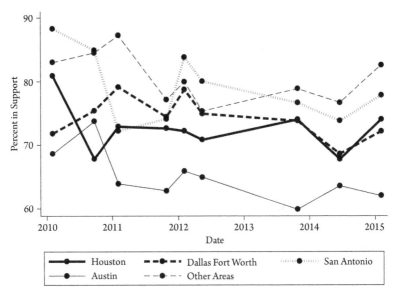

Figure 13.8 Support for Death Penalty in the Major Cities of Texas. Note: Question text: Do you strongly support, somewhat support, somewhat oppose, or strongly oppose the death penalty? Source: Texas Tribune.

Conclusion

In response to general survey questions about the death penalty, large percentages of US adults routinely express their support. But the death penalty is handed out in only a small fraction of homicide cases, in spite of death qualification. In exploring the many puzzles associated with public opinion and the death penalty, we can say the following. First, aggregate opinion over time has clearly moved substantially during the 40 years since *Gregg*. No matter how the question was asked, opinion drifted upward until the mid-1990s and has been declining since then. Innocence, cost, controversies involving lethal injections, botched executions, and other factors have clearly dampened whatever enthusiasm Americans may once have been said to have for capital punishment. Second, the public has never strongly supported capital punishment for certain vulnerable populations, or at least so they say in surveys. Juveniles, those with mental illness, those with intellectual disabilities, women, and those who were only accomplices to the crime are typically judged less deserving of a death sentence. In some cases, constitutional practice has caught up with the public in these matters (e.g., with *Atkins* in 2002 and *Roper* in 2005, barring the execution of those with intellectual disabilities and of juveniles), and in other cases (those with mental illness, women, non-triggerman accomplices), it has not. Third, every state with the death penalty also has LWOP. But when survey respondents are asked about their relative preference for death versus LWOP, support for death always goes down significantly. This may be why juries actually impose death in a relatively low percentage of all homicide cases, in spite of juries having been selected to include only those who support the punishment in the abstract. Finally, there is substantial variation in public opinion across the states and even within states. We found no evidence that the cumulative use of capital punishment over the modern period is in any way correlated with geographical variation in public opinion, however.

Further Readings

Baumgartner, Frank R., Suzanna L. De Boef, and Amber E. Boydstun. 2008. *The Decline of the Death Penalty and the Discovery of Innocence*. New York: Cambridge University Press.

Ellsworth, Phoebe, and Samuel R. Gross, 1994. Hardening of the Attitudes: Americans' Views on the Death Penalty. *Journal of Social Issues* 50 (2): 19–52.

Enns, Peter K. 2016. *Incarceration Nation: How the United States Became the Most Punitive Democracy in the World*. New York: Cambridge University Press.

Fagan, Jeffrey, and Valerie West. 2005. The Decline of the Juvenile Death Penalty: Scientific Evidence of Evolving Norms. *Journal of Criminal Law and Criminology* 95 (2): 427–500.

Gross, Samuel R. 1998. Update: American Public Opinion on the Death Penalty—It's Getting Personal. *Cornell Law Review* 83 (6): 1448–1475.

Pacheco, Julianna. 2014. Measuring and Evaluating Changes in State Opinion across Eight Issues. *American Politics Research* 42 (6): 986–1009.

Peffley, Mark, and Jon Hurwitz. 2007. Persuasion and Resistance: Race and the Death Penalty in America. *American Journal of Political Science* 51 (4): 996–1012.

———. 2010. *Justice in America: The Separate Realities of Blacks and Whites*. New York: Cambridge University Press.

Price, Melynda J. 2015. *At the Cross: Race, Religion and Citizenship in the Politics of the Death Penalty among African Americans*. New York: Oxford University Press.

Stimson, James A. 1998. *Public Opinion in America: Moods, Cycles, and Swings*. 2nd ed. Boulder, CO: Westview Press.

Vidmar, Neil, and Phoebe Ellsworth. 1974. Public Opinion and the Death Penalty. *Stanford Law Review* 26 (2): 1245–1270.

14

Why Does the Death Penalty
Cost So Much?

(WITH JUSTIN COLE)

When New Jersey abolished the death penalty in 2007, one of the reasons was a surprising study that had appeared in 2005, just as the debate over the punishment was developing.[1] The study assessed the aggregate expenses for the state in having the death penalty as opposed to prosecuting all homicides non-capitally, covering the period of 1982 to 2005. During that time, 197 capital trials had occurred; 60 death sentences were handed down, 10 individuals remained on death row, and no executions had taken place. The total cost of the system, leading to no executions? $253 million (see Forsberg 2005). The state had spent a quarter of a billion dollars on a system that had produced not a single execution. We cannot say, of course, exactly why New Jersey abolished; certainly there were many reasons. But the waste of public funds on a system that carried out not a single execution was one of the main arguments among those who pushed for abolition.

A recent media analysis of Pennsylvania's death penalty (see Migdail-Smith 2016) found that the state had spent more than $800 million on a system that generated 408 death sentences but only 3 executions from 1977 through 2015. The math is simple here: each death sentence cost approximately $2 million, and the cost was more than $200 million for each execution. In California, the most recent overall cost estimate, covering the period of 1978 through 2010, was more than $4 billion (Alarcón and Mitchell 2011). In that time, the state has carried out just 13 executions, as we saw in previous chapters, though it maintains the country's largest death row population. Particularly for states with low rates of execution, the aggregate costs of the death penalty are staggering. As Migdail-Smith writes in the article describing the Pennsylvania situation, that money could have been put to many alternative uses, including tax relief, additional services for citizens, victim compensation, or police investigations of cold cases.

These high costs for seemingly little benefit have led to a shift in the debate on the death penalty, as organizations such as the newly formed Conservatives Concerned about the Death Penalty have been established in many states (see Cogan 2016). Nebraska state senator Colby Coash came to oppose the death penalty as a young conservative for religious reasons, but he pushed to have Nebraska abolish in 2015 using economic arguments about wasteful government spending: the state had spent more than $100 million on a death penalty system that had yielded, as in many other states, only a small number of executions. Calculating the costs per execution, and including the full costs of the entire statewide death penalty system, provides a perspective on the death penalty that few had considered previously. Of course, one could argue that there should be no attention to cost in such a matter; justice demands retribution, and we should not even enter into such a debate. Indeed, this was typically the case in the past. The cost of the death penalty was never a significant part of the national debate for many decades, indeed, until recent years (see Baumgartner, De Boef, and Boydstun 2008). But, as Cogan described in June 2016, Republican lawmakers had sponsored legislation in the previous 12 months to abolish the death penalty in Nebraska, Utah, Missouri, Kentucky, Kansas, Ohio, Wyoming, Montana, South Dakota, and New Hampshire. Thus, cost is a new battleground in the fight about the death penalty. Nebraska's legislature voted to abolish in 2015, so at least in that case the cost argument was quite effective. The governor was a strong supporter of the death penalty, however, and fought to bring the issue to a statewide referendum in 2016 where it was reinstated.

Most Americans would assume that it would be less expensive to execute an inmate after a trial and some appeals rather than hold an inmate in prison for the remainder of his or her life. Indeed, it would be less expensive if, as some might prefer, the accused were tried, found guilty, judged deserving of death, allowed perhaps one appeal, and then promptly executed. In fact, the death penalty is extremely expensive, for many reasons. The act of execution by itself is not particularly expensive, but maintaining a system of capital punishment is surprisingly so: the trial is bifurcated and therefore takes longer; generally there are more resources allocated to the defense; of course the prosecution therefore allocates more resources to capital cases as well; more experts tend to be used, including mitigation experts who would not be involved if there were no penalty phase; juries have to be death-qualified, leading to longer pretrial procedures; death rows themselves are generally more expensive to maintain than the general prison population; and since 1976, the Supreme Court mandates automatic appeals. In sum, there are many possible sources of increased costs. The fact that only 16 percent of death sentences are eventually carried out is perhaps the most important factor in generating the extremely high cost estimates we observe throughout the United States. Individuals like Henry McCollum, whose wrongful conviction was discovered only 30 years after his death sentence, make clear that efforts to "streamline" and reduce appeals inevitably raise the chances of executing factually innocent individuals. Further, the fact that most death sentences are overturned certainly suggests that their review during the appellate process should be done carefully, not with a process limiting independent review, which of course is expensive. In this chapter we review published empirical studies to describe and explain these surprising facts. In the following sections we first explain how we identified the studies we use, then we review their estimates of overall cost, breaking down these estimates where possible to show what parts of the process seem to be generating most of the cost or savings, and finally we conclude.

A Literature Review

In order to find studies on the cost of the death penalty, we followed a strategy similar to that of Baumgartner, Grigg, and Mastro (2015), who compiled a list of every major study on race-of-victim effects in the likelihood of capital prosecution or death sentence (see chapter 4). These authors began with a prominent published study, then worked from there, doing a Google Scholar search and reviewing results until there was a relatively complete set of every major study on the topic. For cost studies, our work was facilitated by a page on the Death Penalty Information Center (DPIC) website that focuses specifically on cost (www.deathpenalty.org/ costs-death-penalty). We started with all the articles listed on that page and also conducted Google Scholar searches for relevant terms such as "death penalty costs," "cost of capital punishment," and "price of capital punishment." Because the DPIC site is relatively complete, these additional searches yielded few hits that were not already included. We identified 21 published studies, most of which focus on a single state. The results of the vast majority of the studies were published in academic journals or law reviews, but a few were published in highly professional and systematic journalistic reviews. We did not include any studies that focused on individual cases or that were of relatively small empirical scope. All the studies we reviewed focus on comparisons of the cost of capital cases with non-capital murder trials. Some provide overall cost estimates, and many of them break down the source of the costs to the different phases of the trial or postconviction appeals. In the following sections, we provide a tabular summary of the studies, their time and geographical scopes, the number of cases reviewed, and their cost estimates.

Overall Cost Estimates

Of the 21 studies we reviewed, 7 provide some estimate of the overall cost of a death sentence, an execution, or the entire death penalty system as compared with a first-degree murder trial or a system where capital punishment is not considered. Table 14.1 summarizes these results. Where it is possible to give a precise dollar amount, we do so. Where there is only an indication of "more" spending in the capital case, we indicate this with a plus sign (+). We use a minus sign (–) in the rare cases where

Table 14.1 Overall Cost Estimates

| | Basic Characteristics of Cost Studies | | | | Comparative Costs | |
Author and Year	Geographical Scope	Time Period Examined	Cases Sampled	Death Penalty Trials as Compared to Non–Death Penalty Trials	Death Sentence as Compared to a Sentence of Life without Parole	Death Penalty as Compared to a Scenario Where the Maximum Punishment Is Life without Parole
California Commission on the Fair Administration of Justice (2008)	California	1978–2007	1,644	+	+	+$125,500,000 per year
American Civil Liberties Union of Northern California (2009)	California	1996–2006	338	+	+	
Alarcón and Mitchell (2011)	California	1978–2010	1,940	+	+	+$4,000,000,000 over 31 years
Marceau and Whitson (2013)	Colorado	1999–2010	154	+123.5 days per case		
Dieter (2010)	Pennsylvania	1976–2009		+	+	
Gould and Greenman (2010)	Federal	1998–2004	214	+$308,376 per case		
Palm Beach Post Capital Bureau (2000)	Florida	1979–1999		+		+$51,000,000 per year
Office of Performance Evaluations (2014)	Idaho	1998–2013	251	+3.1 months per case		
Legislative Division of Post Audit (2003)	Kansas	1994–2003	22	+$316,000 per case	+	+
Judicial Council (2014)	Kansas	1994–2011	63	+17.1 days per case		

Roman et al. (2008)	Maryland	1978–1999	1,136	+640,000 per case	+$851,000 per death sentence	+$1,491,000 per case
Goss, Strain, and Blalock (2016)	Nebraska	1973–2014	119		+	+$14,600,000 per year
Miethe (2012)	Nevada	2009–2011	138			
Nevada Legislative Counsel Bureau (2014)	Nevada	2000–2012	28	+$375,000–$389,000 per case	–$5,000 per death sentence to +$86,000 per death sentence	$375,000–$475,000 per case
Forsberg (2005)	New Jersey	1982–2004		+	+	+$253,300,000 over 24 years
Cook and Slawson (1993)	North Carolina	1990–1991	77	+$47,793 per case		
Cook (2009)	North Carolina	2005–2006	1,034	+		+$11,000,000 per year
Kaplan (2013)	Oregon	1984–2013		+	+	+
Dieter (2009)	National Survey			+	+	+
Morgan (2004)	Tennessee	1993–2003	240	+	+	+
Washington State Bar Association (2006)	Washington	1981–2005	254	+	+	
Collins et al. (2015)	Washington	1997–2014	147	+		+$1,150,000 per case

Note: See appendix E, available at our website, for details on our calculations.

there are savings. See appendix E on our website for a replication of the three tables in this chapter with footnotes explaining each cost estimate.

The first column of the table lists the author or authors of the study, as well as the date that the study was published. All but one of these studies was published in the twenty-first century, indicating that the cost of the death penalty has only begun to attract attention in recent years. The second column notes the geographical scope of each cost study. Most of the studies (19 of 21) limit their analysis to one state. The study by Gould and Greenman (2010) focuses solely on federal death penalty cases and that by Dieter (2009) is a national survey of police chiefs. The third column contains the time period that was examined by each study. There are two important points to highlight here. First, most of the studies focus on a time period of a decade or more, but a fair number limit their analysis to a period of only a few years. Second, the vast majority of the studies examine the death penalty prior to 2012, and the data reported do not take into account inflation. For these reasons, it would be fair to consider the cost estimates as low or conservative ones. Real costs are undoubtedly higher.

The fourth column lists the total number of cases examined in each study. The number listed is the total number of homicide cases. For the first entry in the table, the study reviewed 1,644 homicide cases in California between 1978 and 2007. Only a fraction of these cases were prosecuted capitally, and then only a fraction of those led to a death penalty. The N reported in the table is the total number of homicide cases reviewed, not the number of death sentences. The fifth column compares the cost of a death penalty trial to the cost of a first-degree murder trial where the death penalty was not sought. Of course, not every death penalty trial ends in a death sentence, and trials that end in death sentences are more expensive than those that do not. To appropriately account for this, a weighted average of trial costs in these two categories was compiled and then compared to the costs of first-degree murder trials where the death penalty was not sought to get this figure. Some studies examined both trials and pleas. When pleas were included, they were incorporated through a weighted average into both the costs of death penalty trials and the costs of first-degree murder trials where the death penalty was not sought.

The sixth column compares the cost of a capital trial that ends without a death sentence and a capital trial that ends with a death sentence. The costs encompassed by this category are appellate costs garnered in direct appeals, state postconviction proceedings, and federal postconviction proceedings as well as incarceration costs. This category is especially interesting because most people who receive death sentences do not actually end up being executed, as we saw in chapter 7; thus, the death penalty is effectively an expensive form of life without parole (LWOP), at least in those cases. The seventh column looks at both the trial and the postconviction phases of a death penalty case and compares the overall cost of a death sentence, an execution, or the entire death penalty system with a first-degree murder trial where capital punishment is not considered.

Given those definitions, and considering that these studies include many conducted by journalists, by legislative research bureaus, and by academics, what are the trends? In summary, the costs are staggering no matter how we look at them. Overall costs of the entire system are perhaps the most important indicators, and these are summarized in the last column. The lowest estimates were several hundred thousand dollars per capital trial in Nevada, more than a million dollars per case in Washington, and about $1.5 million in Maryland. More typical are annual estimates for the entire state: these run in the tens of millions of dollars, such as $51 million per year in Florida alone. Finally, overall estimates of the cumulative cost of having the death penalty are truly staggering: for example, $250 million in New Jersey and $4 billion in California. And these numbers do not take inflation into account. With such surprising numbers, one must wonder where the costs come from. In the next sections we review studies that have broken down these costs in terms of the different stages or parts of the process. We start with trial costs and move to appellate costs in the subsequent section.

Trial Phase Cost Estimates

The 21 studies listed in Table 14.1 also break down the costs associated with the different phases of the trial process. Table 14.2 summarizes these results.

Just as in Table 14.1, the first four columns of Table 14.2 provide the basic characteristics of all the studies. The fifth column is also contained within Table 14.1. The remaining columns, however, deal specifically with various phases of a death penalty trial as compared with a first-degree murder trial where capital punishment is not considered.

Seven studies provide some estimate of the costs associated with the defense, and five studies provide some estimate of the costs associated with the prosecution. Each of these shows that attorney costs are substantially higher for capital trials than for first-degree murder trials where capital punishment is not considered. Often, two attorneys and two investigators are required for capital trials, which is twice as many as are typically used in ordinary first-degree murder trials. Mitigation specialists may also work in a capital case, but they do so less often in non-capital ones. Because capital trials are more complex, both the defense and the prosecution must spend more time outside of the courtroom preparing their cases. Capital trials also simply last longer than other first-degree murder trials, which increases costs for the defense, the prosecution, and the court system itself. Unsurprisingly, among those studies that provide a precise cost estimate for the defense, costs range from an additional $116,600 per case to an additional $493,500 per case. For those that provide information on the prosecution, costs range from an additional $7,212 per case to an additional $217,000 per case.

Table 14.2 Costs Associated with Each Phase of the Death Penalty Trial

	Basic Characteristics of the Studies				Costs of the Various Parts of Death Penalty Trials					
Author and Year	Geographical Scope	Time Period Examined	Cases Sampled	Death Penalty Trials as Compared to Non–Death Penalty Trials	Defense	Prosecution	Experts	Court	Jury
California Commission on the Fair Administration of Justice (2008)	California	1978–2007	1,644	+	+				+
American Civil Liberties Union of Northern California (2009)	California	1996–2006	338	+	+	+	+	+	+
Alarcón and Mitchell (2011)	California	1978–2010	1,940	+$1,000,000 per case	+	+	+	+	+
Marceau and Whitson (2013)	Colorado	1999–2010	154	+123.5 days per case	+			+	+24.5 days per case
Dieter (2010)	Pennsylvania	1976–2009		+	+	+	+		+
Gould and Greenman (2010)	Federal	1998–2004	214	+$308,376 per case	+$231,753 per case		+$77,754 per case		+
Palm Beach Post Capital Bureau (2000)	Florida	1979–1999		+	+	+			

Study	State	Years	N					
Office of Performance Evaluations (2014)	Idaho	1998–2013	251	+3.1 months per case				+
Legislative Division of Post Audit (2003)	Kansas	1994–2003	22	+$316,000 per case	+	+	+	+
Judicial Council (2014)	Kansas	1994–2011	63	+17.1 days per case				
Roman et al. (2008)	Maryland	1978–1999	1,136	+640,000 per case	+		+	+
Goss, Strain, and Blalock (2016)	Nebraska	1973–2014	119	+	+		+	+
Miethe (2012)	Nevada	2009–2011	138	+1,166 hours per case+ $116,600–$145,750 per case				
Nevada Legislative Counsel Bureau (2014)	Nevada	2000–2012	28	+$375,000–$389,000 per case	+$176,891–$225,834 per case	+$7,212–$10,699 per case	+$49,000–$61,025 per case	+
Forsberg (2005)	New Jersey	1982–2004		+	+$2,300,000 per year	+$4,600,000–$7,800,000 per year	+	+
Cook and Slawson (1993)	North Carolina	1990–1991	77	+$47,793 per case	+	+	+	+

(continued)

Table 14.2 Continued

	Basic Characteristics of the Studies				Costs of the Various Parts of Death Penalty Trials				
Author and Year	Geographical Scope	Time Period Examined	Cases Sampled	Death Penalty Trials as Compared to Non–Death Penalty Trials	Defense	Prosecution	Experts	Court	Jury
Cook (2009)	North Carolina	2005–2006	1,034	+	+$13,180,385 over 2 years	+26,680 hours over 2 years	+$3,024,000 over 2 years	+691 days over 2 years	$224,640 over 2 years
Kaplan (2013)	Oregon	1984–2013		+	+	+	+		
Dieter (2009)	National Survey			+	+	+	+	+	+
Morgan (2004)	Tennessee	1993–2003	240	+	+	+	+	+	+
Washington State Bar Association (2006)	Washington	1981–2005	254	+	+$246,000 per case	+217,000 per case		+$46,640–$69,960 per case	+
Collins et al. (2015)	Washington	1997–2014	147	+	+$493,500 per case	+$55,900 per case	+	+$80,000 per case	

Note: See appendix E, available on our website, for details on our calculations.

Steiker and Steiker (2016) suggest that the "new" death penalty mandates several factors that dramatically increase the cost of the defense as well as that of the prosecution. First, the law is specific, arcane, and complicated. Attorneys on both sides must specialize in it. Second, the goal of the defense must be more complicated than in a non-capital trial. Rather than being focused only on guilt or seeking a conviction on a lesser charge, the defense must be prepared for the penalty phase of the trial. So, of course, must the state. Therefore, mitigation specialists and investigators are brought onto defense legal teams in a process that had no equivalent (and no costs) in the pre-*Furman* period. Mitigation specialists scour school and hospital records for indications that there may have been a diagnosed mental illness, disability, or abuse, as such documentation may save the life of their client. A typical capital defense today involves an entire team of specialists, with multiple attorneys working with investigators and mitigation specialists. Faced with this, state prosecutors of course respond with resources of their own. According to Steiker and Steiker (2016, 196ff.), the creation of the specialized capital bar with associated teams of specialists had no counterpart in the pre-*Furman* period. New organizations such as the Equal Justice Initiative and the Southern Center for Human Rights took up where state indigent defense offices were not able to go, creating an entirely new area of the law and attracting ambitious young attorneys from the nation's top law schools. While these individuals are not, on average, highly paid, the Court's post-*Furman* jurisprudence has led to the creation of an entirely new legal specialty, and that does not come cheap even if the individuals involved may not become wealthy.

Three studies provide some estimate of the costs associated with expert testimony, and three studies provide some estimate of court costs. Each of these shows that both expert and court costs are substantially higher during capital trials than during first-degree murder trials where capital punishment is not considered. Even studies that do not provide specific numerical data provide some indication that these components are more expensive in capital trials. As science has improved, the defense has increasingly relied on experts who specialize in everything from mental health to hair follicle analysis to bite marks to eyewitness testimony in an attempt to avoid the death penalty for their client. As a result, the prosecution has naturally countered with its own array of experts. Court costs are also higher in capital trials. More capital trials change venues, which is also costly. More important, capital trials last much longer, which means not only that daily costs of writing transcripts or providing security increase but also that opportunity costs arise. The more time a capital trial takes, the less time there is for other trials in that same courtroom or by that judge. This does not appear as a direct cost in a state budget, but it is nonetheless important, particularly as many states are experiencing significant delays in their criminal justice system. With this in mind, additional expert costs range from $49,000 to $77,754 per case, and additional court costs range from $46,640 to $80,000 per case.

Two studies provide some estimate of the costs associated with voir dire, or jury selection. Marceau and Whitson (2013) compared 6 capital prosecutions with 148 noncapital cases in Colorado and found that jury selection took 24.5 days longer in the capital trials. Many more potential jurors are required; individuals who are categorically opposed to the death penalty and would refuse to consider a death sentence will be excused, as will many others who are excused because of financial hardship, a problem that is far more severe because of the greater length of capital trials. (Missing work or childcare responsibilities for a longer time is also more onerous.) As Steiker and Steiker (2016) emphasize, jury selection is such an important part of a capital trial that experts focus just on that process, seeking to identify those potential jurors who are not so opposed to the death penalty that they will be excluded by the judge (see chapter 2), but not overly inclined toward the prosecution, either. Once the trial begins, jurors are paid for every day they work, which added up to $224,640 over two years in North Carolina, according to Cook (2009).

Although we do not put too much emphasis on precise dollar figures in this table, particularly because they are not adjusted for inflation, it is clear that costs are high and that they stem not from a single easily controlled source but from virtually every element of the trial and investigation. Contrary to popular belief, the costs of the death penalty are not limited to the appeals that come after a conviction; rather, the costs accumulate from the very instant that a case becomes capital. Of course, appeals costs are high as well.

Postconviction Cost Estimates

We found 17 studies that break down the costs associated with the different phases of the postconviction process; these are a subset of those listed in the previous table. Table 14.3 summarizes these results.

Just as in Table 14.1, the first four columns of Table 14.3 describe the basic characteristics of all the studies. The fifth column is also contained within Table 14.1. The remaining columns, however, deal specifically with various phases of the postconviction process when a death sentence was handed down as compared with the postconviction process when a sentence of LWOP was issued.

Four studies provide some estimate of the costs associated with direct appeals; three provide some estimate of the costs associated with postconviction proceedings at the state level; and three provide some estimate of the costs associated with postconviction proceedings in federal courts. Each of these shows that the various appeals are expensive. For direct appeals, costs range from an additional $13,561 to $340,000 per death sentence; for postconviction appeals at the state level, an additional $43,000 to $300,000 per death sentence; and for postconviction appeals at the federal level, from $96,000 to $1.1 million per death sentence.

Table 14.3 **Costs Associated with Each Phase of the Death Penalty Postconviction Process**

	Basic Characteristics of the Cost Studies			Costs of the Various Phases of the Postconviction Process of the Death Penalty					
Author and Year	Geographical Scope	Time Period Examined	Cases Sampled	Costs of a Death Sentence as Compared to a Sentence of Life without Parole	Direct Appeal	Postconviction at the State Level	Postconviction at the Federal Level	Incarceration	New Death Row Complex
California Commission on the Fair Administration of Justice (2008)	California	1978–2007	1,644	+	+	+		+$90,000 per inmate per year	+$402.6 million overall
ACLU of Northern California (2009)	California	1996–2006	338	+	+	+		+$90,000 per inmate per year	+$356 million overall
Alarcón and Mitchell (2011)	California	1978–2010	1,940	+	+	+$200,000–$300,000 per death sentence	$1.11 million per death sentence	+$90,000 per inmate per year	+$402.8 million overall
Dieter (2010)	Pennsylvania	1976–2009		+	+	+		+	
Office of Performance Evaluations (2014)	Idaho	1998–2013	251		+1.2 years per death sentence	+1.4 years per death sentence			

(continued)

Table 14.3 Continued

	Basic Characteristics of the Cost Studies				Costs of the Various Phases of the Postconviction Process of the Death Penalty					
Author and Year	Geographical Scope	Time Period Examined	Cases Sampled	Costs of a Death Sentence as Compared to a Sentence of Life without Parole	Direct Appeal	Postconviction at the State Level	Postconviction at the Federal Level	Incarceration	New Death Row Complex
Legislative Division of Post Audit (2003)	Kansas	1994–2003	22	+	+			-	
Judicial Council (2014)	Kansas	1994–2011	63		+			+$24,690 per inmate per year	
Roman et al. (2008)	Maryland	1978–1999	1,136	+851,000 per death sentence	+$340,000 per death sentence	$43,000 per death sentence	+$96,000 per death sentence	+$372,000 per inmate over a lifetime	
Goss, Strain, and Blalock (2016)	Nebraska	1973–2014	119	+	+	+	+	+$619,000 per year	
Nevada Legislative Counsel Bureau (2014)	Nevada	2000–2012	28	–$5,000 per death sentence to +$86,000 per death sentence	+	+	+	=	

Study	Location	Time period					
Forsberg (2005)	New Jersey	1982–2004	+	+	+	+	+
Cook and Slawson (1993)	North Carolina	1990–1991	77	+$13,561 per death sentence	+	+	–$17,000 per inmate over a lifetime
Cook (2009)	North Carolina	2005–2006	1,034	+	+	+	+$169,617 over the 2-year time period
Kaplan (2013)	Oregon	1984–2013	+	+	+	+	
Dieter (2009)	National Survey		+`	+	+	+	+
Morgan (2004)	Tennessee	1993–2003	240	+	+	+	=
Washington State Bar Association (2006)	Washington	1981–2005	254	+$118,511 per death sentence	+	+	
Collins et al. (2015)	Washington	1997–2014	147	+	+	+	–$474,000 per inmate over a lifetime

Note: See appendix E, available on our website, for details on our calculations.

Eight studies provide some estimate of the costs associated with incarceration. Six of these indicate that incarceration is more expensive for those who are given the death penalty. Not only are very few death row prisoners actually executed, but death row prisons are far more expensive to operate than other prisons. Three studies from California all noted that the construction of a new death row would cost hundreds of millions of dollars. Of course, when we consider the findings from chapter 7, which showed that California (like Pennsylvania, the federal government, and many other jurisdictions) rarely executes those it condemns, it is clear that costs accumulate but there are few or no offsetting savings. Virginia and Texas, which execute a higher proportion of their death row inmates, may see some savings in incarceration rates. But even these are lower than many uninitiated readers may expect. Just two studies found what many would assume to be true logically: that incarcerating prisoners who had received LWOP was more expensive because death row prisoners are executed prior to their natural death. We saw in chapter 8 that the time spent on death row before execution is often measured in decades. So while theoretically one might expect to see lower incarceration costs for those sentenced to death as opposed to LWOP, several factors make this less likely: few of those condemned are executed; death rows are expensive to operate; and many inmates spend decades on death row before being executed (or seeing their sentence reversed).

Before concluding, we refer briefly to the issue of plea bargaining. It would seem reasonable to assume that when prosecutors have the death penalty to use as a bargaining chip, the defense may be more willing to plea to a lengthy sentence or even LWOP. Therefore, it is common to hear that the availability of the death sentence as an option is useful to the state, and that it can avoid costly trials by leading to more plea agreements. The flaw in this logic is simply that lawyers on both sides prepare for the capital trial even as they may engage in bargaining or be open to the possibility. Before accepting a plea, a defense attorney would want to do a full mitigation investigation to be able to make an informed decision about the likelihood of a death sentence following a trial. Cook (2009) showed in his study of North Carolina that because neither side can afford to bluff, pretrial costs in potentially capital cases are very high, making even death cases ending in a plea bargain more expensive than if death had not been an option.

Conclusion

Bullets are cheap, but numerous studies show that the death penalty is not. From the moment the state declares its intent to seek death, a range of protections and costs come into play. Given what we saw in chapter 7 on how frequently death sentences are overturned and in chapter 9 on how often individuals sentenced to death are later discovered to have been wrongfully convicted, we must have strong defense rights for those facing the ultimate punishment. But most Americans are probably unaware of just how high these costs really are. The ballooning cost of the death penalty has been an important element in many state-level debates where abolition has been on the table. In New Jersey, the first state in modern times to see a legislative vote in favor of abolition (rather than a Supreme Court decision to abolish, as in New York [2006] or Delaware [2016]), the law enforcement community did not mobilize powerfully to protect one of its most important priorities because the death penalty simply was not such a priority (on police placement of the death penalty as a law enforcement priority, see Dieter 2009); the state had never carried out an execution. In Connecticut, which abolished in 2012, just one execution had occurred in the 40 years since the state had reestablished the death penalty in 1973 almost immediately after the *Furman* decision. A reduction in actual use of the death penalty, a rise in reversal rates, difficulties in getting drugs to carry out lethal injections (see chapter 10), concerns about innocence (see chapter 9), and the costs enumerated in this chapter have combined to change the politics of the death penalty. Among law enforcement professionals, it is a lower priority than it was at the time of *Gregg* (see Dieter 2009). Among state legislators, it is a budgetary nightmare. The surprising facts summarized in the three tables included in this chapter help to explain why the politics of the death penalty has moved so far. Opponents are strongly mobilized, though that is not so new. Ideological proponents are just as strongly mobilized in favor. But among law enforcement and judicial professionals, it has become an expensive luxury coming far behind much more pressing criminal justice needs.

Further Readings

Alarcón, Arthur L., and Paula M. Mitchell. 2011. Executing the Will of the Voters? A Roadmap to Mend or End the California Legislature's Multi-Billion-Dollar Death Penalty Debacle. *Loyola of Los Angeles Law Review* 44:41–224.

Collins, Peter A., Robert C. Boruchowitz., Matthew J. Hickman, and Mark A. Larrañaga. 2015. *An Analysis of the Economic Costs of Seeking the Death Penalty in Washington State.* January 1. Seattle: Department of Criminal Justice, Seattle University. http://www.deathpenaltyinfo.org/documents/WashingtonCosts.pdf.

Cook, Philip J. 2009. Potential Savings from Abolition of the Death Penalty in North Carolina. *American Law and Economics Review* 11 (2): 498–529.

Dieter, Richard C. 2009. *Smart on Crime: Reconsidering the Death Penalty in a Time of Economic Crisis.* October. Washington, DC: Death Penalty Information Center. http://www.deathpenaltyinfo.org/documents/CostsRptFinal.pdf.

Marceau, Justin F., and Hollis A. Whitson. 2013. The Cost of Colorado's Death Penalty. *University of Denver Criminal Law Review* 3:145–163.

Roman, John, Aaron Chalfin, Aaron Sundquist, Carly Knight, and Askar Darmenov. 2008. *The Cost of the Death Penalty in Maryland.* Washington, DC: Urban Institute, Justice Policy Center. http://www.deathpenaltyinfo.org/CostsDPMaryland.pdf.

15

Does the Death Penalty Deter?

Many people believe that the death penalty deters crime.[1] After all, it stands to reason that someone contemplating a crime would "think twice" if they knew that the consequence might be death. On the other hand, we have reviewed statistics throughout this book that make it clear why this might not be the case: death is rarely the sentence for homicide; most death sentences are overturned; it is hard to predict which homicide offenders will be tried for a capital crime and which will face lesser punishments; individuals who commit murder are often high or drunk; those who commit such crimes are often mentally ill and not likely to weigh pros and cons of the situation very clearly; and so on. All this is complicated since every state with the death penalty now also has the alternative of life without parole (LWOP), making the "rational calculus" of deterrence the difference between the likelihood of death versus LWOP, not death versus freedom. One could consider LWOP to be a harsher penalty than death, after all. As an extremely harsh penalty, LWOP itself could deter. If so, then the relevant empirical question is, What is the additional deterrent effect of capital punishment, over and above that of LWOP? This question is rarely posed in the literature, as we will see later in this chapter.

If a potential murderer were fully informed about the statistics laid out in this book, he or she might behave somewhat strategically. But in fact, we have no reason to believe that the typical homicide perpetrator is aware of the facts and figures we have reviewed here, nor necessarily thinking much about such things. (As we saw in chapter 12, many have mental illness, and even greater numbers are intoxicated at the time of their crimes.) Certainly, there is little in public life or common knowledge to suggest that any homicide will be followed by a swift execution. And, indeed, such has never been the case. And considering how many black men are the victims of homicide, but how rarely their killers face the death penalty, one could wonder if the system is even designed with the hope of deterring homicide in those cases where it occurs most frequently.

Scholars and activists have debated deterrence for many decades. We saw in chapter 13, for example, that deterrence is cited as the second most common answer for why individuals support the death penalty. The most common answer was retribution ("an eye for an eye"), but 19 percent said deterrence in 1991. This number has declined over time, reaching just 6 percent in 2014 (see chapter 13), possibly for reasons related to what we explain in this chapter. There is much disagreement in the public about whether the death penalty system deters. However, among strong proponents of the death penalty, deterrence is sometimes taken as an article of faith. It makes sense, after all, that such a punishment would give pause. And if the death penalty does not deter because it is too rare, uncertain, and slow, then those problems should be rectified, argue some proponents. It is a highly charged issue, to say the least. Here, we review public opinion on the topic before turning to expert studies and evidence.

Public Opinion

No matter what the evidence may indicate, many Americans believe the death penalty has a deterrent effect. From the comprehensive database on public opinion polling related to the death penalty described in chapter 13, we identified 12 national polls that relate to this question, and we present the results in Table 15.1. These questions ask whether there is a deterrent effect, and in Table 15.2 we show the results of two surveys that asked whether such a fact, if it were true, would make the respondent support or oppose the death penalty. Before we turn to that, let us review Americans' beliefs on whether there is a deterrent effect. Table 15.1 presents the results, and Figure 15.1 then shows them in graphical form.

Large numbers of Americans indicated belief in deterrence at the beginning of the data series: a two-to-one majority through the 1980s and early 1990s. The number responding that they did not believe there was a deterrent effect exceeded the number believing in it for the first time in 1997, and from there it continued to grow. Note that one question, highlighted in italics in the table, shows an apparent reversal: by 67 to 33, in June 2000, members of the public said it is either a "major" or a "minor" deterrent rather than "not a deterrent at all." We coded both of the positive responses as pro-deterrence, but the middle response may imply some skepticism. In any case, the other questions typically have just two response categories, and so this one is not perfectly comparable. In Figure 15.1 we plot the results of the data from the table. We include the best fit regression line showing the general trends; this solid line excludes from its calculation the June 2000 question with three response categories.

Support for the idea of deterrence declines by 1.5 points per year during the time between 1985 and 2006, based on all available data. By early in the first decade of the twenty-first century, less than 40 percent were expressing support for the idea that capital punishment deters crime.

Of course, we saw earlier in this chapter and also in chapter 13 that people can support the death penalty for many reasons, and that the most common reason for support is retribution, not deterrence. So coming to the conclusion that the punishment

Table 15.1 **Public Opinion Polls on Deterrence**

Question Text	Date	Yes, Deters	No, Does Not Deter
Do you feel that the death penalty acts as a deterrent to the commitment of murder, that it lowers the murder rate, or not?	1/11/1985	67	33
Do you feel that the death penalty acts as a deterrent to the commitment of murder—that it lowers the murder rate, or not?	1/10/1986	66	34
Do you think that capital punishment—the death penalty—is or is not a deterrent to murder?	3/30/1990	66	34
Do you think that capital punishment—the death penalty—is or is not a deterrent to murder?	8/16/1990	65	35
Do you feel that the death penalty acts as a deterrent to the commitment of murder, that it lowers the murder rate, or not?	6/13/1991	55	45
Do you think having the death penalty deters people from committing crimes, or don't you feel that way?	6/4/1997	46	54
Whatever your position on the death penalty, do you think it is a major deterrent to violent crime, a minor deterrent, or not a deterrent at all?	6/1/2000	67	33
Do you feel that the death penalty acts as a deterrent to murder—that it lowers the murder rate—or not?	4/20/2001	45	55
Do you think that capital punishment—the death penalty—is or is not a deterrent to murder?	5/10/2001	47	53
Do you feel that the death penalty acts as a deterrent to the commitment of murder, that it lowers the murder rate, or not?	5/2/2004	36	64
Do you feel that the death penalty acts as a deterrent to murder—that it lowers the murder rate—or not?	6/23/2005	42	58
Do you feel that the death penalty acts as a deterrent to the commitment of murder, that it lowers the murder rate, or not?	5/8/2006	35	65

Note: All surveys were conducted with representative samples of US adults with samples ranging from 750 to more than 1,500, generally around 1,000. Most of the surveys were done by Gallup, CBS News, ABC News, and other major organizations. See Appendix D on our website for more information. As in chapter 13, we have eliminated all neutral/neither/don't know responses and recalculated the directional responses to sum to 100 percent.

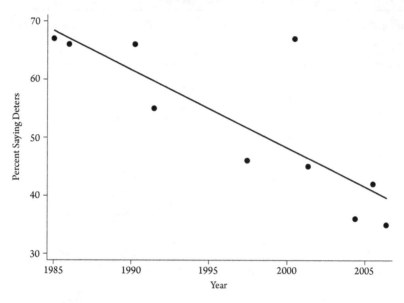

Figure 15.1 Public Opinion on Deterrence. See Table 15.1 for data sources. See text for explanation of the survey in 2000.

Table 15.2 **Two Polls on Deterrence and Support for the Death Penalty**

Question Text	Date	Favor	Oppose
Suppose new evidence showed that the death penalty does not act as a deterrent to murder, that is does not lower the murder rate. Would you favor or oppose the death penalty?	2/8/1999	57	43
Suppose new evidence showed that the death penalty does not act as a deterrent to murder, that is does not lower the murder rate. Would you favor or oppose the death penalty?	5/2/2004	71	29

Note: See note to Table 15.1.

does not deter does not necessarily imply that one would not (or should not) support it anyway. In fact, that is what we find. Table 15.2 shows the results from two polls asking whether individuals would support or oppose the death penalty even if it were shown that there was no deterrent effect. In both cases, a majority supports.

Expert Opinion and Social Scientific Studies

If members of the public have been highly split on the questions of whether the death penalty deters crime and if it would change their opinion on the death penalty if it did, criminologists also have been divided. As we saw in chapter 3, homicides were rapidly increasing throughout the country during the period when the 1972 and 1976 *Furman* and *Gregg* decisions were made in 1972 and 1976, respectively. From the early 1960s to the time of *Gregg*, homicides increased from fewer than 10,000 to approximately 20,000 per year. Perhaps that was because of the decline in capital punishment; after all, there were no executions from 1965 until the first one of the modern period, in 1977. On the other hand, we also saw that homicides, death sentences, and executions have all been declining since the mid-1990s. A fundamental problem is that we do not know whether rising homicide numbers (or rates) might lead prosecutors to seek death more often, or if rising death sentence numbers might lead criminals to commit fewer homicides. That is, we do not know if A causes B, or perhaps B causes A. This, in a nutshell, is why social scientific studies on whether there is a deterrent effect have been inconclusive, mutually contradictory, and/or confusing. Of course, given the highly charged nature of these debates, activists on either side have not hesitated to use those studies that happen to reach a favored conclusion. Here we review some of the social scientific literature on deterrence.

Before we start, it is worth considering that there are really only three possible ways of assessing evidence for or against the deterrence argument. The first approach is to conduct a longitudinal study. Based on data gathered over a long period of time, does the homicide rate increase when execution rates decline? If so, and particularly if the decline in execution rates came before the rise in homicides, then one could suggest there is support for the deterrence idea. The challenge here is to gather enough data over a long enough period, and to control for other variables that may affect either homicides or executions. Most of these variables are studied on a yearly basis; one does not look week by week to see if an execution reduced the homicide rate immediately thereafter. Rather, typically one looks over many years to see if rises and falls in executions and homicides are inversely related; thus, this requires many years of data and the analysis of control variables to ensure that the demonstrated relationship is not spurious. For example, scholars often look at some indicator of the poverty rate, income, unemployment, or another factor that is assumed to affect the motivation of a potential killer: the need for financial gain. What if the homicide rate goes up in response to economic distress, but this is also correlated with changes in the number of executions? The answer in the literature is to gather more years of data. (Of course, many homicides have nothing to do with robbery or financial gain at all, which is another issue.) But inevitably any longitudinal study is limited in how many rival variables it can consider and by its necessary assumption that trends of many years ago continue to affect the system in the same manner today.

A second generic methodological approach is cross-state comparisons. If state X has the death penalty and state Y does not, then homicide offenders should be aware of that. These studies, of course, often show that states with the death penalty have much higher homicide rates, calling into question the deterrent effect but also highlighting the logical possibility that the high homicide rate is what causes the state to adopt the death penalty in the first place; there is less need for such punitive measures in states with less of a homicide problem. Just as in the first example, the generic problem here is that we do not know which comes first: Do high homicide levels cause a state to adopt the death penalty, or do they reflect the lack of deterrent effect? Of course, perhaps all they really indicate is that southern states traditionally have both high homicide rates, compared with northern ones, and also the death penalty.

A third approach is called an "interrupted time series," or more simply a before-and-after study. No state in America had the death penalty in July 1972, but many states enacted new laws in the following years. What happened to their homicide rates? Similarly, states have abolished: New Jersey in 2007, Massachusetts in 1984, and so on. Did their homicide rates go up after abolition? If so, what about neighboring states that had no change in their laws? Again, in these studies we commonly see a problem of causal direction, or endogeneity. States that abolish might be more likely to do so during a time of declining crime rates, rather than in a period of increasing rates. So even if the absence of a death penalty had no effect whatsoever, a pre- and postabolition comparison might show a (continued) decline in homicides. Of course, the same could occur for adoptions, and indeed in the 1970s when the states adopted their post-*Furman* death penalty laws, homicide rates were increasing nationwide, as we saw in chapter 3.

There are other important problems with any deterrence studies. First, there is the absolute rarity of executions, or death sentences, compared with the huge numbers of homicides. As we saw in chapter 3, the United States regularly sees more than 10,000 homicides per year but, with 1,422 executions over 40 years, just about 36 executions in an average year. Divide that number by 50 states, and the number per state is very low. Further, Texas is the only state with relatively large numbers, as we saw in chapter 6. So the very concept of deterrence requires that one accept the idea that moving from no executions in a given state (the most common value in any given year), to one or two will be a salient and widely understood element of the news, coming into the consciousness of those considering homicide. And, of course, we need good data for any study. While we have very accurate data for the number of executions, scholars typically use FBI reports for homicides, and these rely on the cooperation of local authorities for reporting. These are relatively accurate, of course, but far from perfect. Considering the great number of methodological issues involved in these studies, imperfections in the underlying homicide data by state and by year only add to the difficulty.

The Deterrence Argument and Its Critics

During the 1970s, many prominent economists, including some who went on to win the Nobel Prize, began working far afield from business and consumer choices to analyze such topics as divorce rates, voting, and abortion, applying models of rational choice behavior to a number of fields (see Posner 1974; Coase 1978; Becker 1993). In 1975, in the thick of national debate about the death penalty's return, Chicago economist Isaac Ehrlich published "The Deterrent Effect of Capital Punishment" in that discipline's most prestigious journal, the *American Economic Review*. Because the assumption goes largely unquestioned in economics, he used price theory to assess deterrence. Price theory is simply the idea that as the price of something increases, people want less of it. In this case, the good in question is homicide (see Coase 1978; for an excellent review of this body of work, including that which followed in the 1990s and beyond, see Fagan 2006). If the "price" of committing homicide is higher, will people want less of it? Such is the question that Ehrlich posed.

Ehrlich analyzed national homicide and execution data from 1933 through 1969, looking at such factors as the number of homicides per 1,000 population; the percent of homicides "cleared" by police (at the time, more than 89 percent); the percent of those charged who were convicted (43 percent); and the number of executions as a percent of the number of convictions in the previous year (2.6 percent). In his models he used statistical controls for the following variables: labor force participation, unemployment, fraction of the population aged 14 to 24, income per capita, time (to account for trends), percent nonwhite population, population size, government spending, and police spending (see Ehrlich 1975b, 409, Table 2). His idea was that a temptation to commit homicide is often related to financial need, so controlling for the state of the economy is important; similarly, killing is a "young man's game," so he controlled for the proportion of the population in the most relevant age group. With all these variables in mind, the idea is that those considering homicide then rationally calculate the conditional odds of execution as compared with a lesser punishment, based on murder clearance rates, guilty verdicts, and the odds of execution given being found guilty of murder. In the end, while Ehrlich emphasized the tentative nature of his findings and its sensitivity to various assumptions, he estimated that "an additional execution per year of the period in question may have resulted, on average, in 7 or 8 fewer murders" (414). He continued: "The weakness inherent in these predicted magnitudes is that they may be subject to relatively large prediction errors" (414). On the same page of the article, he provides estimates ranging from 1 to 17 or 0 to 24, using a relatively lax 90 percent confidence interval. Using a more standard 95 percent confidence interval would have suggested that the last illustration, at least, would have been statistically insignificant. Of course, the study is subject to the normal ceteris paribus assumption: holding constant all other factors in the model. Ehrlich notes that "the assumption that the values of all other variables affecting the murder rate are held constant as the probability of execution varies" may not hold true "in practice" (415). In spite of all these caveats, the idea that one execution saves eight lives was seen as the take-home message from this study.

Response to the Ehrlich study was swift. Indeed, the *Yale Law Review* convened a panel for a special issue devoted to the topic, rushing it to print in 1975, the same year as the original article was published. In the lead article David Baldus and James Cole (1975) refer to the use of the Ehrlich estimate ("7 or 8 fewer murders") by the US solicitor general in his brief to the US Supreme Court in *Fowler v. North Carolina* (1975),[2] as well as to a previous deterrence study by Thorsten Sellin, criticized by Ehrlich, which had concluded that there was "no measurable deterrent effect beyond that of life imprisonment" (Baldus and Cole 1975, 170). The US solicitor general in 1975, Robert Bork, favorably cited Ehrlich and criticized Sellin for various methodological flaws. Baldus and Cole review the two studies, which used different methodological approaches. (Sellin compared states with and without the death penalty with regard to their murder rates; Ehrlich analyzed the entire nation over the 1933–1969 time period.) Their conclusion: "It is quite possible that because of the complexity of the social phenomenon involved, we will never know with certainty whether capital punishment does or does not deter murder" (Baldus and Cole 1975, 185). In the same special issue, William Bowers and Glenn Pierce (1975) focus largely on inadequacies in federal reporting of homicides over much of the period studied by Ehrlich, making any resulting analysis suspect.

Comparing Sellin's nonfinding with Ehrlich's tentative finding of a deterrent effect, two things stand out. First, the statistical techniques available for such a study cannot be conclusive. Ehrlich's study, for example, included 13 variables (see Ehrlich 1975b, 409, Table 2) and just 37 time points (1933 to 1969). Given that there was a one-year lag in the model, he had 36 annual observations, which means, with 13 variables, that his analysis had just 24 "degrees of freedom"; in other words, there is very little statistical power in such a model. By the same token, Sellin's comparison of contiguous states with and without the death penalty had a significant but unavoidable flaw in that all states surrounding many of the biggest death penalty states (e.g., those in the South) are also death states. So, matched comparisons were either impossible or questionable. Ehrlich compared homicides nationally, even including states where there is no death penalty. And, of course, his driving theoretical assumption was that homicide offenders are motivated by financial need, moderated by a series of calculations about the odds of execution as compared with a punishment of life in prison as an alternative. (Ehrlich expanded on his time-series analysis in a later article that also included cross-sectional state comparisons [see Ehrlich 1977]; he also responded strongly to his critics in the *Yale Law Journal* [see Ehrlich 1975a].)

Second, if Ehrlich's analysis were right, that every execution saves seven or eight American families from the murder of a loved one, then there would be a moral and ethical argument strongly in favor of capital punishment. This was exactly the argument of Robert Bork and others responding to the deterrence findings. It had both a philosophical and a legal impact. In a *Stanford Law Review* article in 2005, Cass Sunstein and Adrian Vermeule asked, "Is the Death Penalty Morally Required?" and answer in the affirmative: if each execution saves *x* lives, then the government has a moral imperative to increase executions, as doing so saves innocent lives. If executing the guilty can save the innocent, it is virtually a sin to oppose capital punishment. The fact that the Sunstein-Vermeule article was published 30 years after the Ehrlich piece suggests that some things have not changed. Because of the timing of the Ehrlich study, coming right as the Court was hearing the most important cases leading up to *Gregg* and during a national moratorium on capital punishment, it gave the credibility of a University of Chicago economist and the imprimatur of the discipline's most prestigious journal to the idea that executions save lives. Critics pounced on the methodological shortcomings at the same time as supporters focused on the moral argument now *in favor* of capital punishment not only from the perspective of retribution but also as a means of lowering the rapidly growing homicide rate. The Supreme Court, of course, responded in 1976 by reinstating the death penalty.

Ehrlich's "seven or eight lives saved" estimate proved extremely powerful, if provocative and highly questionable. Later studies also attempted to attach particular numbers of "lives saved" to their estimates. Another prominent study was that of Dezhbakhsh, Rubin, and Shepherd (2003), whose often-cited estimate was 18. Reinstatement of the death penalty in 1976 did little to quell the disputes among academics and advocates over any possible deterrent effect. Debates continued in academic circles for decades (for an excellent review, see Fagan 2006). Indeed, the National Research Council concluded in 1978 that "available studies provide no useful evidence on the deterrent effect of capital punishment" (quoted in Nagin and Pepper 2002, ix). By that time, however, the Court had spoken. There is no question that the debates about the deterrent effect of capital punishment were prominent parts of the decision to reinstate in 1976, as they were explicitly part of the amicus brief by none other than the US solicitor general.

In oral arguments concerning *Furman*, Solicitor General Bork had made his presentation to the justices and was prepared to sit down when Justice Powell called him back to the stand, saying: "[Y]ou haven't had an opportunity to address in your oral argument the issue of deterrence." The justice then went on to discuss the slaughter of so many thousands of Americans, pointing out that more had been killed by violence in the United States since 1968 than had died in the war in Vietnam. The Court was well aware of the trends in violence that we reviewed in chapter 1: homicides were on the increase. And if each death sentence or execution saved *x* innocent lives, then perhaps there was a moral duty to execute more individuals. Solicitor General Bork had "never heard a question from the bench he liked better" and gave this response:

> Mr. Justice Powell, it seems to me that it cannot rationally be questioned that the death penalty has a deterrent effect. Mankind has always thought so throughout its history. We know, as a matter of common sense—that

all other aspects of human behavior, as you raise the cost and the risk, the amount of the activity goes down. I don't know why murder should be any different. I wouldn't have thought that anybody would have doubted that or listened to a couple of academicians who doubted it. We introduce the Ehrlich study to show that there is respectable academic evidence on the side of deterrence. But I would have thought that the judgment of the legislatures of this country—that they think it deters— is enough. It is a rational judgment. We think it is enough for this Court. (quoted in Mandery 2013, 388)

In fact, this argument was an important element of the Court's reasoning. No matter what "a couple of academicians" might say, common sense tells us that deterrence must be a fact. Although the Court found this argument to be quite persuasive, social scientists have not found it so. Studies on deterrence are inherently limited by the fact that they are "quasi-experiments"—careful comparisons, perhaps, but inherently limited to comparisons before and after reinstatement, of trends over time, or of matched jurisdictions with and without the death penalty. Finally, in 2001, the National Research Council decided to settle the matter of what we can conclude about the accumulated literature on the topic.

The National Research Council Study of Deterrence

Because of the continuing debate on the matter, and the importance of the topic, the National Research Council, an arm of the US National Academy of Sciences, convened a blue-ribbon committee to review all the available evidence for and against deterrence and to provide conclusions from the accumulated literature. The committee was established with support from the National Institute of Justice, and its members were leading scholars in criminal justice, law, and statistics. Their charge was "to address whether the available evidence provides a reasonable basis for drawing conclusions about the magnitude of the effect of capital punishment on homicide rates" (Nagin and Pepper 2002, ix).

The committee made a number of sweeping critiques about the entire literature on deterrence. First, the death penalty should properly be compared to the alternative punishment that would most likely be used in its place. After all, the alternative to death is not freedom but life in prison (with or without the possibility of parole, depending on the state and the time period). However, the committee noted: "One major deficiency in all the existing studies is that none specify the noncapital sanction components of the sanction regime for the punishment of homicide" (3). That is, the studies cannot be interpreted as measuring the deterrent effect of the death penalty as compared with a non-death punishment. If the potential homicide offender is to be deterred by the possibility of death for his crime, he must compare this not to freedom but to whatever the alternative punishment would be if the death penalty were not an option. The committee noted that no previous study had incorporated this logic.

Second, the committee noted that none of the existing studies had a strong (or often even a plausible) assessment of "potential murderers' perceptions of and response to the capital punishment component of a sanction regime" (3). That is, if the model is about whether the threat of capital punishment would dissuade a potential murder from committing a crime, we need a model of how that individual is thinking. In the literature, this is almost always lacking or is extremely implausible (e.g., the potential homicide offender is assumed to have full information about homicide clearance rates, chances of being found guilty, and the conditional probability of death, given a guilty verdict; see Ehrlich 1975b). For example, the committee notes that for deterrence to be occurring, variability in execution rates would be affecting change in murder rates. For that to occur, potential murderers must be aware of variation in execution rates. There is no evidence that they are (Nagin and Pepper 2002, 6).

Third, the committee noted that studies finding no significant deterrent effect were often interpreted as having demonstrated that there was no effect: "A fundamental point of logic about hypothesis testing is that failure to reject a null hypothesis does not imply that the null hypothesis is correct" (3). That is to say, studies refuting a deterrent effect cannot be said to demonstrate that there was none. Rather, there simply was not sufficient evidence to demonstrate that there was such an effect. The importance of this critique may be lost on many but not on those familiar with the scientific method.

Fourth, the committee noted that death sentences are very rare, compared with homicides, and further that executions are even more so. In many states with small populations, the number of homicides is lower than 50 per year, on average. Given the very low rates of death sentences per homicide, these numbers simply mean that estimates are often highly uneven because they are based on small numbers of observations (23). Small absolute differences across "high-use" and "low-use" states are the analytical leverage to discern a possible deterrent effect, but often these differences are so small as to be potentially due to random fluctuation.

The committee went on to review a great number of additional problems with the existing studies, but fundamentally came back to the lack of any serious model of how prospective homicide offenders may be thinking. Are they looking at executions, as opposed, say, to death sentences, news about prominent cases, or highly publicized Supreme Court decisions? (The models all implicitly assume that executions are the key indicator, but they give no evidence for this.) In sum, we really do not know what factors might be considered by those contemplating homicide, so it is virtually impossible to assess whether the statistical models used accurately capture that decision-making process (98–99).

One telling element in the committee's report is its use of Cohen-Cole et al.'s (2009) summary of existing estimates of the number of lives saved per execution.

That study shows hundreds of estimates, each from a different set of assumptions and methodological techniques displayed as a histogram. The takeaway message is that it is an almost perfect normal distribution (e.g., a bell curve), with its peak right at zero but with tails extending down to below −100 on the left side, and to more than 300 on the right side (see Cohen-Cole et al. 2009, 362; Nagin and Pepper 2002, 118). Indeed, the 95 percent confidence interval for the histogram, based on multiple estimates with different specifications, was −24 to +124, with heavy bunching around 0. It is tempting to conclude from such a demonstration that the findings simply come out randomly, and the few that strongly support a given position are then given great weight by proponents of the position supported. Unfortunately, public policy is being driven by such a process.

Statistical problems also abound, but these can perhaps be summarized by simple methodological issues: low numbers of executions (leading to a great deal of fluctuation in rates when one does occur); intercorrelations among various indicators typically used (e.g., homicide rates go up and down over time, as does the economy); a lack of control in panel studies (e.g., no random assignment to death and non-death status); too few time periods for analysis; and no measure of the potential murderer's assessment of the likelihood of a lesser punishment if death is avoided or of the degree to which he or she perceives, for example, LWOP as a lesser punishment in the first place. In sum, demonstrating a deterrent effect, or the lack thereof, is a tall order. In fact, the committee concluded that it cannot be done and that the existing literature essentially should be ignored.

The committee began its report by summarizing the previous research:

In the immediate aftermath of *Gregg*, a National Research Council report reviewed the evidence relating to the deterrent effect of the death penalty that had been published through the mid-1970s. That review was highly critical of the available research, concluding (1978, p. 9):

"The flaws in the earlier analyses finding no effect and the sensitivity of the more recent analysis to minor variations in model specification and the serious temporal instability of the results lead the panel to conclude that available studies provide no useful evidence on the deterrent effect of capital punishment." (Nagin and Pepper 2002, 9)

The final conclusion in 2002? Virtually identical:

CONCLUSION AND RECOMMENDATION: The committee concludes that research to date on the effect of capital punishment on homicide is not informative about whether capital punishment decreases, increases, or has no effect on homicide rates. Therefore, the committee recommends that these studies not be used to inform deliberations requiring judgments about the effect of the death penalty on homicide.

Consequently, claims that research demonstrates that capital punishment decreases or increases the homicide rate by a specified amount or has no effect on the homicide rate should not influence policy judgments about capital punishment. (102)

Given the power of the findings by the National Research Council, and the prestige of its collective authority, it is perhaps surprising that Jeffrey Fagan (2006) was able to conduct a review of the "new" deterrence literature including many citations to articles published in 2003 through 2006. As Fagan concludes:

> The new deterrence studies claim that each execution prevents anywhere from three to thirty two murders. This is hardly a new claim: about 30 years ago, similar claims about the death penalty were made just before executions resumed following the post-*Furman* moratorium. One thousand executions later, the claim has been revived by a small group of researchers touting advances in econometric techniques and new data sources that resolve technical problems in the earlier work. Endorsing these claims, Sunstein and Vermeule suggest that this evidence "morally" requires executions, a conclusion echoed by Becker and Posner. These arguments too are neither new nor correct. (2006, 314)

Perhaps all we can say is, "The more things change the more they stay the same." Clearly, the deterrence argument is so desirable, or so desired, that the scientific difficulties in documenting it give way to the hope that these fundamental problems can be solved. And, as Fagan makes clear, many major academic journals seem to have no trouble publishing these questionable results. Perhaps the reason is that any individual study appears to be well done, but the accumulated mass of dozens or scores of them leaves us no better informed than if we had not read any of them. Scholars disagree, sometimes for good methodological reasons. But in the highly charged world of death penalty litigation, each study is used by advocates on one side or another.

Conclusion

Scores of empirical studies have come to various estimates on the possible deterrent effect of the death penalty. Whenever an estimate has been published showing a significant deterrent effect, supporters have seized upon the finding to suggest that there is a moral obligation to execute more individuals, since the study "proves" that doing so will save lives in the future by preventing x number of homicides. It is, of course a tempting conclusion: we can extract our retributive goals even while also generating a moral benefit and potentially reducing the crime rate as well. However, almost no study has even attempted to "get into the mind" of a potential homicide offender and understand if such individuals are aware of their odds of getting caught, their assessment of the pain of various possible "sanction regimes" (punishments, in plain English), with their relative odds of occurrence. Further, given what we know about other elements of the death penalty from other chapters of this book, what about the range of published studies that show there is no statistically significant deterrent effect? By the same moral logic used by those responding to the studies suggesting that there is an effect, in response to those showing no effect, can the huge costs and flaws of the death penalty system be justified? With such heavy moral questions on the table, but an inherently flawed methodology at the core of every deterrence study, it should be no surprise that the literature has been fraught with confusion and contradiction.

We saw at the beginning of this chapter that public opinion on deterrence has come slowly to share the conclusion of the experts at the NAS: deterrence simply cannot be assessed by existing studies. The flaws in the deterrence literature are not mostly attributable to errors by the scholars involved; rather, as the NAS makes clear, they were related to unavoidable characteristics of such studies. They should be ignored.

Further Readings

Dezhbakhsh, Hashem, Paul H. Rubin, and Joanna M. Shepherd. 2003. Does Capital Punishment Have a Deterrent Effect? New Evidence from Postmoratorium Panel Data. *American Law and Economics Review* 5 (2): 344–376.

Donohue, John J., and Justin J. Wolfers. 2005. Uses and Abuses of Empirical Evidence in the Death Penalty Debate. *Stanford Law Review* 58 (3): 791–845.

———.2009. Estimating the Impact of the Death Penalty on Murder. *American Law and Economics Review* 11 (2): 249–309.

Ehrlich, Isaac. 1975. The Deterrent Effect of Capital Punishment: A Question of Life and Death. *American Economic Review* 65 (3): 397–417.

Fagan, Jeffrey. 2006. Death and Deterrence Redux: Science, Law and Causal Reasoning on Capital Punishment. *Ohio State Journal of Criminal Law* 4:255–320.

Nagin, Daniel S., and John V. Pepper, eds. 2002. *Deterrence and the Death Penalty*. Washington, DC: National Academies Press.

National Research Council. 1978. *Deterrence and Incapacitation: Estimating the Effects of Criminal Sanctions on Crime Rates*. Washington, DC: National Academies Press.

Sellin, Thorsten. 1959. *The Death Penalty: A Report for the Model Penal Code Project of the American Law Institute*. Philadelphia: American Law Institute.

Sunstein, Cass R., and Adrian Vermeule. 2005. Is the Death Penalty Morally Required? Acts, Omissions, and Life-Life Tradeoffs. *Stanford Law Review* 58 (3):703–750.

Steiker, Carol S. 2005. No, Capital Punishment Is Not Morally Required: Deterrence, Deontology, and the Death Penalty. *Stanford Law Review* 58 (3): 751–790.

Is the Death Penalty Dying?

In Figures 1.1 and 1.2, we began this book with an overview of execution counts per year from 1800 to the present.[1] Executions generally rose with the population until approximately 1935, when they reached their maximum historical value of 197, after which they declined precipitously. In the modern period, 1999 saw the peak of 98 executions, and numbers have been declining again since then. Whether we look at the past 100 years, or the past 20 years, the death penalty has been in steep decline. It did, of course, see a resurgence in the 1980s and 1990s following *Gregg*, which saw increased sentencing and subsequent executions. In this chapter, we assess the trends. All point toward the dwindling usage.

Looking at the long-term trends first, historians have outlined several key stages of the decline in capital punishment: (1) a reduction in the range of capital-eligible offenses, (2) the abolition of aggravated death sentences (i.e., death with torture or mutilation of the body), (3) the removal of execution from the public gaze, (4) efforts to reduce pain and suffering during executions, (5) divisions in public opinion on the death penalty, (6) adoption of safeguards in the legal proceedings, (7) a steady decline in its use, and, finally, (8) the movement toward partial and then complete abolishment (Garland 2005; see also Radzinowicz 1948; Gatrell 1994; Evans 1996; Banner 2002; Council of Europe 1999; Hood and Hoyle 2015).

The death penalty in the United States appeared to be following this trajectory in the pre-*Furman* era, and despite its reinstatement, we could argue that a similar pattern is emerging in the current era of decline. In fact, history may well judge the period immediately following *Gregg* and lasting approximately 20 years as being anomalous. From 1935 to 1966, fewer and fewer executions took place until there were none at all. The United States led the Western world in the area of abolition, and while the country was not technically abolitionist until 1972, it was well ahead of the curve of international abolitions, which began only slowly in the 1960s then shot upward in the 1980s and 1990s (see Baumgartner, De Boef, and Boydstun, 2008, 25). France, for example, abolished in 1981. Many thought that *Furman* would be the US abolition, but the divided Court, its multiple disparate logics for the majority ruling, and the powerful political response to re-establish the nation's death penalty laws proved this expectation fanciful. With *Gregg*, the United States bucked a trend of which it had been a leader. For many reasons, particularly the response in the South to a series of Supreme Court rulings that were unpopular there (see Garland 2010; Mandery 2013), the death penalty gained new life, as we discussed in chapter 1. But the enthusiasm that the states showed for capital punishment grew only from 1976 through about 1996: just 20 years. Beginning in the middle to late 1990s, all trends have been toward reduced use, similar to what we saw in the 1940s through 1960s.

Evolving Standards: *Atkins v. Virginia* (2002) and *Roper v. Simmons* (2005)

Trends in the use of the death penalty are important because the US Supreme Court recognizes that "evolving standards" matter. In this section we briefly review what this concept means. We saw in chapter 1 that the Court first recognized this concept in its decision in *Weems v. United States* (1910), in which the Court wrote that the Eighth Amendment "is not fastened to the absolute but may acquire meaning as public opinion becomes enlightened by a humane justice." In 1958 the Court returned to this concept about the Eighth Amendment when Chief Justice Earl Warren interpreted the amendment as drawing "its meaning from the evolving standards of decency that mark the progress of a maturing society" (*Trop v. Dulles* (1958)). Since then, the concept of "evolving standards" has been important in death penalty jurisprudence, though neither *Weems* nor *Trop* was a death penalty–related case.

If it is clear that evolving standards matter, it is not clear what constitutes evidence that standards have evolved. After all, the framers clearly envisioned a system in which capital punishment was an option, but they also envisioned a system where the public stockade, chains, and irons were used—punishments that are no longer acceptable. So how has the Court considered this concept in the recent past with regard to the death penalty? Two important cases—*Atkins* and *Roper*—help us better understand what the Court draws upon when making an evolving standards argument. These two cases invalidated the death penalty for those with intellectual disabilities and for juveniles in 2002 and 2005, respectively. Leading up to the Court's decisions, movements against executing those with intellectual disabilities and juveniles had developed with surprising rapidity. This reinforced the importance of the Court's overruling of former opinions, which were as recent as the late 1980s.

The Court ruled in *Thompson v. Oklahoma* (1988) that executions could not follow crimes committed by those under the age of 16. The following year, in *Stanford v. Kentucky*, the Court ruled that the execution of offenders who were 16 or 17 at the time of their crime was acceptable. During that same year, the Court ruled in

Penry v. Lynaugh (1989) that the execution of those with intellectual disabilities was acceptable. However, these opinions were short-lived, and by 2005, both *Penry* and *Stanford* had been overruled by *Atkins* and *Roper*, respectively. This means that between 1989 and 2002, when the *Atkins* decision was published, and between 1989 and 2005, when the *Roper* decision was published, evidence against the execution of those with intellectual disabilities and juveniles became increasingly clear. However, it is difficult to quantify the amount of change that actually occurred. In fact, this issue was contentious among the justices because "evolving standards" could not be clearly demonstrated through an applied mathematical test.

In *Roper*, Justice Kennedy, who wrote the majority opinion, cited a range of social science research to bolster his argument that the standards of the nation had shifted away from executing juveniles. Records showing how many states actually carried out juvenile executions showed only six states had done so since 1989 and three since 1994; further, five of the states that allowed juvenile capital punishment in 1989 had since abolished (*Roper v. Simmons*, 10–11). The Court noted that at the time of *Stanford v. Kentucky*, contemporary standards did allow the execution of juveniles, since 22 of 37 death states allowed it for 16-year-olds and 25 allowed it for 17-year-olds, "thereby indicating there was no national consensus." However, by 2005, 30 states prohibited the execution of juveniles, including 12 that had no death penalty, as well as 18 death states who exempted juveniles from the punishment. The Court continued in its *Stanford* decision: "Moreover, even in the 20 states without a formal prohibition, the execution of juveniles [was] infrequent" (3). But, as Justice Scalia noted in his scathing dissent, of those states with capital punishment, a majority included juveniles; further, only four states had recently abolished capital punishment by legislative action. In Scalia's opinion (joined by Chief Justice Rehnquist, Justice Thomas, and on this issue by Justice O'Connor), this was woefully thin material on which to base an argument of "consensus."

Similarly, the Court's views on executing those with intellectual disabilities went through a rapid transformation. At the time of its *Penry* decision, there was no consensus against executing those with intellectual disabilities, since only two states banned it. By 2002, however, legislative enactments, which the Court deemed to be "objective indicia of society's standards," had "demonstrated that such executions" were truly unusual insofar "that it was fair to say that a national consensus has developed against them" (2). Responding to the majority in *Atkins*, Chief Justice Rehnquist specifically took issue with the reference to foreign actors, professional associations, and public opinion polls as being relevant to the issue of "evolving standards" (see his dissent in *Atkins*, 322). For the chief justice, legislative actions present the official position of a state; juries, to a lesser extent, also reflect "a significant and reliable index of contemporary values" (323). So while certain elements were open to question, he agreed that the actions of legislatures and juries are important indicators that deserve significant weight.

By the time the Court ruled in *Atkins*, 16 states had abolished the death penalty for those deemed to have intellectual disabilities; in *Roper*, the number was not as great, but there were general movements away from executing juveniles. Parts of the Court's decisions in *Atkins* and *Roper* were influenced by the number of states rejecting the use of the death penalty against these vulnerable groups. However, while the number of states trending away was significant, "the consistency of the direction of change" played a more important role (*Atkins*, 315; *Roper* 11–12). In *Roper*, Justice Kennedy noted how the governor of Kentucky had pardoned Mr. Stanford, the very petitioner whose death penalty the Court affirmed in *Stanford v. Kentucky*. Other indicators pointing in the same direction were the fact that no state having previously abolished juvenile death sentences had reinstated them, and that juvenile death sentences were increasingly rare at a time when concerns about juvenile crime were on the rise. All these trends reinforced the idea that the United States was moving in a consistent direction away from executing juveniles. Clearly, it was not an ephemeral legislative fad but a deeper reasoned, moral reassessment against executing juveniles. Just as clearly, there was no single indicator. The number of states using the punishment, trends in that number, the numbers or trends in actual usage, public opinion, or advice or standards from professional associations—many things could potentially enter into a calculation of evolving standards. Recall from chapter 1 that in *Furman* Justice Brennan wrote that "[t]he acceptability of a severe punishment is measured not by its availability, for it might become so offensive to society as never to be inflicted, but by its use" (*Furman*, 279). For Brennan, actual usage was key. In this chapter, we will therefore review a number of different indicia of usage, ranging from state legislative actions to death sentences to executions.

In addition to trends in the state legislatures and the nation's courtrooms, the Court uses its own judgment in deciding what is cruel and unusual according to contemporary standards. As Justice O'Connor noted in her *Roper* dissent, "The Constitution contemplates that the Court's own judgment be brought to bear on the question of the acceptability of the death penalty" (*Roper*, 3; the justice also refers to *Coker*, 597). For example, under no circumstances today could a state execute a child as young as seven years old, but during the era of the framers, this was at least a theoretical possibility (see Justice Ginsburg's concurring opinion in *Roper* and Justice Scalia's dissent in the same case). In many cases, the Court has ruled unconstitutional a practice that was already extremely rare, essentially acting after, not before, the states. For example, in *Coker v. Georgia* (1977, prohibiting the death penalty for rape of an adult woman), just one jurisdiction allowed it. In *Enmund v. Florida* (1988) prohibiting it for some crimes of aiding and abetting a felony murder), just eight jurisdictions allowed it. In *Ford v. Wainwright* (1986, prohibiting the execution of an inmate who is mentally incompetent to understand the punishment of execution), no jurisdiction allowed it at the time. (See O'Connor's dissent in *Roper v. Simmons*, 11–12; see also Justice Stevens in his majority opinion in *Atkins v. Virginia* (2002), 312.)

The Court considers a wide range of indicators as it seeks to assess where "contemporary standards" may be situated. Clearly, the actions of state legislative bodies are relevant. More contentiously, public opinion polls, actions of professional associations, and international trends have been used by the majority of the Court to justify such conclusions. Finally, the Court uses its "own judgment" in declaring that standards have evolved. With this background, let us look at what the Court might call various indicia of usage.

State Legislative Bills

We can assess legislative attention to the death penalty by looking at bills introduced on the topic throughout the 50 states. Alex Loyal, a student at the University of North Carolina at the time, conducted such a study for his senior honors thesis in 2013, working closely with the senior author here (see Loyal 2013). Using the Lexis-Nexis State Legislative Universe database, which includes all legislative bills introduced across the 50 states, he first identified all bills directly related to the death penalty from 1990 through 2011. For each bill, he assessed whether the bill contained elements that restricted or expanded the use of capital punishment, and the ways in which it did so. For 1990, for example, he found 39 bills on the topic. Five of these bills sought to establish capital punishment; 2 sought to abolish it. But there were many other elements in the bills, such as expanding or restricting the range of crimes for which death was a possible punishment, expanding or restricting the legal options for inmates seeking to appeal their sentences (e.g., establishing strict time limits on appeals or loosening such restrictions, or restricting the total number of appeals allowed, or doing away with such restrictions), expanding or restricting funding for capital defense, and so on. Loyal coded each provision of each bill, understanding that some bills might expand capital punishment by enlarging the list of capital-eligible crimes, but the same bills might restrict it by allowing increased funding for capital defenders. In 1990, with a total of 39 bills, 25 included provisions expanding the use of capital punishment, and 25 included provisions restricting it. In 2011, the last year for which figures were included in Loyal's study, 98 bills were introduced, of which 38 expanded and 70 restricted the use of the death penalty.

Figure 16.1A shows the number of state legislative bills, and Figure 16.1B shows the percent of those bills that restricted, rather than expanded, the use of the death penalty.[2]

Looking first at the number of bills, the totals ranged from just 34 bills introduced across the 50 states in 1992 to 103 bills in 2009. While there is a slight increase in legislative attention over time, there is also great annual variation and no strong pattern with regard to the degree of legislative attention to the death penalty.

The proportion of bills restricting use of the death penalty starts the series at exactly 50 percent in 1990 and 1991 and declines to as low as 21 percent in 1996,

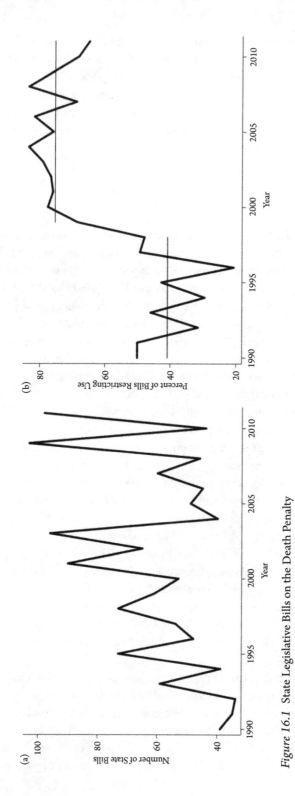

Figure 16.1 State Legislative Bills on the Death Penalty
A. Total Number of Bills Introduced. Source: Loyal 2013.
B. Percent of Bills Restricting Use. Note: Through 1998: 40.85; 1999 and after: 75.36; t = –9.58, df = 20; p < .0000. Source: Loyal 2013.

remaining at 50 or below through the period to 1998. In 1999, however, it jumps to 68 percent, and from that point it has never been lower than 50 percent. The difference before and after 1998 is highlighted in Figure 16.1B: the average value in 1998 or before is 41, and after 1998 it is 75; this difference is highly significant statistically using a simple t-test as shown. In other words, legislative action, like public opinion or the number of death sentences, trended in the direction of expansion in the use of capital punishment until about 1996 or 1998, the same period in which the number of death sentences (1996) and executions (1999) reached their respective peaks. Since then, it has declined sharply. Later we show similar trends with regard to public opinion, death sentences, executions, and the number of jurisdictions initially imposing or finally carrying out these penalties. Here we see that the actions of state-level elected officials followed the same trend: the typical bill on the death penalty expanded its use before 1999, but since then about three-quarters of all legislative provisions have been in the direction of restriction.

Of course, we should note some prominent countervailing actions; a consensus and an emerging trend are not the same as unanimity. When Nebraska's legislature voted to abolish in 2015, it was immediately countered with a voter initiative on the ballot in November 2016 where it was reinstated; one prominent supporter of the initiative was the elected and sitting governor. After North Carolina passed the Racial Justice Act in 2009, it was later met with powerful opposition, and when legislative control switched to the Republican Party after 2012, the law was rescinded. Further, the legislature passed the Restoring Proper Justice Act in 2015, designed to bring back the death penalty following an effective moratorium since 2006. This act focused on simplifying lethal injection procedures and relaxing requirements that trained medical professionals be present. These are but two examples, but clearly many state-level actors have moved to buck the trends that are illustrated in Figure 16.1.

The Rise and Decline of the Modern Death Penalty

There are two distinct periods in the use of capital punishment in the modern death penalty period. Following the *Furman v. Georgia* decision in 1972, there was rapid expansion in the use of the death penalty, and the trends of capital punishment were, across the board, expanding. However, this trend took a swift turn and began to decline in the middle to late 1990s. Figure 16.2 shows the trends of capital punishment use from 1973 to 2016. The variables that have been included in the figure have had their peak usage set to 100, meaning that the trends can be interpreted as the percentage of maximum value of each given indicator. For example, death sentences reached 315 in 1996, and executions reached 98 in 1999. To make all these series fit on the same scale, we present each as a percentage of the maximum value. Table 16.1 indicates what those peak values are for each of the series displayed.

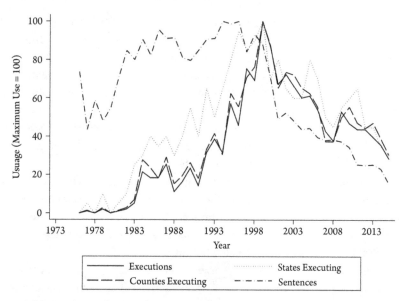

Figure 16.2 Death Penalty Trends, 1976–2015

As shown in Figure 16.2, all the indicators of death penalty peaked within a three-year period, between 1996 and 1999, and then all followed a similar downward trajectory, entering the capital punishment era of decline. Whether we look at death sentences, executions, or the numbers of jurisdictions executing, we see similar trends. Death sentences were extremely erratic in the early years; only Florida had rewritten its death penalty law as of the end of 1973, so death sentences were momentarily and artificially low in that year. They rose dramatically as the states rewrote their laws, then grew throughout the 1970s and 1980s. Executions lagged substantially after death sentences, of course, and represent only a fraction of all the sentences for reasons we explained in chapter 7 (i.e., only 16 percent of death sentences are carried out; most are overturned because of faults in the trial of guilt or the penalty phase). Then, no matter how we look at it, the decline from the mid-1990s is precipitous. Table 16.1 lists the indicators displayed in Figure 16.2., the value and year of their maximum usage, the value occurring in 2015, and the percentage decline from the maximum value to its most recent. In addition, the table adds a number of other relevant indicators that show the declining usage of the death penalty over time.

While death sentences peaked in 1996, executions peaked in 1999, with 98 executions occurring across 72 counties and 20 states. By 2015, these numbers had declined by 70 to 80 percent: just 28 executions in 22 counties found in 6 different states. Accompanying this decline was the number of states with official death penalty laws on the books. We saw in Figure 1.4 that most previous death penalty states rapidly reinstated their capital punishment systems after *Furman*, and these

Table 16.1 **Declining Usage Indicators**

Indicator	Maximum Value	Year of Maximum Value	Recent Value (2015)	Percent Decline
Death sentences	315	1996	49	84.4
Executions	98	1999	28	71.4
States executing	20	1999	6	70.0
States with more than 5 executions	5	1999	2	60.0
Counties executing	72	1999	22	69.4
Counties with more than 3 executions	5	1999	0	100.0
Jurisdictions with death penalty laws	40	2006	33	17.5
States having executed any inmates over the previous five years	30	2001	14	53.3
States having executed 5 or more inmates over the previous five years	12	2003	9	25.0
States having executed 10 or more inmates over the previous five years	10	2006	7	30.0
States having executed 20 or more inmates over the previous 5 years	5	2000	2	60.0
Executions in Texas	40	2000	13	67.5
Executions in Oklahoma	18	2001	1	94.4
Executions in Virginia	14	1999	1	92.9

Note: In cases where the maximum value occurred in more than one year, the most recent year is indicated.

numbers remained very steady for almost 30 years. Beginning in 2007, however, with the New York Supreme Court decision invalidating the death penalty, New Jersey, New Mexico, Illinois, Connecticut, Maryland, and Nebraska have abolished. And the remarkable thing about these abolitions is that they were legislative and political acts, not judicial ones. So state abolitions are one powerful indicator, but as we see later, actual usage has declined much more precipitously.

Decline in Number of Executing Counties

Executions are very concentrated in just a few counties, as we know from chapter 6. In fact, in any given year, it is rare for any county to execute more than a single inmate, even in states with the most active death chambers.[3] As is apparent from Table 16.1, at the peak use of the death penalty, in 1999, while 72 counties

executed, only 5 counties executed more than three inmates. Five executions were
carried out stemming from crimes in Harris and Dallas Counties, Texas, and in
Chesterfield County, Virginia, and 4 executions stemmed from Tarrant County,
Texas, and St. Louis County, Missouri. This was the only year in which as many
as 5 counties carried out more than 3 executions. Sixty counties had just 1; six
had 2; one had 3; two had 4; and three had 5 executions. The maximum number
of executions in any single county in a single year was 1997, when 11 executions
stemmed from cases emanating from Harris County, Texas. So, for any given location, an execution is rare, extremely so. Homicides, on the other hand, as we saw in
chapter 6, are quite common. Los Angeles County had more than 1,900 homicides
in 1992 alone and has never seen a year from 1984 to 2012 with fewer than 500
homicides. Harris County had more than 700 homicides in 1991; it typically has
fewer than in Detroit, Chicago, or Los Angeles, but the numbers are large nonetheless. Of course, not all of these were capital-eligible crimes. But the number of
homicides differs from the number of death sentences or executions by orders of
magnitude. And this is true in Houston, the epicenter of the US death penalty system, just as it is in Chicago, Los Angeles, or Brooklyn, areas (unlike Detroit) where
the death penalty is available (or was for most the modern period, in Brooklyn and
Chicago) but is rarely used.

Decline in Number of Executing States

We see the same pattern when we look at states rather than counties. In 2006, 38
states, the federal government, and the US military had active death penalty statutes. Since then, 7 states have abolished, leaving 33 jurisdictions remaining.[4]
However, as Table 16.1 shows, only 14 states have executed an inmate in the period
of 2011 through 2015; only 9 states have executed an average of 1 inmate per year in
that time; and only 7 states have executed 20 inmates over the most recent five-year
period. So while the movement in terms of legislative authority has been modest,
actual use is very low and declining. Only Missouri and Mississippi have increased
their numbers of executions during the most recent five-year period, though
Mississippi has executed no prisoners after 2012, when 6 were executed. Missouri
executed 16 in 2014 and 2015, the only state to have increased its use of the death
penalty dramatically in the most recent five-year period.

   Table 16.1 shows that 1999 was the peak use across states. During that year, 35
executions took place in Texas; 14 in Virginia; 9 in Missouri; 7 in Arizona; and 6
in Oklahoma. This was the only time when as many as five states each carried out
more than 5 executions. These trends are similar when we look at a moving window
of five years in each state. Twenty executions over five years implies an execution
each quarter: hardly a high rate of usage, considering the numbers of homicides.
But only five states have ever reached that level of usage, and just two states did so
in the 2011–2015 period. Of course, we know from chapter 6 that executions are

highly concentrated in Texas, Oklahoma, and Virginia. These are the only states to have executed more than 10 inmates in any single year. Texas has done so 22 times, Oklahoma 3 times, and Virginia twice. The final three rows of the table therefore concentrate on those states and show that, just as in the rest of the nation, executions are in steep decline. Each state reached its peak number of executions in the period of 1999 to 2001, and each has declined sharply: almost 70 percent for Texas, and down to just one execution each in Virginia and in Oklahoma.[5] Even in the states with the greatest historical use of the death penalty, the trends are consistent: it was always rare when compared with homicides, and today it stands at values from 70 to more than 90 percent below its peak of approximately 15 to 20 years ago.

Declining Public Opinion

In chapter 13 we introduced our summary index of public opinion, scored to a value of zero in 1976; see Figure 13.3. Like the usage indicators just reviewed, our index of public opinion also reached a peak in the mid-1990s. Figure 16.3 presents a general summary of the decline in usage, the increased concentration, and the decline in popularity of the death penalty in the past 20 years. The capital punishment usage series are all scaled to be compared to their maximum historical value during the 1977–2015 period, which is assigned a value of 100. The public opinion index is scaled in relation to its value (scored as zero) in 1976. All the usage series decline to 20 to 40 percent of their maximum values.

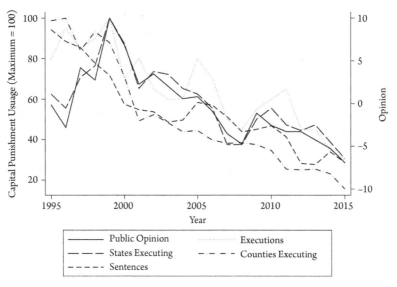

Figure 16.3 Decline of the Death Penalty

Conclusion

In October 2015, Justice Antonin Scalia stated in an appearance at the University of Minnesota Law School that he would not be surprised if the Supreme Court struck down the death penalty. At the event, Justice Scalia said that it has become "practically impossible for states to impose the death penalty" (Kaste 2015), referring to the recent complications in the drug cocktail used in executions. The justice was perhaps also referring to the dissent in *Glossip* by his colleague Justice Breyer, who wrote: "But rather than try to patch up the death penalty's legal wounds one at a time, I would ask for a full briefing on a more basic question: whether the death penalty violates the Constitution" (Breyer, in *Glossip*, 1). Justice Scalia's own opinion in that case began with the following statement: "I . . . write to respond to Justice Breyer's plea for judicial abolition of the death penalty" (Scalia, in *Glossip*, 1). Notably for the discussion in this chapter, Justice Scalia strongly rejected the notion of evolving standards, writing, "I would ask that counsel also brief whether our cases that have abandoned the historical understanding of the Eighth Amendment, beginning with *Trop*, should be overruled. That case has caused more mischief to our jurisprudence, to our federal system, and to our society than any other that comes to mind" (6). For Justice Scalia, it was clear: the death penalty is constitutional, it always has been, and it always should be going into the future.

This chapter has reviewed trends in use. In the long term, trends have been on a steady historical decline from 1935. There was a very powerful and generation-long response to the earthshaking *Furman* decision; trends increased for 20 years following *Gregg*. But now we have seen another 20 years of decline. Evolving standards are but one, and a highly controversial, means of assessing the value of the death penalty. In our final chapter, we assess the evidence we have presented throughout the book in the attempt to draw some conclusions from these trends and patterns.

Further Readings

Fagan, Jeffrey, and Valerie West. 2005. The Decline of the Juvenile Death Penalty: Scientific Evidence of Evolving Norms. *Journal of Criminal Law and Criminology* 95 (2): 427–500.

Garrett, Brandon. 2017. The Decline of the Virginia (and American) Death Penalty. *Georgetown Law Journal* 105:661–729.

Steiker, Carol S. 2002. Capital Punishment and American Exceptionalism. *Oregon Law Review* 81 (1): 97–130.

17

Does the Modern Death Penalty Meet the Goals of *Furman*?

Throughout the chapters of this book, we have focused on particular aspects of the modern death penalty system, one issue at a time.[1] In this chapter, we ask a simple question. If the Court ruled in *Furman* that existing laws were unconstitutional because of certain flaws, but then ruled 4 years later in *Gregg* that the laws had been sufficiently improved to avoid those flaws, then where do we stand today? In the 40 years since *Gregg*, does the evidence show that we have met the promise of this ruling, or is the modern system prone to the same or similar problems as were ruled unacceptable in *Furman*? We also consider whether other concerns, not noted in *Furman*, call into question the constitutional acceptability of the modern death penalty; for example, we discussed in chapter 8 the issue of delays, leading to the question (not discussed in *Furman*) of whether there is a limit to how long an inmate may be expected to wait on death row before being executed.

Is the Modern Death Penalty "Wanton and Freakish"?

Justice Stewart expressed concern in *Furman* (309–310; see chapter 1) that the death penalty was imposed so rarely that it was akin to being struck by lightning, and that such a "wanton and freakish" process could not be squared with the Constitution's prohibition on cruel and unusual punishments.[2] There had to be some greater logic to the system.

Frequency with Respect to Homicides

We reviewed in chapter 1 the numbers of homicides, death sentences, and executions over time during the modern period. We can make a simple comparison by combining the annual numbers into the total over the entire time period. Figure 17.1 shows the total cumulative numbers of homicides, death sentences, and executions.

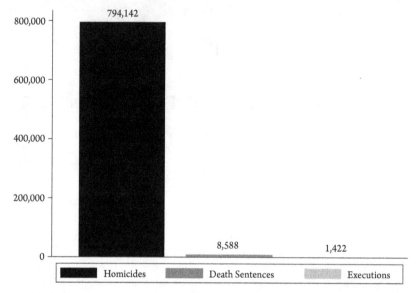

Figure 17.1 Cumulative Homicides, Death Sentences, and Executions. Note: Homicides, 1973–2014; sentences 1973–2015; executions 1976–2015.

Overall, we have had almost 800,000 homicides in the United States since *Furman,* as well as more than 8,500 death sentences and 1,422 executions. Death sentences therefore represent 1.08 percent of homicides, and executions 0.18 percent. In other words, we have had 18 executions per 10,000 homicides. On the face of it, then, we know that death is not the expected punishment for homicide. We know as well that not all of these homicides were death-eligible crimes, that many of them occurred in states without the death penalty, and that many of the offenders were never arrested. On the other hand, if the moral question is whether those thinking of homicide will be deterred by the threat of death, or if those who commit homicide should be killed for reasons of retribution, the point of comparison makes more sense. (In Ehrlich's [1975b] study of deterrence, homicide offenders consider the odds of being caught—the "clearance rate"—the odds of being found guilty, and the odds of receiving death as punishment.) We also saw in chapter 5 that many states make the vast majority of homicides eligible for death because of aggravators such as "lying in wait," "pecuniary gain," or "underlying felony" (or elements defining what is a capital or first-degree murder). In any case, a simple comparison of homicides to executions provides the ratio of 18 executions per 10,000 homicides. Before turning to the question of whether the executions are narrowly targeted at the most depraved, heinous, or deserving killers, we assess rarity and geography in more detail.

The Rarity of Execution in Any Given State in Any Given Year

Thirty-four states and the federal government have carried out executions in the modern time. But the typical state carries out none in any given year. In fact, the distribution of executions per year, for any given jurisdiction, is heavily weighted toward zero, suggesting that no state has capital punishment as a significant part of its criminal justice system, judging by the numbers and considering the number of homicides. Texas, for example, had more than 1,100 homicides in 2013, based on FBI data; there were just nine death sentences, according to the Death Penalty Information Center. Table 17.1 shows how rare it is for states to execute even a single individual in any given year, even in those states that execute. Considering the entire modern period (40 years) and all those jurisdictions with any executions, more than 70 percent of the state-year combinations have a value of zero.

The preceding data show that, across 35 jurisdictions executing and 40 years of observations from 1976 through 2015, by far the most common situation is that there is not a single execution in any given state: 73 percent of the observations are zeros. It is unclear what a large number might be, given that many states have several

Table 17.1 **Annual Executions in States Having Executed in the Modern Period**

Number of Executions per Year	Number of State-Years	Percent	Cumulative Percent
0	1,018	72.7	72.7
1	164	11.7	84.4
2	69	4.9	89.4
3	39	2.8	92.1
4	30	2.1	94.3
5	18	1.3	95.6
6	17	1.2	96.8
7	7	0.5	97.3
8	6	0.4	97.7
9	2	0.1	97.9
10	3	0.2	98.1
More than 10	27	1.9	100.0
Total	1,400	100.0	100.0

Note: Includes only those states (and the federal government) that have carried out at least one execution in the modern period. Numbers refer to states x years.

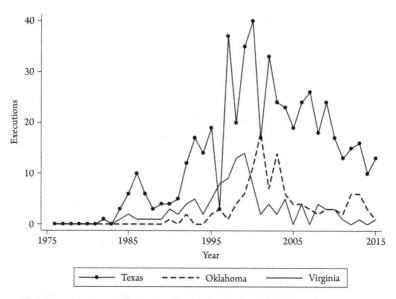

Figure 17.2 Executions per Year in the Three Most Active Death Penalty States

hundred or even more than 1,000 homicides in any given year. But 90 percent of the time, a given state executes fewer than three individuals, and 95 percent of the time fewer than five.

Texas, Oklahoma, and Virginia are the only states where the maximum number of executions has risen above 10 in any given year, with maximum values of 40, 18, and 14, respectively. Figure 17.2 shows how frequently these active death penalty states have carried out executions each year.

Even in what could be considered the epicenter of the death penalty system, the punishment has always been rare. The three top executing states typically generate fewer than 10 executions in any given year, with Texas the only state that has ever surpassed 20. Oklahoma had as many as 400 homicides (in 1995); Texas, 2,652 (in 1991); and Virginia 483 (also in 1991).[3] With thousands of homicides but dozens of executions, or hundreds of homicides and handfuls of executions (often none), even in the three most active death penalty states, it is clear that death is not the usual punishment for murder. And, in each case the trends are toward even lower rates of use since the middle to late 1990s, reflecting national trends.

Geographical Arbitrariness

The Court was concerned in *Furman* that the death penalty was "like being struck by lightning"—completely arbitrary in various ways. One of those ways is by geography. There is no question that this remains an important element of the modern death penalty system. In fact, today's death penalty may be more strongly divided by geography than ever before. After the 1972 ruling, 37 states rapidly enacted new laws allowing the death penalty, and as we saw in the maps presented in chapter 6, this included virtually the entire South. However, adoption of death statutes was not limited to the South. New York, New Jersey, Ohio, Illinois, Pennsylvania, and other northern states adopted them as well. California and Pennsylvania have among the largest death rows in the nation. Many states outside of the South had long histories of active use of the death penalty in previous eras. But as we reviewed in chapter 6, the actual use of the death penalty in the modern period has been extremely focused on just a few jurisdictions. Further, the particularly *southern* character of the punishment is new.

We can use the Espy file (see Espy and Smykla 2005) combined with our own modern era database to compare top-executing states before and after *Gregg*. Figure 17.3 shows the top executing states during the period of 1900 through 1976, on the one hand, using historical data from the Espy file, and then the equivalent data for the top executing states in the post-*Gregg* period.

In the twentieth century through the time of the *Furman* decision, New York was the top executing state (as well as the innovator with regard to the electric chair, as we saw in chapter 10). Other top executing states included Pennsylvania, California, Ohio, and Illinois. In the post-*Gregg* period, the distribution is obviously much more concentrated in just one state, but only one nonsouthern state is included. While New York was the top executing state in the earlier period, only a few executions separated it from the second most active state, Georgia. In the modern period, Texas stands alone. In fact, Ohio (ranked eighth in the modern period, with 53 executions) is the only nonsouthern state to have a large number of executions, compared with other states. If anything, based on the extreme concentration of executions from just a few jurisdictions, and the particular geographical focus of the modern death penalty system, the death penalty seems to have even greater geographical arbitrariness in the modern period than it did earlier. In no period in American history has the death penalty been as highly concentrated as in the modern period.[4] This analysis, which can be confirmed by looking at counties rather than states, has been widely reported; see chapter 6; Baumgartner, Gram et al. 2016; Dieter 2013; Fair Punishment Project 2016a, 2016b, 2016c).

Are There Unacceptable Extralegal Disparities?

As Scott Phillips and Alena Simon (2014) have noted, the justices in *Furman* were concerned about two types of arbitrariness: simple randomness (e.g., the freakish nature of being struck by lightning) and bias. Bias could be intentional or not, but the question was whether unacceptable factors such as race affected the system. The Court ruled in *Furman* that substantial racial disparities infected the application of the death penalty. However, faced with a powerful statistical study in *McCleskey*

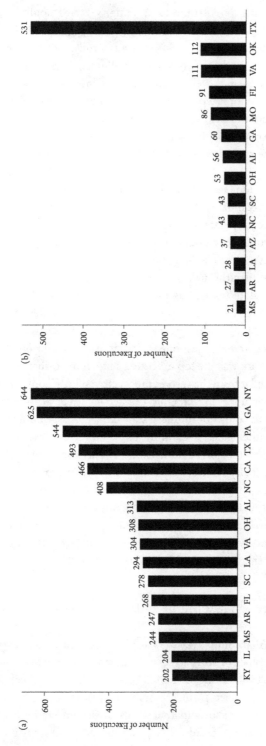

Figure 17.3 Top Executing States before and after *Gregg*

A. 1900 through 1976. Source: Espy and Smykla 2005.

B. Modern period (1977–2015). Source: Carolina Execution Database.

v. Kemp (1986), the Court ruled that statistical patterns revealed by studies such as those conducted by Baldus and others (reviewed in chapter 4 here) were essentially irrelevant. Mr. McCleskey would have to prove that prosecutors, judges, or others involved in his particular death sentence had acted with the intent to discriminate against him because he was black. There can be little doubt that racial and gender disparities are extremely powerful.

We reviewed evidence in chapter 4 and throughout the book that makes clear that, statistically speaking, certain types of victims are more associated with the death penalty: female victims and white victims in particular. Of course, it is possible that such factors could be explained by justifiable legal factors: whether the crime included a sexual assault, for example, or was aggravated in other ways. The studies reviewed in chapter 4 were carefully conducted and typically reviewed hundreds or thousands of death-eligible crimes within particular states, often over many decades. Virtually every published study on the topic, we showed, confirms that legally relevant factors do matter: crimes committed by those with previous violent felonies and crimes that involve torture, sexual assault, or multiple victims are indeed statistically more likely (though not certain) to lead to a death sentence. However, controlling for these factors, many extralegal factors were also found to be relevant: in particular, where the crime occurred, and the race and gender of the victim. The simple comparison of rates of execution per homicide presented in Figure 4.3 shows that killers of black males, statistically, have a 0.10 percent likelihood of execution, whereas those who kill white females have a rate of execution of 1.24: more than 12 times as great. We also noted in chapter 4 that many states had never seen a white offender executed for killing a black victim, particularly a black male. Louisiana, for example, last saw a white executed for a crime against a black in 1752; no white in Louisiana has ever been executed for killing a black male. But black males constitute more than 60 percent of all homicide victims in the state from 1976 through 2011 (see Baumgartner and Lyman 2015). These patterns are reflected in many states, some more accentuated than others, but none suggesting anything close to racial neutrality, and certainly none suggesting the crimes against males and females have been treated equally in the modern death penalty system (see chapter 4; Baumgartner, Grigg, and Mastro 2015; Baumgartner, Johnson, et al. 2016).

Is the Death Penalty Narrowly Targeted at the "Worst of the Worst"?

We noted in chapter 1 Justice White's expressed hope and expectation in *Gregg* that, with its revised laws, Georgia's new death penalty law (and others like it) would target a "narrowly defined" set of crimes and then sentence to death a "substantial portion" of offenders of these particularly deserving crimes. If large proportions of all homicides are death-eligible, but just a few of those who are eligible receive it, there is just too much room for various prejudices and biases to come into play, or for neutral but essentially "freakish" legally indefensible distinctions reserving life for some but death for an unlucky few. Such was the logic in *Furman*, and the hope of *Gregg* was to avoid this by narrow targeting and high sentencing rates within those particularly deserving categories of crime.

We have reviewed a range of materials that suggest we are far from reaching these goals. First, we saw in chapter 5 that states have not, in fact, "narrowly targeted" their lists of death-eligible crimes. Rather, these lists specify a range of vague and broad aggravators or factors making a crime death-eligible, such as "lying in wait," "pecuniary gain," "commission of felony," "heinous" or "depraved," and the like; large percentages of homicides are death-eligible, but very low percentages of such offenders see a capital prosecution. In sum, the evidence suggests we have failed both the "narrow targeting" and the "substantial proportion" standards that the justices collectively seemed to be expecting in *Gregg*.

Second, careful empirical comparisons such as those conducted by Baldus and followers (see the review in chapter 4) have found that while legally relevant aggravators, including measures of heinousness, often increase the odds of a death sentence, these correlations are not as strong as the justices may have been expecting in *Gregg*. For example, in his study of Connecticut's death penalty, Donohue (2014) reviewed the "egregiousness" of the crimes associated with each of 205 death-eligible cases. He did this both by asking 18 law student coders to give a general ranking from 1 to 5 and also to rank victim suffering, victim characteristics, defendant culpability, and number of victims separately on scales ranging from 1 to 3, summing them for a composite ranking from 4 to 12. He found that the general index and the composite index correlated at .88, demonstrating very high reliability (Donohue 2014, 645). Nine individuals had sustained death sentences in the period of his study, based on 205 death-eligible cases. Their composite egregiousness scores ranged from 7.11 to 11.17, on the scale going from 4 to 12. Clearly, the most egregious case was near the top of the scale. But, in fact, 4 non-death cases had higher egregiousness scores than that case. In the lowest case, 170 of the 205 death-eligible homicides had higher egregiousness values (679, Table 13). That is to say, there was little tendency overall to see the most egregious, most heinous, or most aggravated homicides lead to a death sentence.[5] The death cases seem drawn from the higher ranges of the distribution, on average, but the linkage between egregiousness and death sentencing is very weak.

Is the Death Penalty Reliably Applied?

Closely related to the issue of "narrow targeting" is that of applying the penalty in a "substantial proportion" of cases that meet the narrowly defined criteria making a given case eligible for the ultimate penalty. The evidence we have reviewed clearly shows that only small percentages of those committing even eligible crimes actually receive a death sentence, and then even lower numbers are executed. But we would be remiss if we did not return to a fundamental and perhaps unavoidable problem: Can the Court clearly define which crimes and which criminals *should* be sentenced to death? The Court has always said no. In *McGautha* (1971), Justice Harlan wrote that such a complete enumeration was "beyond present human ability," and later the Court refused to allow limitations on jury consideration of mitigators, arguing that it would be impossible to provide a complete list. It is hard to avoid the conclusion that the lack of a clear line between which cases legally do and do not deserve death not only imbues the system with an indispensable role for the jury (or sentencing authority) but also smacks of pixie dust. If the line is invisible, unknowable, and philosophically impossible to verify, but inmates nonetheless are to be subjected to these rules, then we cannot possibly expect a system that is reliable. Two juries faced with the same facts need not come to the same conclusion: one uses its judgment to impose death; another, life. This is the definition of unreliable, and yet it has not been found to be constitutionally faulty. This "tension" between the need for individualized sentencing and jury discretion on the one hand and reliable results on the other exploded in the 1990s. For Justices Scalia and Thomas, it led to the decision to offer blanket rejections of any claims of restricted jury discretion (i.e., complaints of arbitrary outcomes). For Justice Blackmun, four years later, it led to the opposite conclusion: if it cannot be administered in a reliable manner, then " 'the death penalty cannot be administered in accord with our Constitution' " (see Steiker and Steiker 2016, 180–181; the cases were *Walton v. Arizona* (1990) and *Callins v. Collins* (1994)). The Western legal tradition of "mercy" and the long-standing understanding that the causes of mercy cannot ever be listed beg the question of whether the causes for declining mercy can be listed, and if guided discretion statutes seeking to guarantee that denial or exercise of mercy not be done with regard to sympathies based on race, class, or other features. But more generally they beg a more general question of whether we want the state to select prisoners for death while exempting others from that punishment on the basis of criteria that cannot be explained.

Deterrence

Deterrence was a hotly debated item in the *Gregg* decision, and much research has continued on the topic. The National Research Council (NRC) review of these published studies clearly indicated that the consensus assessment among the experts, unfortunately, was that no conclusions either way can be sustained by this accumulated research (see chapter 15). Thus, judicial opinions should not be driven by studies one way or another on this question, and we will follow the NRC advice here by simply not including the issue of deterrence in our assessment. There is no conclusive evidence that the death penalty deters; there is none that it does not.

Innocence

Justice Marshall expressed his concerns in *Furman* that the death penalty was imposed against innocent individuals (364ff.) and that "we have no way of judging how many innocent persons have been executed but we can be certain that there were some . . . . Surely there will be more as long as capital punishment remains part of our penal law" (Marshall, in *Furman*, 367–368). Justice Marshall was the only one to give significant attention to the issue of innocence, however.

Today, if the Court were to give a general review of capital punishment as it did in *Furman*, it would be inconceivable that so little attention would be paid to this issue. It has come to be a major element of all debate about the death penalty, perhaps appropriately given that the penalty of death is of course the only one that cannot be corrected after it is applied. In fact, we noted in Figure 9.3 that 156 individuals have spent a total of 1,923 years on death row or in prison after they were condemned to die, but before they were found to be innocent. One thing has not changed since Justice Marshall wrote: aside from acknowledging that it has certainly happened, we do not know how often innocent individuals have been executed. No human institutions are perfect. In this context, that simple truism takes on greater meaning than it seems to have elicited in previous generations of jurisprudence.

Collateral Damage

Robert Bohm (2013) notes that the death penalty imposes costs on many individuals beyond the inmate. Jurors are faced with life-and-death power but in retrospect may find out that the evidence presented to them was partial, or that the defense attorney was incompetent, incomplete, or mistaken in his or her legal strategy. Jurors could potentially find themselves unwittingly involved in a wrongful conviction, with another person's life on the line. Going through each actor in the system from homicide investigators to family members of both accused and victims, attorneys on both sides, trial and appellate judges up to the US Supreme Court, jurors, prison staff and wardens, execution team members and their families, and governors, Bohm reviews systematically the increased psychological and emotional cost of operating within the death penalty system. The stakes are high, and the emotional cost is extreme.

Jurors in a capital trial pay a particular price, as they are neither professionals having chosen a career in the law nor family members brought into the horrors of a murder and its aftermath by some act beyond their control; they are brought in by the government of which they are a part. But they are asked to look at a person across the room and decide on his or her future life or death. And they play only a passive role in the process, as they cannot ask their own questions but must base their fateful decision on the evidence presented to them and the arcane legal instructions given to them for the first time during the trial and their deliberations. Robin Conley quotes two capital jurors in her review of these costs:

> "That's the hardest thing I've ever had to do, to look at a man and, you know, know that I'm saying, you know, I don't think you should live." (2016. 4)

> "I've always felt that the death penalty you know, was a good thing? This process here is kinda, makes you wanna, makes you wanna think about it . . . . I, it's like I say, that's the hardest thing I ever had to do. And I never thought that it would be that hard." (4)

Most of us will never serve on a capital jury. But for those who do, the price is enormous. (For another study of the high cost of capital jury service, see also Fleury-Steiner 2004.)

Evolving Standards of Decency

We reviewed in the previous chapter various indicia of usage that all point in the same direction. While *Gregg* put in place a system that grew for 20 years, it has been declining now for 20 years. States have abolished their death penalty laws through legislative action several times since 2007; no state had done that previously. Usage, never high when considered in reference to homicides, has dwindled. Literally, lightning strikes are more common today than executions. Whether we look at national figures on death sentences, executions, jurisdictions executing any inmates (or more than a few), the number of jurisdictions retaining the death penalty even in theory, or the number of executions in the three most active death penalty states, it is clear in Table 16.1 that trends since the mid-1990s have been uniformly downward, and sharply so.

Public Opinion Responsiveness

Two elements of public opinion are potentially of interest: whether "evolving standards" suggest that the death penalty is no longer acceptable to a wide swath of Americans, and whether local variation in the use of the death penalty can be attributed to differing "community norms" or values.

We reviewed a range of data in chapter 13 on public opinion. It is hard to disagree with Justice Marshall's assertion that Americans do not know much about the death penalty. In response to simple questions, large numbers of Americans have consistently stated that they support the death penalty. However, when provided the choice between death and life without parole (LWOP), or a lesser punishment for the crime of murder, only a minority (28 percent in a 2014 poll in Houston; see Table 13.6) choose death. Of course, we know that every state with the death penalty also has the option of LWOP. Most important for any discussion of "evolving standards," our best estimate of the dynamics of public opinion is that support for the death penalty generally rose after *Gregg* and that since about 1996 it has been in steep decline. Today, it stands significantly lower than in 1976, according to the evidence we gathered in such a painstaking manner and presented in chapter 13.

Beyond "evolving standards," it is also important to assess "community values." Our empirical evidence in chapter 13 clearly demonstrated that there are virtually no linkages between local (or state-level) opinion in the aggregate and the number of executions. Whether we look at the variability in use across the states, or within the most active state across the various metropolitan areas where public opinion data can reliably be collected, we see no correlation with public opinion.

Death qualification, a process unique to capital punishment, breaks any possible linkage between community norms and jury decision-making, because only certain members of the public are allowed to sit on capital juries. If survey respondents in Houston, Texas, routinely indicate that they prefer LWOP to death, sometimes even preferring life with parole after 25 years, in responses to repeated public opinion polls (see Table 13.6), showing less support for the death penalty than in other parts of Texas, and no more than Americans in general (see Figure 13.7), then why is Houston the epicenter of the nation's death penalty system? It cannot be because of local public opinion. Death penalty usage is driven by prosecutors, not by citizens. Prosecutors start a process, and death penalty supporters serve on juries to the exclusion of those opposed to the punishment.

Previous discussions on the Court of local norms have used juries as the reflection of local norms and noted that the elected nature of the district attorney ensures that such officials remain in tune with local values. But juries do not reflect the full range of opinion, since those on one side of the issue are systematically deprived of their right to sit on them, even in the guilt phase of the trial where their opposition to capital punishment is irrelevant to the decision at hand. And, with regard to the desire of a DA to reflect local opinion, the distribution of public opinion across American communities simply does not correspond to the distribution of use of the death penalty. One is relatively moderate, with some communities slightly more supportive and some slightly less so, but the other is highly skewed. A small number of prosecutors generate outsized numbers of death sentences and executions, as we saw in chapter 6. In sum, there is much less public opinion responsiveness than many have previously assumed.

Possible Elements of Cruelty not Discussed in *Furman*

Previous sections in this chapter have reviewed the accumulated evidence about whether the modern death penalty would pass the *Furman* tests for proportionality, arbitrariness, narrow targeting, and other issues. Evidence suggests that the modern system would fail each of these tests. But our book has also brought to light a number of issues not powerfully addressed in *Furman*. Most important, this involves the possibility that several aspects of the modern death penalty system may be akin to torture. Here we refer to reversals, delays, stays, and botches. No system with these elements designed into it would be considered constitutionally acceptable. But the system we have developed and now can assess with 40 years of experience shows serious deficiencies, which we reviewed in various earlier chapters. We would not argue that any systems have been designed purposefully to create the patterns we describe in the following, but these patterns are clear.

Reversals, Delays, Stays, and Botches

The vast majority of duly imposed death sentences are reversed on appeal. While this is good news from the perspective of the condemned inmate, the extremely high probability of reversal raises powerful ethical questions. As we showed in chapter 7, official government statistics covering every death sentence from 1973 through 2013 show that execution is the outcome of a death sentence only 16 percent of the time (25 percent when we consider only "finalized" dispositions). Commutations are not the cause; they represent just 7 percent of finalized outcomes. Rather, 16 percent of inmates see their convictions overturned, and 32 percent see their death sentence overturned on appeal. On retrial, some of these reversals are reinstated. These reversals are not typically related to actual innocence (through 156 of them have been). Rather, they call into question the reliability and surety of the death penalty system itself. No other public policy functions with an error or reversal rate of 66 percent.

The website of North Carolina's Department of Corrections includes a list of all inmates removed from death row, and the reason they were removed (see North Carolina Department of Public Safety 2016). Inmate 0314959, Randy Joe Payne, was received on death row on January 25, 1985. Payne's sentence was reversed, and a new trial was ordered on July 27, 1987; he received a second death sentence on February 11, 1988. This sentence was also vacated, and a resentencing hearing was ordered on April 23, 1991. A third death sentence was imposed on September 28, 1992. Mr. Payne committed suicide on August 28, 1998.

An on-again off-again death penalty cannot be what the framers had in mind. Neither was a system like the one we documented in chapter 8 in which the average delay from crime to execution is more than 20 years (see Figure 8.1). The Court considered whether excessive delay was unconstitutional and declared it was not in the case of *Lackey v. Texas* (1995). More recently a federal judge ruled that California's system, in which the state itself guarantees decades of delay by its own procedures, particularly in how long it waits before appointing counsel and in scheduling appellate hearings, was unconstitutional (see *Jones v. Chappell* (2014)). While the California case was later overturned, it seems apparent that the increasing delays we documented in chapter 8 will lead to further claims that a punishment of 30 or more years in prison, accompanied by a statistically improbable chance at execution, is not acceptable. The long delay calls into question what is the additional value of execution, given the long period on death row. And the low statistical odds of execution raise the same issues of arbitrariness that so troubled the justices in *Furman*. There, they said death sentences that are imposed "only" on 15 to 20 percent of those having committed a given class of crime were too low, allowing for too much arbitrariness to creep into the system. Today we have a similar rate of execution among those initially condemned to die.

In chapter 11 we documented some surprising facts about last-minute stays of execution. In fact, more scheduled executions are canceled than are carried out. Certain states, such as Pennsylvania, routinely schedule executions though there is no reasonable chance they will be carried out, considering that it has never happened even a single time for a nonvolunteer inmate in the modern history of the commonwealth. We showed that it is not uncommon for individual inmates, such as Troy Davis, to endure three or four dates with death, and for these to be in question until the last minute. One might imagine that by the time an inmate has a last meal, says goodbye to his or her mother, has last rites, and is strapped to the gurney, the legal wrangling would be over. But it is not.

Finally, a significant percentage of executions have been botched. Whether this has been an electric chair that fails to conduct electricity, a gas chamber that creates a slow asphyxiation rather than a painless death, or a lethal injection process gone wrong, we do not have to search the archives for long to find numerous examples of executions leading to suffering; legal arguments typically center on whether these were unavoidable one-time errors or part of a pattern and practice. Perhaps the main reason for the undeniable fact that many inmates have suffered during botched executions is that most states have little experience with the process. The lethal injection protocols in use in most states demand some degree of medical training, but the logical personnel to administer these procedures will not participate.

While we cannot argue that systems were designed purposefully to generate this situation, we must nonetheless ask if there can be a constitutional logic to a punishment that typically consists of (1) a sentence of death solemnly intoned by a judge and jury but routinely overturned on appeal; (2) a delay of at least 20 years on death row, and perhaps much longer; (3) continued legal fighting until the last minute, with stays of execution statistically more likely than seeing the punishment carried out; (4) inmates enduring more than one and sometimes several dates with death, last meals, and family goodbyes; (5) litigation about whether the state's execution protocol is sufficient to guarantee that the inmate will not be subject to excruciating pain, given that the procedure will typically be highly medicalized, but major drug companies will not supply the needed drugs, and professional anesthesiologists will not participate in monitoring the level of consciousness; and (6) substantial numbers of inmates, many with suicidal tendencies, demanding death and finally being allowed to put an end to their lives by publicly assisted suicide.

Are the Costs Justified?

In *Furman* and *Gregg,* cost was not a significant part of the conversation, and it is possible that in future considerations the Court could ignore it. But, as we reviewed in chapter 14, the modern death penalty system has become extremely costly. Partly as a result of the "death is different" jurisprudence required by the Court in order to assure that the new penalty would avoid the flaws of its historical predecessor, costs have skyrocketed. This by itself perhaps poses no constitutional issue. But the high rates of reversal, long delays between sentencing and execution, and extremely low execution rates per homicide raise questions about the penological value of the death penalty system. If the Court is unlikely to be concerned with cost matters, we should nonetheless point to excessive cost as a new flaw in the modern death penalty not recognized by *Furman* and one that citizens and state legislators, if not the Court, should consider.

One reason for the dramatically increased costs associated with the modern death penalty as compared with its historical version is that the Court has generated such a complex and changing regulatory structure, as Steiker and Steiker (2016) have explained in detail. The specialized nature of the habeas process, the need for extensive mitigation work, and myriad other factors that were not part of the death penalty historically and are not part of the process in non-capital cases have generated not just the high cost but in fact a regulatory structure with constant involvement of the highest Court, even until the last minute when inmates await execution on the gurney. Rather than clarify, the new death penalty jurisprudence has created a complicated machine in which the justices are constantly being called to tinker.

Who Gets Executed? Who Does Not?

Some Americans would not support the death penalty in any circumstance. Whether it be because they do not trust the government to get it right every time, because they believe only a higher being should have the power of deciding between life and death, or because they think that the alternative of LWOP is a sufficient punishment or one that takes away any additional deterrent or retributive value of execution, or because of another reason, this book will have convinced them of nothing. On the other hand, many Americans, indeed most Americans according to numerous public opinion polls, support the death penalty. It is fair to think that this group expects the punishment to be meted out to those killers who deserve it. Some might argue that all killers deserve it. Others might say it should be reserved for the worst of the worst. Having reviewed so many facts and figures over the course of the previous pages, what can we say, then, about which killers are executed?

The first answer to the question is: very few. As we saw in chapter 3, there have been more than 800,000 homicides in the United States since 1973, and only about 1 percent of those were followed by a death sentence. Then we saw in chapter 7 that most of those death sentences were overturned on appeal. Just 0.18 percent of all homicides are followed by an execution. That is, for every 10,000 homicides, we would expect 18 executions. So, the first point is that it is extremely rare. What are the factors that move these odds up?

First if the victim is a white female, odds are substantially higher (though still low). We saw in chapter 4 that killers of whites are much more frequently executed than killers of blacks, despite the fact that blacks are much more likely statistically to be the victims of homicide. Similarly, killers of women are more likely to be executed than killers of men. Again, this is despite the fact that women represent only about one-quarter of all homicide victims. When the victim has both of these characteristics, odds are more than 10 times higher than if the victim is a black male.

Second, if the perpetrator is black and the victim is white, odds go up substantially. The inverse statement is equally important: whites who kill blacks rarely get punished with death. Most homicides are within race and within gender, as we saw in chapter 3. And most are committed by men; whites kill whites, and blacks kill blacks, and most of those involved are men. However, on those occasions where a black man kills a white female, the odds of execution go up dramatically.

Third, if the crime occurs in Houston, Texas, or a select few other jurisdictions, it is much more likely to be followed by execution. We saw in chapter 6 that vast discrepancies characterize the geographical distribution of the death penalty. The greatest number of homicides occur in Los Angeles County. The five counties that constitute New York City together have even more. Chicago has high numbers of homicides. And while all these areas had the death penalty as an option throughout the bulk of the post-*Gregg* period (New York abolished the death penalty in 2007, and Illinois in 2011), none of these places has as many executions as Houston. In fact, no state other than Texas has more executions than Harris County. So, the old real estate adage that "location matters" is true here as well.

Fourth, if the crime took place in the 1980s, it was much more likely to be followed by execution. The United States executed 391 individuals in the five-year period between 1997 and 2001, but fewer than half that number between 2011 and 2015. So timing matters as well; it can double the odds of death, so these are not small effects. One of the reasons for the dramatic decline in death sentences in recent years is that states have enacted reforms limiting the scope of the death penalty, provide greater resources for the defense, or otherwise have tended to reduce the frequency of death sentences (see Figure 16.1). For example, North Carolina required prosecutors to seek death in all death-eligible cases until July 1, 2000; at that point, it became optional. Further, it created a statewide Indigent Defense Services unit to provide trained capital defense services working under a consistent compensation system to all those facing capital charges across the state. In response to these two reforms, the number of capital prosecutions and death sentences declined precipitously. As a result, the vast majority (74 percent) of inmates on North Carolina's death row as of 2015 were sentenced under procedures that are no longer valid under state law (see Baumgartner 2015). If they were to be executed, a primary cause of their death would be bad timing. Their crimes occurred during a period when current safeguards were not in place.

Fifth, inmates with various types of vulnerabilities are more likely to be targeted successfully for execution than those who can better defend themselves. Those with serious mental illness, those with no family, those with no funds to hire private attorneys to defend them, or those who in various ways are the most vulnerable are more likely to be executed. Mentally ill offenders may face a jury that finds them to be hard to understand, and they may be unable or unwilling to assist in their own defense. The Court no longer allows the execution of juveniles (but did allow it until 2005) or those with serious problems of intellectual capacity (though it did allow this until 2002). But there is no rule against targeting those who cannot defend themselves: the poor, those with mental illness, or those who cannot find a competent lawyer to help them. Some inmates have suicidal tendencies and therefore ask their attorneys to drop all appeals; unsurprisingly, this increases the odds of execution. We saw in chapter 7 that less than 16 percent of those condemned are executed. One way to increase these odds is to "volunteer," and about 10 percent of all executed inmates have been volunteers, as we saw in chapter 12. Surprisingly, the implication of this is that we execute a class of offender for reasons that have nothing to do with the crime. Mental illness is rampant on death row, and particularly so among inmates who have volunteered for the death chamber.

This is not a comprehensive list of what increases the odds of execution, but in the preceding chapters we have shown that these are indeed key elements in the process. What are some things that don't matter much?

First, the death penalty is not reserved for the "worst of the worst." As we saw in chapter 1, in order to meet constitutional concerns, states theoretically targeted their death penalty statutes on the worst offenders or the most serious murders. However, as we saw in chapter 5, these laws, in the aggregate, have not narrowly targeted those who, for example, may have tortured their victims, showed particular depravity in their crimes, or had multiple victims. These elements are important aggravators, to be sure. However, the states also added other elements to their death penalty statutes. For example, Texas, Oklahoma, and Virginia (the top three executing states) all include an assessment of "future dangerousness" as an element in assessing whether the defendant should be sentenced to life or to death. It is, of course, impossible to state with accuracy what will happen in the future, but these states require a jury to do just that, with a life on the line. Further, future dangerousness may stem from mental illness. In any case, it cannot be predicted very well. Given that the inmate has just been convicted of a capital-eligible crime, it would be hard for that same jury immediately to turn around and say that he or she is unlikely to be a future danger. While "future dangerousness" is a consideration in only five states, three of those five are the top executing ones; this may not be a mere coincidence.

Many states have "felony murder," "pecuniary gain," or "lying in wait" statutes. The practical implication of such laws is that vast numbers of relatively routine homicides become eligible for a capital prosecution. So, rather than necessarily focusing on the most depraved crimes or those against a police officer or prison guard, for example, these laws open up the capital punishment system to any routine robbery gone wrong. Indeed, as we saw in chapter 5, the felony murder law even allows something that very few Americans support (see chapter 13): executing a nontriggerman accomplice. Ten such individuals in fact have been executed, as we discussed in chapter 5.

Academic studies have found that the heinousness of the crime, the number of victims, and whether the inmate had previous violent criminal convictions or was a previous murderer do indeed affect the chances of receiving a death sentence. (We reviewed studies by Baldus, Donohue, Radelet, Phillips, and others in chapter 4.) Therefore, we do not want to suggest that the heinousness of the crime does not matter. However, when we take a step back and ask why 40 percent of the executions occur in Texas, and why they are particularly concentrated in a single jurisdiction within that state, it strains credulity to think that it could be determined by heinousness. Are the crimes in Houston systematically so much more heinous than those in Austin? Are the crimes in Los Angeles, New Orleans, Philadelphia, Atlanta, Tallahassee, Brooklyn, Chicago, or Seattle "garden variety" whereas those in Houston are "aggravated"? Of course not.

Killers of multiple victims are not especially likely to be executed, compared with those with just one victim. We saw in chapter 5 that 73 percent of inmates executed had just one victim, and 96 percent had three or fewer victims. So execution is not reserved for killers with multiple victims.

Execution is not reserved for blacks; in fact, it is unlikely in cases in which a black homicide offender has a black victim (as most of them do). Blacks who kill whites are dramatically over-represented among those executed, on the other hand. Whites who kill blacks are dramatically under-represented; indeed, such executions have occurred only in a relative handful of cases, and in many states there has never been such an execution. Overall, but for complicated reasons, then, black offenders are not over-represented on death row or among those executed. However, if they have a white victim, they are, and dramatically so.

Furman, Gregg, and the Future of the Death Penalty

There need be no guarantee that a future US Supreme Court would follow the same logic that led five justices to conclude in 1972 that the system in place at that time was unconstitutionally biased, arbitrary, and flawed. Since their ruling, more than 800,000 Americans have been victims of homicide. Many elected officials want to maintain the option of a death penalty, even if it is rarely used; indeed, it seems to be de rigueur for political leaders who support the death penalty to suggest that it should be narrowly targeted only for the worst of the worst, as candidate Hillary Clinton stated during the 2016 presidential primary season. Having reviewed the evidence through 17 chapters of this book, we should be able to conclude a few things based on the evidence. First, on the morality of retribution, the hope for deterrence, and many other aspects of the death penalty, facts simply do not matter. Eight hundred thousand homicides is too many. Emotions can run high. People can get angry. All this is fully understandable, desirable even. If we did not get angry at the vast scope of senseless homicide in our country, we would have strong grounds for worry.

Second, to the extent that we do want our criminal justice system to be based on facts, evidence, and fairness, we cannot countenance the flaws that we have documented in each chapter of this book. There is no question that the modern death penalty has continued with the flaws of its historical predecessor, and then some. Not only is it just as arbitrary, just as biased, and just as flawed as the pre-*Furman* system, but it has added to these flaws increased levels of geographical focus on the South, even more concentration in just a few jurisdictions, astronomical financial costs unimagined in the earlier period, average periods of delay now measured in the decades, odds of reversal well over 50 percent, routine and often successful last-minute legal maneuvering even while the inmate is in the execution room and has been prepared to be executed, and a medicalization paradox that was not even imagined in the pre-*Furman* period. Further, while the risk of executing innocent individuals has been present throughout history, evidence is clear that if we have not executed such individuals (and we probably have), we do know for sure that we have condemned many innocents to death. A reasoned assessment based on the facts suggests not only that the modern system flunks the *Furman* test but that it surpasses the historical death penalty in the depth and breadth of the flaws apparent in its application.

Epilogue

How This Book Came About

Teaching, Research, and Teaching Research

This book could not have been produced but for the linkage of teaching and research in America's best universities. Frank Baumgartner has spent a career studying public policies of various types, and this is his second book on the topic of the death penalty. In fall semester 2010, he developed a new class based on a current research project: POLI 495, "The Decline of the Death Penalty." Twenty-five students were enrolled, of whom several continued on to law school: Arielle Reid at Columbia, BJ Dworak and Lindsey Stephens at Duke, and Allisa Ellis at UNC. Dworak, Stephens, and Ellis continued to write senior theses under Baumgartner's direction. The reason there was so much motivation among the students in that initial class had little to do with the instructor but rather to the invited speakers: James Woodall, the local district attorney, came to class and surprised the students by explaining how one of his ancestors had been executed by the State of North Carolina. Ed Chapman came next; he had served more than 14 years on death row for a crime he did not commit. Ellie Kinnaird, a North Carolina state senator, came to discuss criminal justice and her role in the recent passage of the Racial Justice Act. Next was Ken Rose, director (at the time) of the Center for Death Penalty Litigation. Dick Dieter from the Death Penalty Information Center followed, as did Shabaka WaQlimi (who spent 13 years on Florida's death row but was innocent of the crime that sent him there); Steve Dear of People of Faith against the Death Penalty; and Jeremy Collins, main lobbyist behind the passage of the Racial Justice Act in 2009. In sum, it was not your normal undergraduate seminar.

The class was offered again in spring 2013; this time the list of exonerees included Ed Chapman, Bill Dillon, Greg Taylor, and LaMonte Armstrong. They were joined by elected officials, attorneys, family members of death row inmates, and a prison warden who had supervised Florida's electric chair, including some botched executions. Enrollment was 81 this time. In fall 2014 the course entered the regular list of courses in the UNC registry of classes as POLI 203; new speakers included Kim Davis, sister of executed inmate Troy Davis; Darryl Hunt, a Winston-Salem exoneree; and Beverly Monroe, who had been convicted of murdering her long-time partner when in fact he had committed suicide. She was joined by her daughter Katie, who devoted 11 years shortly after law school to getting her mother out of jail. Enrollment was 233. In spring 2016 the class met again, this time with 256 students, and the new speakers included Anthony Ray Hinton, who had just recently been released from Alabama's death row after 30 years in solitary confinement. Mr. Hinton's grace, humor, and strength inspired well over half the class members to ask if they could write him a note to express their amazement; he soon received a huge packet of tear-stained scribbles. He was joined by Fernando Bermudez from New York and Gary Griffin from Mississippi; Jennifer Thompson and Ronald Cotton were accompanied by both the police investigator who was involved in the wrongful conviction of Mr. Cotton and Richard Rosen, a retired UNC law professor who was one of Mr. Cotton's appellate attorneys. Thompson and Cotton together wrote the memoir *Picking Cotton*, the UNC common read in 2010. (Thompson also made Baumgartner the luckiest man in the world, by far, by marrying him in 2011.) It is fair to say that the exonerees and others with personal experience with the wrong end of the judicial system made the biggest impact, but some of the attorneys who addressed our students are luminaries. Ken Rose, Rich Rosen, Jim Coleman, Chris Mumma, Theresa Newman, Jamie Lau, Tye Hunter, and Judge Gregory Weeks could not fail to have a powerful impact.

The book you have in your hands will certainly be used in future iterations of POLI 203 at UNC–Chapel Hill. It is, in fact, a product of that class and the teaching, senior honors theses, and student work that have followed it. In fall 2015, Baumgartner invited some of the best students who had taken the class in 2014 to participate in a "research seminar." Twenty-two students took the challenge, and each paired up with others to work on semester-filling projects that provided much of the basis for this book. Students worked in small groups and produced research projects in the forms of chapters. Some were rough, and we started over later. But some contain the gist of the materials that you have in your hands. Those students were Chris Armistead, Kelsey Britton, Danielle Buso, Marty Davidson, Elizabeth Grady, Candice Holmquist, Emma Johnson, Kaneesha Johnson, Arvind Krishnamurthy, Caroline Lim, Chandler Mason, Brandon Morrissey, Dean Murphy, Betsy Neill, Lanie Phillips, Elizabeth Schlemmer, Sarah Tondreau, Ty Tran, Emily Vaughn, Clarke Whitehead, Emily Williams, and Colin Wilson. Thanks to each of them for the work we collectively accomplished in the class. Students got their hands dirty with data collection, seeing the difficulties of doing high-quality social science and the importance of getting things right. They got a crash introduction into research, and most of them loved the experience.

At the end of fall semester 2015, we had a 370-page manuscript with 20 chapters. But it was rough, not a final version. Since that time, some students have stayed with the project, and others have moved on to study abroad, work, different majors, and other things that college students do. The students listed on the title page of this book have earned that recognition by their continued commitment to the project, working on various chapters as the need arose. Moving from a rough cut to a publishable project involves a lot of work. We have attempted to give credit to each student at the beginning of each chapter where their work and research were essential. In chapter 12 on mental illness, we have made Betsy Neill a full co-author because she did extensive research and writing, though her work was limited to that one chapter. Justin Cole did similarly excellent work and is our co-author on chapter 14, on cost. If we have omitted any names, as we inevitably and unintentionally will have done, we hope that the explanation here makes clear to every reader that this was a large effort and one conducted largely by UNC undergraduate students. At a research university, why would students not be learning research? At one of the nation's best public universities, why would a professor not engage these brilliant minds into the world of research and social impact? We hope this book will be a model for that. Because of the student and teaching-focused nature of this project, each of the authors has agreed to forgo any royalties from it. Rather, these will be directed to the Political Science Department at UNC. Whatever monies are collected will be spent to enhance the student experience of our majors.

Some Personal Notes

One cannot write about the death penalty without someone asking why you do so, and what your views are. This book is not about the personal opinions of any of the authors. However, readers may be curious. For Baumgartner, it is simple. Growing up in Detroit, Michigan, as the youngest of six with a single mother who had a career as a social worker in the Detroit public school system, he was raised far from the world of the death penalty. Detroit had a lot of homicides—it was known as the murder capital of America during the time he was growing up—but Michigan did not have the death penalty. And, like most Americans, there was something in the family background that indicated a general orientation to the death penalty, at the same time without making much of it or being based on very many specifics. In 2008 he published a book on the topic, but the focus there was an intellectual puzzle: If most Americans continue to say they support the death penalty, why was it disappearing, and what was the impact of the new innocence argument that arose in the 1990s? Following the publication of that book, he got more deeply involved in other aspects of the death penalty in terms of both teaching undergraduate students and conducting original research, the results of which are published here. He also met and later married Jennifer Thompson, a prominent crime survivor, a speaker on criminal justice reform, and the founder of Healing Justice, an organization that seeks to address some of the harm caused by errors in the criminal justice system to all those affected by them. Together they have a professional network and social circle that includes many activists, exonerees, crime survivors, and attorneys. This has certainly put a more personal touch on much of the research. However, Thompson is the one who is especially skilled at empathy and personal connection; Baumgartner is relatively good at counting things. As a scholar and a teacher, he has always believed that it should make no difference what his beliefs are: we learn collectively from the evidence, not from prejudgments and assumptions. Thus, this book is focused on the facts, and whether one of us is morally in favor of or opposed to the death penalty is not the question. For Baumgartner, one of the main lessons of this long period of research into the topic has nothing to do with the death penalty. It has to do with homicide: we have far too much of it.

For Marty Davidson, to compare his original academic plans at the beginning of his first year of college with his current research collaborations on the death penalty is to witness a large shift of interests over time. At the beginning of his undergraduate career, he wanted to devote his academic ambitions to the natural and life sciences because completing a bachelor of science degree in chemistry was his primary long-term goal. However, life manages to steer people in interesting directions, and he eventually began taking political science courses during his junior year. These courses piqued his interest in how our public institutions either promote, or fail to promote, justice in society. For Davidson, understanding the institutional and legal development of the death penalty over time was the most fascinating part of research. Until the end of the nineteenth century, the death penalty was generally administered at the local level. To standardize its administration, ensure due process, and preclude local-level biases, states aggregated control of the death penalty toward the state level. However, this did not rid the system of its original problems. Even with provisions set forth in *Gregg*, the death penalty has continually presented new issues raising contemporary concerns, which begs the question: Can the system persist?

For Colin Wilson, a keen interest in politics had been a constant throughout his adolescence and has continued to deepen into his adulthood. His undergraduate career at UNC–Chapel Hill not only gave him the opportunity to immerse himself in a variety issues facing our political system but also allowed him to explore the role of politics in the formation of public policy. In this regard, few topics are more fascinating, in Wilson's view, than capital punishment, an institution surrounded by political contradictions. Evidence suggests that the death penalty is considerably more expensive than the alternative of life in prison without parole, yet you will rarely find a fiscal conservative willing to disavow the practice in the interest of cutting costs. Trends in violent crime indicate that the death penalty does little in the way of deterrence, yet many politicians, liberal and conservative alike, hesitate to disavow the practice for fear of appearing soft on crime. Further still, in a political environment that has featured an apparent erosion of public faith in government institutions, a majority (though a diminishing portion) of the population still trusts a government system with the power to condemn citizens to death. With these considerations and many more in mind, Wilson has considered it an honor to collaborate with such great minds in an effort to delve into the details of such a peculiar institution.

For Arvind Krishnamurthy, his journey toward this project began in the summer of 2013. At that time, he was a first-year student at Ohio State University, unsure of his future goals and majoring in political science for the politics far more than the science of studying them. His family had just moved to Chapel Hill, and in an effort to stay busy in the summer he interned at the Odum Institute for Social Science Research with Dr. Thomas Carsey. That experience helped convince him to transfer to UNC–Chapel Hill, where Dr. Carsey recommended that Krishnamurthy take a course with Dr. Baumgartner. Once Krishnamurthy took POLI 203—Baumgartner's course on the death penalty—he fell in love with the way research could marry narrative with data and has worked as a research assistant ever since. He is fascinated by the paradoxical nature of capital punishment and is thankful for the opportunity to study, learn, and explore the topic with such fantastic collaborators.

Kaneesha Johnson's participation in the project grew from a lifelong interest in the criminal justice system. Having grown up in the United Kingdom, far away from the practice of capital punishment, and seeing the damaging effects of poverty and the biased and unequal application on the law in her hometown, she wanted to understand how deep those inequalities ran and if it was a trend that extended globally. After moving to the United States to pursue her bachelor's degree in political science, and enrolling in Dr. Baumgartner's undergraduate seminar on the death penalty, she could not help but continue to return to the question of how the state grapples with inconsistencies and inequalities when the stakes for punishment are so high, and the threshold of where inequality becomes unacceptable in the eyes of the law. This project allowed her not only to build her own knowledge in the area of capital punishment with a team of dedicated individuals and answer some of her long-standing questions, but also to recognize the wider need, and her own desire, to continue research on inequality and the criminal justice system.

NOTES

Chapter 1

1. Generally, we refer to US Supreme Court decisions in the traditional format of *Furman v. Georgia* (1972), and our list of references provides the full citation to these. On our website, we also provide a link to the actual decisions for every Court decision we reference. Because we refer to them so often, however, we refer to the 1972 decision invalidating the nation's death penalty laws simply as *Furman* and to the 1976 reinstitution as *Gregg*.
2. Johnson did much of the original research for this chapter, and Baumgartner finalized.
3. We end the data series in Figure 1.1 at December 31, 2015. Throughout the book, we follow this convention, so that we do not present results based on a partial year of data. Our website with the replication material for the figures in this book will be updated annually.
4. Evan Mandery's *A Wild Justice* (2013) chronicles the development of the Court's decision-making through the antecedents to the *Furman* decision through to *Gregg*.
5. We do not provide here a full interpretation of the opinions but highlight only certain elements central to the analysis to follow. Our website provides a link to the full text of every Supreme Court decision referenced in the book. We encourage readers to follow those links to read the full decisions themselves. Mandery (2013) provides the best explanation of the background and logic of the various decisions, including the run-up to *Furman* and *Gregg*, both on the Court and among those who were presenting the arguments on both sides. Steiker and Steiker's (2016) analysis is the fullest and most compelling legal analysis of the situation, arguing that the Court has created a jurisprudence regarding proportionality review that would make abolition a strong possibility.
6. A common saying on death rows throughout the United States is "If you ain't got the capital, you goin' to get the punishment." Poverty, class, and race are part of the picture throughout the system (see Bright 1994; Stevenson 2014).
7. Puerto Rico abolished in 1927; for the purposes of this section, jurisdictions include the 50 states, the District of Columbia, the federal government, and the US military.
8. Nebraska voters overturned the legislative repeal of capital punishment in November 2016. The Delaware Supreme Court invalidated that state's death penalty in 2016, leaving the number at 33 at the end of 2016 as well.
9. The Texas scheme is different: "special circumstances" are considered to determine whether the defendant shall be sentenced to death. The scheme is similar only in that it is bifurcated: guilt is separated from the punishment phase.
10. We have excluded footnotes and citations in this quotation.

11. Looking at the facts may not change the opinion of those abstractly opposed to the death penalty, but it could do so for those with an abstract support of it. In any case, we think it helpful for all to know the facts.

Chapter 2

1. Johnson and Baumgartner wrote and finalized this chapter.
2. Before the adoption of LWOP, which occurred mostly in the 1990s, the alternative sentence was typically life with the possibility of parole. Today, each state that has the death penalty also has the alternative of LWOP.
3. Most states require the judge to abide by the punishment determined by the jury, and typically this must be unanimous. Florida's law that allowed nonunanimous death verdicts was struck down by the US Supreme Court in *Hurst v. Florida* (2016). Alabama retains a system whereby judges may impose death even if a jury did not endorse it; given the *Hurst* decision in 2016, this may also be struck down. Delaware was the third state with a similar process of "judge overrule," and its supreme court declared the state's death penalty unconstitutional in August 2016, based largely on the *Hurst* decision; see Reyes 2016.
4. Judges typically have complete immunity for their actions on the bench, as do prosecutors for their actions as prosecutors. Police officers, investigators, and prosecutors when working as investigators have only partial or qualified immunity: their actions are immune from prosecution unless their actions not only were wrong but also were done in bad faith or were unreasonable. While the degree of immunity differs, in fact, the bar is high in all cases. For judges, it is virtually unobtainable. For police and others who may be involved in an investigation, it is rarely reached.

Chapter 3

1. Clarke Whitehead, Elizabeth Grady, and Emma Johnson did much of the research that is reported in this chapter. Wilson and Baumgartner finalized.
2. In Figure 1.3 and Table 1.1 we show that Florida acted more rapidly than the others, reinstating before the end of 1972. We use 1973 as the most appropriate year to identify the "modern" period for homicides and death sentences; no executions took place until 1977.
3. Criminologists differ in their use of UCR homicide reports, which are perhaps the most easily available official statistics but not perfectly accurate. Local law enforcement agencies report to the FBI, but the decentralized manner in which such data are collected, and the lack of enforcement mechanisms to ensure that each agency reports render the statistics imperfect. The Centers for Disease Control and Prevention also generates estimates of deaths by various causes, including homicide, and these differ to some extent from the UCR numbers. In this chapter we use the UCR statistics, but we do so with the understanding that they can be incomplete. Also, for our purposes they have another flaw: they are not limited to death-eligible crimes. They include states without the death penalty, and they include first-degree murder, second-degree murder, and other "nonnegligent homicides." Clearly, the number of death-eligible crimes is much lower than this. On the other hand, these numbers are valuable for several reasons. First, assessing trends over time, the number of homicides (reported here) and the number of death-eligible crimes tend to move in parallel, as death-eligible crimes are a roughly similar proportion of all homicides in any given state over time. Second, it is up to the political process to determine which crimes are death-eligible and which are not, so using all homicide as a baseline makes intuitive and theoretical sense. Finally, in chapter 4 we will review a number of carefully constructed studies, such as those of Baldus, Woodworth, and Pulaski (1990), Donohue (2014), S. Phillips (2008, 2009, 2012; Phillips and Simon 2014), in which the researchers carefully identify every

death-eligible crime in a given state or locality and track which ones led to capital prosecutions, death sentences, and execution. These studies reach remarkably similar conclusions as those we document with the comparisons used here. Therefore, here we provide a simple overview of homicides, but the reader should be aware that the comparisons we make in other chapters, and which have been made in the death penalty literature, are consistent with this baseline, though other scholars often use different and sometimes more accurate indicators.

4. Randolph Roth (2009) has written perhaps the most complete overview and history of homicide, including estimates of the surprisingly high rates of killing in previous historical periods. Steven Pinker (2011) discusses what he calls the dramatic decline in violence that has occurred over time. Randall Collins (2008) provides a very useful overview of violence and a theory of what causes it, at the individual level.

5. The data are available at http://www.icpsr.umich.edu/icpsrweb/NACJD/studies/9119?q=county-level&archive=NACJD. UNC student Wallace Gram compiled these data for his senior thesis, written under Baumgartner's direction; see Gram 2015 for more detail. Gram extrapolated a few dozen observations by taking the average number of homicides in five adjacent years in those few cases where numbers were missing in a county for a single year. He also carefully matched county FIPS codes year by year, including for those few observations, such as Miami–Dade County, where the Census Bureau FIPS code changed over the period of study. FIPS codes are unique identifiers of US counties, cities, and other places as defined by the Census Bureau. A few small counties in Arkansas were missing throughout the entire period, but this would likely not affect our findings as we limit ourselves to counties with at least a total of 100 homicides. Our website provides a complete copy of the county-level homicide data set that we compiled.

6. Note that the list of abolitionist states was relatively constant from the early 1980s, when any jurisdiction that was going to re-establish the death penalty after the *Furman* decision had already done so, to the middle of the first decade of the twenty-first century, after which New York, New Jersey, New Mexico, Illinois, Connecticut, Maryland, and Nebraska abolished (as of 2016). Those states are listed as retentionist in the maps because they were so during most of the study period.

Chapter 4

1. Emily Williams and Colin Wilson did much of the research for this chapter. Krishnamurthy did the literature review and the "Baldus-type" study comparisons in the last section. Wilson and Baumgartner finalized.

2. For example, whites committed about 45 percent of all homicides from 1976 through 1999 according to the Fox 2001 compilation of the UCR; this is true, with slight variation, in each year.

3. We include serial killer Aileen Wuornos here with just a single victim. Although Wuornos murdered seven victims, only one is included here because that was the case for which she was executed. Subsequent death sentences followed the first. In any case, all seven of Wuornos's victims were strangers. The Wuornos case is the only serial murder case among women and clearly is an exception to the pattern.

Chapter 5

1. UNC graduate student Liz Schlemmer assisted with the research reported in this chapter. Krishnamurthy and Baumgartner finalized.

2. In his *Glossip* opinion, Justice Thomas strongly took issue with Donohue's methodology, suggesting that it is impossible for the coders to quantify the heinousness of each victim's suffering. He suggested, however, that jurors would not have this difficulty. Jurors are certainly

exposed to more details of the case than were Donohue's coders. However, jurors see only one case, and the coders reviewed all the cases, allowing exactly the type of proportionality review that the Court has mandated since *Gregg*.

3. In 2009, the ALI rescinded its support for the death penalty section of its model code. It no longer supports use of the death penalty.

4. Most states give a single list of "aggravating factors or aggravating circumstances," whereas others give a separate list as part of a definition of capital-eligible crimes. Note that states have minor variations in how they refer to these concepts: capital murder, aggravated murder, murder with special circumstances, first-degree murder with special circumstances, and so forth. For an individual to be sentenced to death, a jury must find that at least one aggravating factor or eligibility criterion be proven beyond a reasonable doubt. On the other hand, mitigating factors generally need not be proven beyond a reasonable doubt. Typically, no instructions are provided to juries on how to weigh aggravating and mitigating factors.

5. On August 19, 2016, the Texas Court of Criminal Appeals canceled the execution of Mr. Jeffrey Wood scheduled for August and sent the case back to the lower court to review the validity of claims by a "since-discredited psychiatrist that Wood would certainly post a future risk to public safety." As discussed later, Wood is intellectually disabled and was an accomplice to the crime, not the triggerman. See Associated Press 2016.

6. See, for example, California Pen. Code § §37; 190.

7. See http://www.deathpenaltyinfo.org/those-executed-who-did-not-directly-kill-victim.

8. See *White v. Dugger*, 483 U.S. 1045 (1987)

9. See http://murderpedia.org/male.H/h1/hatch-steven-keith.htm.

10. Information on Donald Gaskins is easily available on the Internet, but see Leblanc 2015 for a recent summary.

Chapter 6

1. Baumgartner compiled the county-level database used in this chapter over many years, with the assistance of many UNC students and the cooperation of DPIC. Woody Gram wrote a senior thesis on this topic in 2015, and Gram, Krishnamurthy, Johnson, Wilson, and Baumgartner presented a paper updating the analysis at a Duke University conference in 2016. Baumgartner then finalized.

2. We also include the District of Columbia and the US federal government in these analyses, though they are of course not states. The US military also has a death penalty, but it has not carried out any executions in the modern period, and we do not include it here. So, rather than 50 states, we have 52 jurisdictions in the following section.

3. Note that Montana, with just 538 homicides over the period of study, has had only three executions; thus, while its rate of execution per 100 homicides is high, the absolute numbers of each are very low compared with more populous states.

Chapter 7

1. Anna Dietrich wrote an award-winning senior thesis on this topic in 2014. Emily Vaughn helped update the data. Johnson and Baumgartner finalized.

2. In this chapter we rely on annual publications from the US Department of Justice, the most recent of which was published in 2014 and includes data on the disposition of all death sentences handed down under the post-*Furman* procedures. This is why the number of executions, 1,359, is slightly lower than the 1,422 used in other chapters; those chapters use our own data set, which includes every execution through 2015.

3. Some inmates have had their death sentence successfully overturned only to have it reimposed in a subsequent penalty phase trial. Note, however, that the BJS statistics we use here refer only to final outcomes, so any inmate resentenced to death at a second trial would not be listed as

having had his or her sentence overturned at all, as this was not the final disposition. The numbers we use in this chapter refer to the final decision for each inmate, not any intermediate decisions.

4. Maryland governor Martin O'Malley commuted the sentences of the four inmates remaining on death row before leaving office, on December 31, 2014. Maryland had abolished the death penalty in 2013. New Jersey governor John Corzine and Illinois governor Pat Quinn commuted the sentences of those on death row when their states abolished capital punishment in 2007 and 2011, respectively. Two individuals remain on death row in New Mexico, potentially eligible for execution, though the state abolished the death penalty in 2009. Connecticut abolished in 2012, leaving 11 inmates on death row. They were resentenced to LWOP in 2015 when the state supreme court ruled that the statute was unconstitutional. See state-by-state information at www.deathpenaltyinfo.org.

Chapter 8

1. Chris Armistead helped with the research in this chapter. Davidson and Baumgartner finalized.
2. We were not able to locate the exact date of sentencing for 18 cases, leaving the N for calculations involving that variable at 1,404.
3. See http://www.clarkprosecutor.org/html/death/US/gilmore001.html.
4. See http://www.clarkprosecutor.org/html/death/US/knight1360.htm.
5. See http://www.deathpenaltyinfo.org/innocence-list-those-freed-death-row.
6. See http://www.deathpenaltyinfo.org/innocence-list-those-freed-death-row.
7. See http://www.deathpenaltyinfo.org/node/6277.
8. See http://www.deathpenaltyinfo.org/node/6349.
9. Louisiana: 10 exonerations and 28 executions, 35.71; Tennessee, 3/6: 50.00; Illinois, 20/ 12: 166.67; Pennsylvania, 6/3: 200; New Mexico, 4/1: 400; Massachusetts, 3 exonerations and no executions: indeterminate.

Chapter 9

1. Sarah Tondreau, Lanie Phillips, and Candice Holmquist helped with the research for this chapter. Krishnamurthy and Baumgartner finalized.
2. We should note that some exonerees are sentenced to death, later have their death sentence reversed and so are removed from death row, and then later are exonerated. Kirk Bloodsworth, the first DNA exoneree and a former US Marine, falls in this category, as does Leon Brown from North Carolina. Brown, with his brother Henry McCollum, was sentenced to death but at a second trial was convicted only of rape and was then sentenced to life in prison and so was removed from death row. However, he was not exonerated until after 39 years of wrongful imprisonment. The figure shows the entire elapsed time from wrongful death sentence to exoneration for all inmates.
3. The Bureau of Justice Statistics does not distinguish between nonwhite Hispanics/Latinos and Latinos/Hispanic whites when determining the racial composition of death row. The data used here *do* distinguish. However, even if all Latino exonerees were classified as white, whites would still make up 46.9 percent of all exonerations, a 9 percent difference in representation.
4. For information about Butler and Monroe, see the National Registry of Exonerations.
5. See the Clark County Prosecutor website: http://www.clarkprosecutor.org/html/death/ usexecute.htm.
6. These cases come from the DPIC listing: http://www.deathpenaltyinfo.org/executed-possibly-innocent#cam.
7. DNA Exonerations in the United States—Innocence Project (n.d.), http://www.innocenceproject.org/dna-exonerations-in-the-united-states/ (accessed July 31, 2016).

Chapter 10

1. UNC students Emma Johnson, Elizabeth Grady, Clarke Whitehead, and Ty Tran provided research assistance for this chapter. Davidson and Baumgartner finalized.

2. See Chief Justice Roberts in *Baze v. Rees*, 24: various execution methods "have each in turn given way to more humane methods," leading to today's use of lethal injection.

3. For an excellent review of the history and problems with particular forms of execution, as reviewed in the chapter, see the amicus curiae brief of the Fordham University School of Law in *Baze v. Rees*. We rely on this brief for a number of details throughout and refer to it as Nathan and Green 2007 in the text.

4. For a review of the various methods used throughout history, see Galvin 2015, chap. 3. Galvin reviews the proceedings of New York's Gerry Commission, established in 1886 and charged with recommending the most humane method of execution to replace hanging. The committee was chaired by Elbridge T. Gerry (1837–1927), grandson with the identical name of the fifth vice president of the United States and governor of Massachusetts (1744–1814), from whose name the term "gerrymander" originated. The Gerry Commission eventually recommended the introduction of the electric chair, as we discuss later. But their deliberations included a review of 34 different methods of execution known to human history, as Galvin's chapter explains. These ranged from defenestration to shooting from a cannon.

5. Lynching data collected and compiled by This Cruel War (http://www.thiscruelwar.com/). It is a compilation of inventories collected by the NAACP, Michael J. Pfeifer's Lynching beyond Dixie, and E. M. Beck and Stewart Tolnay. This database contains complete information for all known lynchings between 1889 and 1924 and partial information for lynchings between 1877 and 1950. For more information, consult http://www.thiscruelwar.com/the-long-list/.

6. On botched executions generally, see Sarat 2014, which is a book-length treatment, and also the DPIC page with examples of botched executions post-*Furman*, created by Michael Radelet: http://www.deathpenaltyinfo.org/some-examples-post-furman-botched-executions. For a discussion of the horrors of botched hangings, leading to the introduction of electrocutions as the solution to that problem, see Brandon 1999, chap. 2

7. See the DPIC page on firing squads here: http://www.deathpenaltyinfo.org/descriptions-execution-methods?scid=8&did=479.

8. There was even discussion of coining a new term in the language: "to westinghouse" an inmate was proposed by an associate of Edison as the term to be used for execution by electric chair, just as "to guillotine" had been coined with reference to Dr. Guillotin, who first proposed that machine. Of course, George Westinghouse fought to avoid having any association with the process and was opposed to capital punishment in general. For discussions of what this new process would be called (Edison proposed "ampermort," "dynamort," or "electromort"; *Scientific American* suggested a number of possible terms for the new methodology), see Bernstein 1973; Brandon 1999).

9. The circus elephant had killed three people and was deemed a dangerous "murderer." Note that Kemmler had already been executed by this time, but Edison was still intent on linking alternating current with mortal danger.

10. Tafero was found guilty of killing two police officers, but after his execution Walter Rhodes confessed to the crime. Rhodes had been found guilty of a lesser crime and had been released on parole in 1994. Sunny Jacobs, Tafero's partner, was also sentenced to death but later saw that reversed and agreed to plead to second-degree murder and was freed on time served. Tafero was the only one of the three to be executed, and his execution was notoriously botched.

11. The Espy file and several Internet sources list Nathan (Wilson), a slave executed in Tyler County, West Virginia, in 1821 as having been killed by lethal injection. However, little additional information seems available about this case.

Chapter 11

1. Danielle Buso, Chandler Mason, Emily Vaughn, and Colin Wilson contributed research used in this chapter. Wilson and Baumgartner finalized.
2. The DPIC site for "upcoming executions" (http://deathpenaltyinfo.org/upcoming-executions) had this information as of June 2017.
3. Mr. Wilson also visited Penn State University while Baumgartner was teaching there, spending a day with students and explaining his remarkable story; he was an active member of Witness to Innocence, an advocacy and speaking organization focused on the experiences of innocent people who have been sentenced to die.

Chapter 12

1. Chris Armistead, Caroline Lim, and Lanie Phillips did research for this chapter. Neill took the leading role in this research, and Neill and Baumgartner finalized.
2. We limit our review to those executed since 2000 only because of problems in collecting information for those with earlier execution dates.
3. See http://www.clarkprosecutor.org/html/death/usexecute.htm.
4. More detailed information on our coding, as well as our spreadsheet showing which executed inmates were found with which characteristics, is included in appendix C on our website.
5. Our point here is just that our data are conservative, generally understating the real differences we document. Women may be diagnosed more often with mental illness than men because they seek help more often, because mostly male doctors are more apt to diagnose it among women, or for other reasons.
6. We rely on the Clark County Prosecutor website for information about Brown: http://www.clarkprosecutor.org/html/death/U.S./brown879.htm.
7. The following section draws on the Clark County Prosecutor website profile of Coleman: http://www.clarkprosecutor.org/html/death/U.S./coleman771.htm.
8. See the Clark County Prosecutor page on Chapman at http://www.clarkprosecutor.org/html/death/U.S./chapman1135.htm.
9. See Lewis's Clark County Prosecutor web page here: http://www.clarkprosecutor.org/html/death/U.S./lewis1326.htm.
10. See the National Registry of Exonerations pages on Brown and McCullom athttps://www.law.umich.edu/special/exoneration/Pages/casedetail.aspx?caseid=4493 and https://www.law.umich.edu/special/exoneration/Pages/casedetail.aspx?caseid=4492.
11. See his complete case file, along with others released through the North Carolina Innocence Inquiry Commission, at the commission's web page: http://www.innocencecommission-nc.gov/cases.html.
12. See the Womble case at http://www.innocencecommission-nc.gov/womble.html. Quotation from "Handouts provided to the Commission during the hearing" (p. 52).
13. See http://www.cdc.gov/violenceprevention/pdf/suicide-datasheet-a.PDF.
14. For this section we again rely on the Clark County Prosecutor's web page about the inmate: http://www.clarkprosecutor.org/html/death/US/boyd1000.htm.
15. It is also noteworthy that Thuesen's crime occurred in Brazos County, Texas, home of Texas A&M University. Not only were the two victims college students and potentially very sympathetic to the jury, but as we saw in chapter 6, Brazos County has the highest rate of execution per homicide among all US counties above a threshold of 100 homicides cumulatively from 1984 through 2012. Prosecutors are unlikely to "give a pass" to anyone.

Chapter 13

1. Caroline Lim and Emily Williams provided research assistance. Lim worked particularly on the Houston and Texas data collection. Williams helped construct the index of opinion over time. Krishnamurthy and Baumgartner finalized.

2. We can attest to the lack of information even well-educated individuals have. In teaching a class on the death penalty for several years, Baumgartner has started each semester with an anonymous test on basic facts such as the annual number of homicides, death sentences, and executions in the United States, which states execute, whether the death qualification is law, typical delays and rates of reversal, and other facts now laid out in this book. In spring 2016, the median score was 6 of 25, or overwhelming failure. This is typical.

3. See various resources associated with Gallup's polling on the death penalty over time: http://www.gallup.com/poll/1606/death-penalty.aspx.

4. Later we show that in Harris County, Texas, the nation's leading jurisdiction in the use of the death penalty, public opinion support for the death penalty is surprisingly low. In response to the question "What do you think should generally be the penalty for the persons convicted of first-degree murder: the death penalty, LWOP, or life imprisonment with a chance of parole after 25 years?," just 30 percent said the death penalty in 2012; see https://kinder.rice.edu/content.aspx?id=2147485825.

5. See the Gallup page referenced earlier: http://www.gallup.com/poll/1606/death-penalty.aspx.

6. Susan Smith was a mother convicted of driving her car into a lake with her two sons strapped in their car seats; both boys died. She was sentenced to life in prison after a defense that focused on her acknowledged mental illness.

7. Some questions were posed more than once in the same year. Table 13.2 lists the average for the two administrations. However, in generating our index, we use all the data.

8. Figure 13.1 shows pro-, anti-, and "no answer/don't know" responses. In the analyses later in this chapter, we eliminate the "no response" or "don't know" category and present the percent favorable as a percent of all those expressing an attitude. That is, pro- plus anti- sums by definition to 100 percent.

9. Note these numbers are slightly different from those in Figure 13.1 because we eliminate the "don't know" responses here and calculate the percent support based only on the two remaining categories of response.

10. This index updates and expands with more questions the index generated by Baumgartner, De Boef, and Boydstun (2008). Their index covered the years of 1953 through 2006. This one is compiled with all available survey data from 1976 through 2015. Including or excluding the earlier years makes very little difference in the trends apparent in the index. See Stimson 1998 for the original explanation of the procedure.

11. For information on the Houston Area Survey, see https://kinder.rice.edu/has/purposeandmethods/. For results pertaining to the death penalty, see https://kinder.rice.edu/KHAS/Death_Penalty/.

Chapter 14

1. Several students helped gather the studies for this chapter, including Dean Murphy. Justin Cole, however, did the lion's share of compiling and organizing the results of this literature review in a systematic manner. He worked closely with Baumgartner throughout the research. Cole and Baumgartner finalized.

Chapter 15

1. Baumgartner did the research and finalized this chapter.

2. *Fowler* was a 1975 case heard before the Court in which the petitioner appealed North Carolina's mandatory death sentence law. The Court decided in *Woodson v. North Carolina* (1976) that such mandatory laws were unconstitutional, and Fowler was resentenced to life.

Chapter 16

1. Johnson helped compile the data associated with this chapter; Johnson and Baumgartner finalized.
2. Because the same bill may contain elements that both restrict and expand, the "percent restrict" variable is calculated as follows: percent restrict = (number of bills with provisions that restrict × 100) / (number of bills with provisions that restrict + number of bills with provisions that expand). So, in the 2011 example, there are 98 bills, but 70 restricting and 38 expanding bills. So the calculation is $(70 \times 100) / (70 + 38) = 64.81$. If we calculate the percent restricting on the basis of total bills, the two versions of the variable correlate at $r = .9797$, so it makes little difference either way.
3. Executions are carried out by states, not counties. In this discussion we refer to the counties from which the death sentence was imposed.
4. Delaware can be added to the list of abolitionist jurisdictions as of a 2016 state supreme court decision.
5. Because of problems with the lethal injection protocol, the governor declared that there will be no executions in Oklahoma in 2016.

Chapter 17

1. Baumgartner compiled the information and finalized this chapter.
2. According to the US government, an average of 32 people have been killed by lightning strikes in the United States from 2005 through 2015, down from an average of 81 during the period from 1959 to 2004 (see www.lightningsafety.noaa.gov). In 2015, there were 28 executions (see Figure 1.1).
3. Calculated from this source; homicides include murder as well as nonnegligent manslaughter: http://www.bjs.gov/ucrdata/Search/Crime/State/RunCrimeStatebyState.cfm.
4. In another publication, many of the same authors here compared similar data for the colonial period through 1799, the 1800s, and the two periods shown in Figure 17.3; see Baumgartner, Gram et al. 2016. We also showed there the numbers for each state in the 1900–1976 period compared with the modern period. Comparing a statistical index of concentration, the modern period had a score of .168, and the early twentieth century had a score of .046. This confirms and extends the point made here.
5. The nine death-sentenced individuals had the following number of non-death-sentenced individuals ranked higher than them on composite egregiousness of their homicides: 4, 33, 33, 34, 38, 54, 65, 148, and 170. Because there were 205 homicides in the study, the last two cases were below the median value.

REFERENCES

Academic Sources

Abrams, David S., Marianne Bertrand, and Sendhil Mullainathan. 2012. Do Judges Vary in Their Treatment of Race? *Journal of Legal Studies* 41 (2): 347–383.

Adler, Moshe. 1985. Stardom and Talent. *American Economic Review* 75 (1): 208–212.

Alarcón, Arthur L., and Paula M. Mitchell. 2011. Executing the Will of the Voters? A Roadmap to Mend or End the California Legislature's Multi-Billion-Dollar Death Penalty Debacle. *Loyola of Los Angeles Law Review* 44:41–224.

Allen, Howard W., and Jerome M. Clubb. 2008. *Race, Class, and the Death Penalty: Capital Punishment in American History.* Albany: State University of New York Press.

Alschuler, Albert W. 1968. The Prosecutor's Role in Plea Bargaining. *University of Chicago Law Review* 36 (1): 50–112.

———. 1979. Plea Bargaining and Its History. *Columbia Law Review* 79 (1): 1–43.

American Bar Association (ABA). 2013. The State of the Modern Death Penalty in America: ABA Death Penalty Due Process Review Project, Key Findings of State Death Penalty Assessments 2006–2013. www.americanbar.org/dueprocess.

American Civil Liberties Union Capital Punishment Project. 2004. *The Forgotten Population: A Look at Death Row in the United States through the Experiences of Women.* American Civil Liberties Union. https://www.aclu.org/files/FilesPDFs/womenondeathrow.pdf.

———. 2007. *The Persistent Problem of Racial Disparities in the Federal Death Penalty.* June. American Civil Liberties Union. https://www.aclu.org/persistent-problem-racial-disparities-federal-death-penalty.

———. n.d. *Mental Illness and the Death Penalty.* American Civil Liberties Union. https://www.aclu.org/issues/capital-punishment/mental-illness-and-death-penalty.

American Civil Liberties Union of Northern California. 2009. *The Hidden Death Tax: The Secret Costs of Seeking Execution in California.* San Francisco: ACLU of Northern California. https://www.aclunc.org/sites/default/files/the_hidden_death_tax.pdf.

American Law Institute (ALI). 1962. *Model Penal Code.* Philadelphia: ALI.

American Psychiatric Association. 2013. *Diagnostic and Statistical Manual of Mental Disorders.* 5th ed. Arlington, VA: American Psychiatric Publishing.

Aronson, Jay D., and Simon A. Cole. 2009. Science and the Death Penalty: DNA, Innocence, and the Debate over Capital Punishment in the United States. *Law and Social Inquiry* 34 (3): 603–633.

Bak, Per. 1996. *How Nature Works: The Science of Self-Organized Criticality.* New York: Copernicus.

Baker, David V. 2007. American Indian Executions in Historical Context. *Criminal Justice Studies* 20 (4): 315–373.

Baldus, David C., and James W. L. Cole. 1975. A Comparison of the Work of Thorsten Sellin and Isaac Ehrlich on the Deterrent Effect of Capital Punishment. *Yale Law Journal* 85 (2): 170–186.

Baldus, David C., Catherine M. Grosso, George F. Woodworth, and Richard Newell. 2012. Racial Discrimination in the Administration of the Death Penalty: The Experience of the United States Armed Forces (1984–2005). *Journal of Criminal Law and Criminology* 101 (4): 1227–1335.

Baldus, David C., Charles A. Pulaski, and George F. Woodworth. 1983. Comparative Review of Death Sentences: An Empirical Study of the Georgia Experience. *Journal of Criminal Law and Criminology* 74 (3): 661–753.

Baldus, David C., and George F. Woodworth. 2003. Race Discrimination and the Death Penalty: An Empirical and Legal Overview. In *America's Experiment with Capital Punishment: Reflections on the Past, Present and Future of the Ultimate Penal Sanction*, edited by James R. Acker, Robert M. Bohm, and Charles S. Lanier, 501–552. Durham, NC: Carolina Academic Press.

Baldus, David C., George F. Woodworth, Catherine M. Grosso, and Aaron M. Christ. 2002. Arbitrariness and Discrimination in the Administration of the Death Penalty: A Legal and Empirical Analysis of the Nebraska Experience (1973–1999). *Nebraska Law Review* 81 (2): 486–756.

Baldus, David C., George F. Woodworth, and Charles A. Pulaski. 1990. *Equal Justice and the Death Penalty: A Legal and Empirical Analysis*. Boston: Northeastern University Press.

Baldus, David C., George F. Woodworth, David Zuckerman, Neil Alan Weiner, and Barbara Broffitt. 1998. Racial Discrimination and the Death Penalty in the Post-*Furman* Era: An Empirical and Legal Overview, with Recent Findings from Philadelphia. *Cornell Law Review* 83 (6):1638–1770.

Banner, Stuart. 2002. *The Death Penalty: An American History*. Cambridge, MA: Harvard University Press.

Barnes, Katherine, David L. Sloss, and Stephen C. Thaman. 2009. Place Matters (Most): An Empirical Study of Prosecutorial Decision-making in Death-Eligible Cases. *Arizona Law Review* 51:305–379.

Baumgartner, Frank R. 2015. North Carolina's Wasteful Experience with the Death Penalty. *University of North Carolina, Department of Political Science*. February 1. http://www.unc.edu/~fbaum/Innocence/Baumgartner_NC_Death_Reversals-1-Feb-2015.pdf.

Baumgartner, Frank R., Suzanna L. De Boef, and Amber E. Boydstun. 2008. *The Decline of the Death Penalty and the Discovery of Innocence*. New York: Cambridge University Press.

Baumgartner, Frank R., Woody Gram, Kaneesha R. Johnson, Arvind Krishnamurthy, and Colin P. Wilson. 2016. The Geographic Distribution of US Executions. *Duke Journal of Constitutional Law and Public Policy* 11 (1–2): 1–33.

Baumgartner, Frank R., Amanda J. Grigg, and Alisa Mastro. 2015. #BlackLivesDon'tMatter: Race-of-Victim Effects in US Executions, 1977–2013. *Politics, Groups, and Identities* 3 (2): 209–221.

Baumgartner, Frank R., Emma Johnson, Colin P. Wilson, and Clarke Whitehead. 2016. These Lives Matter, Those Ones Don't: Comparing Execution Rates by the Race and Gender of the Victim in the US and in the Top Death Penalty States. *Albany Law Review* 79 (3): 797–860.

Baumgartner, Frank R., and Tim Lyman. 2015. Race-of-Victim Discrepancies in Homicides and Executions, Louisiana 1976–2015. *Loyola University of New Orleans Journal of Public Interest Law* 17:128–144.

———. 2016. Louisiana Death-Sentenced Cases and Their Reversals, 1976–2015. *Southern University Law Center Journal of Race, Gender, and Poverty* 7:58–75.

Beck, E. M., James L. Massey, and Stewart E. Tolnay. 1989. The Gallows, the Mob, and the Vote: Lethal Sanctioning of Blacks in North Carolina and Georgia, 1882 to 1930. *Law and Society Review* 23 (2): 317–331.

Becker, Gary S. 1993. Nobel Lecture: The Economic Way of Looking at Behavior. *Journal of Political Economy* 101 (3): 385–409.

Bedau, Hugo Adam, ed. 1997. *The Death Penalty in America: Current Controversies*. New York: Oxford University Press.

Bedau, Hugo, and Paul Cassell, eds. 2004. *Debating the Death Penalty.* New York: Oxford University Press.

Bedau, Hugo Adam, and Michael L. Radelet. 1987. Miscarriages of Justice in Potentially Capital Cases. *Stanford Law Review* 40 (1): 21–179.

Bernstein, Theodore. 1973. A Grand Success. *IEEE Spectrum,* 10 (2): 54–58.

———. 1975. Theories of the Causes of Death from Electricity in the Late-Nineteenth Century. *Medical Instrumentation* 9 (6): 267–273.

Bibas, Stephanos. 2004. Plea Bargaining outside the Shadow of Trial. *Harvard Law Review* 117 (8): 2463–2547.

Bienen, Leah B., Neil Alan Weiner, Deborah W. Denno, Paul D. Allison, and Douglas Lane Mills. 1988. The Reimposition of Capital Punishment in New Jersey: The Role of Prosecutorial Discretion. *Rutgers Law Review* 41 (27): 27–372.

Blalock, Hubert M., Jr. 1979. *Social Statistics.* 2nd ed. New York: McGraw-Hill.

Blanco, Juan Ignacio. n.d. Steven Keith Hatch. *Murderpedia.* http://murderpedia.org/male.II/h1/hatch-steven-keith.htm Accessed July 13, 2016.

Blank, Stephen. 2006. Killing Time: The Process of Waiving Appeal. The Michael Ross Death Penalty Cases. *Journal of Law and Policy* 14 (2): 735–777.

Blecker, Robert. 2013. *The Death of Punishment: Searching for Justice among the Worst of the Worst.* New York: St. Martin's Press.

Blume, John H. 2005. Killing the Willing: "Volunteers," Suicide and Competency. *Michigan Law Review* 103:939–1009.

———. 2006. AEPDA the "Hype" and the "Bite." *Cornell Law Review* 91 (2): 259–302.

Blume, John, Theodore Eisenberg, and Martin T. Wells. 2004. Explaining Death Row's Population and Racial Composition. *Journal of Empirical Legal Studies* 1 (1): 165–207.

Bohm, Robert. 2012. *Deathquest: An Introduction to the Theory and Practice of Capital Punishment in the United States.* 4th ed. Waltham, MA: Anderson.

———. 2013. *Capital Punishment's Collateral Damage.* Durham, NC: Carolina Academic Press.

Bohm, Robert M., Louise J. Clark, and Adrian F. Aveni 1991. Knowledge and Death Penalty Opinion: A Test of the Marshall Hypothesis. *Journal of Research in Crime and Delinquency* 28 (3): 360–387.

Borchard, Edwin M., and E. R. Lutz. 1932. *Convicting the Innocent: Sixty-Five Actual Errors of Criminal Justice.* Garden City, NY: Garden City Publishing.

Bowers, William. 1993. Research Note: Capital Punishment and Contemporary Values: People's Misgivings and the Court's Misperceptions. *Law and Society Review* 27 (1): 157–176.

Bowers, William J., and Glenn L. Pierce. 1975. The Illusion of Deterrence in Isaac Ehrlich's Research on Capital Punishment. *Yale Law Journal* 85 (2): 187–208.

Bowers, William J., Glenn L. Pierce, and John D. McDevitt. 1984. *Legal Homicide: Death as Punishment in America, 1864–1982.* Boston: Northeastern University Press.

Brandon, Craig. 1999. *The Electric Chair: An Unnatural American History.* Jefferson, NC: McFarland.

Bright, Stephen B. 1994. Counsel for the Poor: The Death Sentence Not for the Worst Crime but for the Worst Lawyer. *Yale Law Journal* 103 (7):1835–1883.

Bureau of Justice Statistics (BJS). 2005. *State Court Sentencing of Convicted Felons.* Washington, DC: US Department of Justice.

———. 2007. *Drug Use and Dependence, State and Federal Prisoners, 2004.* Washington, DC: Bureau of Justice Statistics. http://www.bjs.gov/content/pub/pdf/dudsfp04.pdf.

———. 2014. *The Nation's Two Measures of Homicide.* Washington, DC: Bureau of Justice Statistics.

Caldwell, H. Mitchel. 2003. The Prostitution of Lying in Wait. *University of Miami Law Review* 57:311–376.

California Commission on the Fair Administration of Justice. 2008. *Report and Recommendations on the Administration of the Death Penalty in California.* June 30. California Commission on the Fair Administration of Justice. http://deathpenalty.org/downloads/FINAL%20REPORT%20DEATH%20PENALTY%20ccfaj%20June%2030.2008.pdf.

Canes-Wrone, Brandice, Tom S. Clark, and Jason P. Kelly. 2014. Judicial Selection and Death Penalty Decisions. *American Political Science Review* 108 (1): 23–39.

Cardno, Alastair G., and Irving I. Gottseman. 2000. Twin Studies of Schizophrenia: From Bow-and-Arrow Concordances to Star Wars Mx and Functional Genomics. *American Journal of Medical Genetics* 97 (1): 12–17.

Castelliani, C. A., M. G. Melka, L. J. Gui, R. L. O'Reilly, and S. M. Singh. 2015. Integration of DNA Sequence and DNA Methylation Changes in Monozygotic Twin Pairs Discordant for Schizophrenia. *Schizophrenia Research* 169:433–440.

Center for Death Penalty Litigation (CDPL). 2015. *On Trial for Their Lives: The Hidden Costs of Wrongful Capital Prosecutions in North Carolina.* Durham, NC: CDPL.

Christianson, Scott. 2004. *Innocent: Inside Wrongful Conviction Cases.* New York: New York University Press.

Chummah, Maurice. 2016. What You Need to Know If the Supreme Court Takes the Case of Duane Buck. *The Marshall Project.* June 6. https://www.themarshallproject.org/2016/04/20/what-you-need-to-know-if-the-supreme-court-takes-the-case-of-duane-buck#.8kX6yWh09. Accessed August 17, 2016.

Coase, Ronald H. 1978. Economics and Contiguous Disciplines. *Journal of Legal Studies* 7 (2): 201–211.

Cohen, G. Ben, and Robert J. Smith. 2010. The Racial Geography of the Federal Death Penalty. *Washington Law Review* 85 (3): 425–492.

Cohen-Cole, E., Steven Durlauf, Jeffrey Fagan, and Daniel Nagin. 2009. Model Uncertainty and the Deterrent Effect of Capital Punishment. *American Law and Economics Review* 11 (2): 335–369.

Collins, Peter A., Robert C. Boruchowitz, Matthew J. Hickman, and Mark A. Larrañaga. 2015. *An Analysis of the Economic Costs of Seeking the Death Penalty in Washington State.* January 1. Seattle: Department of Criminal Justice, Seattle University. http://www.deathpenaltyinfo.org/documents/WashingtonCosts.pdf.

Collins, Randall. 2008. *Violence: A Micro-sociological Theory.* Princeton, NJ: Princeton University Press.

Conley, Robin. 2016. *Confronting the Death Penalty: How Language Influences Jurors in Capital Cases.* New York: Oxford University Press.

Cook, Philip J. 2009. Potential Savings from Abolition of the Death Penalty in North Carolina. *American Law and Economics Review* 11 (2): 498–529.

Cook, Philip J., and Donna B. Slawson. 1993. The Costs of Processing Murder Cases in North Carolina. Terry Sanford Institute of Public Policy Duke University. May. http://www.deathpenaltyinfo.org/northcarolina.pdf. Accessed August 17, 2016.

Council of Europe. 1999. *The Death Penalty: Abolition in Europe.* Strasbourg: Council of Europe Publications.

Cowan, Claudia L., William C. Thompson, and Phoebe C. Ellsworth. 1984. The Effects of Death Qualification on Jurors' Predisposition to Convict and on the Quality of Deliberation. *Law and Human Behavior* 8 (1/2): 53–79.

Cullen, Francis T., Bonnie S. Fisher, and Brandon K. Applegate. 2000. Public Opinion about Punishment and Corrections. *Crime and Justice* 27:1–79.

Cunningham, Mark D., and Mark P. Vigen. 1999. Without Appointed Counsel in Capital Postconviction Proceedings: The Self-Representation Competency of Mississippi Death Row Inmates. *Criminal Justice and Behavior* 26 (3): 293–321.

———.2002. Death Row Inmate Characteristics, Adjustment, and Confinement: A Critical Review of the Literature. *Behavioral Sciences and the Law* 20 (1–2): 191–210.

Death Penalty Information Center (DPIC). 2015. *Battle Scars: Military Veterans and the Death Penalty.* November 11. Washington, DC: Death Penalty Information Center. http://deathpenaltyinfo.org/veterans. Accessed August 17, 2016.

———. 2016a. *Descriptions of Execution Methods.* Washington, DC: Death Penalty Information Center. http://www.deathpenaltyinfo.org/descriptions-execution-methods. Accessed November 27, 2016.

————.2016b. *Those Executed Who Did Not Directly Kill the Victim.* Washington, DC: Death Penalty Information Center. http://www.deathpenaltyinfo.org/those-executed-who-did-not-directly-kill-victim. Accessed July 13, 2016.

————.2017. *States with and without the Death Penalty.* Washington, DC: Death Penalty Information Center. https://deathpenaltyinfo.org/states-and-without-death-penalty. Accessed June 20, 2017.

————. n.d. *State by State Lethal Injection.* Washington, DC: Death Penalty Information Center. http://www.deathpenaltyinfo.org/state-lethal-injection. Accessed November 11, 2015.

Denno, Deborah W. 2007. The Lethal Injection Quandary: How Medicine Has Dismantled the Death Penalty. *Fordham Law Review* 76 (1): 49–128.

Devers, Lindsey. 2011. *Plea and Charge Bargaining: Research Summary.* Washington, DC: US Department of Justice, Bureau of Justice Assistance.

Dezhbakhsh, Hashem, Paul H. Rubin, and Joanna M. Shepherd. 2003. Does Capital Punishment Have a Deterrent Effect? New Evidence from Postmoratorium Panel Data. *American Law and Economics Review* 5 (2): 344–376.

Dieter, Richard C. 2008. Methods of Execution and Their Effect on the Use of the Death Penalty in the United States. *Fordham Urban Law Journal* 35 (4): 789–816.

————.2009. *Smart on Crime: Reconsidering the Death Penalty in a Time of Economic Crisis.* October. Washington, DC: Death Penalty Information Center. http://www.deathpenaltyinfo.org/documents/CostsRptFinal.pdf.

————. 2010. *Testimony before the Pennsylvania Senate Government Management and Cost Study Commission.* June 7. Washington, DC: Death Penalty Information Center. http://www.deathpenaltyinfo.org/documents/PACostTestimony.pdf.

————. 2013. *The 2% Death Penalty: How a Minority of Counties Produce Most Death Cases at Enormous Costs to All.* October. Washington, DC: Death Penalty Information Center. http://www.deathpenaltyinfo.org/documents/TwoPercentReport.pdf.

Donohue, John J., III. 2011. *Capital Punishment in Connecticut, 1973–2007: A Comprehensive Evaluation from 4686 Murders to One Execution.* National Bureau of Economic Research.

————. 2014. An Empirical Evaluation of the Connecticut Death Penalty System since 1973: Are There Unlawful Racial, Gender, and Geographic Disparities? *Journal of Empirical Legal Studies* 11 (4): 637–696.

Donohue, John J., III, and Justin Wolfers. 2005. Uses and Abuses of Empirical Evidence in the Death Penalty Debate. *Stanford Law Review* 58 (3): 791–845.

————.2009. Estimating the Impact of the Death Penalty on Murder. *American Law and Economics Review* 11 (2): 249–309.

Dow, David R. 2005. *Executed on a Technicality: Lethal Injustice on America's Death Row.* Boston: Beacon Press.

————.2010. *The Autobiography of an Execution.* New York: Twelve.

Dow, David R., and Mark Dow, eds. 2002. *Machinery of Death: The Reality of America's Death Penalty Regime.* New York: Routledge.

Doyle, James M. 2005. *True Witness: Cops, Courts, Science, and the Battle against Misidentification.* New York: Palgrave.

Drimmer, Frederick. 2014. *Executions in America.* New York: Skyhorse.

Dunham, Robert B. 2015. Testimony of Robert Brett Dunham Executive Director Death Penalty Information Center Concerning the Pennsylvania Death Penalty. June 11. Death Penalty Information Center. http://www.legis.state.pa.us/WU01/LI/TR/Transcripts/2015_0113_0013_TSTMNY.pdf.

Durham, Alexis M., H. Preston Elrod, and Patrick T. Kinkade. 1996. Public Support for the Death Penalty: Beyond Gallup. *Justice Quarterly* 13 (4): 705–736.

Eberhardt, Jennifer L., Paul G. Davies, Valerie J. Purdie-Vaughns, and Sheri Lynn Johnson. 2006. Looking Deathworthy: Perceived Stereotypicality of Black Defendants Predicts Capital-Sentencing Outcomes. *Psychological Science* 17 (5): 383–386.

Edens, John F., John Clark, Shannon Toney Smith, Jennifer Cox, and Shannon E. Kelley. 2013. Bold, Smart, Dangerous and Evil: Perceived Correlates of Core Psychopathic Traits among Jury Panel Members. *Personality and Mental Health* 7 (2): 143–153.

Edens, John F., Karen M. Davis, Krissie Fernandez Smith, and Laura S. Guy. 2013. No Sympathy for the Devil: Attributing Psychopathic Traits to Capital Murderers Also Predicts Support for Executing Them. *Personality Disorders: Theory, Research, and Treatment* 4 (2): 175–181.

Ehrhardt, Charles W., and L. Harold Levinson. 1973. Florida's Legislative Response to Furman: An Exercise in Futility? *Journal of Criminal Law and Criminology* 64:10–21.

Ehrlich, Isaac. 1975a. Deterrence: Evidence and Inference. *Yale Law Journal* 85 (2): 209–227.

———.1975b. The Deterrent Effect of Capital Punishment: A Question of Life and Death. *American Economic Review* 65 (3): 397–417.

———. 1977. Capital Punishment and Deterrence: Some Further Thoughts and Additional Evidence. *Journal of Political Economy* 85 (4): 741–788.

Ellis, Michael. 2012. The Origins of the Elected Prosecutor. *Yale Law Journal* 121 (6): 1528–1569.

Ellsworth, Phoebe, and Samuel R. Gross. 1994. Hardening of the Attitudes: Americans' Views on the Death Penalty. *Journal of Social Issues* 50 (2): 19–52.

Enns, Peter K. 2014. The Public's Increasing Punitiveness and Its Influence on Mass Incarceration in the United States. *American Journal of Political Science* 58 (4): 857–872.

———.2016. *Incarceration Nation: How the United States Became the Most Punitive Democracy in the World.* New York: Cambridge University Press.

Equal Justice Initiative. 2015. *Lynching in America: Confronting the Legacy of Racial Terror.* 2nd ed. Montgomery, AL: Equal Justice Initiative.

Espy, M. Watt, and John Ortiz Smykla. 2005. *Executions in the United States, 1608–2002: The Espy File* [computer file]. ICPSR version. Ann Arbor: University of Michigan [distributor], 2016.

Evans, R. J. 1996. *Rituals of Retribution: Capital Punishment in Germany 1600–1987.* New York: Oxford University Press.

Fagan, Jeffrey. 2006. Death and Deterrence Redux: Science, Law and Causal Reasoning on Capital Punishment. *Ohio State Journal of Criminal Law* 4:255–320.

Fagan, Jeffrey, and Valerie West. 2005. The Decline of the Juvenile Death Penalty: Scientific Evidence of Evolving Norms. *Journal of Criminal Law and Criminology* 95 (2): 427–500.

Fagan, Jeffrey, Franklin E. Zimring, and Amanda Geller. 2006. Capital Punishment and Capital Murder: Market Share and the Deterrent Effects of the Death Penalty. *Texas Law Review* 84:1803–1867.

Fair Punishment Project. 2016a. *America's Top Five Deadliest Prosecutors: How Overzealous Personalities Drive the Death Penalty.* June. Cambridge, MA: Harvard University Law School.

———.2016b. *Too Broken to Fix: Part I. An In-depth Look at America's Outlier Death Penalty Counties.* August. Cambridge, MA: Harvard University Law School.

———. 2016c. *Too Broken to Fix: Part II. An In-depth Look at America's Outlier Death Penalty Counties.* September. Cambridge, MA: Harvard University Law School.

FBI. 2015. FBI Testimony on Microscopic Hair Analysis Contained Errors in at Least 90 Percent of Cases in Ongoing Review. April 20. Washington, DC: Federal Bureau of Investigation.

Fins, Deborah. 2015. *Death Row U.S.A. Spring 2015.* Baltimore: NAACP Legal Defense and Educational Fund.

Flanagan, T., and K. Maguire. 1990. *Sourcebook of Criminal Justice Statistics, 1989.* Washington, DC: US Department of Justice, Bureau of Justice Statistics.

Fleury-Steiner, Benjamin. 2004. *Jurors' Stories of Death: How America's Death Penalty Invests in Inequality.* Ann Arbor: University of Michigan Press.

Flynn, Kathleen M. 1997. The "Agony of Suspense": How Protracted Death Row Confinement Gives Rise to an Eighth Amendment Claim of Cruel and Unusual Punishment. *Washington and Lee Law Review* 54 (1): 291–333.

Forsberg, Mary E. 2005. Money for Nothing? The Financial Cost of New Jersey's Death Penalty. November. New Jersey Policy Perspective. http://sentencing.nj.gov/downloads/pdf/articles/death3.pdf.

Forst, Brian. 2004. *Errors of Justice*. New York: Cambridge University Press.

Fox, James Alan. 2001. *Uniform Crime Reports [United States]: Homicide Victimization and Offending Rates, 1976–1999*. [computer file]. ICPSR version. Boston: Northeastern University, College of Criminal Justice [producer], 2001. Ann Arbor, MI: Inter-university Consortium for Political and Social Research [distributor], 2001.

Fox, James Alan., Michael L. Radelet, and Julie L. Bonsteel. 1991. Death Penalty Opinion in the Post-*Furman* Years. *New York University Review of Law and Social Change* 18:499–528.

Frierson, R. L., D. M. Schwartz-Watts, D. W. Morgan, and T. D. Malone. 1998. Capital versus Noncapital Murderers. *Journal of the American Academy of Psychiatry and Law* 26 (3): 403–410.

Galvin, Anthony. 2015. *Old Sparky: The Electric Chair and the History of the Death Penalty*. New York: Skyhorse.

Garland, David. 2005. Capital Punishment and American Culture. *Punishment and Society* 7 (4): 347–376.

———. 2010. *Peculiar Institution: America's Death Penalty in an Age of Abolition*. Cambridge, MA: Harvard University Press.

Garrett, Brandon. 2011. *Convicting the Innocent: Where Criminal Prosecutions Go Wrong*. Cambridge, MA: Harvard University Press.

———. 2017. The Decline of the Virginia (and American) Death Penalty. *Georgetown Law Journal* 105:661–729.

Gatrell, V. 1994. *The Hanging Tree: Execution and the English People 1770–1868*. New York: Oxford University Press.

Gelman, Andrew, James S. Liebman, Valerie West, and Alexander Kiss. 2014. A Broken System: The Persistent Patterns of Reversals of Death Sentences in the United States. *Journal of Empirical Legal Studies* 1 (2): 209–261.

General Accounting Office (GAO). 1990. *Death Penalty Sentencing: Research Indicates Pattern of Racial Disparities*. Report to Senate and House Committees on the Judiciary. GGD-90-57. February. Washington, DC: US GAO.

Goss, Ernest, Scott Strain, and Jackson Blalock. 2016. *The Economic Impact of the Death Penalty on the State of Nebraska: A Taxpayer Burden?* Denver, CO: Goss and Associates.

Gould, Jon B., and Lisa Greenman. 2010. *Report to the Committee on Defender Services Judicial Conference of the United States Update on the Cost and Quality of Defense Representation in Federal Death Penalty Cases*. September. Washington, DC: Judicial Conference of the United States. http://www.uscourts.gov/file/fdpc2010pdf. Accessed February 23, 2017.

Gould, Jon B., and Richard A. Leo. 2010. One Hundred Years Later: Wrongful Convictions after a Century of Research. *Journal of Criminal Law and Criminology* 100 (3): 825–868.

Gram, Wallace. 2015. A Power-Law Analysis of the Uneven Geographic Distribution of Executions in the Post-Furman Era of the Death Penalty. Senior honors thesis, Department of Political Science, University of North Carolina at Chapel Hill. http://www.unc.edu/~fbaum/teaching/Misc/Gram2015Thesis.pdf.

Grinshteyn, Erin, and David Hemenway. 2016. Violent Death Rates: The US Compared with Other High-Income OECD Countries, 2010. *American Journal of Medicine* 129 (3): 266–273.

Gross, Samuel R. 1998. Update: American Public Opinion on the Death Penalty—It's Getting Personal. *Cornell Law Review* 83 (6): 1448–1475.

Gross, Samuel R., Kristen Jacoby, Daniel J. Matheson, and Nicolas Montgomery. 2004. Exonerations in the United States 1989 through 2003. *Journal of Criminal Law and Criminology* 95 (2): 523–560.

Gross, Samuel R., Barbara O'Brien, Chen Hu, and Edward H. Kennedy. 2014. Rate of False Conviction of Criminal Defendants Who Are Sentenced to Death. *Proceedings of the National Academy of Sciences* 111 (20): 7230–7235.

Gross, Samuel R., and Michael Shaffer. 2012. *Exonerations in the United States, 1989–2012. Report by the National Registry of Exonerations.* June 22. Ann Arbor, MI: National Registry of Exonerations.

Hammel, Andrew. 2002. Diabolical Federalism: A Functional Critique and Proposed Reconstruction of Death Penalty Federal *Habeas. American Criminal Law Review* 39 (1): 1–99.

Haney, Craig. 2005. *Death by Design: Capital Punishment as a Social Psychological System.* New York: Oxford University Press.

Haney López, Ian F. 2015. Equal Protection as Intentional Blindness. In *Controversies in Equal Protection Cases in America,* edited by Anne Richardson Oakes, 67–84. New York: Routledge.

Harmon, Talia Roitberg. 2004. Race for Your Life: An Analysis of the Role of Race in Erroneous Capital Convictions. *Criminal Justice Review* 29 (1): 76–96.

Hatch, Virginia Leigh, and Anthony Walsh. 2016. *Capital Punishment: Theory and Practice of the Ultimate Penalty.* New York: Oxford University Press.

Hawkins, Darnell F., ed. 2003. *Violent Crime: Assessing Race and Ethnic Differences.* New York: Cambridge University Press.

Hedden, Sara L., Joel Kennet, Rachel Lipari, Grace Medley, and Peter Tice. 2015. *Behavioral Health Trends in the United States: Results from the 2014 National Survey on Drug Use and Health.* September. Washington, DC: Substance Abuse and Mental Health Services Administration. http://www.samhsa.gov/data/sites/default/files/NSDUH-FRR1-2014/NSDUH-FRR1-2014.pdf. Accessed August 17, 2016.

Hill, David B., and State of New York. 1885. *Public Papers of David B. Hill.* Albany, NY: Argus Company, Printers.

Hillman, Harold. 1993. The Possible Pain Experienced during Executions by Different Methods. *Perception* 22:745–753.

Hood, Roger, and Carolyn Hoyle. 2015. *The Death Penalty: A Worldwide Perspective.* 5th ed. New York: Oxford University Press.

IRS. 2008a. Additional Enhancements Could Be Made to Strengthen Lockbox Security. Washington, DC: Department of Treasury.

IRS. 2008b. Program to Protect Hardcopy Personally Identifiable Information Is a Work-in-Progress. Washington, DC: Department of Treasury.

Judicial Council. 2014. *Report of the Judicial Council Death Penalty Advisory Committee.* February. Washington, DC: Death Penalty Advisory Committee. http://www.deathpenaltyinfo.org/documents/KSCost2014.pdf.

Junkin, Tim. 2004. *Bloodsworth: The True Story of the First Death Row Inmate Exonerated by DNA.* Chapel Hill, NC: Algonquin Books.

Kaplan, Aliza B. 2013. Oregon's Death Penalty: The Practical Reality. *Lewis and Clark Law Review* 17 (1): 2–68.

Kaufman-Osborn, Timothy V. 2002. *From Noose to Needle: Capital Punishment and the Late Liberal State.* Ann Arbor: University of Michigan Press.

Keys, David P., and John F. Galliher. 2016. Nothing Succeeds Like Failure: Race, Decisionmaking, and Proportionality in Oklahoma Homicide Trials. In *Race and the Death Penalty: The Legacy of McCleskey v. Kemp,* edited by David P. Keys and R. J. Maratea. 123–142. Boulder, CO: Lynne Rienner.

Kirchmeier, Jeffrey L. 1998. Aggravating and Mitigating Factors: The Paradox of Today's Arbitrary and Mandatory Capital Punishment Scheme. *William and Mary Bill of Rights Journal* 6 (2): 345–459.

———. 2006. Dead Innocent: The Death Penalty Abolitionist Search for a Wrongful Execution. *Tulsa Law Review* 42 (2): 403–436.

Koniaris, Leonidas, Teresa Zimmers, David Lubarsky, and Jonathan Sheldon. 2005. Inadequate Anaesthesia in Lethal Injection for Execution. *Lancet* 365:1412–1414.

Kovarksy, Lee. 2016. Muscle Memory and the Local Concentration of Capital Punishment. *Duke Law Journal* 66 (2): 259–330.

Kuziemko, Ilyana. 2006. Does the Threat of the Death Penalty Affect Plea Bargaining in Murder Cases? Evidence from New York's 1995 Reinstatement of Capital Punishment. *American Law and Economics Review* 8 (1): 116–142.

Legislative Division of Post Audit. 2003. *Costs Incurred for Death Penalty Cases: A K-GOAL Audit for the Department of Corrections.* Topeka: State of Kansas Legislative Division of Post Audit. http://www.kslpa.org/assets/files/reports/04pa03a.pdf.

Leonard, Elizabeth Dermody. 2002. *Convicted Survivors: The Imprisonment of Battered Women Who Kill.* Albany: State University of New York Press.

Lewis, D. O., J. H. Pincus, B. Bard, E. Richardson, L. S. Prichep, M. Feldman, and C. Yeager. 1988. Neuropsychiatric, Psychoeducational, and Family Characteristics of 14 Juveniles Condemned to Death in the United States. *American Journal of Psychiatry* 145:584–589.

Liebman, James S., and the Columbia DeLuna Project. 2014. *The Wrong Carlos: Anatomy of a Wrongful Execution.* New York: Columbia University Press. http://thewrongcarlos.net/.

Liebman, James S., Jeffrey Fagan, Andrew Gelman, Valerie West, Garth Davies, and Alexander Kiss. 2002. *A Broken System, Part II: Why There Is So Much Error in Capital Cases, and What Can Be Done about It.* February 11. Columbia University Law School. http://www2.law.columbia.edu/brokensystem2/index2.html.

Liebman, James S., Jeffrey Fagan, and Valerie West. 2000. *Error Rates in Capital Cases, 1973–1995.* June 12. Columbia University Law School. http://www2.law.columbia.edu/instructionalser-vices/liebman/liebman_final.pdf.

Liebman, James, Jeffrey Fagan, Valerie West, and Jonathan Lloyd. 2000. Capital Attrition: Error Rates in Capital Cases, 1973–1995. *Texas Law Review* 78:1839–1865.

Liebman, James S., and Lawrence C. Marshall. 2006. Less Is Better: Justice Stevens and the Narrowed Death Penalty. *Fordham Law Review* 74 (4): 1607–1682.

Loyal, Alex D. 2013. The Decline of the Death Penalty as Seen through a Legislative Perspective. Senior honors thesis, Department of Political Science, University of North Carolina at Chapel Hill. http://www.unc.edu/~fbaum/teaching/Misc/Loyal_Thesis_2013.pdf.

Lumer, Michael, and Nancy Tenney. 1995. The Death Penalty in New York: An Historical Perspective. *Journal of Law and Policy* 4 (1): 81–142.

Lyon, Andrea D. 2010. *Angel of Death Row: My Life as a Death Penalty Defense Lawyer.* New York: Kaplan.

Mandery, Evan J. 2012. *Capital Punishment in America: A Balanced Examination.* 2nd ed. Sudbury, MA: Jones and Bartlett Learning.

———. 2013. *A Wild Justice: The Death and Resurrection of Capital Punishment in America.* New York: Norton.

Mandery, Evan, Amy Shlosberg, Valerie West, and Bennett Callaghan. 2013. Compensation Statutes and Post-exoneration Offending. *Journal of Criminal Law and Criminology* 103 (2): 553–584.

Marceau, Justin, Sam Kamin, and Wanda Foglia. 2013. Death Eligibility in Colorado: Many Are Called, Few Are Chosen. *University of Colorado Law Review* 84:1069–1115.

Marceau, Justin F., and Hollis A. Whitson. 2013. The Cost of Colorado's Death Penalty. *University of Denver Criminal Law Review* 3:145–163.

Marlowe, Jen, Martina Davis-Correia, and Troy Davis. 2013. *I Am Troy Davis.* Chicago: Haymarket Books.

Martens-Lobenhoffer, J. 1999. Stability of Thiopental and Pentobarbital in Human Plasma Determined with a New Easy and Specific Gas Chromatography–Mass Spectrometry Assay. *Pharmazie* 54:597–599.

Miethe, Terance D. 2012. *Estimates of Time Spent in Capital and Non-capital Murder Cases: A Statistical Analysis of Survey Data from Clark County Defense Attorneys.* February 21. Department of Criminal Justice, University of Nevada, Las Vegas. http://www.deathpenaltyinfo.org/docu-ments/ClarkNVCostReport.pdf.

Moody, Christopher Z., and Mei Hsien Lee. 1999. Morality Policy Reinvention: State Death Penalties. *Annals of the American Academy of Political and Social Science* 566:80–92.

Morgan, John G. 2004. *Tennessee's Death Penalty: Costs and Consequences.* July. State of Tennessee, Comptroller of the Treasury, Office of Research. http://www.deathpenaltyinfo.org/documents/deathpenalty.pdf.

Murphy, E. L. 1984. Application of the Death Penalty in Cook County. *Illinois Bar Journal* 93:90–95.

Nagin, Daniel S., and John V. Pepper, eds. 2002. *Deterrence and the Death Penalty.* Washington, DC: National Academies Press.

NASA. n.d. Space Shuttle Mission Information. Washington, DC: NASA. http://www.nasa.gov/mission_pages/shuttle/shuttlemissions/list_main.html. Accessed August 21, 2016.

Nathan, Alison J., and Bruce A. Green. 2007. Brief for the Fordham University School of Law, Louis Stein Center for Law and Ethics as *Amicus Curiae* in Support of Petitioners. *Baze v. Rees* 07-5439, November 13.

National Research Council. 1978. *Deterrence and Incapacitation: Estimating the Effects of Criminal Sanctions on Crime Rates.* Washington, DC: National Academies Press.

Nevada Legislative Counsel Bureau. 2014. *State of Nevada Performance Audit: Fiscal Costs of the Death Penalty.* Reno: State of Nevada. http://www.deathpenaltyinfo.org/documents/NevadaCosts.pdf.

Norris, Robert J. 2012. Assessing Compensation Statues for the Wrongly Convicted. *Criminal Justice Policy Review* 23 (3): 352–374.

North Carolina Department of Corrections. 2013. *Execution Procedure Manual for Single Drug Protocol (Pentobarbital).* Raleigh: North Carolina Department of Public Safety. https://www.ncdps.gov/div/AC/Protocol.pdf. Accessed November 7, 2015.

North Carolina Department of Public Safety. 2016. *People Removed from Death Row.* Raleigh: North Carolina Department of Public Safety. www.nccrimecontrol.org/index2.cfm?a=000003,0022 40,002327,002338. Accessed August 30, 2016.

Oberer, Walter E. 1961. Does Disqualification of Jurors for Scruples against Capital Punishment Constitute Denial of Fair Trial on Issue of Guilt? *Texas Law Review* 39: 545–567.

O'Brien, Robert M. 1996. Police Productivity and Crime Rates: 1973–1992. *Criminology* 34 (2): 183–207.

Office of Performance Evaluations. 2014. *Financial Costs of the Death Penalty.* Boise, ID: Idaho legislature. http://www.legislature.idaho.gov/ope/publications/reports/r1402.pdf.

Office of the Governor. 2015. *Governor Tom Wolf Announces a Moratorium on the Death Penalty in Pennsylvania.* (February 13. https://www.governor.pa.gov/moratorium-on-the-death-penalty-in-pennsylvania/.

Ogletree, Charles J., Jr., and Austin Sarat, eds. 2009. *When Law Fails: Making Sense of Miscarriages of Justice.* New York: New York University Press.

Oklahoma Death Penalty Review Commission. 2017. *The Report of the Oklahoma Death Penalty Review Commission.* Washington, DC: The Constitution Project.

Olney, Maeve, and Scott Bohn. 2014. An Exploratory Study of the Legal and Non-legal Factors Associated with Exoneration for Wrongful Conviction: The Power of DNA Evidence. *Criminal Justice Policy Review* 26 (4): 400–420.

O'Shea, Kathleen A. 1999. *Women and the Death Penalty in the United States, 1900–1998.* 2nd ed. Westport, CT: Praeger.

———. 2000. *Women on the Row: Revelations from Both Sides of the Bars.* New York: Firebrand.

Oshinsky, David M. 2010. *Capital Punishment on Trial:* Furman v. Georgia *and the Death Penalty in Modern America.* Lawrence: University Press of Kansas.

Pacheco, Julianna. 2014. Measuring and Evaluating Changes in State Opinion across Eight Issues. *American Politics Research* 42 (6): 986–1009.

Palm Beach Post Capital Bureau. 2000. The High Price of Killing Killers. January 4. Death Penalty Information Center. http://www.deathpenaltyinfo.org/node/2289.

Pareto, Vilfredo. 1965. La courbe de la répartition de la richesse. In *Oevres complètes de Vilfredo Pareto,* edited by G. Busino, 1–5. 1896. Geneva: Librairie Droz.

Paternoster, Raymond. 1983. Race of Victim and Location of Crime: The Decision to Seek the Death Penalty in South Carolina. *Journal of Criminal Law and Criminology* 74 (3): 754–785.

Paternoster, Raymond, Robert Brame, Sarah Bacon, and Andrew Ditchfield. 2004. Justice by Geography and Race: The Administration of the Death Penalty in Maryland, 1978–1999. *University of Maryland Law Journal of Race Religion Gender and Class* 4 (1): 1–97.

Paternoster, Raymond, Robert Brame, Sarah Bacon, Andrew Ditchfield, David Biere, Karen Beckman, Deanna Perez, Michael Strauch, Nadine Frederique, Kristin Gawkoski, Daniel Ziegler, and Katheryn Murphy. 2003. *An Empirical Analysis of Maryland's Death Sentencing System with Respect to the Influence of Race and Legal Jurisdiction, Final Report*. http://www.aclu-md.org/uploaded_files/0000/0377/md_death_penalty_race_study.pdf.

Paternoster, Raymond, Jacqueline Ghislaine Lee, and Michael Rocque. 2016. Capital Case Processing in Georgia after McCleskey: More of the Same. In *Race and the Death Penalty: The Legacy of McCleskey v. Kemp*, edited by David P. Keys and R. J. Maratea, 89–108. Boulder, CO: Lynne Rienner.

Peel, Diana. 2013. Clutching at Life, Waiting to Die: The Experience of Death Row Incarceration. *Western Criminology Review* 14 (3): 61–72.

Peffley, Mark, and Jon Hurwitz. 2007. Persuasion and Resistance: Race and the Death Penalty in America. *American Journal of Political Science* 51 (4): 996–1012.

———. 2010. Justice in America: The Separate Realities of Blacks and Whites. New York: Cambridge University Press.

Perlin, Michael L. 2013. *Mental Disability and the Death Penalty*. Lanham, MD: Rowman and Littlefield.

Phillips, Charles. 1987. Exploring Relations among Forms of Social Control: The Lynching and Execution of Blacks in North Carolina, 1889–1918. *Law and Society Review* 21:361–374.

Phillips, Scott. 2008. Racial Disparities in the Capital of Capital Punishment. *Houston Law Review* 45:809–842.

———. 2009. Legal Disparities in the Capital of Capital Punishment. *Journal of Criminal Law and Criminology* 99 (3): 717–756.

———. 2012. Continued Racial Disparities in the Capital of Capital Punishment: The Rosenthal Era. *Houston Law Review* 50:131–156.

Phillips, Scott, Laura Potter, and James E. Coverdill. 2012. Disentangling Victim Gender and Capital Punishment: The Role of Media. *Feminist Criminology* 7:130–145.

Phillips, Scott, and Alena Simon. 2014. Is the Modern American Death Penalty a Fatal Lottery? Texas as a Conservative Test. *Laws* 3 (1): 85–105

Pierce, Glenn L., and Michael L. Radelet. 2002. Race, Region, and Death Sentencing in Illinois, 1988–1997. *Oregon Law Review* 81 (1): 39–96.

———. 2005. The Impact of Legally Inappropriate Factors on Death Sentencing for California Homicides, 1990–1999. *Santa Clara Law Review* 49:1–31.

Pierrepoint, Albert. 1974. *Executioner Pierrepoint*. London: Harrap.

Pinker, Steven. 2011. *The Better Angels of Our Nature: Why Violence Has Declined*. New York: Penguin.

Posner, Richard A. 1974. Theories of Economic Regulation. *Bell Journal of Economics and Management Science* 5:335–358.

Prejean, Sister Helen. 2005. *The Death of Innocents*. New York: Random House.

Price, Melynda J. 2015. *At the Cross: Race, Religion and Citizenship in the Politics of the Death Penalty among African Americans*. New York: Oxford University Press.

Radelet, Michael L. 1989. Executions of Whites for Crimes against Blacks. *Sociological Quarterly* 30 (4): 529–544.

Radelet, Michael L., Hugo Adam Bedau, and Constance E. Putnam. 1992. *In Spite of Innocence*. Boston: Northeastern University Press.

Radelet, Michael L., and Glenn L. Pierce. 1991. Choosing Those Who Will Die: Race and the Death Penalty in Florida. *Florida Law Review* 43 (1): 1–34.

Radzinowitz, I. 1948. *A History of English Criminal Law*. London: Stevens and Sons.

Rakoff, Jed S. 2014. Why Innocent People Plead Guilty. *New York Review of Books*, November 20.

Rattan A., C. S. Levine, C. S. Dweck, and J. L. Eberhardt. 2012. Race and the Fragility of the Legal Distinction between Juveniles and Adults. *PLoS ONE* 7 (5): e36680.

Redlich, Allison D., James R. Acker, Robert J. Norris, and Catherine L. Bonventre, eds. 2005. *Examining Wrongful Convictions: Stepping Back, Moving Forward.* Durham, NC: Carolina Academic Press.

Riedel, Marc, and Wayne Welsh. 2014. *Criminal Violence: Patterns, Explanations, and Interventions.* 4th ed. New York: Oxford University Press.

Risinger, D. Michael. 2007. Innocents Convicted: An Empirically Justified Factual Wrongful Conviction Rate. *Journal of Criminal Law and Criminology* 97 (3): 761–806.

Roman, John, Aaron Chalfin, Aaron Sundquist, Carly Knight, and Askar Darmenov. 2008. *The Cost of the Death Penalty in Maryland.* Washington, DC: Urban Institute, Justice Policy Center. http://www.deathpenaltyinfo.org/CostsDPMaryland.pdf.

Rosen, Richard A. 1986. The "Especially Heinous" Aggravating Circumstance in Capital Cases—The Standardless Standard. *North Carolina Law Review* 64:941–992.

———. 1990. Felony Murder and the Eighth Amendment Jurisprudence of Death. *Boston College Law Review* 31 (5): 1103–1170.

Roth, Randolph. 2009. *American Homicide.* Cambridge, MA: Harvard University Press.

Rountree, Meredith Martin. 2012. "I'll Make Them Shoot Me": Accounts of Death Row Prisoners Advocating for Execution. *Law and Society Review* 46 (3): 589–622.

Royer, Caisa Elizabeth, Amelia Courtney Hritz, Valerie P. Hans, Theodore Eisenberg, Martin T. Wells, John H. Blume, and Sheri Lynn Johnson. 2014. *Victim Gender and the Death Penalty.* Cornell Law Faculty Publications, 838. http://scholarship.law.cornell.edu/facpub/838.

Sarat, Austin. 1999. *The Killing State: Capital Punishment in Law, Politics, and Culture.* New York: Oxford University Press.

———. 2001. *When the State Kills.* Princeton, NJ: Princeton University Press.

———. 2014. *Gruesome Spectacles: Botched Executions and America's Death Penalty.* Stanford, CA: Stanford University Press.

Sarat, Austin, and Neil Vidmar. 1976. Public Opinion, the Death Penalty, and the Eighth Amendment: Testing the Marshall Hypothesis. *Wisconsin Law Review* 17:171–207.

Scalia, Justice Antonin. 1987. *Memorandum to the Conference Re: No 84-6811, McCleskey v. Kemp, January 6.* Reprinted in Erwin Chermerinsky, Eliminating Discrimination in Administering the Death Penalty: The Need for the Racial Justice Act. *Santa Clara Law Review* 35 (1995): 519, 528.

Scheidegger, Kent S. 2011. *Mend It Don't End It: A Report to the Connecticut General Assembly on Capital Punishment.* http://www.cjlf.org/deathpenalty/deathpenalty.htm.

Schulhofer, Stephen J. 1992. Plea Bargaining as Disaster. *Yale Law Journal* 101 (8): 1979–2009.

Scott, Charles L., and Phillip J. Resnick. 2006. Violence Risk Assessment in Persons with Mental Illness. *Aggression and Violent Behavior* 11:598–611.

Sellin, Thorsten. 1959. *The Death Penalty: A Report for the Model Penal Code Project of the American Law Institute.* Philadelphia: American Law Institute.

Sharma, Hemant, John M. Scheb, David J. Houston, and Kristin Wagers. 2013. Race and the Death Penalty: An Empirical Assessment of First Degree Murder Convictions in Tennessee after *Gregg v. Georgia. Tennessee Journal of Race, Gender and Social Justice* 2 (1): 1–39.

Sharon, Chelsea Creo. 2011. The "Most Deserving of Death": The Narrowing Requirement and the Proliferation of Aggravating Factors in Capital Sentencing Statutes. *Harvard Civil Rights–Civil Liberties Law Review* 46:223–251.

Sharp, Susan F. 2005. *Hidden Victims: The Effects of the Death Penalty on Families of the Accused.* New Brunswick, NJ: Rutgers University Press.

Shatz, Steven F., and Nina Rivkind. 1997. The California Death Penalty Scheme: Requiem for Furman. *New York University Law Review* 72 (6): 1283–1343.

Sheffer, Susannah. 2013. *Fighting for Their Lives: Inside the Experience of Capital Defense Attorneys.* Nashville, TN: Vanderbilt University Press.

Shirley, Kenneth E., and Andrew Gelman. 2015. Hierarchical Models for Estimating State and Demographic Trends in US Death Penalty Public Opinion. *Journal of the Royal Statistical Society: Series A* 178 (1): 1–28.

Silbersweig, D.A., E. Stern, C. Frith, C. Cahill, A. Holmes, S. Grootoonk, J. Seaward, P. McKenna, S.E. Chua, L. Schnorr, T. Jones, and R. S. J. Frackowiak. 1995. A Functional Neuroanatomy of Hallucinations in Schizophrenia. *Nature* 378:176–179.

Simms, Tina. 2016. Statutory Compensation for the Wrongly Imprisoned. *Social Work* 61 (2): 155–162.

Smith, A. 2007. Not Waiving but Drowning: The Anatomy of Death Row Syndrome and Volunteering for Execution. *Boston University Public Interest Law Journal* 17:237–254.

Smith, Robert. 2011. The Geography of the Death Penalty and Its Ramifications. *Boston University Law Review* 92 (1): 227–289.

Snell, Tracy L. 2014. *Capital Punishment, 2013—Statistical Tables.* Washington, DC: Bureau of Justice Statistics.

Songer, Michael J., and Isaac Unah. 2006. The Effect of Race, Gender, and Location on Prosecutorial Decisions to Seek the Death Penalty in South Carolina. *South Carolina Law Review* 58:161–210.

Steiker, Carol S. 2002. Capital Punishment and American Exceptionalism. *Oregon Law Review* 81 (1): 97–130.

———.2005. No, Capital Punishment Is Not Morally Required: Deterrence, Deontology, and the Death Penalty. *Stanford Law Review* 58 (3): 751–790.

Steiker, Carol S., and Jordan M. Steiker. 2016. *Courting Death: The Supreme Court and Capital Punishment.* Cambridge, MA: Harvard University Press.

Stevenson, Bryan A. 2002. The Politics of Fear and Death: Successive Problems in Capital Federal Habeas Corpus Cases. *New York University Law Review* 77 (3): 699–795.

———.2014. *Just Mercy: A Story of Justice and Redemption.* New York: Spiegel and Grau.

Stimson, James A. 1998. *Public Opinion in America: Moods, Cycles, and Swings.* 2nd ed. Boulder, CO: Westview Press.

Stuntz, William J. 2004. Plea Bargaining and Criminal Law's Disappearing Shadow. *Harvard Law Review* 117 (8): 2548–2569.

Sunstein, Cass R., and Adrian Vermeule. 2005. Is the Death Penalty Morally Required? Acts, Omissions, and Life-Life Tradeoffs. *Stanford Law Review* 58 (3): 703–750.

Swallows, Beverly Bryan. 1993. Stays of Execution: Equal Justice for All. *Baylor Law Review* 45 (4): 911–932.

Temple, John. 2009. *The Last Lawyer: The Fight to Save Death Row Inmates.* Jackson: University of Mississippi Press.

Thaxton, Sherod. 2016. Un-*Gregg*-ulated: Capital Charging and the Missing Mandate of *Gregg v. Georgia. Duke Journal of Constitutional Law and Public Policy* 11:145–182.

Unah, Isaac, and Jack Boger. 2001. *Race and the Death Penalty in North Carolina: An Empirical Analysis: 1993–1999.* Chapel Hill: University of North Carolina. http://www.deathpenalty-info.org/race-and-death-penalty-north-carolina. Accessed August 19, 2016.

Vidmar, Neil, and Phoebe Ellsworth. 1974. Public Opinion and the Death Penalty. *Stanford Law Review* 26 (6): 1245–1270.

Vito, Gennaro F., and Thomas J. Keil. 1988. Capital Sentencing in Kentucky: An Analysis of the Factors Influencing Decision Making in the Post-*Gregg* Period. *Journal of Criminal Law and Criminology* 79 (2): 483–503.

Washington State Bar Association. 2006. *Final Report of the Death Penalty Subcommittee of the Committee on Public Defense.* December. Seattle: Washington State Bar Association. http://www.wsba.org/~/media/Files/WSBA-wide%20Documents/wsba%20death%20penalty%20report.ashx. Accessed August 17, 2016.

Welty, Jeffrey B. 2013. *North Carolina Capital Case Law Handbook.* 3rd ed. Chapel Hill: University of North Carolina School of Government.

Wermiel, Stephen. 2012. SCOTUS for Law Students (Sponsored by Bloomberg Law): Handling Stay Applications. October 26. http://www.scotusblog.com/2012/10/scotus-for-law-students-sponsored-by-bloomberg-law-handling-stay-applications/.

White, Welsh S. 2006. *Litigating in the Shadow of Death: Defense Attorneys in Capital Cases.* Ann Arbor: University of Michigan Press.

Williams, Marian R., and Jefferson E. Holcomb. 2001. Racial Disparities and Death Sentences in Ohio. *Journal of Criminal Justice* 29 (3): 207–218.

Wright, Ronald. 2008. How Prosecutor Elections Fail Us. *Ohio State Journal of Criminal Law* 6 (2): 581–610.

Xu, Jiquan, Sherry L. Murphy, Kenneth D. Kochanek, and Brigham A. Bastian. 2016. Deaths: Final Data for 2013. February. *National Vital Statistics Reports* 64 (2).

Zalman, Marvin. 2012. Qualitatively Estimating the Incidence of Wrongful Convictions. *Criminal Law Bulletin* 48 (2): 221–279.

Zimring, Franklin E. 2003. *The Contradictions of American Capital Punishment.* New York: Oxford University Press.

———.2007. *The Great American Crime Decline.* New York: Oxford University Press.

Zimring, Franklin. E., and Gordon Hawkins. 1986. *Capital Punishment and the American Agenda.* Cambridge: Cambridge University Press.

News Sources

Associated Press. 2016. Texas Court Halts Execution of Man Who Didn't Pull Trigger. *New York Times,* August 19.

Bauerlein, Valerie. 2016. Church Gunman Dylann Roof Sticks to Plan to Represent Himself. *Wall Street Journal,* December 28.

Bazelon, Emily. 2016. Where the Death Penalty Still Lives. *New York Times Magazine,* August 23.

Berman, Mark. 2015a. Georgia Executes Kelly Gissendaner after Supreme Court Denies Stay Requests. *Washington Post,* September 30.

———. 2015b. Oklahoma Governor Halts Execution of Richard Glossip Due to "Last Minute Questions" about the Drugs Involved. *Washington Post,* September 30.

———. 2016. Oklahoma Lethal Injection Process Muddled by "Inexcusable Failure," Grand Jury Finds. *Washington Post,* May 19.

Beutler, Brian. 2014. Antonin Scalia Used This Wrongful Conviction to Defend the Death Penalty. *New Republic,* September 4.

Brambila, Nicole C. 2016. Executing Justice: The Discretionary Nature of the Death Penalty in Pennsylvania. *Reading Eagle,* June 20.

Brewer, Graham Lee. 2015. Oklahoma Department of Corrections Director Resigns. *NewsOK.com,* December 4.

Campbell, Katie. 2017. Execution Policy Changes Meet Death-Row Inmates' Demands. *Arizona Capitol Times,* June 12.

Carrigan, William D., and Clive Webb. 2015. When Americans Lynched Mexicans. *New York Times,* February 20.

Christie, Bob. 2017. Arizona, Prisoners Reach Deal to Settle Death Penalty Suit. *New Republic,* June 12.

Cogan, Marin. 2016. Meet the Red-State Conservatives Fighting to Abolish the Death Penalty. *Washington Post,* June 3.

Connor, Tracy. 2015a. Georgia Executes Warren Lee Hill Despite Low IQ Claim. *NBC News,* January 27.

———. 2015b. Oklahoma Execution: Baby's Mom Says Killer Charles Warner Should Live. *NBC News,* January 15.

———. 2015c. Oklahoma Governor Halts Richard Glossip Execution at Last Minute. *NBC News,* September 30.

Cross, Phil. 2016. Executions Will Not Resume in Oklahoma in 2016. *KOKH Fox News 25,* August 3.

Denver Post. 2013. Nathan Dunlap Granted "Temporary Reprieve" by Governor. May 22.

DiIulio, John J., 1995. The Coming of the Super-predators. *Weekly Standard,* November 23.

Feldman, Noah. 2016. Death-Penalty Drugmaker Shouldn't Be Anonymous. Bloomberg.com, September 26.

Ford, Matt. 2015. The Troubling Case of Richard Glossip. *Atlantic*, September 16.

Forsyth, Jim. 2012. John Balentine, on Texas Death Row, Has Execution Delayed 3 Times. *Huffington Post*, August 26.

Gallman, Stephanie. 2015. Georgia Executes Man Despite Disability Claim. *CNN.com*, January 28.

Grann, David. 2009. Trial by Fire: Did Texas Execute an Innocent Man? *New Yorker*, September 7.

Grissom, Brandi. 2015. Ex-Marine on Death Row Says Jurors Should Have Been Told More about PTSD. *Dallas Morning News*, August 2.

Hasselle, Della, and John Simerman. 2016. Questions over Conduct of Louisiana Prosecutors Is before Supreme Court. *The Lens*, June 12.

Hedayati, Hooman. 2016. In Texas Death Row Case, Punishment Does Not Fit Crime. *Austin American-Statesman*, July 18.

Hoberock, Barbara. 2016. Oklahoma Gov. Mary Fallin Signs Bill Adding Nitrogen Gas as State Execution Method. *Tulsa World*, May 31.

Hsu, Spencer S. 2016. FBI Admits Flaws in Hair Analysis over Decades. *Washington Post*, April 18.

Johnson, John, Jr. 2011. How Los Angeles Covered Up the Massacre of 17 Chinese. *LA Weekly*, March 10.

Kaste, Martin. 2015. Justice Scalia: "Wouldn't Surprise Me" If Supreme Court Strikes Down Death Penalty. National Public Radio, October 21.

Khalek, Rania. 2013. The Death Row Torture of Warren Hill. *Nation*, August 14.

King, Gilbert. 2011. Edison vs. Westinghouse: A Shocking Rivalry. *Smithsonian.com*, October 11.

Leblanc, Clif. 2015. South Carolina's Infamous Serial Killer, "Pee Wee" Gaskins. *The State*, November 10.

Liptak, Adam. 2016a. Justices Hear Texas Death Penalty Case Involving Intellectual Disability. *New York Times*, November 29.

———.2016b. Supreme Court Rules Right to Speedy Trial Ends at Guilty Verdict. *New York Times*, May 19.

———.2016c. Supreme Court Skeptical on a Speedy Trial Argument. *New York Times*, March 28.

———. 2017. Citing Racist Testimony, Justices Call for New Sentencing in Texas Death Penalty Case. *New York Times*, February 22.

Lucero, Jordann. 2015. Timeline of Events in Richard Glossip's Case. *Fox 25*, September 28.

McCullough, Jolie. 2016. Rally Questions Death Penalty for Texas Man Who Didn't Pull Trigger. *Texas Tribune*, July 23.

McDaniel, Chris, and Chris Geidner. 2016. Pharmacy Argues There's a First Amendment Right to Secretly Sell Execution Drugs. *Buzzfeed.com*, September 25.

McGarrahan, Ellen. 1999. Florida Juice: The Sunshine State's Love Affair with the Electric Chair. *Slate.com*, July 22.

Migdail-Smith, Liam. 2016. Executing Justice: A Look at the Cost of Pennsylvania's Death Penalty. *Reading Eagle*, June 19.

New York Times. 1890. Far Worse Than Hanging. August 7.

Peralta, Eyder. 2015. Oklahoma Used the Wrong Drug to Execute Charles Warner. National Public Radio, October 8.

Pilkington, Ed. 2011. Manuel Valle Execution Carried Out amid Fight over "Cruel" Injection. *Guardian*, September 29.

Redden, Molly. 2015. Why Is It So Hard for Wrongfully Convicted Women to Get Justice? *MotherJones.com*, July/August.

Reyes, Jessica Masulli. 2016. Court: Delaware's Death Penalty Law Is Unconstitutional. *Delaware News Journal*, August 2.

Richinick, Michele. 2015. Supreme Court Grants Stay of Execution for Three Oklahoma Inmates.*MSNBC.com*, January 28.

Robertson, Campbell. 2014. South Carolina Judge Vacates Conviction of George Stinney in 1944 Execution. *New York Times*, December 17.

Robertson, Campbell, and Adam Liptak. 2011. Supreme Court Looks against Methods of D.A.'s Office in Louisiana. *New York Times*, November 2.

Sack, Kevin, and Alan Blinder. 2017. Dylan Roof Himself Rejects Best Defense against Execution. *New York Times*, January 1.

Sanburn, Josh. 2014. Creator of Lethal Injection Method: "I Don't See Anything That Is More Humane." *Time*, May 15.

Weisberg, Jacob. 1991. This Is Your Death. *New Republic*, July 1.

Welsh-Huggins, Andrew. 2015. Problems Obtaining Lethal Injection Drugs Force Ohio to Delay Executions until 2017. *U.S. News & World Report*, April 12.

Wilgoren, Jodi. 2003. Citing Issue in Fairness, Governor Clears Out Death Row In Illinois. *New York Times*, January 12.

Court Cases

Atkins v. Virginia, 536 U.S. 304 (2002)

Barefoot v. Estelle, 463 U.S. 880 (1983)

Barnard v. Collins, 13 F.3d 871 (1994)

Callins v. Collins, 510 U.S. 1141 (1994)

Coker v. Georgia, 433 U.S. 584 (1977)

Connick v. Thompson, 563 U.S. ___ (2011)

Ford v. Wainwright, 477 U.S. 399 (1986)

Furman v. Georgia, 408 U.S. 238 (1972)

Godfrey v. Georgia, 446 U.S. 420 (1980)

Gregg v. Georgia, 428 U.S. 153 (1976)

Hall v. Florida, 572 U.S. ___ (2014)

In re Troy Anthony Davis, 557 U.S. ___ (2009)

Jones v. Chappell, F.3d, CD. Cal. No. CV 09-02158-CJC (2014)

Kennedy v. Louisiana, 554 U.S. 407 (2008)

Lockett v. Ohio, 438 U.S. 586 (1978)

Maynard v. Cartwright, 486 U.S. 356 (1988)

McCleskey v. Kemp, 481 U.S. 279 (1987)

McGautha v. California, 402 U.S. 183 (1971)

People ex. rel. Kemmler v. Durston, 119 N.Y. 569, 24 N.E. 6 (1890)

People v. Edwards, 54 Cal. 3d. 787 (1991)

People v. Morales, 48 Cal. 3d 527 (1989)

Pulley v. Harris, 465 U.S. 37 (1984)

Skipper v. South Carolina, 476 U.S. 1 (1986)

Trop v. Dulles, 356 U.S. 86 (1958)

Walton v. Arizona, 497 U.S. 639 (1990)

White v Dugger, 483 U.S. 1045 (1987).

Woodson v. North Carolina, 428 U.S. 280 (1976)

Zant v. Stephens, 462 U.S. 862 (1983)

INDEX

ineffective assistance of counsel, 31, 176, 226, 238, 342
  in post-conviction appeals, 37, 39–40
  and reversals, 143, 148–149, 152, 172, 174
infrequency of capital punishment, 333–334
  in *Furman v. Georgia* (1972), 5, 9, 14, 94
  across states, 122, 335–336
innocence, 191-193, 215, 255
  and the Constitution, 189, 342
  and executions, 21, 153, 184–187, 192, 216, 351
  and exonerations, 172–173, 175, 178
  financial compensation after, 45, 187
  and pardons, 43, 144
  and public opinion, 152, 183, 267–269, 287
insanity, 236, 240, 247
intellectual disability, 177, 258–259
  in *Atkins v. Virginia* (2002), 23, 236, 239, 253, 322–324
  difficulty in demonstrating, 225, 253–254, 299
  and future dangerousness, 89, 227, 240, 254–255, 362
  as a mitigating factor, 103, 235, 238,
  and prevalence on death row, 240–241, 260
  and public opinion, 263, 266, 278, 280, 287, 362
Internal Revenue Service, 154, 192
iPoll, 268, 273
IQ tests
  after *Atkins v. Virginia* (2002), 236, 239, 253
  among death row inmates, 225, 241–242, 254–255, 258
IRS. *See* Internal Revenue Service
"Is the Death Penalty Morally Required?", 314

Jackson, Lucius, 5
Jackson, Ricky, 181
Jackson v. Georgia (1972), 4
Johnson, Emma, 85
Johnson, John, Jr., 198
Johnson, Kaneesha R., 137, 339
Johnson, Sheri Lynn, 85
Jon, Gee, 205
Jones, Ernest Dewayne, 160, 166
Jones v. Chappell (2014), 157–158, 160, 346
judge overrule, 99, 360
Judicial Council, 292, 297, 302
judicial error, 39, 142, 148, 154
judicial immunity, 45, 360
Junkin, Tim, 178
Jurek v. Texas (1976), 13–14, 89, 99–100
jury consultants, 28
Justia.com, 242
juveniles, death penalty for
  and neurological dysfunction, 241, 253
  and public opinion, 266–268, 278–280, 287
  in *Roper v. Simmons* (2005), 101, 144, 263, 322–324, 349

Kagan, Elena, 189
Kamin, Sam, 91, 93, 108
Kammer, Brian, 225
Kansas v. Marsh (2006), 184, 192
Kaplan, Aliza B., 293, 298, 303
Kasich, John, 222
Kaste, Martin, 332
Kaufman-Osborn, Timothy V., 79–80, 169
Keil, Thomas J., 92
Kelley, Shannon E., 261
Kelly, Jason P., 131
Kemmler, William, 202–204, 213, 364
Kennedy, Anthony, 190, 323–324
Kennedy, Edward H., 194
Kennedy, Robert, 1
Kennedy v. Louisiana (2008) 95, 111
Keyes, David, 84
King, Gilbert, 202–203, 214
Kinkade, Patrick T., 266
Kirchmeier, Jeffrey L., 104, 106, 116, 185
Kiss, Alexander, 155
Khalek, Rania, 225, 234
Knight, Carly, 305
Knight, Thomas, 162, 217
Koniaris, Leonidas, 208–209
Kovarsky, Lee, 81
Krishnamurthy, Arvind, 137
Krone, Ray, 176
Kumph, Diane, 158
Kuziemko, Ilyana, 33

Lackey, Clarence Allen, 158–159, 160, 166
Lackey v. Texas (1995), 157, 159, 217, 346
Larrañaga, Mark A., 305
Law and Society Review, 257
law of parties, 109–111, 227
lay in wait statutes
  as an aggravating circumstance, 98, 334
  overbroadness of, 91, 104–105, 107, 340, 350
Lee, Jacqueline Ghislaine, 82, 84
Lee, Mei Hsien, 10–11, 25
Legislative Division of Post Audit, 292, 297, 302
Leo, Richard A., 193
Leonard, Elizabeth Dermody, 79, 85
lethal injections, 327
  botched executions, 211–212, 222–224, 346
  compared to other methods of execution, 198, 210
  as a cruel and unusual punishment, 208, 210–211, 213–214, 287, 367
  development of, 195–197, 199, 204–207, 209–210, 364
  and drug scarcities, 196, 201, 210, 305
  and stays, 168, 220–222, 226
Leuchter, Fred, 210
Levine, C. S., 86

CPSIA information can be obtained
at www.ICGtesting.com
Printed in the USA
BVHW080057190922
646946BV00004B/5

9 780190 841546